SEXUAL POLITICS AND FEMINIST SCIENCE

signale
========

modern german letters, cultures, and thought

Series editor: Peter Uwe Hohendahl, Cornell University

Signale: Modern German Letters, Cultures, and Thought publishes new English-language books in literary studies, criticism, cultural studies, and intellectual history pertaining to the German-speaking world, as well as translations of important German-language works. *Signale* construes "modern" in the broadest terms: the series covers topics ranging from the early modern period to the present. *Signale* books are published under a joint imprint of Cornell University Press and Cornell University Library in electronic and print formats. Please see http://signale.cornell.edu/.

SEXUAL POLITICS AND FEMINIST SCIENCE

Women Sexologists in Germany, 1900–1933

KIRSTEN LENG

A Signale Book

CORNELL UNIVERSITY PRESS AND CORNELL UNIVERSITY LIBRARY
ITHACA AND LONDON

Cornell University Press and Cornell University Library gratefully
acknowledge the College of Arts & Sciences, Cornell University, for
support of the Signale series.

First published 2018 by Cornell University Press and Cornell University
Library

Library of Congress Cataloging-in-Publication Data

Names: Leng, Kirsten, 1979– author.
Title: Sexual politics and feminist science : women sexologists in
    Germany, 1900–1933 / Kirsten Leng.
Description: Ithaca, NY : Cornell University Press : Cornell University
    Library, 2017. | Series: Signale : modern German letters, cultures, and
    thought | Includes bibliographical references and index.
Identifiers: LCCN 2017031562 (print) | LCCN 2017036376 (ebook) |
    ISBN 9781501713248 (pdf) | ISBN 9781501713231 (epub/mobi) |
    ISBN 9781501709302 | ISBN 9781501709302 (cloth : alk. paper) |
    ISBN 9781501709319 (pbk. : alk. paper)
Subjects: LCSH: Women sexologists—Germany—History—20th century. |
    Feminists—Germany—History—20th century. | Sexology—Germany—
    History—20th century. | Women—Sexual behavior—Germany—
    History—20th century. | Sex role—Germany—History—20th century. |
    Feminism and science—Germany—History—20th century.
Classification: LCC HQ60 (ebook) | LCC HQ60 .L46 2017 (print) |
    DDC 305.420943/0904—dc23
LC record available at https://lccn.loc.gov/2017031562

For Max

CONTENTS

ACKNOWLEDGMENTS

I am grateful for this opportunity to thank the many people and institutions that helped this book come into being. At the University of Michigan, I thank Kathleen Canning, Scott Spector, Geoff Eley, and Elizabeth Wingrove, whose insights have enriched my work, and whose encouragement and support have been invaluable. I thank them for their thoughtful and lively engagement with my arguments, and for modeling interdisciplinary scholarship. I benefited enormously from the breadth of their knowledge, their strong commitment to feminist scholarship, and their theoretical and empirical rigor.

I couldn't have asked for a better postdoctoral landing ground than the Sexualities Project at Northwestern University (SPAN). Steve Epstein and Héctor Carrillo provided an exciting and nurturing intellectual environment that enabled me to move between the worlds of modern European history, gender and sexuality studies, and science and technology studies. I am grateful to them for the opportunities they afforded me to present my work and receive multifaceted and challenging feedback, and for providing support and incredibly helpful and astute advice. My thanks go out to the community brought together by SPAN; special notes of thanks go to Evren Savci, Alex Owen, Tessie Liu, Ken Alder, Tania Munz, Teri Chettiar, and Mary Weismantel for their thoughts and company. The American Council of Learned Societies' New Faculty Fellowship provided me the chance to write, teach, and present my work at the Institute for Research on Women, Gender, and Sexuality (IRWGS) at Columbia University under the direction of Alondra Nelson, whom I thank for her continued advice, feedback, and support. Currently, I am grateful for the support, understanding, comradeship, and good humor of my colleagues in the Department of Women, Gender, Sexuality Studies at the University of Massachusetts Amherst: Kiran Asher, Abbie Boggs, Laura Briggs, Alex Deschamps, Tanisha Ford, Lezlie Frye, Linda Hillenbrand, Miliann Kang, Karen Lederer, Svati Shah, Banu Subramaniam, Mecca Sullivan, and Angie Willey.

This book has benefited from feedback offered by various other communities and readers. I thank the members of the Max Planck Institute for the History of Science's Working Group on Gender and Knowledge beyond the Academy, which convened in 2010–2011, in particular Christine von Oertzen, Maria Rentetzi, and Elizabeth S. Watkins. Over the course of our meetings, Sally Gregory Kohlstedt provided especially pivotal feedback that helped reframe the project. Participants in the Five College Feminist Science and Technology Studies Initiative, and in the Five College Women's Studies Research Center colloquia, provided helpful thoughts on various chapters. Dagmar Herzog proved an engaging, insightful, and stimulating discussant of a paper I presented at IRWGS that became chapter 7. Melissa Kravetz thoroughly read and gave supportive and friendly critique of chapter 6. Kathleen Kearns read the entire manuscript more than once, and provided indispensable insights. Additionally, I thank audience members at the various conferences where I presented portions of this book, including meetings of the German Studies Association, the American Historical Association, the History of Science Society, the Social

Science History Association, the Berkshire Conference on the History of Women, Genders, and Sexualities, the Christina Conference on Gender Studies at the University of Helsinki, and the Canadian Congress of the Social Sciences and Humanities, as well as audiences at Hampshire College, the University of Florida, and Harvard University.

Many institutions supported the research and writing of this project. I am thankful for the recognition and support of the Social Science and Humanities Research Council of Canada, the Social Science Research Council, the German Academic Exchange Service, the Council for European Studies, the University of Michigan (through its Center for European Studies and International Institute), Northwestern University (through its Faculty Research Grant), the Max Planck Institute for the History of Science (through a Visiting Fellowship), and the American Council of Learned Societies. I also thank librarians, volunteers, and archivists at institutions in Germany, Austria, the Netherlands, Britain, and the United States; special thanks go to Jens Dobler at the Schwules Museum in Berlin for being on the lookout for rare documents on female homosexuality and same-sex love during the Wilhelmine era, and to the volunteers at the Spinnboden Lesbian archive in Berlin, who allowed me to peruse their undocumented files. At Cornell University Library and Cornell University Press, I am grateful for the help, understanding, and boundless patience of Kizer Walker and Mahinder Kingra, as well as the thorough and generous reports provided by two anonymous readers. Thanks also to Marian Rogers's and Kate Mertes's keen eyes.

This project received less formal yet integral support from various quarters that deserve acknowledgment. I am incredibly grateful to Christiane Leidinger, who shared with me her voluminous knowledge on Johanna Elberskirchen. Marti Lybeck and Kirsten McGuire also shared their expertise on early twentieth-century German gender politics at a critical stage. Likewise, the members of the Magnus Hirschfeld Society in Berlin shared rare, painstakingly acquired research documents, as well as their encyclopedic knowledge of Wilhelmine-era sexology. In particular, I thank Ralf Dose for facilitating my visits and sharing his knowledge, and Andreas Pretzel for alerting me to the existence of Mathilde Vaerting.

Last but certainly not least, I thank my friends and family for their companionship and encouragement over this long process: Marianna Ritchey, Kimberlee Pérez, April Trask, Melissa Kravetz, the Roys (Elissa, Donald, Nicolas, Sebastian, and Alexandre), Huxley, Rosa and Rue, and James and Ruth Styles. My grandmother, Ruth, gave me the invaluable life lesson to "knock 'em down as they come"; I am grateful to her for that mantra. This book could not have been completed without the support and love of my parents, Christine and Siegfried Leng, and especially my partner, Kevin Young. What can I say to thank people who have proven remarkable intellectual interlocutors, who have been willing to discuss the finer points of Wilhelmine-era German grammar and syntax and the idiosyncrasies of sexological terminology, and who have cooked and cared for and comforted me? Words fail. Above all, I'm grateful to Kevin, who not only inspires me every day with his love of researching and writing, but also reminds me of how lucky we are to participate in the process of producing knowledge.

Finally, I dedicate this book to my son, Max, who passed away during the final stages of finishing this project. Although his existence was cruelly brief, he nonetheless proved the greatest teacher I have known. I thank him forever for his gifts of love and pure possibility.

Portions of this book originally appeared in different form in the following: "An 'Elusive' Phenomenon: Feminism, Sexual Science, and the Female Sex Drive, 1880–1914," special issue, *Centaurus: An International Journal of the History of Science and Its Cultural Aspects* 55, no. 2 (2013): 131–152; "Permutations of the Third Sex: Sexology, Subjectivity, and Anti-Maternalist Feminism at the Turn of the Twentieth Century," *Signs: Journal of Women in Culture and Society* 40, no. 1 (2014): 227–254; "The Personal Is Scientific: Women, Gender, and the Production of Sexological Knowledge in Germany and Austria, 1900–1931," *History of Psychology* 18, no. 3 (2015): 238–251. Copyright © 2015 by the American Psychological Association. Adapted with permission.

SEXUAL POLITICS AND FEMINIST SCIENCE

Introduction

Women and Sexology: Knowledge, Possibilities, and Problematic Legacies

The decades bookending the beginning of the twentieth century constituted a volatile and decisive period in German history. During this time, Germany transformed from an empire into a fractured republic, and in the process became a laboratory for experiments in democracy, the arts, and sexual expression—until these were dramatically foreclosed by fascism.

In this era of incredible transformation, perhaps nowhere was change sought more urgently than in the realms of sex, gender, and sexuality. Men and women reflecting a range of standpoints publicly debated the true nature of sexual drives and desires, the limits and boundaries of gender, and the implications of new understandings of sex and gender for the reform and regulation of sexual life. Within these debates, science came to play a pivotal role. For many, science held the promise of objectively establishing truths about bodies, minds, and desires that would provide a firm foundation for lasting social and political change. As such, science offered a language of both norms and possibilities.

The centrality of science in these debates precipitated an explosion of research into and theories about sex, gender, and sexuality in fields including (but not limited to) biology, anthropology, psychology, embryology, gynecology, and, later, endocrinology. By the first decade of the twentieth century, knowledge from these disparate disciplines had coalesced to form the unique field of *Sexualwissenschaft*, or sexology, and Germany quickly became established as the vanguard of sexual scientific research and writing. The knowledge produced during this period had long-term consequences: in fact, it helped forge the sexual identity categories and attitudes toward sex that shaped the twentieth (and arguably the twenty-first) century.

In the early years of the twentieth century, however, sexual categories lacked firm contours, taxonomies were still malleable, and the evaluation of sexual identities and desires remained contested. As a field in formation—one that involved an eclectic group of individuals and incorporated information from a wide range of disciplines—consensus on many issues did not exist. As knowledge proliferated, truth claims were rendered up for grabs. It took concerted effort to try and establish orthodoxy within the field (which was never truly achieved), and for the field to achieve a patina of expertise. These efforts involved not only establishing institutions, but also attempting to sideline unruly voices—particularly those of "amateur" women.

This aspect of building the field of sexology was flagged as early as May 1914, as a short article in the German sex reform journal *The New Generation* reveals. In "New Foundations for Sexology," the unattributed author (likely the controversial feminist, pacifist, and sex reformer Helene Stöcker) noted that it was "strange" (*seltsam*) that at the beginning of the twentieth century, after fifty years of the women's movement and almost ten years of the sex reform movement, women were not playing more important and prominent roles in the expansion and consolidation of sexology, particularly in the creation of knowledge about women's bodies and sexualities.[1] In the midst of chronicling the latest innovations

---

1. Helene Stöcker likely wrote the article because she edited *The New Generation* and as editor claimed responsibility for the "general part" of the publication.

in the scientific study of sex and celebrating them as evidence of the public's growing interest in sexual "problems," the author noted that women figured in new journals such as the *Archive for Women's Studies (Frauenkunde) and Eugenics* and the *Journal for Sexual Science* almost exclusively as "object[s]" of research, and were rarely considered as "subjects"—that is, as independent, self-determining agents capable of producing knowledge about their own sexual realities.[2]

Although the author magnanimously conceded that this "one-sidedness" was likely unintentional and ought to correct itself in time, the insertion of this critique into an otherwise purely informational text is illuminating.[3] It indicates that the content, direction, and sociopolitical implications of sexology were highly contested, especially along gendered lines. As many scholars have shown, conservative male sexologists in Germany and beyond actively used science to militate against women's rights claims. They mobilized research on the size and weight of women's brains, their reproductive functions, and their nervous systems to refute feminist demands for access to education, suffrage rights, and reforms to marriage and family law.[4] For many male sexologists, women were precisely objects to be studied, managed, and contained.

But these men did not monopolize sexual scientific knowledge. The fact that the author of "New Foundations for Sexology" believed that the elision and objectification of women would be "corrected" in time suggests that women had already made

2. "Neugründung zur Sexualwissenschaft," *Die neue Generation* 5 (May 1914): 287–289.

3. Ibid., 289.

4. See, for example, Lillian Faderman, "The Morbidifcation of Love between Women by 19th Century Sexologists," *Journal of Homosexuality* 4 (1978): 73–90; Janet Sayers, *Biological Politics: Feminist and Anti-Feminist Perspectives* (London: Tavistock, 1982); Sheila Jeffreys, *The Spinster and Her Enemies: Feminism and Sexuality, 1880–1930* (London: Pandora Press, 1985); Cynthia Eagle Russett, *Sexual Science: The Victorian Construction of Womanhood* (Cambridge, MA: Harvard University Press, 1989); Margaret Jackson, *The Real Facts of Life: Feminism and the Politics of Sexuality, c. 1850–1940* (London: Taylor and Francis, 1994); Lucy Bland, *Banishing the Beast: Feminism, Sex, and Morality* (London: Penguin Books, 1995; London: I. B. Tauris, 2001). Citations from Bland refer to the I. B. Tauris edition.

important contributions to sexology that were worthy of acknowledgment. Furthermore, the author's demand for a continued role for women within sexology reveals that certain women were invested, epistemologically and politically, in the creation of scientific knowledge about sex, gender, and sexuality. Yet 100 years after the publication of this warning against women's exclusion and marginalization from sexology, women remain largely peripheral to prevailing understandings of sexology, and to narratives about its history.

In *Sexual Politics and Feminist Science: Women Sexologists in Germany, 1900–1933*, I seek to correct course by bringing women from the margins to the center of analysis. In what follows, I examine German-speaking women's overlooked contributions to the rethinking of sex, gender, and sexuality taking place within sexology between 1900 and 1933. In so doing, I demonstrate that women not only played active roles in the creation of sexual scientific knowledge, but also made significant and influential interventions in the field that are worthy of rediscovery and engagement. Collectively, I refer to these women as women sexologists and as female sexual theorists, both to disrupt assumptions regarding sexological authorship and expertise, and to acknowledge the sustained intellectual energy these women dedicated to exploring, analyzing, and theorizing sexual subjectivity, desire, behavior, and relationships. Their sustained attention, focused textual output, intertextual and interpersonal connections to male sexologists, and international influence distinguish them from other feminist or female authors who wrote about sex at this time.

Of the nine women whose work I discuss, six were born and lived in Germany—namely, Ruth Bré, Henriette Fürth, Johanna Elberskirchen, Anna Rüling, Helene Stöcker, and Mathilde Vaerting; the others—Rosa Mayreder, Grete Meisel-Hess, and Sofie Lazarsfeld—were Austrian. Although this study focuses on developments within Germany, the close cultural, intellectual, and political ties between Germany and Austria in the early twentieth century allow for an examination of sexual theorizing taking place among Austrian women as well. At this time, ideas and individuals traveled frequently back and forth across relatively recently created territorial borders.[5] Moreover, evidence of interpersonal and organizational interconnection, as well as intellectual influence, exists among some of the women in this book. Mayreder and Meisel-Hess, for example, collaborated with like-minded reformers and intellectuals in Germany: they were active members of German sex reform movements like the League for the Protection of Mothers and Sexual Reform, and their writing exercised considerable influence among German feminists, sex reformers, and sexologists. Meisel-Hess in fact moved to Berlin in 1908.[6] Even Sofie Lazarsfeld, who did not play a central role in any of the organizations

---

5. Acknowledging the links and parallels between German and Austrian female sexual theorists reminds us not only that the sense of "Germanness" was transnational in the early twentieth century, but also that a sense of *European* interconnectedness was particularly pronounced among political, economic, cultural, and intellectual elites especially before the First World War, as Ute Frevert has pointed out. See Ute Frevert, "Europeanizing Germany's Twentieth Century," *History and Memory* 17 (Spring/Summer 2005): 87–116. Moreover, it prompts the question raised by David Blackbourn: "What did it mean around 1900 to be a German who was also a Pfälzer and a (reluctant) Bavarian, the more so when you lived on the French border, probably had family members who had settled in the Banat two centuries earlier, and had an uncle in Milwaukee?" "German" characterizes a broader linguistic and cultural community that included Austrians, German-speaking Swiss, and "ethnically" German inhabitants of Russia, Italy, France, and Hungary, and even extended in the later nineteenth and early twentieth century beyond Europe to Africa and North America as a result of imperialism and emigration. David Blackbourn, "Europeanizing German History: Comment on the Eighteenth Annual Lecture of the GHI, November 18, 2004," *GHI Bulletin* 36 (Spring 2005): 26. It is also important to acknowledge that, at the time this book begins, Germany had only been an independent, sovereign state for approximately three decades. Before that, the states comprising what became Germany had been part of the German Confederation, a loose association of German states established at the Congress of Vienna in 1815. Austria too had been a member of the German Confederation. Within the confederation, Austria and the powerful state of Prussia had fought each other for supremacy over the German territories within the confederation—a struggle that was decided in Prussia's favor following the Austro-Prussian war of 1866, and resolved when southern German states joined with Prussia and other northern German states in 1871 to form the new empire. Yet a sense of "greater Germany," or a kind of transnational "Germanness," first stirred in the nationalist revolutionary fervor around 1848, persisted after 1866 and 1871. Fruitful cultural and interpersonal exchange and political collaboration, particularly between major metropolises like Berlin and Vienna, certainly continued throughout the early twentieth century.

6. Conversely, psychiatrist Richard von Krafft-Ebing, born in the southern German city of Mannheim, made his career in Austrian asylums and universities.

that brought together many of the figures in this book, led education courses and gave lectures on individual psychology in Berlin during the early 1930s.

Several of these women, such as feminist intellectuals Stöcker, Mayreder, and Meisel-Hess, are well-known figures in German and Austrian women's history, while others, like writer-activists Elberskirchen, Rüling, Vaerting, and Lazarsfeld, are only now being rediscovered. Regardless of their relative fame, these women were remarkably productive sexual theorists and researchers who wrote on a range of topics including sexual instincts and desires, homosexual subjectivity, gender expression, sexual difference, and motherhood. Some of these women, like the prolific Johanna Elberskirchen, wrote on almost all of these themes, whereas others like Grete Meisel-Hess focused on particular issues, in Meisel-Hess's case heterosexual desire, maternal welfare, and racial hygiene.

The women sexologists studied in this book did not necessarily all share a common sexual politics, and especially disagreed on the meaning of sexual freedom: borrowing from Isaiah Berlin's famous formulation, some envisioned sexual freedom in "positive" terms, as a freedom to have and enjoy sex, while others treated it in "negative" terms, as a freedom from sexual obligations.[7] The personal and political motivations underlying their investments in sexual knowledge also varied significantly. Whereas Helene Stöcker lived in a common-law relationship with her long-term partner Bruno Springer, Henriette Fürth was a mother of eight who went on to have a career in Frankfurt's municipal politics. Rosa Mayreder was married but took on numerous lovers over the course of her life, and was an important intellectual within avant-garde Viennese circles. Johanna Elberskirchen, an active social democrat, lived openly as a lesbian, an extremely rare and courageous move for a woman of her time.

---

7. Isaiah Berlin, "Two Concepts of Liberty," in *Liberty: Incorporating Four Essays on Liberty*, ed. Henry Hardy (Oxford: Oxford University Press, 2002), 166–217.

Though they diverged in significant ways, these women shared a number of important demographic similarities. By and large, they were born between the 1850s and 1880s, and belonged to the middle classes broadly defined. Four of these women (Elberskirchen, Meisel-Hess, Stöcker, and Vaerting) enjoyed some university education, though they may not have attained a degree; Stöcker was among the first women to receive a PhD in Germany.[8] Though secular, these women tended to come from Protestant or Jewish confessional backgrounds; Catholics Mayreder and Vaerting are exceptional in this regard. They tended to be involved or affiliated with the "progressive" wing of the women's movement as well as scientifically oriented sex reform organizations, such as the Scientific Humanitarian Committee (Wissenschaftlich-humanitäres Komitee), the German Society for the Fight against Venereal Diseases (Deutsche Gesellschaft zur Bekämpfung der Geschlechtskrankheiten), and the League for the Protection of Mothers and Sexual Reform (Bund für Mutterschutz und Sexualreform). All would have been considered representative of the generation of "advanced," "modern," or "New Women" coming into view around the world around the beginning of the twentieth century.

Certainly, these women were not the only ones writing about sex, gender, and sexuality at this time, nor should their ideas be considered representative of "women's ideas"—even the women included

---

8. Women's access to education at this time can be described as spotty at best. The universities of Baden (Freiburg and Heidelberg) began admitting women as full-time (matriculated) students to all faculties in 1901; Prussia did not begin admitting female students until 1908. Before 1897, women who wished to attend lectures at Prussian universities had to obtain permission from the Prussian minister of education. Between 1897 and 1908, individual professors exercised the right to admit women to their classes. Before gaining the right to study in Germany, many German women of means pursued higher education in Switzerland. Once women became able to attend university, their numbers grew rapidly: according to Richard J. Evans, there were 80 full-time female students at German universities in 1905; by 1910, that number had risen to 1,867; by 1914, that number more than doubled to 4,126. See Richard J. Evans, *The Feminist Movement in Germany, 1894–1933* (London: Sage Publications, 1976), 19–20. On the history of German women's education, see James C. Albisetti, *Schooling German Girls and Women: Secondary and Higher Education in the Nineteenth Century* (Princeton, NJ: Princeton University Press, 1988).

in this study held a multiplicity of sometimes radically conflicting views. Nevertheless, all of these women explicitly embraced
the transformative implications of sexual science. At a time when
sexual norms, ethics, and knowledge were unstable, contested, and
quickly changing, these women sexologists saw feminist potential
in the scientization of sex. They intervened in the discursive melee
to articulate new understandings of female sexuality and same-sex
desire, criticize hegemonic expressions of masculinity and male heterosexuality, investigate the effects of war on sexuality, and insist
on the fluidity of gender. Their research and theories underwrote
empowering representations of autonomous, active, female sexual
desire, gender expressions that exceeded the masculine/feminine binary, and new forms of heterosexual relations beyond contractual
marriage and prostitution.

   Scientific knowledge about sex appealed to women sexologists for a number of reasons. Undoubtedly, science's growing social authority, derived from its status as a truth discourse, was a
major factor. The pace of new discoveries during the nineteenth
and early twentieth centuries emboldened scientists to declare
that their work would both enlighten and improve humanity. Scientists claimed that the empirical facts they produced about the
natural world had implications for the social: specifically, they
maintained that their work revealed the illegitimacy of existing
power relations based on "backward" traditions and dangerous
"superstitions." During the early years of Germany's existence
as a unified nation-state, scientists were often among the loud-
est challengers to established social and political powers. Physician, biologist, and anthropologist Rudolf Virchow, for example,
played a leading role in advancing policies aimed at diminishing
the authority of the Catholic Church following Germany's unification as part of what has become known as the "culture wars"
(*Kulturkampf*).[9] Over time, science came to inform a new, modern

---

9. Kevin Repp, *Reformers, Critics, and the Paths of German Modernity: Anti-
Politics and the Search for Alternatives, 1890–1914* (Cambridge, MA: Harvard
University Press, 2000), 40–41.

politics of legitimacy among new social actors vying for greater power and authority.

Power and authority were certainly in short supply for German women at the beginning of the twentieth century, regardless of their class position. Although the Imperial Civil Code of 1900 defined women as legal persons and freed them from the guardianship of their husbands, the Code only really addressed women as wives and mothers, thanks in part to its premise that the family constituted the fundamental unit of the state and society.[10] Despite being legal persons in their own right after 1900, and despite gaining control over their own wages earned from work outside of the home (which would of course have been less than their husbands', even when performing the same job), German women continued in many ways to occupy the status of legal minors. Legal power over children and property remained in husbands' hands, and the rules surrounding divorce were tightened.[11] And of course, until the Revolution of 1918, German women did not have the right to vote in national elections or run for office. Their subordinate legal status, their economic precariousness and dependence, their tenuous access to education and the professions, and their exclusion from formal political life made even middle-class women vulnerable as actors in the public sphere. Understanding their political and legal position alone gives us some sense of how hard women, above all feminist women, had to work to have their voices heard and make them matter; how difficult the task of changing dominant views

10. Myra Marx Ferree, *Varieties of Feminism: German Gender Politics in Global Perspective* (Stanford, CA: Stanford University Press, 2012), 37.

11. Section 1354, Part 1, of the Code stated that "the husband takes the decision in all matters affecting married life." Wives were obligated to transfer their property to their husbands upon marriage, and to submit property accrued during the marriage to their husbands. All legal power over children remained in fathers' hands, and mothers could not legally represent their children in relationships with third parties; as Section 1634 put it, "If the parents disagree, the father's opinion takes precedence." If a widow with children remarried, her new spouse would gain all legal powers over children. Under the Code, the grounds of divorce were tightened and did not allow for divorce by consent for childless couples, or on the grounds of insurmountable dislike. See Evans, *Feminist Movement in Germany*, 13–14.

about proper sexual roles and relationships really was; and what obstacles women faced in having their ideas about the world and its reformation acknowledged as legitimate, particularly when it came to the controversial topics of sex, gender, and sexuality.

Science was therefore strategically valuable for women. Deploying the language of science enabled women to frankly and publicly participate in debates about sex and sexuality and not comprise their respectability—a precious political commodity for disempowered social actors, and one that, for women, was largely premised upon the presumption of sexual ignorance. Science could help women conjoin claims regarding somatic sexual needs and evolutionary imperatives with demands for economic independence and legally inscribed rights and freedoms. Moreover, couching their claims in what Lorraine Daston and Fernando Vidal have termed the "moral authority of nature" enabled women to assert that realizing their demands would improve not only individual but also collective well-being.[12]

Yet the appeal of science was not merely strategic or rhetorical: treating sex objectively and rationally, as science claimed to do, further provided women with an alternative to religious frameworks for discussing sex, and broke with the conception of sex as sin. Many women insisted that gaining "objective" knowledge about sex was a necessary precondition for the formation of moral opinions, and for the proper governance of sexual life. As Johanna Elberskirchen put it, "As long as you rely on metaphysical arguments, which are elastic, a willing person with a good understanding of argumentation can confound you. That ends when you appeal to scientific facts, the results of natural history; they cannot be twisted or turned."[13] In Elberskirchen's view, "The source of every higher ethic, every higher moral is the laws of life."[14] Many women like Elberskirchen believed that science exposed the integral roles women played in sexual and social life, and revealed that women

---

12. Lorraine Daston and Fernando Vidal, eds., *The Moral Authority of Nature* (Chicago: University of Chicago Press, 2004).

13. Johanna Elberskirchen, "Offener Brief an Fräulein Dr. phil. Ella Mensch," *Frauen Rundschau* 5, no. 12 (1904): 382.

14. Ibid.

possessed innate sexual needs and instincts—along with a natural, "biological" right to live as autonomous and self-determining sexual agents. On the basis of its revelations, many women hoped that sexual science would effect a break with the arbitrary authority of the past and resolve long-standing inequalities. By revealing the "laws of life" and replacing ignorance with enlightenment, science could place women's destiny under their own control, and liberate them by opening up new vistas of existential possibility.

For many women, then, sexology seemed to provide resources to conceive of sexual life in ways that transcended the limitations of the "man-made" world—that is, when it was conducted properly. This last point must be stressed, as some women were highly suspicious of the effects of male bias among sexual scientists. As Elberskirchen put it in her 1903 tract, *Feminism and Science*, "When scientists critique women, they do so as men, and not scientists."[15] Women sexologists pitted their supposedly more objective knowledge against what they claimed were male scientists' self-interested assertions. Mathilde Vaerting for one insisted that men, as the dominant group, could not be objective, as their power blinded them from seeing conditions as they truly were.[16] At the same time, women often mobilized their gender as a unique epistemic location from which to produce sexual knowledge. In *Feminism and Science*, for example, Elberskirchen asserted that her experience as a woman, and her (self-proclaimed) authority as a medical specialist (*Medizinerin*), made her more objective when it came to women, and thus better able to read and interpret scientific evidence regarding women.[17] Likewise, in *Woman's Experience of the Male* (1931), Sofie Lazarsfeld declared that her sexological text brought together "feminine attitude" and "personal experience" with specialist knowledge gained from practical,

15. Johanna Elberskirchen, *Feminismus und Wissenschaft*, 2nd ed. (Leipzig: Magazine Verlag Jacques Hegner, 1903), 4.

16. See Kirsten Leng, "The Personal Is Scientific? Women, Gender, and the Production of Sexological Knowledge in Germany and Austria, 1900–1931," *History of Psychology* 18, no. 3 (2015): 238–251.

17. Elberskirchen, *Feminism und Wissenschaft*, 22.

professional experience.[18] These women claimed that their experiences as women and greater knowledge of women, combined with their grasp of scientific facts and their lack of bias regarding women's inferiority, made them better, more reliable producers of knowledge regarding women, sexual difference, and female sexuality. They maintained that their status as women provided them with the opportunity to produce a privileged form of what feminist science studies scholar Donna Haraway has termed "situated knowledge."[19]

In the early twentieth century, women sexologists' journal articles and encyclopedia entries were published alongside men's work. Some of their monographs, such Rosa Mayreder's *Towards a Critique of Femininity* (1905), Grete Meisel-Hess's *The Sexual Crisis* (1909), Mathilde Vaerting's two-volume *New Foundation for the Psychology of Sex* (1921, 1923), and Sofie Lazarsfeld's *Woman's Experience of the Male* (1931), were internationally influential and translated into multiple languages. Women's texts were reviewed and commented upon in major sexological journals, which also reported on lectures delivered by women sexologists. Moreover, whether they agreed with them or not, recognized male sexologists felt compelled to engage with women's ideas and arguments, as was the case for August Forel, who commented upon the work of Ruth Bré in *The Sexual Question* (1905), and Iwan Bloch, who engaged with ideas put forward by Rosa Mayreder in *The Sexual Life of Our Time* (1907).

Despite the fact that women's texts were influential and widely read in their own time, they have since fallen into obscurity. Several factors are responsible for the long-standing neglect of women's sexological writing, including the destructive impact of the Second World War, the general trajectory of the histories of sexology and sexuality, and later twentieth-and twenty-first-century assessments

---

18. Sofie Lazarsfeld, *Woman's Experience of the Male* (London: Francis Aldor, n.d.), 19.

19. Donna Haraway, "Situated Knowledges: The Science Question in Feminism and the Privilege of Partial Perspective," in *The Feminist Standpoint Theory Reader: Intellectual and Political Controversies*, ed. Sandra Harding (New York: Routledge, 2004), 81–102.

of who was or could be a producer of sexual scientific knowledge.[20] In revisiting this lost archive of women's sexual theory and writing, I show how women drew upon languages, conceptual frameworks, and cutting-edge discoveries from the natural and social sciences in order to create new knowledge about bodies, drives, and desires that challenged the sexual status quo and refuted misogynistic scientific pronouncements. In examining their writings, I show that women's ideas were not merely derivative of male authority, and highlight the epistemological consequences of feminist political commitments. Furthermore, in the course of outlining a critical intellectual history of women's engagements with sexology, I interrogate the historically and culturally specific possibilities for feminist politics that were latent in the scientization of sex.

The narrative offered by *Sexual Politics and Feminist Science* is not wholly celebratory, however. Like their male colleagues, women's efforts to understand and theorize sex through science were laced with cognitive biases and social prejudices that ultimately circumscribed the transformative potential of their ideas. Consistent with Haraway's concept of "situated knowledge," it is important to recognize that women's sexological work was always "partial," "radically contingent," and "certainly not innocent."[21] The fact that these women wrote from particular social locations shaped by their race, class status, education, sexuality, and ideological positions should cause us to exercise caution when evaluating their claims made on behalf of women as a whole. In addition to being constrained by their subjectivity, women sexologists' work was conditioned by sexology's discursive imperatives and prescriptive stances. The women I study shared early twentieth-century sexology's overriding concern with the health, improvement, and

---

20. For a thoroughgoing critique of gendered bias among historians of science regarding the questions of "how, where, and by whom knowledge has been produced," see Christine von Oertzen, Maria Rentetzi, and Elizabeth S. Watkins, "Finding Science in Surprising Places: Gender and the Geography of Scientific Knowledge; Introduction to 'Beyond the Academy: Histories of Gender and Knowledge,'" *Centaurus: An International Journal of the History of Science and its Cultural Aspects* 55 (May 2013): 73–80.
21. Haraway, "Situated Knowledges," 81–102.

regulation of individual bodies as a means of safeguarding the health and strength of the "body politic." Particularly in the years before 1918, their work was unmistakably shaped by eugenic logic, and as a result was laden with racial implications. Women's insistence on health and "naturalness" as the fundamental criteria for evaluating sexual actors and behaviors has had long-term ableist consequences, including for radical sexual politics. Consequently, the possibilities inherent in sexology cut both ways for women in general: emancipating for some, inhibiting for others. On the one hand, sexology was a site of productive disruption for female sexual theorists that catalyzed innovative visions of sexual subjectivities, demands for empowerment, and expressions of desire; on the other hand, it encouraged an exclusive and arguably elitist approach to sexual politics, specifically around the question of who was a desirable and valuable sexual subject. Ultimately, *Sexual Politics and Feminist Science* seeks to understand women's ideas in all their complexity in order to appreciate women's intellectual, epistemic, and political investments in sexology, excavate the full range of sexology's discursive effects, and contend with the complex legacy of women's scientized sexual theories.

Reconceptualizing Sexology through the Lens of Gender Politics

In order to make women's writing on gender and sexuality visible and intelligible as sexology, we must acknowledge the breadth and aims of sexology as it came into being in the early twentieth century. We must also engage with conceptual frameworks beyond those that have shaped the existing historiography; specifically, we must work "with and beyond" Michel Foucault in order to grasp sexology's multifaceted and polyvalent character.[22] Moreover, we

---

22. Here I borrow from the title of a recent text dedicated to assessing Foucault's legacy: Scott Spector, Helmut Puff, and Dagmar Herzog, eds., *After the "History of Sexuality": German Genealogies with and beyond Foucault* (New York: Berghahn, 2012).

must situate sexology within historical contexts notoriously over-looked by Foucault, namely, the histories of women and feminism. Together, these moves will demonstrate that approaching sexology through early twentieth-century gender politics offers grounds for a productive reconceptualization of sexology.

The term "sexology" is generally used to signify the knowledge produced as a result of the remarkable expansion of scientific research and theorizing about sex and sexuality over the course of the nineteenth century. During this period and into the twentieth century, researchers across a variety of fields preoccupied themselves with trying to understand the origins, essence, and etiology of sexual subjectivities, desires, and practices. At this time, gender and sexuality enjoyed no separate existence in either science or society: gender, sexual desires, and sexual behaviors were all viewed as properties emanating from particular kinds of bodies. In their pursuit of sexual truths, researchers drew upon new scientific hypotheses and discoveries emanating from the natural and social sciences, including Darwin's theorized mechanisms of evolution; eugenics, racial, and social hygiene; psychiatric theories of degeneration, hysteria, and neurasthenia; anthropological, ethnological, and archaeological investigations into ancient and "primitive" cultures; new findings on the processes of cellular and embryonic development; discoveries from medical fields such as venereology, dermatology, and gynecology; and newly discovered evidence of "internal secretions," or hormones, and their impact on sexual functions. Before (and even after) psychoanalysis established its own institutional trappings, it was also part of the sexological project. Freud certainly recognized his indebtedness to thinkers like Albert Moll in his *Three Essays on the Theory of Sexuality* (1905), and even published his important 1908 essay "Modern Sexual Morality and Modern Nervousness" in the sexological journal *Sexual Problems*.[23] Scientific interest in sex exploded around the

---

23. See footnote 1 to the first essay in Sigmund Freud, *Three Contributions to the Theory of Sexuality*, trans. A. A Brill, 2nd ed. (New York: Nervous and Mental Disease Publishing, 1920); Freud, "Die kulturelle Sexualmoral und die moderne Nervosität," *Sexual-Probleme* 4 (1908): 107–129. Freud also maintained correspondence with *Sexual-Probleme*'s editor, Max Marcuse, who was an early

world as diverse societies endeavored to cope with the transformations wrought by modernity, such as industrialization, urbanization, the consolidation of nation-states, and the solidification of middle-class hegemony.[24] Imperialism also played a critical role in the creation and circulation of sexual scientific knowledge around

---

champion of psychoanalysis. See Bernd Nitzschke, Annelise Heigel-Evers, and Franz Heigl, "Wo es in einer Sache nur Gegner oder Anhänger gibt': Ein bisher unbekannter Brief Sigmund Freuds an Max Marcuse," *Zeitschrift für Sexualforschung* 8 (1995): 241–248.

24. In recent years, scholars have reconstructed histories of sexual scientific research in European states like Germany, Austria, Italy, and Britain; East Asian nations such as China, Japan, and India; Middle Eastern territories formerly dominated by the Ottoman Empire; and twentieth-century North America. Roy Porter and Lesley A. Hall, *The Facts of Life: The Creation of Sexual Knowledge in Britain, 1650–1950* (New Haven, CT: Yale University Press, 1995); Henry L. Minton, *Departing from Deviance: A History of Homosexual Rights and Emancipatory Science in America* (Chicago: University of Chicago Press, 2002); Laura Briggs, *Reproducing Empire: Race, Sex, Science, and US Imperialism in Puerto Rico* (Berkeley: University of California Press, 2002); Sabina Frühstück, *Colonizing Sex: Sexology and Social Control in Modern Japan* (Berkeley: University of California Press, 2003); Volkmar Sigusch, *Geschichte der Sexualwissenschaft* (Frankfurt am Main: Campus Verlag, 2008); Heike Bauer, *English Literary Sexology: Translations of Inversion, 1860–1930* (London: Palgrave Macmillan, 2009); Liat Kozma, "Sexology in the Yishuv: The Rise and Decline of Sexual Consultation in Tel Aviv, 1930–1939," *International Journal of Middle East Studies* 42 (2010): 231–249; Howard Chiang, "Epistemic Modernity and the Emergence of Homosexuality in China," *Gender and History* 22 (2010): 629–657; Naoko Wake, *Private Practices: Harry Stack Sullivan, the Science of Homosexuality, and American Liberalism* (New Brunswick, NJ: Rutgers University Press, 2011); Chiara Beccalossi, *Female Sexual Inversion: Same-Sex Desires in Italian and British Sexology, c. 1870–1920* (London: Palgrave Macmillan, 2012); Britta McEwen, *Sexual Knowledge: Feeling, Fact, and Social Reform in Vienna, 1900–1934* (New York: Berghahn Books, 2012); Peter Hegarty, *Gentlemen's Disagreement: Alfred Kinsey, Lewis Terman, and the Sexual Politics of Smart Men* (Chicago: University of Chicago Press, 2013); Liat Kozma, "We, the Sexologists: Arabic Medical Writing on Sexuality, 1879–1943," *Journal of the History of Sexuality* 22 (September 2013): 426–445; Robert Beachey, "The German Invention of Homosexuality," *Journal of Modern History* 82 (2010): 801–838; Heike Bauer, ed., *Sexology and Translation: Cultural and Scientific Encounters across the Modern World, 1880–1930* (Philadelphia: Temple University Press, 2015). On specific national traditions of sexology, see Robert Nye, "The History of Sexuality in Context: National Sexological Traditions," *Science in Context* 4 (1991): 387–406.

the world, as the bodies and cultural practices of colonized peoples were exploited as empirical resources.[25]

The German terminological equivalent of "sexology" is *Sexualwissenschaft*.[26] Although *Sexualwissenschaft* literally translates to "sexual science," because of the more expansive meaning of the word *Wissenschaft*, it is better understood as the systematic and

---

25. Howard Chiang, "Double Alterity and the Global Historiography of Sexuality: China, Europe, and the Emergence of Sexuality as a Global Possibility," *e-pisteme* 2 (2009): 33–52; Ann Laura Stoler, *Carnal Knowledge and Imperial Power: Race and the Intimate in Colonial Rule* (Berkeley: University of California Press, 2002); I. C Schick, *The Erotic Margin: Sexuality and Spatiality in Alterist Discourse* (New York: Verso, 1999); Kirsten Leng, "Culture, Difference, and Sexual Progress in Turn-of-the-Century Europe: Cultural Othering and the German League for the Protection of Mothers and Sexual Reform, 1905–1914," *Journal of the History of Sexuality* 25, no. 1 (January 2016): 62–82.

26. Tracing the etymology of the term "sexology" is itself a challenge, as descriptors of the field vary across languages. Volkmar Sigusch has identified the Italian physician Paolo Mantegazza as the first sexologist, and noted that although Mantegazza did not use terminology such as sexology or sexual science to describe his work, he did characterize it as belonging to a "science of embraces" (*Geschichte der Wissenschaft*, 122). It is fascinating to note that one of the first recorded uses of the English term "sexology" was in the work of a woman, American writer Elizabeth Osgood Goodrich Willard. Though little is known about Willard herself, the very title of her 1867 book, *Sexology as the Philosophy of Life: Implying Social Organization and Government*, defines sexology in a way that highlights an intrinsic element of the scientization of sex: namely, that the study of sex was prompted by social concerns and endeavored to offer solutions. In 1889, the British mathematician, eugenicist, and Germanophile Karl Pearson wrote in his reflections on the end of the London-based "Men and Women's Discussion Club" that "the possibility of a 'learned society' to collect the facts of *sexualogy* had entered the minds of some of the men before the club was established"; however, he noted that such a society seemed "unfeasible" in the early 1880s because of "the unknown factor of how women would treat the proposal" (University College, University of London, Special Collections, Pearson Papers, 10/1 Minute Book of Men and Women's Club, Karl Pearson concluding reflections; undated but ca. June 1889; emphasis mine). However, in his reflections Pearson added, "Personally I am rather surprised than disappointed in the amount of really good scientific work which has been done by the Club, and I feel it is a real loss that the club has taken no actions to collect, reunite and publish for a wider range of students some of the papers—especially the historical—read at its meetings." On the history of the Men and Women's Club, see Bland, *Banishing the Beast*, 3–47; and Judith Walkowitz, *City of Dreadful Delight: Narratives of Sexual Danger in Late-Victorian London* (Chicago: University of Chicago Press, 1992), 135–170.

scholarly study of sex.[27] One of the earliest mentions of *Sexualwissenschaft* can be found in the writing of little-known author and publisher Karl Vanselow, who declared that one of the goals of his ultimately unsuccessful Association for Sexual Reform was the "establishment of a central point for sexual science under the leadership of qualified subject experts (*berufener Fachgelehrter*)."[28] The content, purpose, and parameters of *Sexualwissenschaft* were not formally elaborated until 1907, by the dermatologist Iwan Bloch in his highly influential monograph *The Sexual Life of Our Times*.[29] In this text, Bloch defined *Sexualwissenschaft* as "part of the general science of mankind," composed of "a union of all other sciences of general biology, anthropology and ethnology, philosophy and psychology, the history of literature, and the entire history of civilization." The "union" of these sciences was necessary, he insisted, to do "full justice to the many sided relationships between the sexual and all the other provinces of human life."[30] Seven years later, in a 1914 article entitled "Tasks and Goals of Sexology," Bloch explained that "sexual science as an independent discipline is the science of sex, that is, of the manifestations and effects of sexuality in physical and emotional, individual and social relationship. This conceptualization does justice to the peculiar double nature of

---

27. For interesting commentary on the historical meanings of science versus *Wissenschaft*, see "Forum: The 'German Question' in the History of Science and the 'Science Question' in German History," *German History* 29 (2011): 628–639.

28. Andreas Seeck, "Aufklärung oder Rückfall? Das Projekt der Etablierung einer 'Sexualwissenschaft' und deren Konzeption als Teil der Biologie," in *Durch Wissenschaft zur Gerechtigkeit? Textsammung zur kritischen Rezeption des Schaffens von Magnus Hirschfeld*, ed. Andreas Seeck (Münster: LIT Verlag, 2003), 174.

29. Intriguingly, Andreas Seeck points out that dermatologist and urologist Hermann Rohleder also called for the establishment of a "Sexologie" or "Geschlechtswissenschaft" in 1907, ostensibly independently of Bloch, in his *Vorlesungen über Geschlechtstrieb und gesamtes Geschlechtsleben des Menschen*. See Seeck, "Aufklärung oder Rückfall?," 174.

30. Iwan Bloch, *The Sexual Life of Our Time*, trans. Eden Paul (New York: Allied Book, 1908), xxi. On the contemporary reception of Bloch's 1907 definition of *Sexualwissenschaft*, see Seeck, "Aufklärung oder Rückfall?," 174–175. See also Sigusch, *Geschichte der Sexualwissenschaft*, 285–307.

the sex drive, its biological and cultural side."[31] Much like Bloch, physician Magnus Hirschfeld viewed sexology as a comprehensive realm of study; in his programmatic article, "Sexual Science as the Foundation of Sexual Reform," he enumerated the following areas of investigation as essential to the sexological project: sexual anatomy, sexual physiology, sexual psychology, sexual evolution, sexual chemistry, comparative sexual biology, sexual hygiene, sexual education, sexual prophylaxis, sexual politics, sexual laws, sexual ethics, sexual ethnology, sexual variation and pathology, and sexual statistics.[32]

Bloch and Hirschfeld's definitions draw our attention to the fact that early sexologists viewed their field as a truly human science that brought together diverse realms of knowledge to comprehensively study human sexuality. It was interdisciplinary avant la lettre, embracing a range of methodologies and subject matter under one rubric.[33] This point is important to stress in order to break the assumption that turn-of-the-century sexology exclusively reflected the medical gaze. German studies scholar Peter Davies has made this point quite bluntly: "There is, in fact, no fundamental method that sets *Sexualwissenschaft* apart from other disciplines. All that united the researchers who thought of themselves as *Sexualwissenschaftler* was the conviction that sexuality was the fundamental determining issue in both human nature and social structures, that it was liberating to discuss these things openly, and that the self-consciously interdisciplinary employment of modern methods . . . could establish fundamental truths about the body and its social meaning and sweep away traditional prejudice and ignorance. However, they agreed on little else."[34]

31. Iwan Bloch, "Aufgaben und Ziele der Sexualwissenschaft," *Zeitschrift für Sexualwissenschaft* 1 (April 1914): 3–4, 10–11.

32. Further description of each subfield can be found in Magnus Hirschfeld, "Sexualwissenschaft als Grundlage der Sexualreform," *Die neue Generation* 8 (1912): 115–126.

33. For a more detailed discussion of sexology's variety, see Seeck, "Aufklärung oder Rückfall?," 173–205.

34. Peter Davies, "Introduction: 'Crisis' or 'Hegemony'? Approaches to Masculinity," in *Edinburgh German Yearbook*, vol. 2, *Masculinities in German Culture*, ed. Sarah Colvin and Peter Davies (Rochester: Camden House, 2008), 10.

Although the rediscovery of fin-de-siècle sexology is largely attributable to the gay rights movement of the 1960s and 1970s,[35] it arguably took the publication of Michel Foucault's pathbreaking *History of Sexuality,* volume 1, not only to incite scholarly interest in what he termed "scientia sexualis," but also to provide the analytical framework that has influenced writing on sexology ever since.[36] In light of the remarkable influence of Foucault's work, and in order to understand how and where I diverge from it, it is worth exploring his analyses in some detail here.

In the *History of Sexuality,* volume 1, Foucault characterized sexual science as a complex discursive and epistemic apparatus dominated by medical men, above all psychiatrists. According to Foucault, scientists sought to develop a "system of legitimate knowledge" about sex, one that treated sexual desires as psychosomatic effects, and was structured by adjudications of normality and abnormality.[37] This "system of legitimate knowledge" played an integral role in defining, classifying, and evaluating sexual behaviors and desires, and provided the foundation for new, modern sexual subjectivities, most famously "the homosexual" but also, according to Foucault, the masturbating child, the Malthusian couple, and the

---

35. Rita Felski, "Introduction," *Sexology in Culture: Labelling Bodies and Desires,* ed. Lucy Bland and Laura Doan (Chicago: University of Chicago Press, 1998), 4. Sexology's history has also attracted interest from later twentieth-century sexologists such as Volkmar Sigusch who have endeavored to establish an intellectual genealogy for their field and identify early "pioneers." In addition to Sigusch's *Geschichte der Sexualwissenschaft,* see Vern Bullough, *Science in the Bedroom* (New York: Basic Books, 1995). For early biographies of sexological "pioneers," see Sheila Rowbotham and Jeffrey Weeks, *Socialism and the New Life: The Personal and Sexual Politics of Edward Carpenter and Havelock Ellis* (London: Pluto Press, 1977); and Phyllis Grosskurth, *Havelock Ellis: A Biography* (New York: Knopf, 1980). More recent biographical treatments include Manfred Herzer, *Magnus Hirschfeld: Leben und Werk eines jüdischen, schwulen und sozialistischen Sexologen* (Frankfurt am Main: Campus Verlag, 1992); Sheila Rowbotham, *Edward Carpenter: A Life of Liberty and Love* (New York: Verso, 2008); Elena Mancini, *Magnus Hirschfeld and the Quest for Sexual Freedom: A History of the First International Sexual Freedom Movement* (New York: Palgrave Macmillan, 2010).

36. For an early discussion of Foucault's influence, see Jeffrey Week's "Foucault for Historians," *History Workshop Journal* 14 (1982): 106–119.

37. Michel Foucault, *The History of Sexuality,* vol. 1, trans. Robert Hurley (New York: Vintage, 1990), 72.

hysterical woman.[38] Foucault argued that those who understood themselves according to the terms sexology provided would also judge themselves in accordance with its precepts, and subsequently regulate their own thoughts and behavior according to sexology's veiled moral prescriptions. As a result, sexology's classificatory schema not only effectively established hierarchies of desirable sexual subjects, but also helped discipline and control sexuality precisely at a time when defining and cultivating a distinctive sense of self was becoming a cultural preoccupation in Europe.[39] Perhaps even more importantly, Foucault maintained that the disciplinary work of sexology served new, insidious, and distinctively modern manifestations of power associated with managing and regulating life itself. According to Foucault, the long nineteenth century marked the first time in history that "biological existence was reflected in political existence," and that this development enabled "the subjugation of bodies and the control of populations" by targeting "life itself."[40] This new form of power, which he termed "biopower," aimed at maximizing the productivity of bodies, and was fundamentally concerned with the health of individual bodies and the body politic.[41]

This preoccupation with life and its maximization subsequently gave rise to the politicization of life, or what Foucault termed "biopolitics."[42] Biopolitics certainly characterizes political, social,

---

38. Foucault, *History of Sexuality*, vol. 1: 43, 104–105, 110. Although "the homosexual" has been the subject of much scholarly intervention and historical research, philosopher Penelope Deutscher has recently investigated the status of the Malthusian couple as one of the four "strategic assemblages" named by Foucault. See Penelope Deutscher, "Foucault's *History of Sexuality, Volume I*: Re-reading Its Reproduction," *Theory, Culture, and Society* 29 (January 2012): 119–137.

39. See Harry Oosterhuis, *Stepchildren of Nature: Krafft-Ebing, Psychiatry, and the Making of Sexual Identity* (Chicago: University of Chicago Press, 2000), 209–258. See also H. G. Cocks, "Historiographical Review: Modernity and the Self in the History of Sexuality," *Historical Journal* 49 (2006): 1211–1227.

40. Foucault, *History of Sexuality*, vol. 1, 142–143.

41. Ibid., 143.

42. Foucault offered an expanded discussion of biopolitics in his 1978–79 lectures at the Collège de France, in which he more explicitly tied the "birth of biopolitics" to the rise of liberalism and neoliberalism. See Michel Foucault, *The Birth of Biopolitics: Lectures at the Collège de France, 1978–1979*, ed. Michel Senellart

and cultural preoccupations in turn-of-the-century Germany. Following national unification in 1871, Germany witnessed rapid rates of industrialization and urbanization, which in turn sparked concerns about public health.[43] Urbanization made especially obvious the corporeal and spiritual ills of the "body politic," which were believed to materially and symbolically manifest themselves in sexual phenomena such as venereal diseases and prostitution. Concerns with public health were not merely or strictly managerial: as Paul Weindling has observed, health had ideological valences, as it was considered the foundation of both individual and national well-being and prosperity.[44] The idea that a healthy population constituted the foundation of national wealth is perhaps best captured by Austrian social democrat and sociologist Rudolf Goldscheid's theory of "human economy" (*Menschenökonomie*), which held that humans constituted "organic capital" and for this reason ought to be protected from exploitation, poverty, and disease.[45]

Beyond political economy, health had broader national and social valences in the early twentieth century, as it signified stability, cohesion, and collective strength. In the early twentieth century the state and civil society were often described in organic terms, endowed with a particular kind of living energy, and construed as

---

and trans. Graham Burchell (New York: Picador, 2008). Here I also want to stress that I am only interested in and engaging with Foucault's particular conceptualization of biopolitics. In recent years, "biopolitics" has attracted diverse scholarly interest, and has assumed a range of new meanings and connotations, particularly through the work of theorists like Giorgio Agamben, Michael Hardt and Antonio Negri, Agnes Heller, Didier Fassin, Paul Rabinow, and Nikolas Rose. For a helpful overview of the intellectual history of "biopolitics," see Thomas Lemke, *Biopolitics: An Advanced Introduction* (New York: New York University Press, 2011).

43. See Volker R. Berghahn, *Imperial Germany, 1871–1914: Economy, Society, and Politics*, rev. and exp. ed. (New York: Berghahn Books, 2005), 305.

44. Paul Weindling, *Health, Race, and German Politics between National Unification and Nazism, 1870–1945* (Cambridge: Cambridge University Press, 1989), 1.

45. Rudolf Goldscheid, *Höherentwicklung und Menschenökonomie: Grundlegung der Sozialbiologie* (Leipzig: Klinkhardt, 1911); Goldscheid, *Frauenfrage und Menschenökonomie* (Vienna: Anzengruber, 1914). See also Gudrun Exner, "Rudolf Goldscheid (1870–1931) and the Economy of Human Beings," *Vienna Yearbook of Population Research*, 2004, 283–301.

interconnected; consequently, any decline in the health and well-being of individuals was viewed as a serious threat to collective survival.[46] Such beliefs were held and promoted not only by state officials, but also by civil society actors, including those belonging to a variegated "life reform" movement (*Lebensreformbewegung*) popular among the German middle-classes that promoted natural therapies such as vegetarianism, therapeutic baths, wandering clubs, and garden cities, as means of realizing individual health and healing society.[47] Life itself even became the object of philosophical intervention at this time: aptly titled "life philosophy" (*Lebensphilosophie*), this tradition of thought is exemplified by the work of Friedrich Nietzsche—a thinker who exercised an extraordinary influence on many female sexual theorists—as well as by that of Henri Bergson and Wilhelm Dilthey.

---

46. Lemke, *Biopolitics*, 9–10. Such biological visions of the social and political can also be found in the writings of scientists themselves, as in physician and anthropologist Rudolf Virchow's concept of the "cell state." See also Paul Weindling, "Theories of the Cell State in Imperial Germany," in *Biology, Medicine, and Society, 1840–1940*, ed. Charles Webster (Cambridge: Cambridge University Press, 1981), 99–155. However, it is important to note that this intellectual tendency was not an exclusively German phenomenon. Thomas Lemke identifies early twentieth-century Swedish political scientist Rudolf Kjellén as one of the first to develop an elaborated "organicist concept of the state"; see Lemke, *Biopolitics*, 9. Biological metaphors for the social also pervade landmark works of sociology, such as Émile Durkheim's *On Suicide* (1897). Such beliefs were especially encapsulated by the doctrine of Monism, a popular belief system that insisted on the inseparability of matter and spirit. See Edward Ross Dickinson, "Reflections on Feminism and Monism in the Kaiserreich, 1900–1913," *Central European History* 34, no. 2 (2001): 191–230.

47. Michael Hau, *The Cult of Health and Beauty in Germany: A Social History, 1890–1930* (Chicago: University of Chicago Press, 2003), 1. On the life reform movement (and life philosophy), see also "Anders Leben: Wilder denken, freier lieben, grüner wohnen; Jugendbewegung und Lebensreform in Deutschland um 1900," in *Die Zeit Geschichte* 2, ed. Christian Staas (Hamburg: Zeitverlag Gerd Bucerius, 2013); Florentine Fritzen, *Gesünder Leben: Die Lebensreformbewegung im 20. Jahrhundert* (Stuttgart: Steiner, 2006); John Alexander Williams, *Turning to Nature in Germany: Hiking, Nudism, and Conservation, 1900–1940* (Stanford, CA: Stanford University Press, 2007); Kevin Repp, *Reformers, Critics, and the Paths of German Modernity: Anti-Politics and the Search for Alternatives* (Cambridge, MA: Harvard University Press, 2000), 266–273.

In his discussion of biopolitics, Foucault focused particular attention on the *"techniques* of power present at every level of the social body and utilized by very diverse institutions," including sexology.[48] According to him, sexology's potency lay in the unique opportunities it created for interventions into one of the most intimate spheres of individual life, namely, that designated by the concept of sex. As Foucault argued, sex constituted a privileged focal point for power because it offered "a means of access both to the life of the body and the life of the species."[49] Additionally, sexology helped to maintain "relations of domination and [the] effects of hegemony" through its adjudications of normality and abnormality, which in turn marked out desirable and undesirable lives and bodies.[50]

Foucault's terminology and conceptual frameworks have become deeply imprinted on the historiography of sexology: sexology is routinely described as "discourse," analyzed as a manifestation of "disciplinary knowledge," represented as a tool of "biopolitics" and "governmentality," and credited with the power of creating, controlling, and condemning sexual diversity and difference.[51] Additionally, the idea that sexual science was primarily interested in studying "deviants" and sexual "pathologies" has become almost axiomatic. Scholars following Foucault have often premised their histories of sexology upon analyses of texts written by a select group of male physicians and psychiatrists, such as Richard von Krafft-Ebing's *Psychopathia Sexualis* (1886), Havelock Ellis and John Addington Symonds's *Sexual Inversion* (1897), and Sigmund Freud's *Three Essays on the Theory of Sexuality* (1905). Within many existing accounts, sexologists and their texts are treated as "always already" authoritative and sharing a common worldview

---

48. Foucault, *History of Sexuality*, vol. 1, 141; emphasis in original.

49. Ibid., 146.

50. Ibid., 141.

51. On Foucault's influence on the history of sexuality generally, see Scott Spector, Helmut Puff, and Dagmar Herzog, eds., *After the History of Sexuality: German Genealogies with and beyond Foucault* (New York: Berghahn Books, 2012); Howard Chiang, ed., "Revisiting *The History of Sexuality:* Thinking with Foucault at Forty," special issue, *Cultural History* 5, no. 2 (October 2016).

and set of attitudes toward sex. Moreover, many analyses obscure or selectively address these texts' larger social contexts.

To be clear, I am not contending that Foucault's claims are untrue, nor do I wish to disparage previous scholars' work; in fact, I draw heavily from Foucault's insights and the existing rich historiography in my examinations of women's contributions and ideas. However, I do maintain that Foucault's narrative and analytical framework offer a rather limited view of what sexology was, who created it, and what its effects were. Analyzing sexology solely in terms of biopolitics, biopower, deviance, and pathology only allow us to tell part of the full story: in particular, such analyses obscure the critical contributions women made to sexology, and leave us utterly incapable of understanding why women would bother to involve themselves in this intellectual project, aside from a "will to power."

Women's interest and investments in sexology begin to make sense once we acknowledge that the expansion of scientific research into sex, gender, and sexuality coincided with the international emergence of the "woman question," the collective term for the widespread debates regarding women's roles and rights.[52] By the later nineteenth and early twentieth centuries, the woman question included discussion of questions pertaining to sex, including differences in the nature of female and male sexuality. In Germany, the upswing in interest in female sexuality coincided with efforts to introduce "protective" labor legislation to regulate female factory workers. As Kathleen Canning has observed, the maternal bodies of women workers constituted a powerful symbol and point of political intervention that connected "the factory to the nation, . . . the conditions of work to the conditions of (national) reproduction and the national birth rate."[53]

---

52. On this point, see Lucy Bland, "Introduction [Gender and Sexual Difference]," in *Sexology Uncensored: The Documents of Sexual Science*, ed. Lucy Bland and Laura Doan (Chicago: University of Chicago Press, 1998), 11.

53. Kathleen Canning, "Social Policy, Body Politics: Recasting the Social Question in Germany, 1875–1900," in *Gender History in Practice: Historical Perspectives on Bodies, Class, and Citizenship* (Ithaca, NY: Cornell University Press, 2006), 162.

Interest in female sexuality also coincided with the expansion and consolidation of the German women's movements.[54] In the late nineteenth century, middle-class German women's groups began to organize themselves into larger coordinating federations: the largest association, the League of German Women's Associations (Bund Deutscher Frauenvereine, BDF), was established in 1894, and represented 137 groups with approximately 70,000 members by 1901.[55] The BDF's diverse members reflected a range of political orientations—aside from social democrats, who were excluded from the BDF and organized their own movement apart from "bourgeois" feminists under the auspices of the Social Democratic Party.[56] A smaller coordinating organization, alternately characterized as left-liberal and progressive, took shape under the aegis of the Union of Progressive Women's Associations (Verband Fortschrittlicher Frauenvereine, VFF) in 1899 following a rift among feminists within the BDF.[57] Although the break between the BDF and VFF was never absolute, this schism defined the dominant ideological divisions within the middle-class German women's movement: while "progressives" were eager to tackle provocative social and sexual issues and demand dramatic reforms, the "moderates" proved more hesitant to deal with sexuality head-on, and more willing to work within the status quo.[58] For

---

54. On the German women's movement, see Evans, *Feminist Movement in Germany*; Theresa Wobbe, *Gleichheit und Differenz: Politische Strategien von Frauenrechtlerinnen um die Jahrhundertwende* (Frankfurt am Main: Campus Verlag, 1989); Ute Gerhard, *Unerhört: Die Geschichte der deutschen Frauenbewegung* (Hamburg: Rowohlt Taschenbuch Verlag, 1990); Ferree, *Varieties of Feminism*. On the history of Austrian feminism, see Agatha Schwartz, *Shifting Voices: Feminist Thought and Women's Writing in Fin-de-Siècle Austria and Hungary* (Montreal: McGill-Queen's University Press, 2008); Harriet Anderson, *Utopian Feminism: Women's Movements in Fin-de-Siècle Vienna* (New Haven, CT: Yale University Press, 1992).

55. Evans, *Feminist Movement in Germany*, 37.

56. On the German Social Democratic women's movement, see Jean Quataert, *Reluctant Feminists in German Social Democracy, 1885–1917* (Princeton, NJ: Princeton University Press, 1979).

57. Evans, *Feminist Movement in Germany*, 47–50.

58. As Richard Evans has pointed out, many radicals stayed in the BDF, and progressive feminist Marie Stritt became a leader within the BDF in the early 1900s

this reason, it is perhaps not surprising that most of the women sexologists examined in this book were affiliated with the progressive faction of the German women's movement.

Yet despite moderates' reluctance to directly focus on sexuality, both factions of the German women's movement addressed social and what they termed "moral" issues, including prostitution and the inequities of marriage and the patriarchal family.[59] There are a number of reasons why German feminists were preoccupied with social and moral issues, as opposed to more obviously and formally political ones, at this time. Part of the reason lies in the German women's movements' strong roots in social welfare work. Performing welfare and charitable work was one of the major ways middle-class women were able to enter public life, as such endeavors were considered appropriately feminine; moreover, undertaking "useful" labor that served the community helped bolster demands for women's rights, as Richard Evans has noted.[60] Another important factor was the legal ban on German women's political participation. Under the Prussian Law of Association of 1851, women were denied the right to join political parties or attend meetings where political issues might be publicly discussed. This ban was maintained until the passage of the Imperial Law of Association in 1908.[61]

A further important consideration lies in the fact that, to paraphrase later generations of feminists, "the personal is political." Moral and social rules help to establish the boundaries of what people think they can do with their lives, and of course, moral

---

(Evans, *Feminist Movement in Germany*, 48–52). The VFF itself ultimately voted to join the BDF in 1907 (Evans, 149–150). In addition to the progressive and moderate wings of the German women's movement, there also existed a conservative right wing, represented by urban and rural Housewives Associations, as well as confessionally defined women's groups like the League of Protestant Evangelical Women, led by Paula Müller.

59. Evans, *Feminist Movement in Germany*, 52–53; Wobbe, *Gleichheit und Differenz*, 23–25. Although the demand for women's suffrage was on the agenda, it attracted much less interest and attention among activists, and only within the progressive wing.

60. Evans, *Feminist Movement in Germany*, 9, 29.

61. Ibid., 11, 73.

standards often concentrate on sexual behavior and vary according to gender. Far from viewing issues relating to sex as esoteric
and trivial, women active in both the moderate and the progressive wings of the movement were highly attuned to their political
importance.[62] Progressives in particular identified sexual relations
as a source of women's broader social, political, and economic oppression, and recognized that beliefs about female and male sexuality served to determine and justify limitations on women's legal
rights, social being, and access to public spaces—limitations that
inhibited women's broader powers of self-determination.[63] Importantly, they identified the ways in which prevailing understandings
of female and male sexuality were underwritten by a patriarchal
sexual logic—a sexual double standard (*doppelte Moral*)[64]—that
simultaneously authorized male dominance in the bedroom and
male control over the state and civil society.[65] Combating sexist
assumptions about the capacity for sexual agency was, in effect, an
act of claiming citizenship: as Isabel Hull has shown, philosophers
and lawmakers had, since the Enlightenment, rationalized men's
greater involvement in civil society and women's exclusion from it
on the grounds of men's sexual potency and self-determination.[66]

62. On this point, see Kirsten Reinert, *Frauen und Sexualmoral* (Herzbolzheim:
Centaurus Verlag, 2000), 15–29.

63. According to Myra Marx Ferree, the question of how women could realize a right to personal and political self-determination was one that had exercised
German feminists since the (ultimately failed) 1848 revolution. See Ferree, *Varieties of Feminism*, 33.

64. On the sexual double standard, see Keith Thomas, "The Double Standard,"
Journal of the History of Ideas 20 (1959): 195–216.

65. On this point, see also Edward Ross Dickinson, "The Men's Christian Morality Movement in Germany, 1880–1914: Some Reflections on Politics, Sex, and
Sexual Politics," *Journal of Modern History* 75 (March 2003): 108.

66. According to Hull, the practitioners of early modern German civil society
"released the foundation of their new society, the male individual, from his social
'fetters' and reconceived him according to dynamics they understood as 'natural.' . . .
They built upon the traditional [gendered] sexual associations, and their creation
became the sexually potent, desiring, self-determining individual fit for active citizenship." While they stressed men's sexual potency, energy, and desire, they put
women in "social fetters" considering her "only as wife and mother." Hull points
out that women's "derivative social status was mirrored in [their] derivative sexual nature"; a woman was not seen as "independent, emancipated or a citizen, she

These issues arguably became more urgent at the turn of the century as a generation of self-consciously modern women attained leadership roles in the women's movement and wrestled with the question of how women could exercise agency over the conditions of their own lives.[67]

Turn-of-the-century debates about sex and gender therefore had profound implications for women's demands for greater autonomy and greater involvement in public life. Women actively participated in these debates in order to advance new, empowering visions of sexual subjectivity that would underwrite their demands for control over their own bodies, lives, and fates. The women who endeavored to establish sexual truths for themselves did so often through recourse to science. Aside from friends and relatives who shared specialized texts of potential interest, as was the case for Rosa Mayreder, women largely gained access to scientific ideas as a result of the widespread popularization of science over the course of the nineteenth and early twentieth centuries.[68] During this time, a variety of scientific ideas, theories, and evidence was made available to lay audiences through circulation within journals, newspapers, lectures, and exhibitions, as well as novels, lyrical texts,

---

could not be sexually self-determining, she could not 'posit' her own desire, will it, and act upon it." In this way, "the civic and the sexual mutually constituted each other." See Isabel V. Hull, *Sexuality, State, and Civil Society in Germany, 1700–1815* (Ithaca, NY: Cornell University Press, 1996), 410–411.

67. On German women's preoccupation with subjectivity and existential possibility in the early twentieth century, see Marti Lybeck, "Gender, Sexuality, and Belonging: Female Homosexuality in Germany, 1890–1933" (PhD diss., University of Michigan, 2007).

68. On the popularization of science, see Bernard Lightman and Aileen Fyfe, eds., *Science in the Marketplace: Nineteenth-Century Sites and Experiences* (Chicago: University of Chicago Press, 2007); and Bernard Lightman, *Victorian Popularizers of Science: Designing Nature for New Audiences* (Chicago: University of Chicago Press, 2007). It should be noted here that the concepts of "popular science" and "popularized science" are contested among historians of science because of the dichotomy the term implies between "professional" and "popular science." For more on this debate, see the essays included in "Focus: Historicizing 'Popular Science,'" special issue, *Isis* 100 (June 2009); as well as Roger Cooter and Stephen Pumfey, "Separate Spheres and Public Spaces: Reflections on the History of Science Popularization and Science in Popular Culture," *History of Science* 32 (September 1994): 237–267.

and inexpensive tracts that made complex ideas comprehensible. The popularization of science through "the means of mass communication that [science] helped to invent" ensured that the public was up-to-date on all of the latest innovations, and that "science and medicine were part of a common cultural context," as Paul Weindling has noted.[69] Enthusiasm for science transcended class and gender boundaries: both women and workers proved avid consumers of science.[70]

Women's engagement of science may be viewed as an example of what Foucault termed "tactical polyvalence."[71] In the *History of Sexuality*, volume 1, Foucault allowed for the resistant use of knowledge through his observation that sexological categories and pronouncements provoked dissent among the target audiences for regulation, and that they often expressed their dissent using the language of sexology itself. Foucault further acknowledged that sexology could be and was redeployed to serve a range of political and rhetorical ends, including those favored by marginalized groups. Yet within Foucault's framework, the "reverse discourses" resulting from such discursive maneuvers remain resolutely oppositional: he did not view them as helping shape sexology itself, and the authors of reverse discourses are not treated as producers of sexological knowledge in their own right. Within Foucault's framework, the boundary marked by medico-scientific expertise appears inviolable: scientific knowledge making is left to accredited scientists, who appear immanently authoritative, while resistant knowledge produced via reverse discourse constitutes a rhetorical strategy, but not real knowledge. However, the women whose work is examined in this book did not simply and uncritically redeploy scientific resources created by men, or use science to footnote potentially contentious claims: they actively produced new information, writing articles and monographs and giving lectures that sought to challenge men's pronouncements, reinterpret existing

---

69. Weindling, *Health, Race, and German Politics*, 3.

70. On the broad popularity of Darwin in Germany at this time, see Alfred Kelly, *The Descent of Darwin: The Popularization of Darwinism, 1860–1914* (Chapel Hill: University of North Carolina Press, 1981).

71. Foucault, *History of Sexuality*, vol. 1, 100–102.

evidence, and develop their own sexual theories and comprehensive analyses of sexual life. Their textual engagements of sex and science exceeded the feminist public sphere: women advanced their feminist sexual science from deep within the sexological milieu, an epistemic and political community constituted by key journals and sex reform organizations.[72] They were engaged in conversation—and at times, in contentious debate—with men, using a common language and set of conceptual resources. Through their own unique engagements with sexual science, women questioned the validity of male-authored knowledge, particularly about women. By advancing their own knowledge, women were fighting to define sexual reality.

For these reason, contra Foucault I argue that women ought to be viewed as not merely appropriating knowledge to forge "reverse discourses," but as sexologists in their own right. Some may resist viewing women in this way by virtue of their lack of professional titles, academic appointments, clinical research experience, and, in some cases, formal education. However, so doing would deny the historical reality that putative amateurs often produced sexological

---

72. I have adopted the concept of the "epistemic community" from Peter Haas. Haas defined epistemic communities as "networks of professionals with recognized expertise and competence in a particular domain and an authoritative claim to policy-relevant knowledge within that domain or issue-area." What bonds members of an epistemic community, he maintained, is "their shared belief or faith in the verity and applicability of particular forms of knowledge." Epistemic communities are further unified by shared normative and principled beliefs, shared ways of knowing, shared patterns of reasoning, shared discursive practices, and shared commitments to the application and production of knowledge. All of these shared traits, Haas argued, "provide a value-based rationale for the social action of community members." While women sexologists may have lacked credentials, they shared with male practitioners of sexual science common ways of knowing, patterns of reasoning, discursive practices, and commitments to the production and application of knowledge for shared sociopolitical ends. Where they disagreed was on the political implications of facts derived from shared ways of knowing. See Peter Haas, "Introduction: Epistemic Communities and International Policy Coordination," *International Organization* 46 (Winter 1992): 18, 3. The concept of "epistemic communities" has also been elaborated by feminist science studies scholars and philosophers of science; see Lynn Hankinson Nelson, "Epistemic Communities," in *Feminist Epistemologies*, ed. Linda Alcoff and Elizabeth Potter (New York: Routledge, 2013), 121–160.

knowledge outside of academic spaces; indeed, the professionalization and specialization of science are themselves relatively recent historical phenomena. The argument that historians should give more attention to male sexologists because more men were accredited as physicians and scientists is specious. Most of the male doctors who figure prominently within the history of sexology had no specialized training for the comprehensive study of sex. Iwan Bloch, for example, was trained in dermatology, as was Max Marcuse. Richard von Krafft-Ebing was a psychiatrist; Albert Moll a neurologist. Magnus Hirschfeld and Havelock Ellis were physicians— and Ellis never practiced medicine. It is also worth noting that a number of men without formal medical or scientific training, such as the British socialist and sexual radical Edward Carpenter, are frequently included within the pantheon of sexological pioneers. The presence of such men makes the absence of women like Johanna Elberskirchen, a German feminist who frequently wrote about sex and actually studied natural sciences at the University of Bern, even more striking.[73] Tellingly, Volkmar Sigusch paid only one woman—Helene Stöcker—any significant attention in his comprehensive and invaluable *History of Sexual Science*, though he curiously does acknowledge many women's contributions in his supplementary *Lexicon of Sexual Researchers*.[74] In reality, the creation of sexological knowledge was a collaborative and polyvocal project, even if the history of sexology has thus far been defined by an exclusive collection of "expert" male voices.

Approaching sexology while attentive to the politics of gender— and with a particular focus on women's intellectual contributions— highlights the importance of considering knowledge production as a complex social act, one engaged by diversely situated authors across multiple, overlapping discursive sites. To effect an analytical

---

73. In her texts Elberskirchen often claimed for herself the title of "Medizinerin." See, for example, Elberskirchen, *Feminismus und Wissenschaft*, 22.

74. See Volkmar Sigusch, "Neue Ethik, Mutterschutz und freie Liebe: Helene Stöckers Kampf gegen Männermoral, Frauenunterdrückung und Krieg," in *Geschichte der Sexualwissenschaft*, 254–260. See also Volkmar Sigusch and Günter Grau, eds., *Personenlexikon der Sexualforschung* (Frankfurt am Main: Campus Verlag, 2009).

shift in this direction, I propose reconceptualizing sexology as a field of knowledge production, rather than as a set of discourses reflecting a consensual worldview. The concept of fields, as initially formulated by Pierre Bourdieu, provides a framework through which to grasp the fundamentally social and contested dynamics of sexological knowledge production.[75] In framing sexology as a field, I draw on Steven Epstein's use of fields as a means of understanding the production of knowledge about HIV in the United States during the 1980s and 1990s. Proceeding from Bourdieu, Epstein characterized fields as "specific, relatively autonomous, domains of social action—domains of social production and reproduction— that both reflect and constrain the interests, positions, strategies, and investments of the actors within them. Inside each field, players compete with one another subject to the current rules of the game, but in so doing they seek to reshape the rules to suit the means at their disposal."[76] One of the benefits of analyzing sexology through the concept of the field is the attention it draws to the actors, sites, and processes involved in knowledge production. According to the field paradigm, the production of knowledge is fundamentally tied to struggles for power and authority, and involves a range of actors united by commonly held epistemologies and broad social connections. Moreover, as Epstein pointed out, the field paradigm militates against any presumptions regarding which groups and which sites create scientific knowledge.[77] It opens up the possibility that science can be created by diversely situated actors through the "encounter—or clash—between members of many different social worlds."[78]

---

75. See, for example, Pierre Bourdieu, "The Specificity of the Scientific Field and the Social Conditions of the Progress of Reason," *Social Science Information* 14 (December 1975): 19–47.

76. Steven Epstein, *Impure Science: AIDS, Activism, and the Politics of Knowledge* (Berkeley: University of California Press, 1996), xxxix.

77. Ibid., xxxvii. Historians of science in Germany, and of gender and science, have also increasingly called upon scholars to pay greater attention to the diverse sites and actors involved in the production and dissemination of scientific knowledge. See "Forum: The 'German Question,'" 628–639; Oertzen, Rentetzi, and Watkins, "Finding Science in Surprising Places," 73–80.

78. Epstein, *Impure Science*, xxxv, xxxix.

Treating sexology as a field facilitates an understanding of sexology as a socially embedded, interactional, and highly contested practice of knowledge production, one that was not limited to a select few (male) authors and canonical texts. By stressing that contests for and over power were key elements in the production of knowledge, the field framework helps illuminate the fact that sexology was animated by competing ideas and theorizations of sexual practices and subjectivities. Framing sexology as a field not only destabilizes our understandings of expertise and authority, but also allows for a fuller exploration of sexology's polyvalent political potential. Thinking of sexology as a field allows us to consider sexology's effects beyond regulation, discipline, and servicing "biopolitics" in the sense articulated by Foucault. Moreover, it offers an expanded understanding of the possible meanings of "biopolitics" itself, which I address in further detail below. Finally, this new conceptualization of sexology, situated within specific historical contexts and sets of social and political relations, allows us to account for women's role as participants in the deeply contested practice of sexological knowledge production.

The Biopolitical Potential and Pitfalls of Sexology

Women's engagements with sexology enabled them to rethink gender and sexuality in new, imaginative, and potentially empowering ways. Within their work, they were able to express ideas that were highly controversial at the time, including the claims that women had innate sexual needs, drives, and desires, both for the opposite and the same sex; that gendered identity exceeded a biologically arbitrary male/female binary and existed in numerous diverse combinations along a spectrum; that male (hetero)sexuality was destructive and in desperate need of reform; and that women should have the right to control their own fertility. All of these ideas had implications for women's rights and social reform; many of them have become widely accepted today.

Women's sexological work arguably demonstrates another possible valence of "biopolitics": namely, an interest in the existential potential embedded in the biological body. Early twentieth-century women were particularly invested in the process of "becoming subjects," that is, becoming self-determining, autonomous individuals empowered, and not limited, by their cultures, societies, and bodies. They wanted to imagine and explore what new kinds of social roles they could occupy, what relationships they could enjoy with men and other women, what intellectual and physical labor they could undertake—and how these might be facilitated or limited by physiology and psychology. Here, new knowledge about bodies and brains would prove an essential resource for efforts to challenge assumptions about women's capacities. Sexual scientific research was constantly undermining limits on women's social roles by revealing, for example, the indeterminacy and contingency of biological sex development and the existence of female sexual desires and needs. Such research suggested that the biological body did not constitute a limit on women's social role, but rather served as a site of multiple subjective possibilities. This strand of biopolitics enabled female sexual theorists to ground sex, love, and desire in the body, theorize new subjectivities, and assert what they believed to be women's "biological right" to sexual expression.

And yet, these powers and possibilities were limited to particular *kinds* of women. Women's sexological ideas have consequently bequeathed an incredibly complicated historical legacy, and this statement is particularly true of the German case. Despite their critical stances on male bias within the sexological field, women's writing was nonetheless infused with the field's norms, values, and concerns. Specifically, concerns with the "quality" of populations and effects of individual acts on collective well-being heavily informed women's writing. Like their male colleagues, women conceived of collective life in organic terms, as a body politic in an almost literal sense. In so doing, they helped contribute to what Ulrich Herbert has termed the "biologization of the social" in early twentieth-century Germany.[79] Women adjudicated and evaluated

---

79. Ulrich Herbert, "Rassismus und rationales Kalkul," in *"Vernichtungspolitik": Eine Debatte über den Zusammenhang von Sozialpolitik und Genozid im nationalsozialistischen Deutschland,* ed. Wolfgang Schneider (Hamburg: Junius,

sex and sexualities in the binary terms of healthy versus sick, regenerative versus degenerative, natural versus unnatural, and normal versus abnormal; as Johanna Elberskirchen put it in her treatise *The Love of the Third Sex* (1904), these women advocated only on behalf of those subjects "of healthy mind, healthy spirit (*Geist*), and healthy morals."[80] The differential standards of value these women assigned to different kinds of subjects clearly circumscribed and undercut the universal emancipatory potential of their work, and even created new forms of exclusions among women along the lines of health. Women sexologists believed such hierarchical treatments of human life were completely consistent with their left-leaning politics.

Questions regarding health, value, and virtue, and concerns with the impacts of individual acts on collective life, did not exist apart from concerns with race. Scholars have devoted much-needed attention to the role of race in sexological writing, and have shown that studying sex simultaneously meant (and means) studying race.[81] The connections between sex and race, as variously defined around the beginning of the twentieth century, will be examined in further detail in chapter 5. Within sexology, racial thinking took place across various registers, with race alternately denoting color, ethnicity, nationality, region, religion, and, at its broadest, humanity itself. Though most German sexologists examined here tended to deploy race as a synonym for nation rather than skin color, it is important to acknowledge the implicit and assumed whiteness that informed men and women's sexological writing.[82]

1991), 28; quoted in Edward Ross Dickinson, "Biopolitics, Fascism, Democracy: Reflections on Our Discourse about 'Modernity,'" *Central European History* 37 (2004): 3.

80. Johanna Elberskirchen, *Die Liebe des dritten Geschlechts: Homosexualität, eine bisexuelle Varietät keine Entartung—keine Schuld* (Leipzig: Max Sport Verlag, 1904), 35–38.

81. See, for example, Siobhan Somerville, *Queering the Color Line: Race and the Invention of Homosexuality in American Culture* (Durham, NC: Duke University Press, 2000); Julian Carter, *The Heart of Whiteness: Normal Sexuality and Race in America, 1880–1940* (Durham, NC: Duke University Press, 2007).

82. Fatima El-Tayeb, *Schwarze Deutsch: Der Diskurs um "Rasse" und nationale Identität 1890–1933* (Frankfurt: Campus, 2001) 149–152; quoted in Laurie

Whiteness in and of itself was no guarantor of normality or biopolitical desirability, however. Attending specifically to women's insistent focus on health in their work highlights one of the most enduring, problematic, and arguably overlooked legacies of women's sexological writing: what we could now describe as their relentless ableism. The sexual delegitimization of people with disabilities cut across numerous axes of difference. Like their male counterparts, women prioritized and highly valued specific understandings of physical and psychological health, both as goals in and of themselves *and* as preconditions for sexual agency, pleasure, and socially legitimate sexual subjectivities. They disavowed supposedly unhealthy subjects, above all those whose bodies and minds had been "disabled" by disease, disadvantageous living conditions, or workplace accidents. Within sexological texts, the "crippled," the "feebleminded" (*schwachsinnig*), the syphilitic, and the alcoholic—of all genders, races, and sexual orientations—were repeatedly marked out as illegitimate sexual subjects out of fear of the potential consequences of their reproduction for the body politic. Assertions of unsuitability were grounded not just in medical claims, but also in aesthetic assertions, as the natural was conflated with the beautiful and the moral. Such tendencies were present in the writing of virtually all the women studied in this book, especially in the years before the end of the First World War.

Women sexologists were thus equally complicit in tying sexual agency to certain notions of ability. Their work articulated and aimed to legitimate a range of new sexual possibilities—as long as they were performed by otherwise healthy, putatively natural bodies. Their writing in turn rendered "disabled" people not only sexually threatening, but also improper sexual subjects. Drawing on disability and queer studies scholar Robert McRuer's critical insights into the intersections of disability and sexuality, it can be observed that women sexologists promulgated "compulsory

Marhoefer, *Sex and the Weimar Republic: German Homosexual Emancipation and the Rise of the Nazis* (Toronto: University of Toronto Press, 2015), 16.

able-bodiedness."[83] They denied supposedly unhealthy bodies the possibility of sexual recognition, validation, or empowerment. The primacy of health in sexologists' adjudications of sexualities—and human lives—had a wide range of damning implications, particularly when it came to reproduction. Though it would be inaccurate and unfair to hold these ideas directly responsible for state policies or for Nazi racism, at the very least the discursive conjunction of ability and sexuality would resonate in the silence around disability issues within discussions of sexual liberation throughout the twentieth century. This silence is only now being challenged, thanks in part to the flourishing of disability studies and disability rights activism in recent years.[84]

At the same time, it is important to attend to change in women's writings over the three decades I explore. Shifts within women's sexological writings become particularly notable during and after the First World War. After the war, women's writings began to shift focus away from a rigid interest in health and racial quality in order to explore the social construction of femininity and masculinity. Yet despite this development, biopolitics haunted sexological writing in a different guise: it is precisely at a time when women's sexology starts to take a more radical perspective on the contingency of gender that it begins to take on a particularly rigid insistence on heterosexuality, and helps firm up sexology's heterosexism.

In order to do justice to women's ideas and their legacies for the present, in the following chapters I examine women's ideas in all of their ambivalence. I take stock of their imaginative, empowering innovations as well as their damning discursive implications. It is important to recognize that this dynamic of possibility and

---

83. Robert McRuer, "Compulsory Able-Bodiedness and Queer/Disabled Existence," in *The Disability Studies Reader*, ed. Lennard J. Davis, 4th ed. (London: Taylor and Francis, 2013), 369–380.

84. On the intersection of disability studies and sexuality studies, see Robert McRuer, *Crip Theory: Cultural Signs of Queerness and Disability* (New York: New York University Press, 2006); and Robert McRuer and Anna Mollow, eds., *Sex and Disability* (Durham, NC: Duke University Press, 2012).

foreclosure was intertwined in women's sexological writings. Aside from chapter 1, which lays out why and how sex became the object of science and politics in Germany as well as the ways in which sexual knowledge and politics were intertwined in the early twentieth century, each chapter examines an emerging line of thought within German-speaking women's sexological writing on gender and sexuality.

Chapters 2–5 focus on ideas circulating between 1900 and 1914, during the so-called Wilhelmine era, when Germany was an empire ruled by Kaiser Wilhelm II. In chapter 2, I examine arguments regarding the true nature of the female sex drive and the physiological need for (heterosexual) intercourse it produced in women. I point out how women sexologists, specifically the radical feminist Ruth Bré, sex reformer and writer Grete Meisel-Hess, feminist and homosexual rights activist Johanna Elberskirchen, and social democrat and sex reformer Henriette Fürth, mobilized such understandings of the female sex drive to assert women's biological right to sexual emancipation and self-determination, and to demand a broad range of sexual reforms. I also show how these sexual theorists' attempts to establish a definition of the natural female sex drive provoked considerable debate among German-speaking feminists. This debate significantly exacerbated existing conflicts among feminists over what constituted a feminist program of sex reform—a debate that remains unresolved.

Chapter 3 examines formulations of alternative female sexual subjectivities. Here I explore how women writers critically engaged theories of female homosexuality to articulate nonnormative, nonheterosexual subjectivities as legitimate social identities with specific social rights and claims to sexual freedoms. Through my analyses of speeches and texts by journalist and homosexual rights activist Anna Rüling, Elberskirchen, and feminist intellectual Rosa Mayreder, I illustrate the diversity of alternative subjectivities that theories of homosexuality informed. I show how, despite their diversity, all of these authors represented their subjects as enjoying a special relationship to the feminist movement, and as superior to average, "normal"—that is, unambiguously feminine, heterosexual—women, whom they viewed as limited in their existential possibilities by virtue of their reproductive sexuality.

Chapter 4 examines how female sexual theorists engaged scientific theories and research to criticize masculinity and male sexuality, specifically heterosexuality. The writers I study in this chapter, including Elberskirchen, Mayreder, and Meisel-Hess, insisted that human male sexuality contravened and exceeded nature, with negative implications for the future of humanity. They also insisted upon the superiority of female sexuality, and sought a greater place for women in the governance of sexual life. While agreeing on these assessments of male and female sexuality, these theorists disagreed on what was required to reform male sexuality, and to emancipate women from men's purportedly excessive sexual demands. Not all of the women sexologists explored in this chapter believed that male sexuality could be reformed.

In chapter 5, I examine the attraction of racial thinking, specifically through the frameworks offered by eugenics and racial hygiene, for women sexologists. I argue that eugenics' appeal can be attributed not only to its stress on women's critical role in racial regeneration, but also to the fact that eugenicists conceived of sexual ethics in ways that resonated with many of the female sexual theorists examined in this book. Based on an in-depth exploration of the work of Meisel-Hess, I show how the new understandings of the female sex drive articulated in chapter 1, combined with eugenics, enabled theorists like Meisel-Hess to argue that women had a right to self-determined sexual experiences—regardless of marital status. In Meisel-Hess's case, this discursive merger further underwrote a sweeping critique of sexual ethics and arrangements under capitalist patriarchy, as well as demands for a comprehensive range of reforms to marriage and family law, and to the welfare state.

Chapter 6 explores women sexologists' reactions to the First World War. Here I show that although women sexologists like Meisel-Hess, Fürth, Helene Stöcker, and German academic Mathilde Vaerting shared many of the same concerns as their male peers, and even agreed with them on certain key points regarding the war's effects and the kinds of reforms that would be needed after the war, they diverged in important ways and contributed a number of unique insights and arguments. Women writers gave greater credence to women's subjective experiences of the war, and decried the double standard inherent in their male colleagues' frequent attempts to blame women for the war's so-called sexual problems, including the spread of venereal diseases, proliferation of prostitution, decline in birth rates, and degeneration of public morality. Although they deplored women's sexual promiscuity, women sexologists also critically analyzed male sexuality and pointed out men's complicity in precipitating a supposed sexual decline. In their writing women intriguingly treated the war not only as a crisis, but also as an opportunity for rethinking and transforming sexual life; nevertheless, as was the case before the war, we find once again that women's understandings and evaluations of sex were fundamentally informed by population concerns and eugenic principles, now heightened by the exigencies of war.

Chapter 7 examines new trends and developments in the postwar era. It explores how revised gender roles, strained heterosexual relations, and ongoing biopolitical concerns regarding the regeneration of the German population following the war, combined with a turn toward social, cultural, and psychological factors in sexology, transformed women's analyses of sex, gender, and sexuality. Focusing on groundbreaking texts written by Vaerting and Adlerian psychologist Sofie Lazarsfeld, this chapter shows how one can begin to identify the emergence of an analytical separation of sex into discreet categories of gender and sexuality. Moreover, one finds in their texts a turn away from eugenic and explicitly racial logics, and a greater attention to power as a factor shaping gender and sexual roles. Nonetheless, both Vaerting and Lazarsfeld retreat to essentialism when it comes to sexuality: in both texts, the radical contingency of gender they espouse is tethered to a foundation of naturalized and essentialized heterosexuality. Vaerting and Lazarsfeld's texts raise questions about the historical-social conditions in which gender and sexuality become open to new forms of scrutiny and analysis.

By way of conclusion, I not only account for the fate of the women whose ideas are examined in this book, but also take stock of the legacies of women's sexological work. I suggest that there is a larger twentieth-century story of women's sexology that can be told, one that is international in its scope. Finally, I argue that revisiting the history of women's sexological work is especially significant at this particular moment in time, as twenty-first-century feminist theorists positively embrace science and nature as intellectual resources once again.

1

THE EMERGENCE OF SEXOLOGY IN EARLY TWENTIETH-CENTURY GERMANY

By the early twentieth century, Germany was internationally recognized as a leader in sexual scientific research, and home to the most unimpeded public discussions of sex. British sexologist Havelock Ellis acknowledged as much in a letter to Edward Carpenter regarding the publication of *Sexual Inversion*. Because it was banned in Britain, *Sexual Inversion* was first published in Germany; however, Ellis wrote that he was "not anxious to publish it in Germany" because it wasn't "required" there. His only hope was that the German publication would "pave the way for English publication."[1] Similarly, British socialist publishers and translators

---

1. See Ellis to Carpenter, 24 April 1896, CARP MSS 358: Letters from Havelock Ellis, Reel 5, Fabian Economic and Social Thought Series One: The Papers of Edward Carpenter, 1844–1929, from Sheffield City Libraries, Part 1: Correspondence and Manuscripts. Later, commenting on the German publication of Edward Carpenter's *Intermediate Sex* in 1907 (prior to its English publication in 1908), Ellis wrote to Carpenter that it is "more needed in England than in Germany; it is

Eden and Cedar Paul declared in their "Translators' Preface" to the English edition of Grete Meisel-Hess's *The Sexual Crisis*, "In freedom of discussion in sexual matters . . . Germany is in the van."[2] The world's first professional sexological societies, the Medical Society for Sexual Science and Eugenics and the International Society for Sexual Research, were established there in 1913 and 1914, respectively. Likewise, the world's first institute dedicated to sexual scientific research opened in Berlin in 1919. Germans were the "prime movers" behind many international, scientifically inclined sex reform movements, such as the International Association for the Protection of Mothers and Sexual Reform established in 1912, and the World League for Sexual Reform, which began to take shape in Berlin in 1921.[3] Researchers across the globe, in sites as diverse as Britain, Japan, and Egypt, not only referenced the authority of German sexologists in their own work, but were inspired by the German example and hoped to develop a comparable culture of sexual scientific research in their own countries.[4]

How and why did sexology develop into such a robust, influential, cutting-edge field in Germany? In this chapter, I address this question by exploring the causes behind sexology's emergence in early twentieth-century Germany, all of which were unique to Germany's development as a nation-state. Here I focus on three

quite true, however, that England is scarcely yet ripe for it." See Ellis to Carpenter, 8 April 1907, CARP MSS 358: Letters from Havelock Ellis.

2. Eden Paul and Cedar Paul, "Translator's Preface," in Grete Meisel-Hess, *The Sexual Crisis: A Critique of Our Sexual Life*, trans. Eden Paul and Cedar Paul (New York: Critic and Guide, 1917), 15.

3. On the international connections between sexologists and sex reformers, see Nicholas Matte, "International Sexual Reform and Sexology in Europe, 1897–1933," *Canadian Bulletin of Medical History* 22 (2005): 253–270. On the World League for Sexual Reform, see Ralf Dose, "The World League for Sexual Reform: Some Possible Approaches," *Journal of the History of Sexuality* 12 (2003): 1–15.

4. See Sabine Frühstück, *Colonizing Sex: Sexology and Social Control in Modern Japan* (Berkeley: University of California Press, 2003), esp. 34, 55, 78–79, 84; Liat Kozma, "We, the Sexologists . . . Arabic Medical Writing on Sexuality, 1897–1943," *Journal of the History of Sexuality* 22, no. 3 (September 2013): 432, 435, 443. As Frühstück and Kozma note, many early twentieth-century sexologists in Japan and the Ottoman Empire had received medical or scientific training in Germany.

essential preconditions: the status and increasingly important political economic role of the sciences and medicine around the beginning of the twentieth century; the growth of interest in and concern
about urbanization, specifically its effects on health and morality;
and the development of a variegated sex reform movement. In
the course of examining these causes, I highlight an important yet
largely overlooked aspect of German sexology that helps to explain
its power and enables us to locate women in its history—namely,
its involvement in and dependence upon the politicization of sex.

The mid- to late nineteenth century was an era of scientific and
medical innovation. Within the biological sciences, for example,
scientists made huge strides in understanding the mechanisms of reproduction and the spread of diseases. During the 1870s and 1880s
alone, scientists made a number of revolutionary discoveries: they
recognized for the first time that fertilization occurred through the
fusion of the ovum and sperm, were able to manipulate chromo-
somes and cell nuclei, and uncovered the connection between bacillus and diseases.[5] The rapid rate of scientific breakthroughs such
as these helped boost the authority and prestige of medicine and
science. Moreover, these advances bolstered hopes that science and
medicine could exercise humanitarian and democratic influences
on social life by eradicating ignorance and superstition and allevi-
ating suffering through remedial therapy and preventative hygienic
measures.[6]

In Germany, such scientific and medical endeavors were encouraged through state and private funding of medical research and the
establishment and expansion of universities, hospitals, and various welfare institutions.[7] According to Paul Weindling, this level

---

5. Paul Weindling, *Health, Race, and German Politics between National
Unification and Nazism, 1870–1945* (Cambridge: Cambridge University Press,
1993), 16.

6. Ibid., 16, 3, 1.

7. Ibid., 4. Figures on the growth in expenditures on science between the 1870s
and 1914 can be found in Volker R. Berghahn, *Imperial Germany, 1871–1914:
Economy, Society, and Politics,* rev. and exp. ed. (New York: Berghahn Books,
2005), 308, table 12, "Growth in Expenditures on Sciences by the Reich and
Major Federal States in 10-Year Averages."

of investment and support aimed at "build[ing] Germany into a *Kulturstaat*" and "gaining international respect."[8] These efforts arguably paid off, as they helped make Germany a leader in scientific and medical research.

Investments in science coincided with the creation of the rudiments of the German welfare state.[9] Beginning in the 1880s, Chancellor Otto von Bismarck introduced legislation that established sickness insurance (1883), invalidity and accident insurance (1885), and pensions (1887).[10] Importantly, physicians proved to be among the groups that benefited from the introduction of the social insurance system. It not only provided a good income, but also proved a boon to professionalization efforts. The creation and expansion of the social insurance system ultimately led to a dramatic increase in the study of medicine—and ultimately to what Weindling has characterized as a "catastrophic overproduction of doctors," who were largely concentrated in towns and cities. Whereas there were 13,728 doctors in 1876, by 1900 that number had grown to 27,374.[11]

Much to the chagrin of newly minted doctors, this overproduction of physicians coincided with the industrial depression of the 1870s and 1880s.[12] Maintaining a medical practice in an urban setting was consequently difficult, and competition for insurance dollars stiff. According to Weindling, many doctors endeavored to make ends meet—and maintain their professional prestige and social status—by "colonizing social spheres related to health and reproduction."[13] That is to say, underemployed physicians sought

8. Weindling, *Health, Race, and German Politics*, 4.
9. On the history of social insurance in Germany from the later nineteenth through the early twentieth century, see Kathleen Canning, *Languages of Labor and Gender: Female Factory Work in Germany, 1850–1914* (Ann Arbor: University of Michigan Press, 2002); David F. Crew, *Germans on Welfare: From Weimar to Hitler* (Oxford: Oxford University Press, 1998).
10. Insurance was funded by mandatory contributions from workers and employers, and administered by autonomous bodies governed jointly by both parties. Weindling, *Health, Race, and German Politics*, 16–17.
11. Weindling, *Health, Race, and German Politics*, 17.
12. Ibid., 35.
13. Ibid., 126.

to establish niches where they could claim specialized knowledge and authority. Although Weindling's assertion is based on physicians' leading roles in new organizations promoting racial and social hygiene, his general argument holds true for sexologists such as Magnus Hirschfeld, Max Marcuse, and Iwan Bloch, who attempted to eke out a living under these conditions. Berlin became the center of sexological niche-building, as Berlin was, in Weindling's words, "a center for avant-garde thought on the social and psychological significance of medicine and biology."[14] As the rapidly growing capital of the German Empire, Berlin was the center of formal political power and a hotbed of reformist energy and intellectual productivity thanks to its esteemed universities and new research institutes.[15] Notably, almost all of the authors examined in this study lived in Berlin for a significant part of their lives, and all of the aforementioned professional sexological associations were founded or based in Berlin.

Practical and ideological investments in science and the niche-seeking behavior of underemployed physicians propelled the scientization of sex, and further help explain how and why scientific *men* became involved in sexology. To understand why and how sex came to be seen as a problem requiring sustained study and activism, we must look to the anxieties surrounding urbanization. By 1910, nearly two-thirds of Germans lived in towns, with more than a fifth living in cities exceeding 100,000. Berlin had over 2 million inhabitants by 1907.[16] The city quickly became a subject of intense fascination and extensive research, specifically as a site of both "pleasure and danger," to reference a tension familiar to feminists.[17] On the one hand, big cities were seen as the

---

14. Ibid., 102.

15. Kevin Repp, *Reformers, Critics, and the Paths of German Modernity: Anti-Politics and the Search for Alternatives, 1890–1914* (Cambridge, MA: Harvard University Press, 2000), 231.

16. David Blackbourn, *History of Germany, 1789–1914: The Long Nineteenth Century* (Malden, MA : Blackwell, 2003), 265.

17. Here I am referencing the title of the classic feminist collection *Pleasure and Danger: Exploring Female Sexuality*, ed. Carole Vance (New York: Routledge and Kegan Paul, 1984).

centers of the psychological, somatic, and moral ills of modernity.[18] Cities were home to prostitution, racy urban entertainment, and commercial venues, all of which supposedly facilitated illicit and "perverse" sexual relations fueled by lust and alcohol. Moreover, crowded urban living conditions, particularly for the poor, were held responsible for causing sexual abuse and even incest according to some social reformers and researchers.[19] In these ways, cities were viewed as threatening the stability and health of marriages and families, and as corrupting youth.

On the other hand, cities represented opportunity and provided spaces for experimentation in new ways of living and being in the world. Specifically, they offered opportunities to explore the possibilities of sexual agency, particularly for a generation of younger women and individuals who wished to pursue same-sex desires. This, again, was particularly true of Berlin, which was home to the cultural and existential avant-garde and to a burgeoning queer culture at the turn of the century.[20] The challenge for many people thus became how to enjoy urban life while avoiding and combating its ills. To do so would require studying and reforming what was believed to be the root cause of many of the city's problems and pleasures: sex.

Indeed, in the early twentieth century, studying sex and reforming sex went hand in hand. Sex reform groups ranged across the ideological spectrum, reflecting positions from the conservative to the progressive, and concerned themselves with issues such as prostitution, venereal diseases, homosexuality, marriage, maternal welfare, and the state of morality and sexual ethics. They represented a diverse constituency of middle-class professionals, including physicians, politicians, pastors, professors, artists, educators, lawyers, and writers, and varied in the tone of their public interventions,

---

18. Andrew Lees, *Cities, Sin, and Social Reform in Imperial Germany* (Ann Arbor: University of Michigan Press, 2002), 2–4.

19. Blackbourn, *History of Germany*, 227–229, 293–294.

20. Repp, *Reformers, Critics, and the Paths of German Modernity*, 260–266; see also Robert Beachy, *Gay Berlin: Birthplace of a Modern Identity* (New York: Knopf, 2014).

from the moralistic to the technocratic to the philosophical and intellectual.

Their emergence was part of an explosion of reform movements at this time. As David Blackbourn has noted, the turn of the century was a "seed time of single issue groups, from the Evangelical League and the Zionists to organized economic interests."[21] Although the reasons behind the growth of reform movements at this time are numerous and complex, an important catalyst was Kaiser Wilhelm II's declaration of the Social Reform Decrees of February 1890.[22] Although the decrees and the "New Course" they announced were intended to improve relations between workers and the state, their political and social effects were much broader— namely, they inspired a new generation to imagine and work toward alternative visions of the future, as Kevin Repp has demonstrated.[23] This "thaw in domestic relations," as Repp put it, suggested that German political culture was beginning to open up to the possibility of new voices and wide-ranging change.[24] This hope infused civil society with a new energy that in turn gave rise to an eclectic array of organizations seeking to shape the future. This statement is particularly true of many educated middle-class actors belonging to the "Bildungsburgertum" who possessed intellectual capital, were not affiliated with or members of political parties, and sought solutions to social problems beyond the realm of formal politics. Although the Kaiser would quickly become disenchanted with the promises he made in February 1890, his decrees nonetheless served

---

21. Blackbourn, *History of Germany*, 314.

22. The so-called February Decrees were meant to create and maintain "peace between employers and employees" by guaranteeing workers "free and peaceful expression of their wishes and complaints" and "equal rights before the law." This included lifting the ban on the Social Democratic Party, which had been enacted by Bismarck twelve years earlier. Through the February Decrees, Kaiser Wilhelm pronounced himself committed to a "New Course" for labor relations certainly, but for the nation generally. Repp, *Reformers, Critics, and the Paths of German Modernity*, 19–25.

23. Repp goes so far as to describe the February Decrees as the "birth certificate of a generation"; Repp, *Reformers, Critics, and the Paths of German Modernity*, 20.

24. Repp, *Reformers, Critics, and the Paths of German Modernity*, 25.

as an enduring source of inspiration for a generation already animated by an anxious discourse on modernity and clearly desiring
change. Their competing solutions to modern problems and visions
for social improvement could now take more concrete and organized expression.

Although they did not play a major role in the development of
sexology—except perhaps as an opposing force—it is important to
note that sexually conservative moral purity organizations (*Sittlich-
keitsvereine*) were among the earliest sex reform groups, and were
incredibly active in early twentieth-century Germany. Already by
1890, a national coordinating body, the General Conference of
German Morality Organizations, had been established in Berlin.[25]
Interestingly, as was the case for progressive and radical sex reform
movements, the main site of purity activism was Berlin.[26] In the
years before the First World War, organizations with titles such
as the White Cross League and the Men's Alliance for Combating
Public Immorality proliferated. Many powerful morality movements were dominated by men, oftentimes Protestant ministers and
other members of the educated bourgeoisie, even though men and
women participated in the moral purity movement at a roughly
equal rate.[27] With their close ties to the Protestant and Catholic
churches, moral purity organizations were formidable and influential champions of the patriarchal sexual status quo.[28]

Purity organizations stressed the moral authority of the Christian church and its teachings in the face of various forms of sexual

25. John C. Fout, "Sexual Politics in Wilhelmine Germany: The Male Gender Crisis, Moral Purity, and Homophobia," *Journal of the History of Sexuality* 2
(January 1992): 404.

26. Edward Ross Dickinson, "The Men's Christian Morality Movement in Germany, 1880–1914: Some Reflections on Politics, Sex, and Sexual Politics," *Journal
of Modern History* 75, no. 1 (March 2003): 63. As Dickinson notes, the Rhineland
was also a site of intense activism.

27. Fout, "Sexual Politics in Wilhelmine Germany," 405; Dickinson, "Men's
Christian Morality Movement," 65.

28. Dickinson, "Men's Christian Morality Movement," 67. As Dickinson has
observed, they were primarily influential among social and political conservatives;
their influence widened after a series of public scandals around 1908 (87–90). It is
also important to note that moral purity movements were often the subject of critique and satire, which Dickinson also helpfully chronicles (83–86).

"perversity" and degeneracy. As John Fout has observed, these organizations "countered the demand for sexual diversity with a pronounced emphasis on the centrality of heterosexual marriage and family."[29] Moral purity groups insisted that sex was exclusively for procreation, and viewed marriage as a holy imperative. They also championed strict and separate gender roles. For them, maintaining male dominance and women's sexual and social subordination was a critical goal. According to Fout, male-dominated purity organizations were particularly perturbed by what they perceived as "an implicit crisis in gender relations, primarily in the form of . . . eroding gender boundaries on the part of a large segment of the middle-class male population as well as part of the male working class."[30] Around the turn of the century, the boundaries of gender were breached in a number of ways, including women's growing numbers in the workforce, the rise and consolidation of women's movements, and the growing opportunities for mixed-sex social interaction in cafés, dance halls, cinemas, and theaters. To countervail these changes, purity groups targeted youth and sought to inculcate teachings about "proper" gender roles. They promoted chastity and sexual self-discipline for young women and men alike.

Despite the influence of moral purity movements, "progressive modernity" was also "an undeniable feature of moral discourse in the German Empire," as Andrew Lees has noted.[31] Beginning in the 1890s, groups began to emerge that sought to fundamentally transform the way sex and sexuality were conceptualized, experienced, and governed in Germany. Many of these groups also sought to radically change relations between the sexes, and to promote women as independent sexual agents. In explicit opposition to moral purity groups, they combated the role of religion in shaping sexual life and turned to science instead. Because of their commitment to secular sexual change, these groups can collectively be described as progressive, though they differed in the kinds and degrees of change they sought.

---

29. Fout, "Sexual Politics in Wilhelmine Germany," 390.
30. Ibid., 391.
31. Lees, *Cities, Sin, and Social Reform*, 5.

Of the groups that emerged during this time, three were especially significant for the history of sexology: the Scientific Humanitarian Committee, the German Society for the Fight against Venereal Diseases, and the League for the Protection of Mothers and Sexual Reform. The Scientific Humanitarian Committee was formed in Berlin in 1897 by physician Magnus Hirschfeld, publisher Max Spohr, lawyer Eduard Oberg, and writer Franz Josef von Bülow. Its specific goal was the removal of Paragraph 175 from the German Criminal Code, which criminalized sex acts between men; its larger ambition was to fight for social recognition and toleration of gay men and, to a lesser degree, lesbians and gender minorities.

Meanwhile, the German Society for the Fight against Venereal Diseases was founded in Berlin in 1902 by physicians Alfred Blaschko and Albert Neisser. Its goal is fairly self-evident from its title: it aimed to serve as a central point of organization for individuals seeking to limit the spread of venereal diseases. The society brought together a number of prominent and learned individuals such as Neisser, the Breslau-based venereologist who discovered the bacteria responsible for gonorrheal infection. Perhaps because of the predominance of eminent physicians and scientists on its membership rosters, the society was rather successful, eventually winning grants from the Prussian and federal governments to support its work.

Finally, the League for the Protection of Mothers and Sexual Reform was founded in Berlin in 1905 by an eclectic mix of feminists, physicians, artists, academics, and social reformers. As suggested by its name, the league was concerned with improving maternal welfare, particularly the welfare of unwed mothers. The league would undertake a number of practical activities toward this end, such as advancing petitions before various state ministers, creating homes for single mothers, and establishing sex and marriage advice counseling centers during the Weimar Republic. It also sought to fundamentally transform sexual norms and ethics, particularly those surrounding female sexuality.

Almost all of the female sexual theorists at the heart of this book belonged to, or were somehow involved in, at least one of these organizations. Some of these women were instrumental in the establishment, organization, and leadership of these groups. German feminist and social democrat Henriette Fürth, for example, was deeply involved in the inner workings of the German Society for the Fight against Venereal Diseases.[32] She and other women participated in the society's meetings and contributed to its journals, where they fought alongside and against their male peers, particularly when it came to the question of the state regulation of prostitution and sexual education.[33] To an even greater extent, radical feminists Ruth Bré and Helene Stöcker helped establish the League for the Protection of Mothers and Sexual Reform, with Stöcker serving variously as the group's president and secretary as well as the editor of its journal, *The New Generation*. Even in the Scientific Humanitarian Committee, an organization largely committed to the decriminalization of same-sex acts between men and the recognition and social toleration of male homosexuality, journalist Anna Rüling, Johanna Elberskirchen, and Helene Stöcker were all chairpersons.

Aside from women's significant participation, what makes these groups important for the history of sexology is their deep investment in sexual scientific knowledge. These groups were populated by a diverse group of men and women who were united by their belief that, in the words of the Scientific Humanitarian Committee's motto, science would lead to justice. Members of these groups, which at various times included now famous male sexologists like Magnus Hirschfeld, Iwan Bloch, Max Marcuse, Havelock Ellis, and even Sigmund Freud, adhered to shared ontological and epistemic beliefs—namely, that sex had a natural, material reality that preexisted and transcended human constructs; that this reality

32. See, for example, letters between Dr. Alfred Blaschko and Henriette Fürth in the Kollektion Fürth at the Internationaal Instituut voor Sociale Geschiedenis in Amsterdam (Folder 5).

33. See, for example, reports of the Congresses of the German Society for the Fight against Venereal Diseases from 1903 to 1911, entitled *Verhandlungen des [Ersten bis Achten] Jahresversammlung der Deutschen Gesellschaft zur Bekämpfung der Geschlechtskrankheiten* (Leipzig: Verlag von Johann Ambrosius Barth, 1911).

could only be accessed via scholarly and scientific methods; and that this knowledge had implications for personal enlightenment and emancipation, and for social order and governance. They even shared a broader belief that sexual science offered the means to both know and regenerate sex: that is, it had the potential to remake subjectivities, relations, and ethics in line with nature, and provide an objective basis for a just and happier world. The regenerative promise of sexual science lay in the fact that its findings sometimes fundamentally contradicted existing beliefs and values surrounding sex, sexuality, and gender. Scientific knowledge constituted a productive source of disruption, and a way of dispelling what its proponents believed to be outmoded beliefs about sexuality. It inspired the imaginations of self-consciously progressive reformers while providing an increasingly authoritative means of legitimizing their demands for reform.

To be clear, sex reformers were not merely appropriating sexual science to their ends. It is worth noting that many early programmatic articles regarding the purpose and goals of *Sexualwissenschaft* recognized the close connection between sexual knowledge and sexual politics, and that their authors were themselves members of sex reform groups at one time or another. These articles usually began with dissatisfied ruminations on the flawed state of sexual life, at the time most starkly represented by prostitution, sexually transmitted diseases, the conditions facing unwed mothers and their children, and the social disparagement and criminal persecution of sexual minorities. This dissatisfaction often led to an insistence that scientific investigation was the only solution to the myriad problems causing sexual dissatisfaction and disease. According to Max Marcuse, one of the primary goals of research into the "Vita sexual" was to awaken people to the "necessity of far-reaching sexual reform."[34] In his view, sexology could help secure emancipation from sexual need and danger; reform relations between the sexes, both inside and outside of marriage, making them happier, healthier, and honorable; and protect the state and

---

34. Max Marcuse, "Ein Wort zur Einführung," *Sexual-Probleme* 4 (January 1908): 1.

society from a further increase of "unfit" and antisocial individuals while increasing the number of strong, capable, socially valuable offspring.[35] Arguably, sexual science's normativity served as a kind of regulative ideal.[36] Many sexological texts contain within them visions of a better future, largely expressed in general and abstract terms, that constituted what could be described as "ends-in-view" that would inform a new, alternative sexual-social order.[37]

Beyond epistemology and ideology, sex reform groups like the Scientific Humanitarian Committee, the Society for the Fight against Venereal Diseases, and the League for the Protection of Mothers and Sexual Reform were strategically invested in sexual science. In addition to typically liberal political tactics such as presenting petitions to Parliament, these groups engaged sexual science as part of a sustained war of ideas they waged through their journals, lectures, and exhibitions. In their view, science provided true and objective support for their reform proposals, many of which were controversial by the standards of the time. By enlightening the public about the truths of sexual nature, they believed they could not only sway public opinion in their favor, but also influence individual behavior, and maybe even transform ethical and cultural beliefs and values around sex, gender, and sexuality. Because they believed that scientific revelations about sex would support and legitimize their struggles for reform and social improvement, sex reform groups produced, collected, and disseminated scientific knowledge on a remarkable range of topics concerning the psychology, biology, anthropology, and history of sex, gender, and sexuality. To this end, all three organizations published journals that featured cutting-edge sexual scientific work, new sexual theories, reviews of major works, and notices of upcoming talks: the Scientific Humanitarian Committee published the *Yearbook for Sexual Intermediaries*; the German Society for the Fight

---

35. Ibid., 3.

36. Ruth Levitas, *Utopia as Method: The Imaginary Reconstitution of Society* (London: Palgrave Macmillan, 2013), 6.

37. For the reference to John Dewey's "end-in-view" I am indebted to Alessa Johns, "Feminism and Utopianism," in *The Cambridge Companion to Utopian Literature*, ed. Gregory Claeys (Cambridge: Cambridge University Press, 2010), 174–199.

against Venereal Diseases produced the *Journal for the Fight against Venereal Diseases*; and the League for the Protection of Mothers published *The Protection of Mothers* and later *The New Generation.*

These journals constituted crucial sites for the creation, contestation, and circulation of scientific knowledge dealing with sex. In assuming the critical roles of collecting, curating, and circulating sexual knowledge, sex reform journals helped to build the sexological field. Importantly, these journals preceded the establishment of specialized sexual scientific journals like *Sexual Problems* (est. 1908) and the *Journal for Sexual Science* (est. 1908). As Magnus Hirschfeld himself noted in his 1908 article "Towards a Methodology of Sexual Science," "The sexual scientific journals . . . have all proceeded from the publication organs dedicated to special questions."[38] Sexology as a field was forged in large part within the public sphere, and involved actors, journals, ideas, and institutions beyond the limited realms of clinical research and medical practice. German sexology actually developed largely outside of academia and other institutionalized settings. No institutions for sexological research existed until 1919, when Hirschfeld opened the Institute for Sexual Science in Berlin; likewise, specifically sexological professional societies did not emerge in Germany and Austria until 1913, with the creation of the Medical Society for Sexual Science and Eugenics. Sex reform organizations helped knit together sexual knowledge, sexual politics, and sexual ethics. The links they established between sexual reform and sexology would persist through the First World War and well into the 1920s.

The Inextricability of Sexual Knowledge and Sexual Politics—and Its Gendered Consequences

The fact that German sexology was a product of the public sphere rendered it porous, contentious, and profoundly unstable—at least before its stricter professionalization. In its early years, sexology

---

38. Magnus Hirschfeld, "Zur Methodik der Sexualwissenschaft," *Zeitschrift für Sexualwissenschaft* 1 (1908): 702.

was open to interventions from a range of actors, which in turn opened up the possibility of making new claims to expertise. The early twentieth century was a markedly polyvocal moment in the history of sexology: both women and men wrote texts that reported and interpreted theories and empirical data regarding sex and extrapolated their social and political implications. Participants in the field, men and women alike, broadly agreed on the importance of creating knowledge about sex rooted in secular scholarship, rather than theology, and on the criteria for adjudicating desirable, healthy sexual subjects. Moreover, they cited—and debated—one another in monographs, pamphlets, and journal articles. Iwan Bloch actually thanked Helene Stöcker and Rosa Mayreder in the acknowledgments of his *The Sexual Life of Our Time*, which clearly suggests that discussions and debates with these women informed the content of this influential work.[39]

Sexology's porousness should not be confused with openness, however: differently situated actors, particularly women, faced distinct challenges to their ability to participate in the field and have their authority recognized by their peers. Although men and women did not belong to fundamentally antagonistic and irreconcilable camps organized along gender lines, and despite the fact that they shared certain beliefs about science, implicitly agreed on the discursive "rules of the game" for participation in the sexological field, and worked together toward common political goals, men and women routinely disagreed on the interpretations and political implications of sexual science, particularly as it affected women's agency and power relations between the sexes. Women had to contend with sexist and misogynist ideas about womanhood and female sexualities, as well as gendered hostility from their male colleagues.

Men and women also disagreed on the questions of who could know sex objectively, whose voices mattered, and what ought to be counted as science. Sexology as it took shape in the early twentieth century constituted a dynamic staging ground for gendered debates

---

39. Iwan Bloch, *Das Sexualeben unserer Zeit, in seiner Beziehungen zur modernen Kultur* (Berlin: Louis Marcus, 1908), vi.

over knowledge and power. Male sexologists clearly enjoyed structural advantages by virtue of their gender, class, and status that undoubtedly endowed their ideas with greater authority within the public sphere. For many men, women's involvement presented a significant obstacle to the professionalization and institutionalization of the field. As male sexologists increasingly insisted on the objective, rational character of their work, they concomitantly dismissed the work of their female colleagues and interlocutors as too "emotional," subjective, amateurish, and political.[40] In fact, it was largely as a result of efforts to ensure the scientific status of sexology that the two branches of German sexology emerged.[41] The different visions for sexology were ultimately organized through dueling professional societies. The Medical Society for Sexual Science and Eugenics, founded in 1913 by Magnus Hirschfeld, Iwan Bloch, Albert Eulenberg, and Hermann Rohleder, stressed sexual science's role in "enlightening" the public and reshaping sexual laws and ethics. Conversely, the International Society for Sexual Research, founded by Max Marcuse, Albert Moll, and jurist Julius Wolff in 1914, pushed for a distinction between pure science and politics—even though some of its positions, such as Max Marcuse's assertion that homosexuality was a sickness or congenital malformation, had definite political implications.[42]

Although this division was ostensibly prompted by debates about the role of politics in scientific work, it was clearly also driven by gendered conflicts and biases. One of the main catalysts of the division in German sexology was the conflict between Max Marcuse and Helene Stöcker over what should be included in

---

40. See, for example, Max Marcuse, "Rundschau: Johanna Elberskirchen, Geschlechtsempfindung und Liebe," *Sexual-Probleme* 4 (1908): 153.

41. For a more detailed discussion of the two branches of German sexology—one that focuses primarily on the conflicts and rivalries between Magnus Hirschfeld and Albert Moll—see Volkmar Sigusch, *Geschichte der Sexualwissenschaft* (Frankfurt am Main: Campus Verlag, 2008), 197–233.

42. Seeck, "Aufklärung oder Rückfall? Das Projekt der Etablierung einer 'Sexualwissenschaft' und deren Konzeption als Teil der Biologie," in *Durch Wissenschaft zur Gerechtigkeit? Textsammung zur kritischen Rezeption des Schaffens von Magnus Hirschfeld*, ed. Andreas Seeck (Münster: LIT Verlag, 2003), 178–181, 194–196.

the League for the Protection of Mothers and Sexual Reform's first journal, *The Protection of Mothers*. This conflict came to a head at the end of 1907, when *The Protection of Mothers* featured a notice from its publisher, Sauerländer, that stated that, as a result of a difference of opinion regarding the future content of the journal, the direction of the journal would be transferred from Helene Stöcker to Max Marcuse. Marcuse, the publishers insisted, would devote less attention to "abstract philosophical" and "literary aesthetic" themes, and would instead shine a critical light on the pressing questions of the day, above all by treating "special sexual political and sexual scientific questions."[43] (It should be noted that sexual scientific articles had featured prominently in *The Protection of Mothers* from its launch in 1905.) In the initial pages of *The Protection of Mothers* under Marcuse's editorship, now published independently of the league and bearing the new title *Sexual Problems,* Marcuse declared, "The sexual question requires and enables a solution only through science (*Wissenschaft*)." Declaring himself "an enemy of all utopias," Marcuse went on to state that the journal would fight against "naïve ideologues" in the pursuit of sexual "Realpolitik" that dealt with the problems of today, and that was based not on feelings but on experience and expert research.[44] It is entirely unclear whether Marcuse orchestrated this editorial coup behind the scenes, or whether it was genuinely the result of the publisher's discomfort, of which Marcuse was the opportunistic benefactor. Regardless, this development within the journal led to Marcuse's expulsion from the League for the Protection of Mothers and Sexual Reform after a special meeting of the General Assembly in December 1907.[45]

That this conflict of opinion between Stöcker and Marcuse was gendered beyond the identities of its protagonists is revealed by Marcuse's comments in the wake of his break from the league. To preface these comments, it is worth noting here that Marcuse was

---

43. Bernd Nowacki, *Der Bund für Mutterschutz (1905–1933)* (Husum: Matthiesen Verlag, 1983), 47.
44. Marcuse, "Ein Wort zur Einführung," 1–4.
45. Nowacki, *Der Bund für Mutterschutz*, 48.

an adherent of the Prague-based Gestalt philosopher Christian von Ehrenfehls, who championed male heterosexual virility, declared that the highest goal of the healthy woman lay exclusively in motherhood (and a remarkably submissive version of motherhood at that), and insisted upon a strict hierarchical separation of sex roles. Throughout his time in the League for the Protection of Mothers and Sexual Reform, Marcuse chafed against women's leadership and disagreed with the league's goal of achieving greater sexual freedom for women. In autobiographical material about Marcuse recently recovered by the sexologist Volkmar Sigusch, Marcuse stated that he sought to break with the league because, in Sigusch's words, he "wanted to operate on the side of the strong and not feminine weaknesses."[46] It is perhaps therefore not surprising that he subsequently allied himself with conservative sexual researchers and theorists like Albert Moll and Julius Wolff. Moreover, as Bernd Nowacki has noted, in the over 6,100 pages published by *Sexual Problems* between 1908 and 1915, the League for the Protection of Mothers and Sexual Reform was only mentioned twice, amounting to a coverage of only six pages.[47] In one of these two mentions, Max Marcuse bemoaned the fact that the league was developing into a "special sect of the women's movement," and that women now constituted the majority of the league. The league was becoming feminized not only in its leadership, Marcuse insisted, but in a "deeper sense":

> It is femininely weak, illogical, shrinks from its own consequences, is happy with half measures and satisfies itself with wishes that do not lead to results. It thinks itself revolutionary . . . and cannot free itself from biological false fundamental principles from the past. . . . It raises protests in the name of morality and nature, makes demands on the state and society without thinking of the means of its realization,—it wants to help the socially outcast and moral degenerates, and knows no other advice but to lower itself to their level.[48]

Marcuse's comments regarding his erstwhile female and feminist colleagues, along with his mission statement for the new journal

---

46. Volkmar Sigusch, "Der Sexualforscher Max Marcuse in bisher unveröffentlichen Selbstzeugnissen," *Zeitschrift für Sexualforschung* 21 (2008): 134.
47. Nowacki, *Der Bund für Mutterschutz*, 49.
48. Quoted in Nowacki, *Der Bund für Mutterschutz*, 49–50.

Sexual Problems, give us some sense of the difficulties women would face when trying to engage in the sexological field as it professionalized, specifically when their ideas, analyses, and arguments contradicted those advanced by their male peers. They show how easily women's work could be dismissed as amateurish, based on feeling, too political, and insufficiently factual—even when women largely obeyed the same disciplinary protocols and generic rules as their male peers. Marcuse's comments further reveal that the question of what exactly constituted legitimate sexual scientific knowledge was the site of intense contestation, one that involved politics, understandings of science, and gendered assumptions regarding who could create valuable and factual knowledge. Tellingly, aside from Stöcker's membership in the Medical Society for Sexual Science and Eugenics, women were largely absent from the membership rosters of the first professional sexological societies and from the editorial boards of the first explicitly sexological journals.

It is important to remember that Marcuse did not speak for all sexologists at this time. Rather, his statements attune us to the fact that the exclusion of women from certain branches of the sexological field, particularly the branch that considered itself strictly and purely scientific, was a process that required work. While it is appropriate perhaps to speak of German "sexologies" after 1910, many of the texts discussed in the following chapters were written before this period, when battle lines were still being drawn. Moreover, the distinctions between the various camps were never absolute, and certain women were included within even the more conservative sexological circles, as long as their research was seen as strictly objective and appropriately scientific. This was the case, for example, with the gynecologist and eugenicist Dr. Agnes Bluhm, who was one of the few women involved in the highly conservative Society for Racial Hygiene founded in 1905, and invited by Marcuse to contribute some entries to his *Encyclopedia of Sexual Science* (1923–26).[49] Mathilde Vaerting, Germany's second female university professor, also proved an exception to the general rule, as her 1922 paper, "Physiological Origins of Intellectual

---

49. Günter Grau, "Agnes Bluhm," in *Personenlexikon der Sexualforschung*, ed. Volkmar Sigusch and Günter Grau (Frankfurt am Main: Campus Verlag, 2009), 68.

High Achievement by Man and Woman," was published in the *Papers from the Field of Sexual Research*, a publication of the International Society for Sexual Research edited by Max Marcuse.[50] Lest one think that these particular women were included because of their professional credentials, and that the International Society was not being sexist but rather adhering to its commitment to rely on "expert knowledge," it is worth noting that Albert Moll reached out to British socialist and supporter of gay rights, Edward Carpenter, inviting him to participate in the society.[51] Carpenter, who eventually became a member of the society, lacked formal credentials.

Yet even when gendered assumptions and divisions between the sexes were at their sharpest and most pernicious, many women were unwilling to accept men's authority and expertise, particularly regarding female sexuality, or to concede that sexual science was an exclusively male preserve. In spite of considerable challenges, German-speaking women produced sexual knowledge throughout the early twentieth century that reimagined the possibilities of sex, gender, and sexuality and highlighted the need for women's sexual empowerment and thoroughgoing social transformation.

50. See Mathilde Vaerting, "Physiologische Ursachen geistiger Höchstleistungen bei Mann und Weib," *Abhandlungen aus dem Gebiete der Sexualforschung*, ed. Max Marcuse (Bonn: Marcus & E. Webers Verlag, 1922).

51. See Moll to Carpenter, May 1914, Carpenter Collection, MS 386, Sheffield City Archives.

2

AS NATURAL AS EATING, DRINKING, AND SLEEPING

Redefining the Female Sex Drive

In 1908, following five years of active involvement in the German Society for the Fight against Venereal Diseases, German feminist and social democrat Henriette Fürth finally felt compelled to publicly criticize the organization's advocacy of premarital chastity and medically regulated prostitution as the best measures to prevent venereal infection and regenerate sexual life. In *The Sex Problem and Modern Morals* (1908), Fürth asserted that these measures were deeply flawed, and not merely because they supported men's sexual pleasure at women's expense. What was more troubling for Fürth, particularly in light of the many "well-educated representatives of science" who populated the society, was the fact that these proposals were premised, she claimed, upon unscientific beliefs regarding female sexuality.[1] Widely held beliefs within and beyond

---

1. Henriette Fürth, *Das Geschlechtsproblem und die moderne Moral* (Gautsch b. Leipzig: Felix Dietrich, 1908), 4. Subsequent citations of this work appear parenthetically in the text.

science regarding men's greater sexual need—and women's lesser sexual desire—were frequently mobilized to defend and legitimize prostitution. According to Fürth, the consensus regarding "the lesser sexual activity of the female and her resulting lesser sexual needs" was not "based on biological facts," but rather upon male bias and male-centered morality (4–5). To counter prevailing views, Fürth drew upon evolutionary theory, physiology, and anthropology to show that the sciences had found no essential difference between the male and female sex drive in either the plant or the animal world (5). For Fürth, science had proven that men and women experienced equal amounts of innate sexual "need" (6, 14, 21).

On the basis of the existence of organic sexual impulses, Fürth argued that women had as much right to sexual experience and pleasure as men (14). Empowering women to act upon their natural sexual needs, Fürth asserted, would undermine the very need for prostitution as so doing would ultimately help to create conditions of sexual equality and establish a new sexual ethic grounded upon mutual love, responsibility, self-determination, and self-control (12, 17). For Fürth, acknowledging women's sexual impulses and needs was not just important to the specific goal of ending prostitution: it was a matter of existential importance and social justice. As she insisted in her text, "Also in sexual things [women] must feel themselves as humans of flesh and blood and also in this realm demand their rights, their human rights" (16).

Henriette Fürth and the male physicians and scientists she challenged were part of a wide-ranging debate regarding the true nature of female sexuality in early twentieth-century Germany. The debate was an outgrowth of the long-standing scientific, social, and political interest in female sexuality that was reinvigorated beginning in the later nineteenth century, and gained in strength in the first decade of the twentieth century as a result of feminists' challenges to the regulation of prostitution, women's unequal status in marriage, and the rights and well-being of mothers, including unwed mothers. Reflecting the crucial role of Darwinian evolution, medicine, and psychiatry in these debates, these turn-of-the-century investigations into female sexuality centered on the female sex drive, alternately referred to as a sex instinct, sex need, sex impulse, sex feeling, and libido.[2]

The general concept of a sex drive was hard to pin down, and uncertainty surrounded its function and manifestation: how it worked, where it was physiologically or psychologically rooted, and whether it was a singular corporeal phenomenon were all unclear. These uncertainties were heightened when it came to the female sex drive: in 1902, British sexologist Havelock Ellis went so far as to characterize the female sex drive as an "elusive" phenomenon, and even as a "mocking mystery."[3] Part of the reason Ellis characterized the female sex drive using such terms stemmed from the fact that social prohibitions against female sexual expression made it extremely difficult to acquire accurate and comprehensive information about it—for male physicians, at any rate.[4] Despite these difficulties, understanding the sex drive was viewed as a crucial task: in the words of German physician Magnus Hirschfeld, sexological writers viewed the sex drive as "the most important property of life." It was responsible for "the happiness of the individual as well as the strength of society," along with "the preservation of mankind [and] the survival of the whole world."[5]

To understand how the female sex drive worked, and what it required for its satisfaction, women and men alike investigated not only the drive itself, but also the effects of its repression on women's physical and psychological health. Through their attempts to divine the true nature of the female sex drive, they sought to establish a standard or norm around which sexual life could be rationally

---

2. In German, the terms were *Geschlechts-* or *Sexualtrieb*, *Geschlechts-* or *Sexualempfindung*, *Geschlechtsgefühl*, and *Libido*. I have chosen to use "sex drive" (*Trieb*) instead of other terms such as "instinct," "impulse," "feeling," or "libido," as it was the term most often used by German commentators throughout the period under study.

3. See Havelock Ellis, "The Sexual Impulse in Women," *American Journal of Dermatology* 6 (March 1902): 47.

4. Ibid., 47, 49–51.

5. Magnus Hirschfeld, "Sexualwissenschaft als Grundlage der Sexualreform," in *Mutterschutz und Sexualreform: Referate und Leitsätze des I. Internationalen Kongresses für Mutterschutz und Sexualreform in Dresden 28./30. September 1911*, ed. Dr. Max Rosenthal (Breslau: Verlag von Preuss und Jünger, 1912), 76.

and justly organized. For women sexologists in particular, this effort to scientifically determine female sexual norms had profound implications for women's rights.

In this chapter, I show how German-speaking women engaged and expanded scientific knowledge to redefine the female sex drive. I specifically focus here on the work of Ruth Bré, Henriette Fürth, Johanna Elberskirchen, and Grete Meisel-Hess. In texts they wrote between 1903 and 1914, against the backdrop of growing feminist agitation for an end to the state regulation of prostitution and the rights of unmarried mothers, Bré, Elberskirchen, Fürth, and Meisel-Hess all represented the female sex drive as a simultaneously physiological and psychological phenomenon that was active, desiring, and naturally in need of satisfaction. Many of these women distinguished the sex drive from a maternal drive, and insisted that the drive for sex was distinct from the impulse to reproduce and nurture.[6]

---

6. This chapter does not investigate turn-of-the-century writing on the maternal drive or instinct. It is, however, worth briefly examining how physicians, scientists, and other commentators thought about this subject at that time. So doing provides further context for their invocations of the maternal drive/instinct, especially as they contrasted it with the sex drive. Reviewing German- and English-language literature from the period, it seems that, for many writers, the maternal instinct or maternal drive (*Mutterinstinkt, Muttertrieb*) was a primary signifier of sexual difference throughout the animal kingdom. The maternal instinct was believed to endow women with a particular psychology and set of behaviors. According to Charles Darwin, the maternal instinct rendered women different from men "in mental disposition, chiefly in [their] greater tenderness and lesser selfishness." Darwin maintained that women displayed such qualities not only toward their children but also "towards [their] fellow-creatures"; Charles Darwin, *The Descent of Man, and Selection in Relation to Sex* (London: John Murray, 1871), 2:326. From the eighteenth into the early twentieth century, naturalists claimed evidence of the maternal instinct in many animal species, even among "females of supposedly cruel and ferocious species, such as the tigress and lioness," who "would subdue their natural ferocity to take care of their young, often perishing with them rather than abandoning them when pursued by hunters"; Elisabeth Badinter, *The Myth of Motherhood: An Historical View of the Maternal Instinct*, trans. Roger DeGaris (London: Souvenir Press, 1981), 156. The maternal instinct was held responsible for women's greatest virtues and altruistic feelings, above all their heightened capacity for sympathy, patience, nurturance, compassion, and care for the sick and vulnerable; see Max Runge, *Das Weib in seiner geschlechtlichen Eigenart*, 4th ed. (Berlin: Verlag von Julius Springer, 1900), 23; also Elisabeth Gnauck-Kühne, *Die Deutsche Frau um die Jahrhundertwende: Statistische Studie zur Frauenfrage*, 2nd ed. (Berlin: Verlag von Otto Liebmann, 1907), 9; Havelock Ellis, *Studies in the*

In representing the female sex drive thusly, these women deployed ideas also put into circulation by their male peers, such as Richard von Krafft-Ebing and Havelock Ellis. However, these women

---

Psychology of Sex, vol. 3, *Analysis of the Sexual Impulse, Love and Pain, the Sexual Impulse in Women*, 2nd ed., rev. and enl. (Philadelphia: F. A. Davis, 1913), 95; Robert Müller, *Das Problem der sekundaren Geschlechtsmerkmale und die Tierzucht: Eine wissenschaftliche Untersuchung* (Stuttgart: Verlag von Ferdinand Enke, 1908), 48. It also supposedly protected women from nervousness, mental illness, and suicide, and actually helped to prolong life; Dr. Grassl, "Die Mutterschaft und die finanztechnische Hilfe für die Mutter," *Zeitschrift für Medizinalbeamte: Zentralblatt für das gesamte Gesundheitswesen für gerichtliche Medizin, Psychiatrie und Irrenwesen* 22, no. 8 (20 April 1909): 297. Others believed that, along with sexual impulse, the maternal impulse was a key element of love itself; Karl Groos, *Aesthetic Genuss* (1902); cited in Havelock Ellis, *Studies in the Psychology of Sex: Erotic Symbolism, the Mechanism of Detumescence, the Psychic State in Pregnancy* (1906; repr., Philadelphia: F. A. Davis, 1920), 249. And yet the maternal instinct appears relatively undertheorized at the time. What it exactly "was" and did remained nebulous. Did it provoke a desire for children? Did it entail a set of behaviors enacted only after the birth of a child? Similarly, the locus of the maternal drive was unclear. Many simply asserted the existence of the maternal instinct: its "naturalness" seemed self-evident, and attempts to prove its existence, redundant. Like sociologist Franz Müller-Lyer, many asserted that the maternal drive was deep-seated, inborn, and biologically inherited; Franz Müller-Lyer, *Phasen der Liebe: Eine Soziologie des Verhältnisses der Geschlechter* (Munich: Albert Langen, 1913), 64. Others identified the brain and the nervous system as the organic roots of the maternal drive; see Thomas Smith Clouston, *Clinical Lectures on Mental Diseases* (Philadelphia: Lea Brothers, 1897), 336. Still others extrapolated the existence of a maternal instinct from little girls' penchant for, and manner of, playing with dolls; see Gnauck-Kühne, *Die Deutsche Frau*, 8; Dr. Georg Lomer, *Liebe und Psychose* (Wiesbaden: Verlag von J. F. Bergmann, 1907), 35.

Interestingly, by the early twentieth century many within the scientific and medical communities were expressing skepticism about the power and even the existence of the maternal drive. American writer E. T Brewster flat out asserted that there is "no such thing" as the maternal instinct in the abstract; rather, each kind of mother has her own bundle of instinctive reactions; E. T. Brewster, "Studying the Animal Mind in Laboratories," *McClure's Magazine* 33 (May–October 1909): 384. Some authors, such as American physician J. Ross Snyder, dismissed the maternal instinct, "whatever that may be," as capable of "overcom[ing] certain deficiencies in the education and in the preparation of a woman for maternity"; J. Ross Snyder, "The Status of the Child," *Journal of the American Medical Association* 49, no. 5 (3 August 1907): 363. German physician Paul Näcke challenged the routine evidence for the existence of the maternal drive, and further pointed out that "no one has spoken at all about a 'paternal instinct,' despite the fact that most men wish for children in marriage, above all heirs"; Medizinalrat Dr. Näcke, "Kleinere Mitteilungen," in *Archiv für Kriminal-Anthropologie und Kriminalistik*, vol. 20

elaborated upon and expanded men's ideas, and extrapolated the political consequences of new understandings of female sexuality. All four of these women had particular political investments in redefining the sex drive, and their work sought to establish as normal a new female sexual subjectivity: that of the desiring, sexually autonomous woman who could engage in personally enriching (hetero)sexual experiences. The creation of this subjectivity is important, as it offered to expand the bounds of sexual opportunity for women beyond the spheres of prostitution, marriage, and motherhood, and to endow women with the same degree of sexual agency enjoyed by men.

The new views of the sex drive that Fürth, Elberskirchen, Bré, and Meisel-Hess offered were highly controversial. They challenged not only prevailing understandings of femininity but also gendered relations of power. Their ideas expanded and radicalized those put forward by male sexological writers and clashed with beliefs held by many within the broader German women's movement. Moreover, their ideas were inflected with the eugenic and homophobic valences of early twentieth-century sexology, which ultimately limited the scope of their analyses and demands. According to Fürth and the others, although all women may have a sex drive, only certain women—above all, heterosexual and "healthy" women— ought to act upon their impulses.

The Female Sex Drive: An Object of Social and Scientific Concern in Early Twentieth-Century Germany

Whereas female sexuality had been characterized as rampant and voracious by previous generations, over the course of the nineteenth century this representation shifted, thanks in large part to

---

(Leipzig: Verlag von F. C. W. Vogel, 1905), 186. In light of the elusiveness of and uncertainty surrounding the concept of the maternal instinct, it is perhaps not surprising that anthropologist Sarah Blaffer Hrdy attributes older scientific views on the maternal instinct to "tensions between males and females" and to "conflicting interests between fathers and mothers"; Sarah Blaffer Hrdy, *Mother Nature: Maternal Instincts and How They Shape the Human Species* (New York: Ballantine Books, 1999), 12.

the consolidation of middle-class identity and power. Discipline and restraint regarding sex and sexuality became key defining features of the German bourgeoisie as it ascended to hegemony; as a consequence of this new paradigm, female sexuality became redefined as chaste, passive, modest, exclusively maternal, and essentially passionless.[7] This standard, or rather ideal, of middle-class female sexuality would ultimately become normative for all women, and the standard by which true and virtuous womanhood would be measured.

Male medical and scientific authorities played critical roles in articulating and legitimizing this new bourgeois definition of female sexuality. From the mid-nineteenth century until the beginning of the twentieth, the prevailing view among German-speaking male physicians and scientists was that female sexuality was primarily meant for reproduction. For example, in *The Sex Drive* (1894), German gynecologist Alfred Hegar claimed that the human sex drive was composed of two distinct impulses, one directed toward copulation, the other toward reproduction.[8] Hegar maintained that males exhibited a greater desire for copulation, whereas the females' primary interest lay in reproduction. He attributed this gendered difference to evolutionary factors, specifically to females' purportedly innate modesty, the menstrual cycle, and the fact that females bear the reproductive consequences of intercourse.[9] Hegar also insisted that women's sexual sensibility is weaker than men's, a fact he claimed was demonstrated by frequent expressions of "disgust" toward sexual intercourse among "strong and healthy" women, even when it involved someone they loved.[10] Hegar further argued that too much sex and too frequent pregnancies caused anemia, malnutrition, muscle deterioration, and nervous

---

7. On middle-class norms regarding sexuality in nineteenth-century Europe, see George Mosse, *Nationalism and Sexuality: Respectability and Abnormal Sexuality in Modern Europe* (New York: H. Fertig, 1985).

8. Alfred Hegar, *Der Geschlechtstrieb: Eine Social-medicinische Studie* (Stuttgart: Verlag von Ferdinand Enke, 1894), 1.

9. Ibid., 5.

10. Ibid., 5–6.

exhaustion in women.[11] The medico-scientific definition of the female sex drive as naturally chaste and essentially maternal was reiterated in landmark sexological texts such as August Forel's *The Sexual Question*.[12]

Contrary to women, men were seen as having a stronger urge and need for sex, and required regular sexual activity in excess, supposedly, of what their virtuous wives wanted or could sustain. It was for this reason that prostitution was a "necessary evil" in the eyes of many commentators. While chastity before and within marriage was treated as ideal for men, their recourse to prostitution was treated as understandable and forgivable in light of their stronger sexual natures. By defining the female sex drive as passionless and exclusively maternal, and the male sex drive as pleasure seeking and in need of regular satisfaction, many physicians posited a fundamental incommensurability between male and female sexuality, as Edward Ross Dickinson has observed.[13] Some male sexual theorists and researchers insisted that men were by nature polygamous, whereas women were inclined to monogamy—a set of claims that female sexual theorists would attack.

By the early twentieth century, however, increasing scrutiny and activism surrounding prostitution helped destabilize such beliefs regarding female (and male) sexuality. As Lynn Abrams notes, prostitution attracted widespread interest and concern at least until the early part of the second decade of the twentieth century, when foreign policy began to dominate public discussions.[14] The incredible growth of urban centers like Berlin and Hamburg as a result of recently unified Germany's rapid economic expansion was largely responsible for the increased interest in sex work and its social

11. Ibid., 20, 46.

12. August Forel, *The Sexual Question: A Scientific, Psychological, Hygienic, and Sociological Study for the Cultured Classes*, trans. C. F. Marshall, M.D. (London: Rebman, 1908), 93–95.

13. See Edward Ross Dickinson, "'A Dark, Impenetrable Wall of Complete Incomprehension': The Impossibility of Heterosexual Love in Imperial Germany," *Central European History* 40 (2007): 467–497.

14. Lynn Abrams, "Prostitutes in Imperial Germany, 1870–1918: Working Girls or Social Outcasts?," in *The German Underworld: Deviants and Outcasts in Germany History*, ed. Richard J. Evans (London: Routledge, 1988), 189.

effects.[15] According to some statistics (which one must, for various reasons, take with a grain of salt—above all because these numbers only accounted for prostitutes registered by the police), the number of prostitutes in Berlin grew from 15,000 in 1871 to approximately 50,000 in 1900.[16]

German states began regulating prostitution in the early 1800s, in accordance with Napoleonic law. The regulatory system, common to many European countries and U.S. states in the nineteenth century, did not make prostitution per se illegal, but criminalized the practice under certain conditions. According to the provisions of the regulatory system, only women who held a permit from the morals police (*Sittenpolizei*) and underwent frequent medical examinations could avoid criminal prosecution, and prostitution could be practiced legally only within designated zones. The morals police were authorized to arrest any woman they suspected of prostitution and subject her to an invasive medical examination.[17] By the 1870s, bordellos were officially illegal yet tacitly sanctioned; clients and, before 1900, pimps were also exempt from legal punishment.[18] In the view of some conservatives, physicians, and hygienists, the regulatory system was the most effective way to control prostitution and, more importantly, the venereal diseases it was held responsible for spreading within the general population.

Prostitution attracted sensational public attention at the end of the nineteenth century as a result of the infamous Heinze murder trial of 1891, wherein it was revealed that the defendant was pimping out his own wife.[19] The legal reforms prompted by the

---

15. Ibid.

16. Ute Gerhard, *Unerhört: Die Geschichte der deutschen Frauenbewegung* (Hamburg: Rowohlt Taschenbuch Verlag, 1990), 249. As Gerhard notes, this number does not account for "secret" prostitution, sex trafficking, underage prostitution, and the sexual violation and exploitation of working-class women such as servants, factory workers, or barmaids.

17. Abrams, "Prostitutes in Imperial Germany," 191.

18. Gerhard, *Unerhört*, 250. As Abrams points out, Hamburg was unique in maintaining state-run brothels. See Abrams, "Prostitutes in Imperial Germany," 191.

19. Gerhard, *Unerhört*, 248; Eva Maria Heberer, *Prostitution: An Economic Perspective on Its Past, Present, and Future* (Wiesbaden: Springer Science and Business Media, 2014), 39–40.

Heinze trial, the notorious Lex Heinze introduced in 1900, not only heightened criminal penalties for pimping, but also exempted prostitutes' landlords from prosecution. The latter move was meant to decrease the presence of prostitution on city streets; however, many feared that it effectively allowed for the revival of brothels, which had been banned since 1876.[20] The Lex Heinze also allowed for the censorship of "immoral" art, literature, and theater.

Reformers across the religious and political spectrums disparaged prostitution for a number of reasons. Prostitution was alternatively framed as a threat to morality, social order, and public health; as a phenomenon produced by the contradictions of bourgeois society that criminalized the working classes; and as the most blatant, symbolic representation of the sexual double standard and men's power over women. Both feminists and moral purity activists had been active in organizing around prostitution since the 1880s. Even at this relatively early stage, feminists promoted divergent approaches to prostitution: whereas Gertrud Guillame-Schack's failed German League for Culture (Deutscher Kulturbund), established in 1880, advocated the abolition of state regulation over prostitution, Hannah Bieber-Böhm's Association for the Protection of Youth (Verein Jugendschutz), founded in 1889, promoted increased punishments for sellers and clients of prostitution.[21]

The number of organizations dedicated to solving the prostitution "problem" expanded considerably after 1898, during discussions of the Lex Heinze.[22] At this time, progressive German feminists revived the abolitionist position, inspired by British feminist Josephine Butler and previously advocated by Gertrud Guillame-Schack. Leaders like Minna Cauer became converts to the abolitionist cause following the 1899 Congress of the International Abolitionist Federation held in London, and the abolitionist position was embraced by organizations such as "Frauenwohl" and the Union of Progressive Women's Associations. Branches of the

20. Heberer, *Prostitution*, 40.
21. Kerstin Wolff, "Herrenmoral: Anna Pappritz and Abolitionism in Germany," *Women's History Review* 17, no. 2 (2008): 227–228.
22. Heberer, *Prostitution*, 41.

International Abolitionist Federation were established in Hamburg (1898), Berlin (1900), and Dresden (1900).[23] The German section of the International Abolitionist Federation was established in 1904, and 1905 saw the publication of the first issue of *The Abolitionist*, a journal coedited by Anna Pappritz and Katharina Scheven.[24]

Abolitionists maintained that the regulatory system constituted a thoroughgoing attack on women's civil rights and bodily autonomy. As leading abolitionist Katharina Scheven put it, the regulatory system helped secure "healthy women for dissipated men."[25] They blamed the existence of prostitution not on the existence of innately immoral, "work shy," or sexually perverse women, but rather on men's economic and sexual dominance over women. Abolitionist feminists pointed to factors such as women's lack of education and professional opportunities, their low and unequal pay, their economic dependency upon men, and greater precariousness as single women; they also criticized prevailing beliefs regarding discrepancies in male and female sexuality, which rationalized prostitution by citing men's greater sexual needs.[26] For these reasons, abolitionists supported the decriminalization of prostitution, rather than its suppression, and demanded that the state retreat from involvement in prostitution. Such a liberal stance, they believed, supported women's freedom and right to their own person. Abolitionists further advocated a common moral standard for men and women—although supporters of abolition did not necessarily agree what that standard ought to be.

Beyond legal changes, many progressive feminists agreed with sexual reformers who argued that the solution to the problems of prostitution lay in reforms to individual behavior via sexual education, particularly among youth. They maintained that frank, comprehensive, and scientific education regarding human sexuality would ultimately give rise to more authentic—and hygienic—relations

23. Gerhard, *Unerhört*, 251, 253.
24. Wolff, "Herrenmoral," 230; Gerhard, *Unerhört*, 251.
25. Gerhard, *Unerhört*, 252.
26. Ibid., 251.

between the sexes. Where these actors disagreed was in their understanding of human sexuality itself—a disagreement that had implications for what constituted desirable sexual behavior and social
reforms. In the eyes of many progressive women, false and biased
beliefs regarding female sexuality underwrote not only flawed ethics, laws, and social policy, but also the reform programs advanced
by some men, including their colleagues in groups like the German
Society for the Fight against Venereal Diseases.

Growing activism surrounding the plight of unwed mothers and
their children also raised provocative questions about the nature
of female sexuality. Motherhood itself was a topic of considerable
debate around the turn of the twentieth century, sparked by concerns over the national birth rate and, among feminists, by the subordinate status of wives and mothers under the newly revised Civil
Code.[27] In both demographic and legal debates, the unwed mother
emerged as a potent symbol of the dysfunctions produced by existing arrangements: demographers and eugenicists decried the loss of
valuable life and national strength that resulted from the stigmati-
zation of "illegitimate" children, while feminist critics of the Civil
Code saw in the unwed mother an extreme example of the vulner-
ability all women faced under patriarchal laws that gave fathers
virtually all rights over children (and no obligations, in the case of
childbirth outside of marriage).[28] Incited by a 1904 statistic that
estimated the number of single mothers in Germany at 180,000,
the League for the Protection of Mothers formed in 1905.[29] At
various times, both Henriette Fürth and Grete Meisel-Hess played
active roles within this organization. The league's goal was the
"protection of motherhood, married as well as unmarried," and

27. Paul Weindling, *Health, Race, and German Politics between National Unification and Nazism, 1870–1945* (Cambridge: Cambridge University Press, 1993),
241–248; Ann Taylor Allen, *Feminism and Motherhood in Germany, 1800–1914*
(New Brunswick, NJ: Rutgers University Press, 1991), 135–145; Allen, "Mothers of the New Generation: Adele Schreiber, Helene Stöcker, and the Evolution
of the German Idea of Motherhood, 1900–1914," *Signs* 10, no. 3 (Spring 1985):
419–420.
28. See also Allen, "Mothers of the New Generation," 425–426.
29. Tracie Matysik, *Reforming the Moral Subject: Ethics and Sexuality in Central Europe, 1890–1930* (Ithaca, NY: Cornell University Press, 2008), 71.

the "improvement of the legal situation of unmarried mothers and their children."[30] To this end, league leadership circulated petitions that they submitted to Parliament, and established the Office for Mother Protection (Büro für Mutterschutz) in 1906, which offered advice and information to unmarried mothers and working-class women.[31] The league also advocated maternity insurance, the development of a system of crèches for working women, and better treatment of single mothers by gynecological clinics.[32] Beyond these practical activities, the league sought thoroughgoing reforms to existing standards of sexual ethics and beliefs regarding female and male sexuality.

In part because of the social politics surrounding prostitution and unwed mothers—and in part because of new research and hypotheses—scientific understandings of the female sex drive started to shift around the beginning of the twentieth century. New theories regarding the very constitution and manifestation of the sex drive began to surface that had significant implications for conceptualizations of female sexuality. In what follows, I highlight key aspects of the emerging new paradigm of female sexuality through the works of famous male sexologists in order to show, first, that the women sexologists examined here were participating in a broader discursive shift in sexological understandings of female sexuality; second, that they shared certain beliefs and understandings with their male peers, while deviating from them in meaningful ways; and third, that they not only expanded but also radicalized the ideas circulated by men.

Around the turn of the century, physicians and scientists increasingly conceptualized the human sex drive as possessing a psychological, emotional component alongside a physiological one. The dual nature of the drive meant that in seeking sex, humans simultaneously sought emotional intimacy and physical contact. Whereas religious interpretations frequently represented love and

---

30. Ibid., 71.

31. Ibid., 72.

32. Weindling, *Health, Race, and German Politics,* 256–257. Further details on the league's practical activities can be found in Allen, "Mothers of the New Generation," 429–431.

intimacy as spiritual and notably distinct from brute animalistic intercourse, physicians and scientists insisted that these emotions were an intrinsic element of sex and sexuality, and that they were materially rooted and inextricable from physical intercourse. Proceeding from German dermatologist Albert Moll's *Research on the Libido Sexualis* (1897), British physician Havelock Ellis claimed in his *Analysis of the Sexual Impulse* (1903) that the sex impulse was comprised of two mutually constitutive phenomena: namely, "tumescence," or physical sexual tension, and "contrectation," an instinct to approach, touch, and kiss another person, usually—but, notably, not necessarily—of the opposite sex.[33] Such reconceptualizations of the sex drive can be partially attributed to the emerging consensus in the late nineteenth century that the brain and the nervous system constituted the anatomical loci of the sex drive. In *Psychopathia Sexualis*, for example, psychiatrist Richard von Krafft-Ebing claimed that the sex instinct is a function of the cerebral cortex, which serves as the "junction" of paths leading to the sex organs and the nerve centers of visual and olfactory sensation. Krafft-Ebing represented the sex drive as connecting mind and body, sensations and emotions—although for him its function remained primarily reproductive.[34]

The belief that the sex drive's primary function was reproductive would come under fire around the turn of the century. As a result of this growing understanding of the sex drive as simultaneously physiological and psychological, sexual theorists increasingly decoupled sex and reproduction. Havelock Ellis was particularly emphatic in his insistence that the sexual impulse was not solely, or even primarily, a reproductive one. Pointing to the intellectual fallacy of defining an object through its ultimate end, Ellis cleverly averred, "We might as well say that the impulse by which young animals seize food is 'an instinct of nutrition.'"[35] He further suggested

---

33. Havelock Ellis, *Studies in the Psychology of Sex*, vol. 3, *Analysis of the Sexual Impulse* (Philadelphia: F. A. Davis, 1903), 17.

34. Richard von Krafft-Ebing, *Psychopathia Sexualis, with Especial Reference to Contrary Sexual Instinct: A Medico-Legal Study*, trans. Charles Gilbert Chaddock, 7th ed. (Philadelphia: F. A. Davis, 1894), 24–25.

35. Ellis, *Analysis of the Sexual Impulse*, 16.

that the term "reproductive instinct" is "vaguely employed as a euphemism by those who wish to veil the facts of the sexual life; it is more precisely employed mainly by those who are unconsciously dominated by a superstitious repugnance to sex."[36] Just as Ellis insisted on the distinction between reproductive and sex drives in general, he also distinguished between women's sexual and maternal instincts. According to Ellis, women's maternal instinct, their "longing to fulfill those functions for which their bodies are constituted," was not the same as the sex drive. Interestingly, he believed that the maternal instinct was ultimately of greater importance to women's lives than the sexual impulse, asserting that "a woman may not want a lover, but may yet want a child."[37]

The conceptual separation of the sexual and reproductive drives was heightened in the early twentieth century as theorists and researchers began positing that the sex drive was not determined by inputs to the central nervous system, but was a more diffuse and complex psychosomatic phenomenon. In his *Three Contributions to the Theory of Sexuality* (1905), Sigmund Freud suggested that the sexual impulse emanated from "all organs of the body" beginning as early as infancy.[38] In subsequent editions of *Three Contributions*, Freud refined his conceptualization of the sexual instinct, characterizing it as "lying on the frontier between the mental and the physical." The sexual instinct was a "psychical representative of an endosomatic, continuously flowing source of stimulation," rather than a response to external stimuli.[39] According to Freud,

---

36. Ibid., 17.

37. Ibid., 16.

38. Sigmund Freud, *Three Contributions to the Theory of Sexuality*, trans. A. A. Brill, 2nd ed. (New York: Nervous and Mental Disease Publishing, 1920), 77. I draw from the English text for translation. Freud's text was originally published in German; see Sigmund Freud, *Drei Abhandlung zur Sexualtheorie* (Leipzig: Deutike, 1905).

39. As footnote 9 in Peter Gay's *The Freud Reader* (1989) points out, this characterization of the sexual instinct dates to 1915, meaning it did not appear in the original version of *Three Contributions*. In accordance with this translation, I use the term "instinct" in the text. See Sigmund Freud, *Three Essays on the Theory of Sexuality*, in *The Freud Reader*, edited by Peter Gay (New York: W. W. Norton, 1989), 256. Notably, 1915 was the same year Freud wrote "Instincts and Their Vicissitudes," which many scholars identify as one of the first comprehensive

instincts lacked intrinsic traits, but assumed particular qualities in relation to their somatic sources and their aims. In later editions of *Three Contributions*, he famously characterized the sexual instinct as a "demand upon the mind for work"—specifically, it sought release of sexual tension, and consequent attainment of sexual satisfaction.[40] Thus, while Freud did not move away entirely from the notion of a (continual, self-generating) somatic source of sexuality, its realization required psychological effort and elaboration.

Freud was among the first to insist that the sex drive's fundamental, essential aim was not reproduction, but pleasure. In his essay "Modern Sexual Morality and Modern Nervousness" (1908), he asserted that "broad vistas open up for us when we bear in mind the fact that man's sexual instinct is not at all primarily meant to serve the purposes of reproduction but is intended to furnish certain forms of gratification."[41] Like Ellis, Freud argued that the sex drive was distinct from reproduction; however, he took this argument a step further by implying that sexual pleasure was a physiological and psychological phenomenon, produced by physiological and psychological processes. However, Freud was not alone in highlighting the role of pleasure as the object of the sex drive. Swiss psychiatrist August Forel also identified a "pleasure principle" at work in the sex drive, and associated the desire for sexual pleasure specifically with women. In so-called normal women, Forel found "a certain sensual desire for caresses, connected more or less with unconscious and ill-defined sexual sensations." Intriguingly, he insisted this desire was "not limited to the male sex but extends to other women, to children, and even to animals." As Forel noted in *The Sexual Question* (1905), "Young normal girls

---

elaborations of his drive theory (alongside "The Unconscious" and "Repression," which also appeared that year). See Joel Weinberger and Jeffrey Stein, "The Drive Theory," in *The Freud Encyclopedia: Theory, Therapy, and Culture*, ed. Edward Erwin (New York: Routledge, 2002), 163.

40. Freud, *Three Essays*, 256. Again, I have quoted here from the 1915 passage.

41. Sigmund Freud, "Modern Sexual Morality and Modern Nervousness," *American Journal of Urology and Sexology* 11 (October 1915): 392. This essay was originally published before the First World War in German as "Die kulturelle Sexualmoral und die moderne Nervosität," *Sexual-Probleme* 4 (1908): 107–129.

often like to sleep together in the same bed, to caress and kiss each other, which is not the case with normal young men." While representing this impulse as a "peculiarity of the sexual sentiments of woman," Forel, like Freud, recognized that the sex drive encouraged nonreproductive sexual behavior aimed at no purpose other than self-satisfaction.[42]

These changing scientific understandings of the sex drive clearly opened up new ways of thinking about female sexuality, and even led male physicians and scientists to suggest that the female and male sex drives may be similar in strength and intensity. According to Havelock Ellis, "We may fairly hold that, roughly speaking, the distribution of the sexual impulse between the two sexes is fairly balanced."[43] Ellis claimed that previous researchers had failed to grasp this fundamental truth because they had not understood that women's "sexual mechanism" was less spontaneous and more complex, variable, and diffuse than men's.[44] On the basis of "a series of twelve cases of women [on] whose sexual development [he] possess[ed] precise information," all of whom "belong[ed] to the middle class" and were "fairly healthy" (though he noted that "two or three might be regarded as slightly abnormal"), Ellis asserted that "all the more highly intelligent, energetic women . . . [are] those with strong sexual emotions."[45] Ellis even noted that of these twelve women, "nine had at some time or another masturbated (four shortly after puberty, five in adult life), but, except in one case, rarely and at intervals."[46] Quite radically, Ellis blamed men for women's sexual unresponsiveness, insisting that "many women may never experience sexual gratification and relief, through no defect on their part, but through the failure of the

42. Forel, *Sexual Question*, 94–95.
43. Ellis, "Sexual Impulse in Women," 57.
44. Ibid., 53–54, 57. Ellis further argued that "a woman can find sexual satisfaction in a great number of ways that do not include the sexual act proper, and in a great number of ways that apparently are not physical at all, simply because their physical basis is diffused or is to be found in one of the outlying sexual zones" (56).
45. Ellis, "Sexual Impulse in Women," 50.
46. Ibid., 50.

husband to understand the lover's part."[47] For these reasons, Ellis asserted,

> a state of sexual anaesthesia, relative or absolute, cannot be considered as anything but abnormal. To take even the lowest ground, the satisfaction of the reproductive function ought to be at least as gratifying as the evacuation of the bowels or bladder; while if we take . . . higher ground than this, an act which is at once the supreme fact and symbol of love and the supreme creative act cannot under normal conditions be other than the most pleasurable of acts, or it would stand in violent opposition to all that we find in nature.[48]

Like Ellis, German dermatologist Iwan Bloch insisted in his influential *Sexual Life of Our Time* (1907) that the intensity of women's "sexual sensibility" was "at least as great as that of man." Bloch claimed that he arrived at this view through consultation with "a great many cultured women" who "without exception . . . declared the theory of the lesser sexual sensibility of women to be erroneous." Bloch reported that "many [women] were even of the opinion that sexual sensibility was greater and more enduring in woman than man."[49] Also like Ellis, Bloch maintained that the female sex drive was more diffuse, and that this trait inhibited the "spontaneous resolution of the libido." He thus concluded that when it came to women's true sexual nature, "behind the veil prescribed by conventional morality, behind the apparent coldness, there is concealed an ardent sexuality."[50]

Freud offered perhaps the most radical statement concerning the similarities of the male and female sex drive in *Three Contributions to the Theory of Sexuality*. Freud maintained that both the male and the female libidos were essentially "masculine"—a term he claimed meant "active"—as a result of humanity's fundamental bisexuality.[51] Freud saw no inherent difference in the character,

---

47. Ibid., 54.
48. Ibid., 51.
49. Iwan Bloch, *The Sexual Life of Our Time*, trans. Eden Paul (New York: Allied Book, 1908), 83–84.
50. Ibid., 86.
51. During this period, "bisexuality" denoted the presence of both female and male physiological properties in the body, rather than a sexual orientation toward both sexes. In Freud's words, "There is no pure masculinity and femininity either

purpose, or strength of the male and female sex drives; instead, he insisted that gendered differences in manifestations of the sex drive were a result of socialization.

These new theories of the sex drive, and specifically new claims that the male and female sex drives and needs were not essentially or fundamentally different, were bolstered by psychiatric research on the detrimental effects of prolonged celibacy on women's physical and psychological health. Whereas physicians such as Hegar claimed that celibacy was physiologically and psychologically beneficial, contributing to longer life and greater intellectual and creative activity, in the 1880s psychiatrists such as Krafft-Ebing began to argue that women's enforced celibacy caused a host of physical and psychological diseases, including hysteria and suicide.[52] In the second edition of his *Textbook of Psychiatry* (1883), Krafft-Ebing unambiguously stated that women were by their nature as much in need of sex as men.[53]

As scientists and physicians continued to link women's forced sexual abstinence to poor mental and physical health, they became openly critical of women's enforced celibacy. Although he had previously insisted that women were passionless, by 1911 Leipzig-based dermatologist and urologist Dr. Hermann Rohleder had become convinced that women's sexual needs and feelings were equal to men's; furthermore, he maintained that the diminishment of a woman's sex drive was a product of culture, not nature.[54] Rohleder actually considered celibacy to be impossible, except among the truly perverse. Like physician Albert Eulenberg and dermatologist Max Marcuse, he maintained that celibacy could never be an absolute phenomenon because sex permeated all realms of physical

---

in the biological or psychological sense. On the contrary every individual person shows a mixture of his own biological sex characteristics with the biological traits of the other sex and a union of activity and passivity." Freud, *Three Contributions*, 79.

52. Hegar, *Der Geschlechtstrieb*, 7–8.

53. See Richard von Krafft-Ebing, *Lehrbuch der Psychiatrie auf klinischer Grundlage für praktische Ärzte und Studirende*, bd. 1, *Die Allgemeine Pathologie und Therapie des Irreseins*, 2nd ed. (Stuttgart: Ferdinand Enke, 1883), 80–90.

54. Hermann Rohleder, "Die sexuelle Veranlagung der Frauen," *Die neue Generation* 7 (July 1911): 266.

and psychological existence.[55] According to Rohleder, even sexual thoughts and longings constituted a breach of celibacy.

Like Rohleder, Eulenberg, and Marcuse, Freud insisted in "Modern Sexual Morality and Modern Nervousness" that most people were "constitutionally incapable of abstinence."[56] He insisted that all humans, regardless of their gender, required not only sexual activity but also sexual gratification for the sake of their mental and physical well-being. He declared that existing social restrictions on the play of sexual instincts were primarily responsible for causing nervous disorders.[57] With respect to women, Freud argued that premarital abstinence, repression of girls' sensuality, and enforced sexual ignorance all caused certain "functional disturbances" and inadequacies in women, including their mental inferiority.[58] Freud was remarkably forthright in suggesting that society consciously repressed women's sexuality to serve its own ends.[59]

Changing understandings of the sex drive—as autonomous and separate from a reproductive drive, driven by desires for emotional intimacy and physical pleasure, and fundamentally similar in men and women—along with the growing belief that celibacy was harmful to women's health, suggested the need to reform the organization of sexual life and constitution of sexual ethics. Nevertheless, male physicians and scientists continued to insist upon distinctly gendered roles and, importantly, power relations in sexual intercourse, despite finding commonalities between the male and female sex drives. For example, in holding men responsible for failing to arouse women's sex drives, Ellis effectively reaffirmed men's dominant and "more active part in coitus," including determination of the conditions of sexual intercourse.[60] Bloch's insistence

---

55. Albert Eulenberg, "Leitsätze zu dem Referate: 'Die sexuelle Abstinenz und die moderne Kultur,'" in Rosenthal, *Mutterschutz und Sexualreform,* 112–114.

56. Freud, "Modern Sexual Morality and Modern Nervousness," 397, 394.

57. Ibid., 392, 398.

58. Ibid., 402.

59. According to Freud, "The double standard which obtains in present day society is the frankest admission that society, much as it may issue decrees, does not believe that its decrees can be enforced" (398).

60. Ellis, "Sexual Impulse in Woman," 53, 54.

that women depend upon men to awaken their latent "erotic sensibilities" held similar implications.[61] According to some scientists like August Forel, women's "sexual sensibility" was fundamentally submissive. In *The Sexual Question*, Forel argued that the female sex drive is not just subordinate to the male, but seeks out and delights in its subordination. According to Forel, when a woman finds the man she loves and with whom she wishes to have children, she is driven "to give herself to him as a slave . . . , to play the part of the one who devotes herself, who is conquered, mastered, and subjugated." Forel even insisted that these "negative aspirations form part of the normal sexual appetite of women."[62] Although Freud did not believe women were innately sexually submissive, he nonetheless insisted that female sexuality *must* be repressed to facilitate the development of the male sex drive. In Freud's view, "The reenforcement of the sexual inhibitions produced in the woman . . . causes a stimulus in the libido of the man and forces it to increase its capacity." If the female sex drive were liberated, it would undermine the power and potency of male sexuality.[63]

Male physicians and scientists also used the naturalization of women's sexual drive and attendant needs to reassert male dominance and sexual privilege in other insidious ways: namely, by imputing alternative meanings and motives to women's sexual behavior. In particular, women's purported sexual passivity, once held as evidence of her passionlessness, became redefined as part of the courtship ritual meant to facilitate sexual activity—even to the point of inviting male sexual domination. In upholding this interpretation of women's passivity, many sexual scientists referenced Darwinian sexual selection and the evolutionary role

---

61. Bloch, *Sexual Life of Our Time*, 83–86.

62. Forel, *Sexual Question*, 93–94.

63. Within the developmental schema outlined in *Three Contributions*, sexual repression is represented as fundamental to both normal female and male sexual subjectivity. While defining all childhood sexuality as diffuse, or "polymorphously perverse," and recognizing the clitoris as the girl's central erogenous zone, Freud states that during the course of sexual maturation, the female youth must effectively abandon the clitoris, or the "male element," as the central erogenous zone, and transfer this sexual excitation to the vagina in preparation for her future maternal role. Freud, *Three Contributions*, 80.

Darwin attributed to female modesty. Ellis, Forel, and Bloch all insisted that women's sexual passivity was only "apparent" or superficial.[64] According to Ellis, "The true nature of the passivity of the female is revealed by the ease with which it is thrown off whenever the male refuses to accept his cue. . . . The aggressiveness of the male, the coyness of the female, are alike unconsciously assumed in order to bring about in the most effectual manner the ultimate union of the sexes! The seeming reluctance of the female is not intended to inhibit sexual activity either in the male or herself, but to increase it in both."[65] Male scientists' recognition of female sexual need had the effect of stigmatizing women's sexual disinterest in men as "frigidity," which men like Ellis, Bloch, and Freud condemned as a sexual abnormality. Echoing Eulenberg, Bloch argued that female frigidity constituted a form of sexual "infantilism" that he attributed to multiple causes including heredity, masturbation, and women's experience of male sexual violence.[66] While at one time a virtue, female passionlessness increasingly became redefined as evidence of underlying pathology. In the hands of many male physicians and scientists, new views of female sexuality as similar in strength, need, and intensity to that of the male became used to support men's sexual aggression and, to borrow from Adrienne Rich, "compulsory heterosexuality."[67] It not only upheld unequal power dynamics within heterosexual relations, but also bolstered existing gendered social roles and inequalities.

Perhaps not surprisingly, women interpreted the implications of new understandings of the sex drive differently. For women sexologists, these new scientific facts seemed to affirm the illegitimacy of the sexual double standard, and opened up the possibility that an equal, more liberal sexual ethic might be appropriate for both sexes. Rather than allowing male physicians and scientists to monopolize the discussion, women like Ruth Bré, Johanna Elberskirchen, Grete Meisel-Hess, and Henriette Fürth began writing and revising understandings of the sex drive, and published

---

64. Forel, *Sexual Question*, 74; Ellis, "Sexual Impulse in Woman," 53.

65. Ellis, "Sexual Impulse in Woman," 52–53.

66. Bloch, *Sexual Life of Our Times*, 86, 430–431.

67. Adrienne Rich, "Compulsory Heterosexuality and Lesbian Existence," *Signs* 5 (1980): 631–660.

monographs, pamphlets, essays, and journal articles to express their ideas. Though these women agreed with male sexologists on many fundamental points, they challenged and expanded aspects of the emerging paradigm by drawing on their own experiences or the experiences of other women, which they suggested provided a truer, more objective perspective than that provided by men. The analyses these women put forward in their writing helped further the shift in understanding of the female sex drive that recognized its coexisting carnal and emotional aspects, as well as its active nature and innate needs. Unlike their male peers, women extended this view of the female sex drive to its logical conclusions in terms of women's rights and sexual reform: that is, they insisted that women had a *biological right* to engage in freely chosen (hetero)sexual encounters. However, these new ideas would prove contentious, above all to other feminists. Moreover, the pathologization of female sexual frigidity and disinterest in heterosexual relations found in men's writing would also inform women's texts in ways that would profoundly impact women's assertions of their "biological" rights.

Women Sexologists Redefine the Female Sex Drive

Ruth Bré, Johanna Elberskirchen, Henriette Fürth, and Grete Meisel-Hess all wrote on the "true nature" of female sexuality between 1903 and 1914. In their writing, they endeavored not only to define female sexuality through the concept of the sex drive, but also to delineate the social and political consequences of understanding women's physiologically and psychologically determined sexual needs. Even though some male researchers such as Max Marcuse disparaged what they viewed as their feminine or feminist bias and eccentricity, as well as the "gullibility" (*Gutgläubigkeit*) of their ideas,[68] many of the texts discussed in this chapter were reviewed in key prewar sexual scientific journals, such as *Sexual Problems, Journal for Sexual Science, Journal for the Fight against Venereal Diseases,* and *Monthly Journal for Urinary Illness and*

---

68. See, for example, Max Marcuse, "Rundschau: Johanna Elberskirchen, Geschlechtsempfindung und Liebe," *Sexual-Probleme* 4 (1908): 153.

Sexual Hygiene.[69] They were even included on bibliographic lists of contemporary sexual scientific literature.[70]

Before turning to their ideas, it is worth briefly introducing these authors (although more comprehensive biographical details can be found in the appendix). Ruth Bré was the pseudonym of schoolteacher Elisabeth Bouness. The contested founder of the League for the Protection of Mothers and Sexual Reform, she left the organization when it did not embrace her idea of settling healthy unwed mothers and their children in German colonies in eastern Europe as a key part of its program. Beyond eugenic convictions, Bré's investment in the fate of single mothers and their children was personal, as she was the daughter of an unwed mother. In spite of her historical liminality, Bré produced a number of contemporarily influential and provocative texts, including *The Right to Motherhood* (1903). Johanna Elberskirchen was born into a lower-middle-class family in Bonn in 1864. After working as a bookkeeper in her early twenties, she moved to Switzerland to pursue a university education. Elberskirchen studied the natural sciences, anatomy, physiology, and philosophy at the University of Bern before switching to law and jurisprudence at the University of Zurich. Following her studies and return to Germany, she became involved in left-leaning organizations and campaigns for women's suffrage. Unusually forthright and public about her same-sex desires, Elberskirchen became one of only four female chairpersons of the Scientific Humanitarian Committee in 1914, following a move to Berlin. Henriette Fürth (née Katzenstein) was born in 1861 to an upper-middle-class family

---

69. Notably, the exchange between Bré and Bluhm was noted in the May 1904 edition of the *Monatschrift für Harnkrankheiten und sexuelle Hygiene*, and Bré's *Staatskinder oder Mutterrecht* was reviewed in the September 1904 edition of the same journal. *Staatskinder oder Mutterrecht* was also reviewed in the *Zeitschrift für Bekämpfung der Geschlechtskrankheiten* (January 1905), as was *Das Recht auf Mutterschaft* (November 1903). Meisel-Hess's *Die sexuelle Krise* was reviewed in the January 1910 edition of *Sexual-Probleme*, and in the December 1909 edition of the *Zeitschrift für Bekämpfung der Geschlechtskrankheiten*. Johanna Elberskirchen's contribution to the essay collection *Mann und Weib* was noted in the January 1908 edition of the *Zeitschrift für Sexualwissenschaft*.

70. See, for example, *Sexual-Probleme* 5, 8, and 11 (1908); *Sexual-Probleme* 2 and 8 (1909); *Sexual-Probleme* 1 (1910).

in Giessen. Before the First World War, she became involved in a range of sex reform organizations, including the German Society for the Fight against Venereal Diseases and the League for the Protection of Mothers and Sexual Reform, and ultimately became a member and representative of the Social Democratic Party. Though lacking a formal university education, Fürth wrote approximately thirty monographs and 200 articles on topics including social and racial hygiene, women's suffrage, home economics, women's work, maternal insurance and welfare, infant welfare, and sexual morality. Finally, Grete Meisel-Hess was born in Prague in 1879. She grew up in Vienna, where she later attended university and studied philosophy, sociology, and biology. Following a move to Berlin in 1908, she became involved in various sex reform organizations, including the League for the Protection of Mothers and Sexual Reform. During her brief life she published numerous successful texts across a variety of genres, all of which addressed feminism and sex reform. Her 1909 study, *The Sexual Crisis*, was especially influential, eventually gaining an international readership.

All four of these writers conceived of the female sex drive as an autonomous and important physiological phenomenon and asserted that female needs, like those of the male, were wholly natural. Grete Meisel-Hess insisted that the sexual impulse constituted "the most primitive and most clearly expressed will in all nature."[71] In her view, "The demands of the sexual impulse are as imperative as those of hunger."[72] Similarly, both Ruth Bré and Johanna Elberskirchen described the sex drive as a function akin to eating, drinking, and sleeping.[73] This analogy between the sex drive and

---

71. Grete Meisel-Hess, *The Sexual Crisis: A Critique of Our Sexual Life*, trans. Eden Paul and Cedar Paul (New York: Critic and Guide, 1917), 170. Though I cite from the English translation, this text was originally published in German in 1909; see Grete Meisel-Hess, *Die sexuelle Krise: Eine sozialpsychologische Untersuchung* (Jena: Diedrichs, 1909).

72. Meisel-Hess, *Sexual Crisis*, 195. Subsequent citations of this work appear parenthetically in the text.

73. Ruth Bré, *Das Recht auf die Mutterschaft: Eine Forderung zur Bekämpfung der Prostitution der Frauen- und Geschlechtskrankheiten* (Leipzig: Verlag der Frauen-Rundschau, 1903), 28; Johanna Elberskirchen, *Geschlechtsleben und Geschlechtsenthaltsamkeit des Weibes* (Munich: Seitz & Schauer, 1905), 3.

drives for other forms of nourishment was in fact widespread. In her 1903 tract, *The Right to Motherhood*, Ruth Bré argued, "The sex drive is a natural drive like every other. It is neither moral, nor immoral. It is simply natural. To satisfy it is a natural law, like eating, drinking, and sleeping. It can only be made immoral through immoderation, like immoderate eating and drinking can become immoral."[74] Likewise, in her 1905 tract, *Sex Life and Sexual Abstinence of Woman*, Johanna Elberskirchen declared, "An active sex life is a function which is, of necessity, characteristic of all sexually differentiated individuals, and is as necessary as eating and drinking. This activity is a physiological feature, necessary for the creation of an individual person and for the preservation of our species—it is a basic law of biology. An individual's sex life can therefore not be restricted or even prohibited, just like eating and drinking."[75] Elberskirchen went so far as to describe women as "sexually hungry," and as possessing a sex drive so overpowering that it leads them to overlook and ignore all social prohibitions against extramarital sex.[76]

Representing the sex drive as akin to eating and drinking enabled Bré and Elberskirchen to assert that the satisfaction of the female sex drive was a physiological necessity: just as eating required food, the sex drive required sex. In Elberskirchen's words, "The active sexual life in itself can therefore be so rarely restricted or forbidden for the single individual, as is the case with eating and drinking."[77] She thus insisted that women's forced sexual celibacy constituted a form of deprivation, declaring that "a sexually mature woman is naturally never voluntarily celibate."[78] Similarly, Ruth Bré made the case in *The Right to Motherhood* that sex itself could be moral because "in Nature all is moral."[79] In a rhetorical move

74. Bré, *Das Recht auf die Mutterschaft*, 28.

75. Elberskirchen, *Geschlechtsleben und Geschlechtsenthaltsamkeit des Weibes*, 3.

76. Johanna Elberskirchen, *Die Sexualempfindung bei Weib und Mann: Betrachtet vom physiologisch-soziologisch Standpunkte* (Berlin: R. Jacobsthal Verlag, 1903), 28.

77. Elberskirchen, *Geschlechtsleben und Geschlechtsenthaltsamkeit des Weibes*, 3.

78. Ibid., 4.

79. Bré, *Das Recht auf die Mutterschaft*, 26.

common at the time, she declared "primitive" peoples (*Naturvölk-ern*) to be the happiest and healthiest, as their sex lives, especially the sex lives of women, were supposedly untouched by civilization, and most accurately reflected true, authentic sexual relations. The "basic evil" bedeviling sexual life, she claimed, was the "distance from nature, from natural laws" that plagued civilized people.[80]

Women sexologists also argued that male and female sex drives did not differ significantly with regard to their strength or the degree of sexual need they created in men and women. As stated at the outset of this chapter, Henriette Fürth was adamant that the male and female sex drives were essentially the same in their features and equal in their intensity. In *The Sex Problem and Modern Morals*, Fürth insisted that "within the plant and animal world there are nowhere indications that the sexual instinct of the male would be completely different from that of a female," as the instinct is essentially biological and functional (5). Referring to behaviors and processes within the "animal world," Fürth maintained that the behaviors of certain animals demonstrated that "the females are stronger and also in sexual relations were the more aggressive [partner]." She cited "herring, bees and ants" as "obvious" (*naheliegend*) examples (5). Like Bré, she too invoked the example of primitive peoples, who, she believed, "show themselves to be closer to the condition of animals" and demonstrated the similarities between male and female sex drives (6). "And in the same way as with animals," she argued, "we too find in some primitive people the woman to be the selecting one in a sexual relationship and . . . nothing that points to a difference in the sexual feelings and desires of both sexes" (6). Fürth implied that this lack of difference in male and female sex drives among "natural peoples" was the result of the fact that secondary sexual characteristics were "not as developed" (*ausgebildet*) as among "civilized people"—a common anthropological assertion in the late nineteenth and early twentieth centuries (6). "In regard to biology," she concluded, "it does not give us, at least in regard to animals and primitive people, any indications that the sex drive is different" among men and women (6).

---

80. Ibid., 25.

By the end of the first decade of the twentieth century, feminists began to insist on the necessity of women's sexual pleasure, often in terms strikingly reminiscent of Freud. In *The Sexual Crisis*, Grete Meisel-Hess held that sensual enjoyment was necessary for the individual, whether male or female, within the limits delineated by the need to release sexual tensions, on the one hand, and the need to preserve energy for social and cultural labor, on the other (36). She also recognized the political implications of this position: "The recognition that the need exists for both sexes," she maintained, "would destroy the false foundation" of the sexual double standard (198). In Meisel-Hess's view, "The sexual life is the focal point of every healthy being whose instincts have not undergone partial or complete atrophy"; indeed, within *The Sexual Crisis* sexual fulfillment is presented as the essential precondition of a balanced and whole personality (117). "Let us admit the truth," Meisel-Hess insisted. "Let us recognize that there is full justification for the desire of every human being to love and to be loved; let us make it socially possible for everyone to satisfy this desire as may best commend itself to the individual judgment—so long as no other person is harmed, and so long as nothing is done injurious to racial welfare" (117). The eugenic qualifications embedded in Meisel-Hess's rousing declaration attune us to the kinds of limitations that buttressed women sexologists' understanding of the normal and desirable female sexual subject.

As part of their efforts to assert the similarities of the male and female sex drives, many women sexologists distinguished between the sex drive and maternal instinct as phenomena, although there was some ambivalence on this point among certain writers. In *The Right to Motherhood*, Ruth Bré characterized woman's sexual drive in line with many male doctors, that is, as indistinguishable from a maternal drive.[81] In making this claim, she offered medical citations from the likes of Richard von Krafft-Ebing. However, Bré

---

81. Bré stressed the concordance between her views and those of male doctors in her 1904 article "Is Forced, Unwilled Sexual Abstinence and Childlessness Damaging for the Healthy, Normal Woman?" by noting the positive notices that her book received from male physicians, including Drs. Wilhelm Erb, Albert Neisser, and Max Flesch. See Ruth Bré, "Ist erzwungene, unfreiwillige Enthaltsamkeit

maintained that the fundamentally maternal nature of the female sex drive did not mean that women's sexual needs are less than those of men; moreover, she leveraged her assertion that the female sex drive was a maternal drive to argue that women's sexual satisfaction ought not be limited to marriage. "It seems to be quite natural for a true, loving girl to surrender to her lover," she asserted; shame had to be taught to her later.[82] For Bré, reproduction and motherhood were "necessary for the physical and spiritual flourishing of woman, as well as the full development of her sexual character";[83] consequently, she believed that attempts to deny a woman the "right" to motherhood—and thus sexual expression and satisfaction—rendered her a "cripple."[84] In a nod to the eugenic convictions she shared with her fellow sexual theorists, Bré maintained that the more capable and "fit" the woman, the more she—and the race—will suffer from her denied instincts.

For Meisel-Hess, significant qualitative differences between the male and female sex drives existed. She maintained that women's sexuality was complicated by maternal desires, writing that "in the case of women, the manifestations of sexual tension are complicated by an organic need additional to that felt for erotic stimulation and erotic satisfaction, the need for motherhood." According to Meisel-Hess, "A healthy young woman who is unable to become a mother is likely to suffer from nervous disorder, for her organism feels the need for the stimulation furnished by the act of parturition, and suffers from the accumulation of tensions that should be discharged in lactation and in her love for her offspring" (322). Meisel-Hess further argued that whereas man's love is individual, woman's love is general: woman is, far more than man, an "instrument in the hands of the species, used for the purposes of the species." She asserted that "by nature, woman lacks the direct pitilessly clear vision that man has of these things. This is just as

---

und Kinderlosigkeit für das gesunde, normale Weib schädlich?," *Deutsche medizinische Presse* 4 (1904): 27.

82. Bré, *Das Recht auf die Mutterschaft*, 28.

83. Bré, "Erzwungene, unfreiwillige Enthaltsamkeit und Kinderlosigkeit," 27; and Bré, *Das Recht auf die Mutterschaft*, 24.

84. Bré, *Das Recht auf die Mutterschaft*, 24.

well, for did women also see sexual relationships as they really are, the continued existence of the human race would become impossible" (124).

Conversely, in *The Sexual Feeling of Woman and Man* (1903), Elberskirchen directly challenged gynecologist Max Flesch's assertion that women's sex drive was nothing more than a physiological impetus to motherhood. Allowing herself "weapons from the scientific armory of male intellectuals," including zoologist Oscar Hertwig, Elberskirchen argued that motherhood must be viewed as a physiological effect of sex.[85] Like Ellis, she asserted that the effects of sex cannot also constitute its origin.[86] Moreover, she pointed out that if the female sex drive was merely a desire for children, there would be no abortion, infanticide, or suicide in the face of unwanted pregnancy or unwed motherhood—and that women would be less discriminating in terms of their mates.[87] Fürth also maintained that women's sex drive was distinct from any maternal longing. Reversing Havelock Ellis's ranking, she asserted that sexual desire is primary in women, and motherhood secondary. According to Fürth, the desire for a child sometimes only emerges after a woman holds her child in her arms for the first time: "A mother's love and a mother's longing, important and beautiful as they are, do not represent something fundamental. They are the obvious results which emerge from a heightened sexual desire caused by the urge to procreate, that feeling and longing innate to women as well as to men."[88]

These writers drew upon representations of the sex drive as simultaneously physical and psychological to stress that physical and emotional intimacy were natural phenomena. In "The Sex Life of the Female" (1908), Elberskirchen paralleled Albert Moll's division of the sex drive into impulses of "tumescence" and "contrectation" to define the normal female sex drive as comprised of innate

85. Elberskirchen, *Die Sexualempfindung bei Weib und Mann*, 13.
86. Ibid., 6–7.
87. Ibid., 26.
88. Fürth, *Das Geschlechtsproblem und die moderne Moral*, 14–15.

impulses to physical and emotional union.[89] Elberskirchen maintained that the sex drive was fundamentally a "Vereinigungskraft,"
or a drive to union, made up of a "Begattungskraft," a drive to
copulation originating from the sexual organs and nervous system,
and a "Liebeskraft," a drive to physical intimacy originating in the
brain.[90] She insisted that even if "the starting point of the sex drive
or its origins is the power of growth or reproduction," the sex drive
must be considered a simultaneously spiritual and physical phenomenon that produces a "sex hunger" in all healthy individuals.[91]
In making such claims, she directly and explicitly challenged male
doctors who treated the female sex drive as congenitally weak and
inhibited; here she named Otto Adler, author of *The Inadequate
Sexual Feeling of Woman*, as the worst offender.[92]

For women sexologists, the dual character of the female sex
drive ennobled sex and sexuality. "The prophets of gloom, those
who refuse to recognize the sex relationship as a means of individual salvation, those who consider the sexual act to be justified
solely when effected for the purposes of the species, must be ignored as fanatics," Grete Meisel-Hess declared. "The processes of
love, the tender mutual intertwining of the two human personalities, must be recognized as valuable, not merely in order to ensure
the physical continuity of the species, but also for the development
of the individual soul" (*Sexual Crisis*, 120). In Grete Meisel-Hess's
view, the sexual impulses of both men and women were in their
"essential nature not evil, but good," although they may be "misused or repressed in our perverted sexual order" (322). She even
asserted that sexual pleasure was "preordained" by nature, writing, "The source of our [sexual] misery is not the existence of such
desires, but the denial of their satisfaction. If sexual pleasures were
not 'preordained,' the 'Divine Creator' would not have provided

89. Elberskirchen,"Das Geschlechtsleben des Weibes," in *Mann und Weib:
Ihre Beziehungen zueinander und zum Kulturleben der Gegenwart*, ed. Dr. R.
Kossmann and Dr. Julius Weiss (Stuttgart: Union Deutsche Verlagsgesellschaft,
1908), 194.
90. Ibid., 188–192, 195.
91. Ibid., 194.
92. Ibid., 210.

us with the organs of sex" (305). As evidenced earlier by Ruth Bré's insistence that that which is natural is also moral, female sexual theorists invoked the supposed naturalness of the sex drive to prove that female sexual expression, even outside of marriage, was both positive and moral. Like Bré, Henriette Fürth declared that "every form of life is morally and aesthetically beautiful and perfect that develops harmoniously out of its natural preconditions and always remains in harmony with itself."[93]

For these reasons, many women sexologists insisted that women possessed what they termed a biological right to both sexual experience and sexual pleasure.[94] Claiming for herself the status of a "Medizinerin," or medical expert, Elberskirchen quite explicitly asserted that "every sexually differentiated individual has a biological right, that is, a natural right to an active sex life, that, logically and obviously, should not be limited or even abolished by any means or any outside influences."[95] Recognition of such a right, Meisel-Hess maintained, would constitute an important form of "erotic enfranchisement" that would "go far to restore [the] independence and self-respect [women have] lost in the modern perversion of courtship."[96] It would also enable women to free themselves from their emotional and erotic dependence upon men, and from their sense of "gratefulness" to men for their sexual satisfaction.[97] Furthermore, it would produce what Meisel-Hess called an "oversurplus of sexual energies" that could be put to other creative uses.[98] She drew direct parallels between intellectual power and

---

93. Henriette Fürth, "Die Frauenbewegung und was ihr not tun," *Neues Frauenleben* 17 (1905): 9.

94. Elberskirchen, *Geschlechtsleben und Geschlechtsenthaltsamkeit des Weibes*, 3; Johanna Elberskirchen, *Mutter! II: Geschlechtliche Aufklärung des Weibes* (Munich: Seitz und Schauer, 1905), 39–49.

95. Elberskirchen, *Geschlechtsleben und Geschlechtsenthaltsamkeit des Weibes*, 3.

96. Grete Meisel-Hess, "Sexuelle Rechte," *Die neue Generation* 8 (1912): 185–186; Meisel-Hess, *Sexual Crisis*, 200.

97. Meisel-Hess, *Sexual Crisis*, 199; see also Meisel-Hess, "Sexuelle Rechte," 185–186.

98. Meisel-Hess, *Sexual Crisis*, 305.

sexual intensity in women, asserting that "in art and in research the ardent woman is the receiver and interpreter of intuitions."[99]

Women sexologists further bolstered their claims regarding women's biological rights by referencing the damaging effects of celibacy on women's health. In *The Right to Motherhood*, Ruth Bré insisted that celibacy caused cancers of the ovaries, uterus, and breast, in addition to "sleeplessness, depression, hysteria, epilepsy, madness, and even suicide."[100] Bré declared such afflictions to be "nature's revenge" for denying the female sex drive its innate needs and outlets.[101] The manifold negative health consequences of abstinence led Meisel-Hess to bluntly exclaim, "Denial to the right of the life of sex—it is hardly possible to conceive the horror of such a fate!" (*Sexual Crisis*, 306). She argued at length in *The Sexual Crisis* that celibacy was responsible for producing hysteria and anxiety. As support, she invoked the research of Berlin-based physician Dr. Wilhelm Hammer to point out that sexual deprivation gives rise to hysterical symptoms in animals (306). She also referenced the work of Josef Breuer and Freud on hysteria in connection with women's sexual repression: "These writers speak with no uncertain voice, and they add that the natural impulses are to such an extent forced into 'abreaction' that 'the psychic unity becomes disordered.' Thus a sexual psychosis is the widely diffused pathological consequence of our sexual misery" (331). To further press her case, Meisel-Hess cited Krafft-Ebing's finding of a higher rate of insanity among single women between the ages of twenty-five and thirty-five: that is, during the years when most women

---

99. Ibid., 240. Elsewhere, however, Meisel-Hess argued that women's sexual needs did not have as far-reaching effects upon women's lives and psyches as some feminists and sexual scientists claimed. Instead, she insisted the exaggerated role of sex in women's lives was a cultural product, created by the restricted life paths provided to women and their dependence upon man. See Meisel-Hess, "Sexuelle Rechte," 185.

100. Bré, *Das Recht auf die Mutterschaft*, 32–33.

101. Ibid., 51. Following attacks by Dr. Agnes Bluhm on the validity of Bré's claims, Bré published her article in the *Deutsche medizinische Presse* in 1904 to fully elaborate both the anecdotal and the medical bases of her claims regarding the negative health effects of forced celibacy and childlessness; see Bré, "Erzwungene, unfreiwillige Enthaltsamkeit und Kinderlosigkeit," 27–28.

marry and presumably become sexually active (323). Like Freud, Meisel-Hess asserted the negative effects of celibacy on women's intellectual development, claiming that women's "artificial desexualization" caused a conflict between their "impulse life" and their reason, which in turn endangered women's "psychic unity" (321). Meisel-Hess claimed that the repression of women's sexuality was the cause of women's purported lack of objectivity. According to her, "The incessant and heavy oppression of her sexual sphere disorders her critical faculties, weakens her power of resistance, obscures her whole intelligence" (317). "Those who have lived out their sexual experiences," she maintained, "can use things according to their nature, objectively, that is to say, freely, independently, and capably; whereas those whose sexual life is in a state of continuous repression must always remain dependent, enslaved to themselves and others" (317).

According to women sexologists, female celibacy and sexual abstinence were both "unnatural" and "forced," and not reflective of women's own instincts and desires. Not surprisingly, many authors insisted that female sexual abstinence, and even their supposed sexual passivity, were simply the products of cultural oppression, and specifically products of the institutions that supported the sexual double standard: namely, prostitution and marriage. According to Elberskirchen, the "cultural phenomenon of the enforced abstinence of women is [simply] . . . the other side of the coin of prostitution." In her view, prostitution was the central institution that upheld the sexual double standard not only by establishing gender-differentiated moral norms, but also by "standing in absolute contradiction to the biological rights and duties of love" and "separating woman from her natural right to love . . . while the man is allowed completely free love, whether healthy or sick."[102] Boldly, Elberskirchen asserted that "if there are no external, artificial barriers or if these are overcome through an inner spiritual-sexual power, the question of copulation is only a question of opportunity. The entire organism of the woman is directed toward

---

102. Elberskirchen, *Geschlechtsleben und Geschlechtsenthaltsamkeit des Weibes,* 6, 11, 15.

her beloved man and ready, whether consciously or unconsciously, to tirelessly unite with him (*sich mit ihm rastlos zu vermählen*)."[103] Under prevailing cultural conditions, Elberskirchen declared that women's sex drive had been "cramped and corrupted" into two forms of sickness: abnormal hypersexuality (here termed "man-craziness") and abnormal hyposexuality (frigidity).[104]

While Grete Meisel-Hess also viewed prostitution as a cause of women's "sexual deprivation," she blamed patriarchy generally. She asserted that the sexual double standard was a "vestige of a primitive institution, the best means available in former days to protect the weaker sex against the strong hand of the male." A sexual double standard had emerged "as a protective wall round woman wherever her maintenance depends exclusively on the male, and wherever there is lacking any *social* provision for the upbringing of the offspring and for the care of women during pregnancy and childbirth" (*Sexual Crisis*, 89; emphasis in original). This "wall" was largely manifested in the form of contractual marriage and monogamic exclusivity—at the very least for women. It was "reasonable" in an early, less evolved time, Meisel-Hess offered, to demand strict monogamy for women to ensure "father-right" over progeny; in return, women secured material support for herself and her children. Meanwhile, men were freed from such a requirement, and could impose sexual restrictions upon women as "the breadwinner for wife and children" (97). This "vestige" persisted into the present through the dueling institutions of marriage and prostitution, the only available forms of sexual expression to women. In light of contemporary social, political, and economic conditions, Meisel-Hess insisted that the need for such institutions had passed: "A higher civilization can dispense with this means of protection, being competent to establish institutions that shall safeguard women without depriving them of their freedom as human beings" (89).

According to these writers, new scientific revelations regarding the nature and needs of the female sex drive and the detrimental

103. Elberskirchen, "Das Geschlechtsleben des Weibes," 197.
104. Ibid., 201.

effects of its repression required wide-ranging sexual reforms that would end the sexual double standard. If the male and female drives were similar and equal, and if sex was distinct from reproduction, these was no reason why women should not have the same sexual rights and privileges as men. Women should share men's socially recognized and scientifically legitimized right to sexual experience and pleasure before, within, and independent of marriage. Moreover, these sexual theorists believed that all women who did pursue sex outside of marriage should not be socially ostracized: prostitution, they argued, should not be the only site for women's extramarital (hetero)sex. At the same time, they recognized that currently, in Meisel-Hess's words, "Because women have no permissible free outlet for their sexual need, they are exposed to misadventures of all kinds" (198). Beyond calling for the abolition of the state regulation of prostitution, they envisioned other reforms to the organization of sexual life. Some demanded the creation of conditions that would facilitate early marriage. Henriette Fürth maintained in *Prostitution: Its Origins and the Way to a Remedy* that early marriages would enable men and women at the height of their sexual powers to satisfy their needs within the (supposedly) disease-free zone of monogamous matrimony.[105] Bré and Meisel-Hess went further and demanded recognition of nonmarital relations of intimacy as well as the legal recognition of children born to unmarried women. Bré advocated monogamous free love based on healthy and conscious sexual selection, asserting that a woman "will breed selectively in the interests of the species, not in the pursuit of her own interests." These unions may not last a lifetime, but rather "perhaps a couple of years, perhaps a few months—or weeks. For some women, perhaps only a night."[106] Such a situation was preferable to prevailing conventions, which she claimed rendered the "union between man and woman today [either] a trade agreement or an exclusive sexual association."[107] According to Bré,

105. Henriette Fürth, *Die Prostitution: Ursachen und Wege zur Abshilfe* (n.d.), 10, Folder 49, Kollektion Henriette Fürth, Internationaal Instituut voor Sociale Geschiedenis, Amsterdam.
106. Bré, *Das Recht auf die Mutterschaft*, 63.
107. Ibid., 66.

"If woman wants to be independent from man in sexual relationships, she must form her own moral laws in harmony with natural
law and become independent of marriage. As long as patriarchal
marriage remains the only legal way to have children, she will
remain dependent as a sexed being."[108] Beyond free unions, Bré
called for the reestablishment of a revised matriarchy, which she
characterized as "the earliest and most natural familial and legal
form" that respected the "natural" and central bond of mother and
child, regardless of marital status. Only within a matriarchy could
women develop "free and proud."[109]

Although Meisel-Hess did not want to revive matriarchy, she did
believe that "unfettering" sexual intercourse would help circum-
vent the need for prostitution *and* mercenary marriages within the
middle classes that were based on money rather than love. She proposed what she called erotic friendships as an alternative to both
contractual marriage and prostitution. In support of this ideal, she
pointed out that "the need for sexual enjoyment without elaborate
preliminaries or far-reaching consequences will never disappear . . .
[and] as long as the woman is used as a mere means to the man's
end, she will in most cases be misused, and every possibility of
true joy will thereby be excluded from the erotic process" (*Sexual
Crisis*, 195). In Meisel-Hess's view, "It is . . . far from impossible
that a healthy, normal, and well-disposed woman should give herself to a friend, each freely choosing the other, in a union in which
neither partner incurs any further and increasing responsibilities
towards the other." "By the simplicity of this process," she insisted,
"the whole sordid paradox of the duplex [double] sexual morality
would be exploded once and for all"(198). In a rather impassioned
appeal on behalf of intimacies beyond prostitution and marriage,
Meisel-Hess wrote, in a passage worth quoting at length:

> Are we to stifle that which so urgently demands expression? We have
> passions, not in order that we may stifle them, but in order that, *if they
> injure no one*, we may experience and enjoy them, as we enjoy any
> other good gift of fortune, as we savor a fine fruit. When two persons

---

108. Ibid., 31.
109. Ibid., 9, 12.

are inspired with passionate mutual desire, the future alone can decide whether their union is destined to afford them complete and enduring satisfaction. But the primary state, that of reciprocal passionate love, is in itself pure happiness, and deserves as such to be sounded to the depths. Time may show that the love is grounded on delusion but so long as the belief is real, real also is the happiness, and every chance of happiness must be taken when it comes, and not cast on the dust heap of life. Should the event prove, in any particular case, that the happiness was the fruit of illusion, let the sometime lovers regain internal and external freedom by dissolving their association, and let them do this without any interference on the part of society, without any public declaration of the fact that an intimate private relationship has been broken off, without any enumeration of the occasions on which either or both may have had earlier and similar experiences, and without the incurring of any obloquy. . . . What two human beings have in common, what draws them together, and what leads them to separate, can be understood by themselves alone, and are matters of purely private concern. (113; emphasis in original)

Meisel-Hess maintained that a number of essential preconditions had to be in place to realize the freer, less formal yet monogamous and intimate sexual arrangements she envisioned. These include economic security for women, particularly in the form of motherhood insurance; moral and social reform to ensure the recognition of free love intimacies; the primacy of the unity of mother and child as the basis of sexual order; and "absolute mastery of sexual hygiene and of the methods of preventing procreation" (326, 197). Such a conjunction of prerequisites for women's sexual freedom was also articulated by Johanna Elberskirchen, who, in stressing women's physiological need for sexual intercourse, also demanded women's right to "preventatives" (by which she meant contraceptives) and women's right of free sexual choice of partner.[110] All the same, Elberskirchen insisted that on "hygienic grounds" all artificial external sexual stimulation should be avoided in order to enable the inner needs of the sex drive to direct human sexual behavior.[111] According to her, it is only through the application of the feminine principles of love, strength, and motherliness that human

---

110. Elberskirchen, *Mutter! II*, 39–49.
111. Elberskirchen, "Das Geschlechtsleben des Weibes," 223.

sexuality can be redeemed and elevated to the higher, spiritual sphere where it belongs.[112]

Additionally, to ensure the healthy and "responsible" use of the sex drive, Henriette Fürth called for sex education, particularly among school-age youth, that would represent sex as a fact of life, undifferentiated from other human functions and drives. In Fürth's view, how one teaches children about sex determines their future sexual behavior, as the early information they receive regarding sexuality shapes their attitude. While emphasizing the need for continued moral pedagogy in sexual education, she maintained in a series of articles published in the *Socialist Monthly Magazine* in 1908 that children should receive factual and scientific sexual education, based on comparisons with the plant and animal worlds. Sexuality, she claimed, should be stressed as a simple natural fact of human life; the dual spiritual-material character of sexuality ought to be especially highlighted in order to emphasize that the sex drive must be brought under control, via the power of the individual will, to fulfill our higher selves. Fürth boldly insisted that the erotic be represented as a vital energy source, both for the individual and for cultural life, and stated that the right of sexually mature adults to sexual satisfaction must be affirmed, even to the young.[113]

Finally, the recognition of women's biological right to sex also required legal reforms, namely, an end to the prohibition against the marriage of female Prussian civil servants and the celibacy it consequently enforced upon them. This demand was put forward most forcefully by the Association of Prussian Schoolteachers, which counted radical feminists like League for the Protection of Mothers and Sexual Reform member Maria Lischnewska among its leaders.[114] Although Henriette Fürth was not a member of this

---

112. Ibid., 230.

113. See Henriette Fürth, "Der Aufklärungsunterricht: Ein Beitrag zur Sexualpädagogik," *Sozialistische Monatshefte* 12 (1908): 243–246; Henriette Fürth, "Sexualpädagogik und Sexualethik," ibid., 564–568.

114. See, for example, Landesverein Preußischer Volksschullehrerinnen, *Die verheiratete Lehrerin: Verhandlungen der ersten Internationalen Lehrerinnen-Versammlung in Deutschland, berufen im Anschluss an den Internationalen Frauenkongreß im Juni 1904* (Berlin: Walther, 1905).

association, in her comprehensive *State and Morality* (1912) she concurred that the enforced celibacy of female state employees was "not only in the deepest sense immoral, because [it] involve[s] the forcible renunciation of a human right, [it is] also highly consequential for the efficiency of the race . . . quite often physically, mentally, and morally good and often outstandingly gifted individuals are thereby excluded from reproduction."[115]

Fürth's critique of the de facto celibacy imposed on female state employees in Prussia highlights a key argument that runs like a red thread through female sexual theorists' visions and arguments regarding the female sex drive and the unnaturalness of celibacy: namely, that sexual reforms endowing women with greater sexual freedom and agency were essential for the health and well-being not only of individual women, but also for the "race" itself.[116] As Grete Meisel-Hess put it in an address to the 1912 Congress of the Monist League, "We demand the right to a healthy, natural love life also for the woman, to a healthy motherhood that would elevate the race, even in those cases where the road to marriage is blocked by a solid dowry or other obstacles."[117] Their invocations of the race here are vague, and it is unclear whether they are

---

115. Henriette Fürth, *Staat und Sittlichkeit* (Leipzig: Hans Wehner, 1912), 62.

116. Among an older generation of feminists, the enthusiastic, eugenic pronouncements and demands of the radicals were viewed with great skepticism. In her 1909 article, "On Biological Love" ("Von der biologischen Liebe"), the progressive feminist Hedwig Dohm expressed pessimism regarding the claim, promulgated by Grete Meisel-Hess and Swedish feminist Ellen Key, that women's greater sexual freedom would lead to "racial improvement" through the exercise of woman's superior, sexual selective instincts, and through the ennobling effects of a child conceived through love rather than compulsion. Dohm asked, "Assuming that all obstacles of free selection would be eliminated, would a woman, guided by a superb biological instinct, then select as a husband the mentally and physically most suitable person for procreation purposes?" She emphatically answered in the negative, and instead insisted that love is "biologically blind." Hedwig Dohm, "Von der biologischen Liebe," *Sozialistische Monatshefte* 13 (1909): 1493. Dohm believed that "actually it is love which prohibits selective breeding; love especially has therefore to be excluded whenever a young woman selects her husband out of biological idealism for the purpose of procreation" (1494).

117. Grete Meisel-Hess, at the Congress of the Monist League in Magdeburg, 6–10 September 1912, reported by Helene Stöcker in "Von Kongressen und Gründungen," *Die neue Generation* 9 (October 1912): 547–548.

meant to denote humanity, Germanness, or whiteness; regardless, women sexologists invoked racial arguments as a kind of trump card in support of their demands for women's sexual rights. They argued that continuing to deny women their biological right to sexual autonomy and expression would have disastrous implications for the future of humanity. Grete Meisel-Hess cautioned specifically against the celibacy of the current generation of modern New Women; citing Ruth Bré, she warned, "If these intellectual and fearless women die without leaving bodily offspring, if they fail to reproduce their forcible individualities, the race necessarily suffers." According to Meisel-Hess, "women of finer clay" must bequeath their finer qualities to the next generation (*Sexual Crisis*, 324). To realize such racial hygienic and sexual liberatory ends, Meisel-Hess insisted that both men and women must be free to "develop themselves as social and erotic forces," to have the "possibility of being desired and loved," to "propagate their kind under favorable biological conditions," and to consecrate free and mutually determined sexual partnerships (343, 326, 343). For Meisel-Hess, sexual morality is, in the final instance, "based upon the interests of the species alone, and the only true sexual morality is that which leads to the procreation of healthy and beautiful human beings" (101).

For women like Bré, Elberskirchen, Meisel-Hess, and Fürth, the female sex drive held innate, powerful political implications. Empowering women to realize their sexuality as a right in turn required the social recognition of women as independent, desiring sexual subjects. However, the women discussed here were not representative of the majority of their contemporaries, including within the women's movement. Some feminists, particularly those affiliated with the moderate League of German Women's Associations (Bund Deutscher Frauenvereine, BDF), disagreed with sexological representations of female sexuality and questioned whether the liberalization of sexual life would benefit women. The scientized redefinitions of female sexuality examined here—and their concomitant demands for liberalizing sexual reforms—actually exacerbated existing conflicts within the women's movement.

The Natural Is Not the Same as the Good: Debates among Women on the Female Sex Drive

Many German feminists rejected attempts to redefine the female sex drive. In pamphlets, essays, and articles published in newspapers and journals affiliated with women's organizations, moderate feminists rejected nature as an arbiter of moral truths, and expressed skepticism as to whether science was the best means of gaining knowledge about female sexuality. They also insisted on distinguishing emotional intimacy from "animalistic" sex, and argued that women ought to downplay the importance of sex and instead focus on developing their minds and personalities. Sexual freedom was a regressive goal in their view because it stressed the only aspect of women that men cared about anyway. Importantly, these critics did not entirely eschew scientific evidence: in fact, when prudent they appealed to facts and theories that supported their positions.

For some members of the moderate German women's movement, the main problem with the new definitions of female sexuality was their reliance on medical and scientific evidence, much of which was produced by men. In her provocative tract *Men's Morals*, German feminist Anna Pappritz criticized male gender bias within scientific pronouncements on female sexuality. Pappritz challenged male physicians' claims that they had better insights into the "secrets of nature" because of their professional expertise, by pointing out the hypocritical contradictions in their assessments of female sexuality. Pappritz was one of the leading campaigners against the state regulation of prostitution, and vehemently fought against the idea, popular in scientific circles at the turn of the century, that there existed a class of "born prostitutes."[118] What frustrated Pappritz was men's rejection of women's subjective experience as a legitimate source of knowledge:

> This is what men, doctors, naturalists, and physiologists, whose eyes were opened to the holy book of nature, who were allowed to probe its

---

118. Anna Pappritz, "Gibt es geborene Prostituierte?," *Der Abolitionist* 2 (1903): 63–67.

secrets by all scientific methods, say. They commit an offense to the divine creative power of nature by stating that it created two categories of women, "abnormal creatures" for satisfying the extramarital needs of man and motherly types for the procreation of the species within a marriage. But if a woman had indeed only a desire for a child, should she not demand with equal right a fulfillment of this desire with which a man demands satisfaction of this desire? A woman, however, who dared to express this objection, is not only met with Homeric laughter: we were then told that we do not understand that a woman experiences things quite differently. Therefore, only men know how women are feeling—we of course do not have the slightest clue![119]

Through this critique, Pappritz intimated that women should be extremely wary of sexual scientific arguments, as well as the kinds of dividing practices they produced. Pappritz believed that sex was a matter of little interest to women, and was certainly less important to their lives and their happiness than other activities.

Many feminists also took umbrage at the claim that celibacy was damaging to women's health. Pappritz for one maintained that negative views of celibacy gave medico-scientific support for the continued state regulation of prostitution, which she claimed facilitated male pleasure, recklessness, and irresponsibility at women's expense. Pappritz was not alone among feminists in fighting the view that celibacy was necessarily injurious to women's health. At the turn of the century, feminists publicly debated the desirability of female celibacy, not only in the feminist counterpublic but also in major medical journals. In a fascinating exchange that took place on the pages of feminist and medical journals, gynecologist and eugenicist Dr. Agnes Bluhm, member of the BDF and the Society for Racial Hygiene, rejected Ruth Bré's assertions that celibacy contributed to physical and mental health problems in women. Over the course of their back-and-forth, Bluhm cited psychiatrist Emil Kraepelin's *Textbook of Psychiatry*, as well as her own clinical experiences and those of other female doctors, to prove that sexual intercourse itself, not celibacy, was responsible for women's

---

119. Anna Pappritz, *Herrenmoral* (Leipzig: Verlag der Frauen Rundschau, n.d.), 7–8, 13–15.

illnesses.[120] According to Bluhm, childless women sought medical attention most often to deal with menstrual problems and, if
married, to deal with infertility.[121] In her various articles attacking
Bré, Bluhm especially objected to claims that celibacy led to cancer.
With her colleague Alfred Hegar, Bluhm maintained that women
who had given birth (and had therefore had sex) suffered a higher
incidence of uterine and ovarian cancer. Throughout her critique,
Bluhm ridiculed Bré's lack of formal medical and scientific training, mockingly writing, "Who would have thought that a question that serious researchers have fruitlessly sacrificed years of their
lives attempting to solve would be answered seemingly overnight
by a woman lacking natural scientific and medical knowledge!"[122]
Bluhm pointed out the lack of experimental and statistical evidence
in *The Right to Motherhood*, and in contrast asserted her own medical credentials and expertise. Yet despite her thorough rejection of
Bré's arguments, Bluhm arrived at the ambivalent conclusion that
sex and motherhood, regardless of their perils, were inevitable for
most women. For her part, Bré undermined Bluhm's authority by
asserting that truly authoritative female doctors ought to be "full
[women], in order to help [other women],—a blossoming mother,
who has experienced in her own body, what a child means for the

120. Agnes Bluhm, "Geschlechtliche Enthaltsamkeit und Frauenleiden: Aerztliche Randbemerkungen zu Ruth Bré's 'Das Recht auf Mutterschaft,'" *Die
Frauenbewegung* 10 (February 1904): 18. The exchange between Bluhm and Bré
continued on the pages of the *Deutsche medizinische Presse*: see Bré, "Erzwungene, unfreiwillige Enthaltsamkeit und Kinderlosigkeit"; Agnes Bluhm, "Zur Erwiderung auf den Artikel von Ruth Bré: 'Ist erzwungene unfreiwillige Enthaltsamkeit
und Kinderlosigkeit für das gesunde, normale Weib schädlich?,'" *Deutsche medizinische Presse* 5 (1904): 34–35; Bré, "Schlusswort zu der Erwiderung von Dr.
Agnes Bluhm," *Deutsche medizinische Presse* 6 (1904): 41–42.
    The exchange appeared in the *Deutsche medizinische Presse* because, accord-
ing to the editors of the journal, "The author would like to share her observations
and thoughts about the above-mentioned topic with medical circles, after the editor of the *Frauenbewegung* cut off further discussions following Frl. Dr. Bluhm's
critiques. We do not take any responsibility for the aetiology of gynaecological disorders espoused by Ruth Bré. However, we ask our informed readers to express
their views on the question raised by the author and offer them our columns for
their comments."
121. Bluhm, "Geschlechtliche Enthaltsamkeit und Frauenleiden," 19.
122. Ibid., 18.

woman. We do not need so-called naturally frigid, homosexual, or onanistic female doctors to solve this problem."[123] (Bluhm did not have children.) She went so far as to challenge medical expertise regarding sexual questions generally by noting that physicians are dependent upon laypeople, including ordinary women, for their knowledge. Citing a Dr. Gleich, she declared that "in the state of science, every educated man (and also every educated woman) is a citizen (*stimmberechtigter Bürger*), because the state is a republic in which there is no dictator, no subordination and no power other than the intellect, which alone rules; not through blind belief in authority, but rather through the foundation of truth, reason, and experience."[124]

Beyond debates over celibacy, treating nature as an arbiter of sexual truth was a major point of contention. In her essay "Sexual-Ethical Principal Questions," BDF member Marianne Weber vigorously argued that nature provides no firm basis for ethical demands. She accused nature enthusiasts of hubris, insisting that they were in no position to divine nature's goals; furthermore, she criticized one-sided definitions of the natural as good, rightly pointing out that nature was also responsible for bad phenomena. According to Weber, nature had proven "consistently indifferent toward that which it created. It teaches us absolutely nothing about the meaning of our lives and leaves us eternally responsible for the question of how we should behave if we want to behave in a meaningful way."[125] Nature in Weber's view was fundamentally amoral, and could not provide guidance when making moral decisions. Weber vehemently insisted that only culture and its stress on the spiritual and chaste elements of love could elevate human sexuality, as it was culture that assigned moral value. Demanding greater sexual freedom for women would only lead to a further brutalization of sexual feeling; in her view, sexual freedom could only ever be a purely masculine goal because women bore more burdens than

123. Bré, "Erzwungene, unfreiwillige Enthaltsamkeit und Kinderlosigkeit," 28.
124. Ibid., 29.
125. Marianne Weber, "Sexualethische Prinzipienfragen," in *Frauenbewegung und Sexualethik: Beiträge zur modernen Ehekritik*, ed. Gertrud Bäumer et al. (Heilbronn: Eugen Salzer, 1909), 27.

benefits in sexual life.[126] Instead of focusing on sexual freedom, Weber advocated training girls to be materially and existentially independent, and demanding a higher sexual-ethical standard of behavior from men.[127]

Finally, many moderate feminists found the radical revision of the female sex drive undesirable and even dangerous because of the undue emphasis it placed on sex in defining womanhood. In her essay "The Women's Movement and the Modern Critique of Marriage," Helene Lange, one of the leaders of the BDF, insisted that the sex drive must be viewed as an individually variable entity and placed within the broader context of a woman's total personality. Lange demanded a more comprehensive view of sex's place in women's lives and in society, noting that the overemphasis of any one drive is detrimental to the health of the others. "Of course we will protest against all approaches which result in a human being torn into two parts, forcing the sublimations of one part while the other is driven into the subhuman sphere," Lange conceded; yet she maintained that the sexual sphere is only one part of an individual's physical and emotional being, and must be subjected to the consideration of other "responsibilities."[128] The sex sphere, she claimed, requires the leadership and discipline of the will to bring it into harmony with other life powers. She further argued that sexual needs are dependent upon the nature of one's personality, and even referenced science to combat representations of all women as sexually needful and desirous. According to Lange, psychology and physiology had proven that sex may be "a hindrance" to one person, while it may be one of "the highest achievements in life" to another; to a third person it could be "something non-essential and insignificant."[129] Finally, she stressed that the so-called sexual question does not exist apart from larger social questions, and asserted that treating sex independently from other sociopolitical issues supports a reorientation of ethics away from collective needs

---

126. Ibid., 41.
127. Ibid., 42.
128. Helene Lange, "Die Frauenbewegung und die moderne Ehekritik," in Bäumer et al., *Frauenbewegung und Sexualethik*, 81.
129. Lange, "Die Frauenbewegung und die moderne Ehekritik," 82.

in favor of individual pleasures. For Lange as for Weber, sex was a profoundly social concern and a historical project, and for these reasons she also rejected nature as a moral arbiter of sexual life. In her view, "We have to consider . . . [that] the rules that [have] been handed down to us . . . [regarding] the form of marriage and family. . . are more than just the invention of one's brain . . . ; life itself has shaped them through the experiences of many generations."[130]

Anna Pappritz similarly sought to downplay the role of sexuality in women's lives in a private letter to Magnus Hirschfeld written in 1908. Here Pappritz argued that Hirschfeld's views on female sexuality, which mirrored those put forward by the women sexologists examined in this chapter, were fatally mistaken because they were based exclusively upon "those softened and sensitive types of women raised in the big city." According to Pappritz, such women not only misrepresented the norm of their sex, but also artificially inflated the importance of sexuality in women's lives. She further chastised Hirschfeld for his diagnosis of "healthy, strong types of women" less interested in sex than in "intellectual matters or healthy movement" as "'abnormal' and 'masculine.'" Pappritz maintained that Hirschfeld's conceptualization of normal female sexuality hampered women's progress because it inhibited them from developing intellectually and physically. In Pappritz's view, it was absolutely essential for women's progress that their interests broaden beyond sex.[131]

Limitations to the Redefinition of the Female Sex Drive

The ideas of Fürth, Bré, Elberskirchen, and Meisel-Hess remain controversial and problematic today in light of the many limitations built into their understandings of the female sex drive—limitations that, as we have already seen, proceeded from the heteronormative

---

130. Ibid., 79.
131. Anna Pappritz to Magnus Hirschfeld, 29 February 1908, B Rep 235–13 MF-Nr. 3448–53, Nachlass Anna Pappritz, Helene-Lange Archiv, Landesarchiv Berlin.

biases and eugenic beliefs that existed within sexual science and society at large. Somewhat ironically, the engagement of these women with science inhibited their understanding of the full range of women's potential sexual desires, experiences, and subjectivities, and ultimately restricted their demands for sexual liberation.

Though new approaches to the female sex drive released it from reproductive impulses, they reinforced heterosexuality as the purportedly natural norm. Women's claim that the sex drive represented a "drive to union" that would strengthen monogamous bonds between men and women meant that the normal could only ever be heterosexual. Women writers went so far as to exclude as abnormal all sexual practices and forms of desire not directed toward men, specifically masturbation and homosexuality. Ruth Bré made this exclusion explicit in her 1904 article, "Is Forced, Unwilled Sexual Abstinence and Childlessness Damaging for the Healthy Normal Woman?" which she wrote to clarify the purpose of *The Right to Motherhood*. Here she stated, "I asserted in my book *The Right to Motherhood* that forced sexual abstinence and childlessness have damaging effects on the normal healthy woman. In claiming this, I of course did not mean the so-called naturally frigid (*sogenannte Naturae-frigidae*), nor did I mean women who disregard the lack of natural sexual relations through the thirst for life and glory on the one hand or masturbation or homosexual satisfaction on the other; rather, I speak for women who are really women, with healthy bodies and healthy desires for human and maternal happiness."[132] Bré even argued that homosexuality and masturbation were consequences of the denial of women's sexual needs and drives: "The natural instinct cannot be smothered and artificially suppressed either in men or women without causing further severe damage to an individual," she warned.[133]

Some writers disparaged frigid or "sexually anaesthetic" women uninterested in sex: Meisel-Hess referenced Freud's research on women's anxiety neuroses to argue that the sexually frigid woman

---

132. Bré, "Erzwungene, unfreiwillige Enthaltsamkeit und Kinderlosigkeit," 27.
133. Bré, *Das Recht auf die Mutterschaft*, 57.

constituted an abnormal specimen.[134] She further maintained that frigid women were "inapt . . . for social and artistic work" because they lacked "the fire of love."[135] While stigmatizing women's frigidity, these writers nonetheless followed Krafft-Ebing in labeling sexually unrestrained women as nymphomaniacs.[136] As Elberskirchen put it, "It is indeed obvious that, when I speak here as a doctor about a biological right to an active sex life, I can only refer to a sex life that is absolutely pure, modest, and healthy and does not lead to illnesses and unhealthy and dirty conditions."[137]

Elberskirchen's clarification raises another crucial point: like their moderate feminist critics, women sexologists feared the eugenic consequences of untrammeled sexual freedom. Although many of them believed that the sex drive was not reproductively motivated, they were nevertheless conscious of the fact that reproduction remained a possible outcome of sex. In their view, conscious sexual decision-making, moderation, and self-control were critically important for sexually free women, and only certain women were capable of exercising good judgment when it came to sex.[138] According to Meisel-Hess, sexual appetites must be limited in cases where individuals were "incompetent to estimate or provide for the consequences of sexual activity or passivity, and so long as there exists incapacity to control some of the pathological manifestations of the sexual life."[139] In her view, such limitations were justified to prevent "dangers to the offspring and to the race that may result from uncontrolled sexual indulgence" by irresponsible actors, and that such limitations fulfilled "the first principles of rational morality."[140] In her view, "It is obvious that a voluntary erotic self-surrender of the kind here under consideration is

---

134. Meisel-Hess, *Sexual Crisis*, 334–337.

135. Ibid., 240.

136. Elberskirchen, *Geschlechtsleben und Geschlechtsenthaltsamkeit des Weibes*, 5.

137. Ibid., 3.

138. Elberskirchen, *Geschlechtsleben und Geschlechtsenthaltsamkeit des Weibes*, 16–17, 22, 31.

139. Meisel-Hess, *Sexual Crisis*, 101.

140. Ibid.

conceivable and desirable only in the case of women who are independent in character, self-controlled, and fully mature."[141] For
Meisel-Hess, only advanced modern women could at present make
responsible sexual choices within the prevailing conditions of sexual life; for all other women, sexuality at present represented a
danger to themselves and to the race.

For Johanna Elberskirchen, however, the answer to the question of which women should exercise their sexual function was
somewhat more complicated. In *Sex Life and Sexual Abstinence
of Woman,* Elberskirchen clarified that her analysis pertained
specifically to women of "middling sexuality." According to her,
they were neither "frigid" nor "hyper-sexual," and constituted
the majority.[142] For women of "middling sexuality," "a love life
within physiological boundaries is for all people something normal and . . . for health reasons more beneficial than chastity."[143] However, Elberskirchen believed that the superior, intellectual (*geistige*)
woman was meant for other, higher pursuits that left little energy
for sex. Within Elberskirchen's understanding, the heterosexual
woman of "middling" sexuality was incapable of the sexual restraint required for intellectual pursuits; she needed sex to give her
personality and to provide her life with a sense of purpose. Sexual
fulfillment was a matter of indifference for the superior woman,
as she was predestined to develop a personality independent of
her sex instinct.[144] Positing a sharp antithesis between the intellect and sexuality, Elberskirchen asserted that "highly intellectual
and outstanding people are never very sexually active; on the other
hand, highly sexual people are never very intellectual."[145] While
Elberskirchen expounded the naturalness of the female sex drive
and insisted upon its realization as a biological right, she nonetheless maintained that such demands were only relevant for women
incapable of advanced intellectual pursuits. The tensions within

141. Ibid., 200.
142. Elberskirchen, *Geschlechtsleben und Geschlechtsenthaltsamkeit des Weibes,* 5.
143. Ibid., 23.
144. Ibid., 5.
145. Ibid., 17.

Elberskirchen's writings demonstrate that the seemingly immanent political implications of sexological knowledge were neither clear-cut nor singular. Women sexologists' texts also illuminate how the feminist potential of sexological knowledge could be undercut by particularistic caveats.

While the definitions of the female sex drive provided by Fürth, Elberskirchen, Bré, and Meisel-Hess responded to contemporary social concerns and were consistent with changing scientific understandings of human sexuality, they uniquely teased out the transformative political ramifications of scientific ideas in ways that offered to empower women sexually. By mobilizing scientific knowledge, they naturalized women's sexual desires and legitimized claims that sexual activity was essential to women's health and the creation of sympathy between the sexes. Ultimately, their efforts to elaborate the new understanding of the sex drive taking shape in sexology helped them define and legitimize a new female sexual subjectivity: that of the sexually autonomous woman who had a biological right to engage in personally enriching sexual experiences. Science thus endowed women's efforts to enhance their sexual agency with legitimacy. However, this redefinition of the female sex drive and the concomitant demands it inspired provoked conflict, particularly among German feminists. Furthermore, the heterosexist and eugenic logics they employed built limitations into the redefined female sex drive. Female sexual theorists stigmatized and disavowed all forms of sexual desire and practice that did not seek satisfaction in intercourse with men, and argued that only certain women were in a position to make conscious, "racially" responsible sexual choices. Still others saw the sex drive and the rights it implied as valuable only to the average, heterosexual woman who was incapable of intellectual or spiritual self-realization. Women sexologists' commitment to the scientific enlightenment of sexual phenomena both expanded and restricted the understanding and potential of female sexuality.

While many of the female sexual theorists examined here insisted on heterosexuality as the natural norm, scientific understandings and evaluations of what constituted natural or normal sexual subjectivities were not fixed or stable at this time. In his discussion of the sex drive, for example, Havelock Ellis took care to note that the sex drive was usually, *but not exclusively*, inclined toward someone of the opposite sex. Likewise, August Forel believed that girls' and women's desires for same-sex intimacy were natural phenomena connected to their feminine constitution. Freud insisted that the libido did not necessarily have a predetermined orientation or object. In fact, the turn of the century saw the rise of theories that posited homosexuality as a natural and congenital phenomenon, and thus a legitimate subjectivity deserving social acceptance. In the next chapter, I examine how some women writers engaged theories of female homosexuality to articulate nonbinary gender and nonheterosexual subjectivities as desirable and superior alternatives to normal female (hetero)sexuality, endowed with their own set of "biological" rights.

3

CHALLENGING THE LIMITS OF SEX

Envisioning New Gendered Subjectivities and Sexualities

Women sexologists' investments in discerning the true nature of female sexuality emerged at a time when both sexual science and the broader culture increasingly associated the demand for women's rights with sexual abnormality. Within Germany, the "women's righter" (*Frauenrechtlerin*) was frequently conflated with another disruptive sexual subject attracting new interest around the turn of the century: namely, the female homosexual.[1] Both subjects were considered transgressive figures who would not, perhaps could not, conform to the expectations of normal

---

1. Terminology is a problem when dealing with turn-of-the-century theories of homosexuality. At this time, individuals believed to be "born" with same-sex desires and/or nonconforming gender identities were referred to variously as Uranians, inverts, contra-sexuals, homosexuals, and members of the third sex. I have used the term "homosexual" as an umbrella term to embrace all of these nomenclatures, as it is most familiar to contemporary readers. Likewise, I have not used "the lesbian" or "lesbianism," as these terms referred at the time to individuals who were believed to engage in homosexual acts as a matter of choice.

womanhood. Both the "women's righter" and the female homosexual were accused of betraying masculine traits such as intellectualism and assertiveness and of harboring masculine desires
for economic, legal, and sexual autonomy. Berlin-based urologist
and so-called doctor for prostitutes (*Dirnenarzt*) Wilhelm Hammer went so far as to call the women's movement a homosexual
women's movement and accused it of "sacrific[ing] normal, man-
loving" women in pursuit of its ends.[2] Likewise, Iwan Bloch held
both the "women's righter" and the female homosexual responsible for undermining the "cultural and evolutionary achievement"
of sexual dimorphism.[3]

Because of the gender nonconformity attributed to these figures,
many male sexologists and conservative cultural commentators diagnosed both as sexually inverted; some even suggested that they
both belonged to a third sex that was neither fully male nor female. In the eyes of many scientific commentators, the apparently
growing prevalence of both subjects signaled nothing less than the
coming of sexual anarchy. Linking women's rights to sexual abnormality and sexual anarchy helped antifeminists represent demands
for women's empowerment as not just improper, but in fact pathological and therefore illegitimate.

Given the stigmatizing effects of this association, it is perhaps
not surprising that many within the German women's movement
responded to imputations of homosexuality with denials, attempts
at distancing, and vigorous assertions of their femininity and heterosexual propriety. However, not all women with ties to feminism
responded in this manner. For some, the discursive conjunction of
women's rights and homosexuality offered an opportunity to challenge the limitations of existing sexual subjectivities and espouse
alternatives. Between 1895 and 1906, women in fact wrote a number of fiction and nonfiction German-language texts that described

---

2. Wilhelm Hammer, "Über gleichgeschlechtliche Frauenliebe mit besonderer
Berücksicthigung der Frauenbewegung," *Monatsschrift für Harnkrankheiten und
sexuelle Hygiene* 4 (1907): 442.

3. Iwan Bloch, *Das Sexualleben unserer Zeit, in seiner Beziehungen zur modernen Kultur* (Berlin: Louis Marcus, 1908), 64.

and championed nonheterosexual, nongender normative sexual subjectivities.[4]

In this chapter, I examine three models of female sexual subjectivity put forward by journalist and homosexual rights activist Anna Rüling, feminist and social democrat Johanna Elberskirchen, and feminist intellectual Rosa Mayreder. All three productively drew upon emerging theories of homosexuality to envision a female subject unmoored from the expectations of reproductive heterosexual womanhood. I collectively refer to these models of subjectivity as nonnormative in order to encompass their remarkable variety. In her now famous speech, "What Interest Does the Women's Movement Have in Solving the Homosexual Problem?" (1904), Anna Rüling articulated a vision of female homosexuality akin to what Heike Bauer has aptly termed a "rational" female masculinity.[5] Conversely, in *The Love of the Third Sex* (1904) and *What Has the Man Made of the Woman, the Child, and Himself? Revolution and the Salvation of Woman: A Reckoning with the Man—a Guidepost to the Future!* (1904; henceforth *Revolution!*), Johanna Elberskirchen represented the female homosexual as the most feminine of subjectivities, a "Woman-Identified Woman" avant la lettre.[6] However, in Rosa Mayreder's *Toward a Critique*

4. See, for example, Anne van den Eken, *Mannweiber-Weibmänner und der §175: Eine Schrift für denkende Frauen* (Leipzig: Verlag von Max Spohr, 1906); Anna Rüling, *Welcher unter Euch ohne Sünde ist . . . Bücher von der Schattenseite* (Leipzig: Max Spohr, 1906); E. Krause, "Die Wahrheit über mich," *Jahrbuch für sexuelle Zwischenstufen* 3 (1901): 292–307; M. F. "Wie ich es sehe," ibid., 308–312; Aimee Duc, *Sind es Frauen?* (Berlin: Amazonen Frauenverlag, 1976); Elisabeth Dauthendey, *Vom neuen Weibe und seiner Liebe: Ein Buch für reife Geister* (Berlin: Schuster u. Loeffler, 1900); [Emma Trosse], *Der Konträrsexualismus inbezug auf Ehe und Frauenfrage* (Leipzig: Verlag von Max Spohr, 1895).

5. Though Bauer never explicitly defines rational female masculinity, she invokes the term to characterize the way New Women authors strategically engaged the concept of sexual inversion to stress the "masculine" traits of the mind, specifically rationality, as a means of overcoming the limitations of the female body. See Heike Bauer, "Theorizing Female Inversion: Sexology, Discipline, and Gender at the Fin de Siècle," *Journal of the History of Sexuality* 18 (January 2009): 89, 99–102.

6. I borrow the term "Woman-Identified Woman" from the eponymous manifesto written in 1970 by the Radicalesbians.

of Femininity (1905), the reader does not encounter a positive articulation of a female homosexual subjectivity, but rather the ideal of the synthetic human, a subject that psychically transcends the physiological limits of sex yet retains femininity or masculinity as a stylized performance of the body.

Notably, all of these texts were published well before the German government attempted to criminalize same-sex acts between women, inspired by the 1909 *Proposal for a German Criminal Code.*[7] In fact, the authors examined here were not terribly vocal during that debate, which provoked the participation of a range of moderate and progressive feminists who had previously eschewed discussion of homosexuality, including Helene Stöcker and Anna Pappritz.[8] These texts were also published before the notorious Eulenburg-Harden trials (1907–9), which revolved around accusations of homosexuality within the Kaiser's inner circle.[9] The timing of Rüling, Elberskirchen, and Mayreder's texts could be entirely coincidental: they could simply be reflective of the upswing in public interest, intellectual attention, and activist energies devoted to the women's movement. The paucity of archival materials

7. The *Proposal* envisioned the creation of a new paragraph, §250, which would have extended the criminal sanction against same-sex acts between men to include women, and would have increased the severity of punishment to include a mandatory sentence of no less than six months and up to five years of jail, in addition to the possible loss of civil rights. Tracie Matysik, *Reforming the Moral Subject: Ethics and Sexuality in Central Europe, 1890–1930* (Ithaca, NY: Cornell University Press, 2008), 153.

8. See, for example, Camilla Jellinek, "Der Vorentwurf zu einem Deutschen Strafgesetzbuch: Vom Standpunkte der Frauen aus betrachtet," *Centralblatt des BDF* 11, nos. 20–22 (1910): 153–155, 161–162, 170–171; Käthe Schirmacher, "Zum §175 des Deutschen Strafgesetzes," *Der Abolitionist* 10, no. 1 (1911): 3–5; Elisabeth Krukenberg, "§175," *Monatsschrift für Kriminalpsychologie und Strafrechtsreform* 7 (1910–11): 612; Anna Pappritz, "Zum §175," *Der Abolitionist* 10, no. 2 (1911): 9–11; Pappritz, "Die Strafrechtsreform," *Der Abolitionist* 9, no. 1 (1910): 1–6; Helene Stöcker, "Die beabsichtigte Ausdehnung des §175 auf die Frau," *Die neue Generation* 7, no. 3 (14 March 1911): 110–123.

9. James D. Steakley, "Iconography of a Scandal: Political Cartoons and the Eulenburg Affair in Wilhelmine Germany," in *Hidden from History: Reclaiming the Gay and Lesbian Past*, ed. Martin Duberman, Martha Vicinus, and George Chauncey Jr. (New York: Meridian, 1990), 233–263.

surrounding the texts makes it difficult to know when their authors began writing them, and whether specific catalysts for the
ideas contained within them existed. However, it is perhaps worth
noting that the texts analyzed in this chapter clustered around the
years 1904 and 1905, which coincides with the International Congress of Women held in Berlin in June 1904. The congress was a
major event that helped put a domestic spotlight on the international women's movement—and an international spotlight on the
German women's movement. Importantly, it greatly enhanced the
visibility of the movement, its leaders, and their demands. As a
side note, this element of visibility seems particularly significant,
as it was this event that sexologists like Albert Moll would cite as
providing evidence of the high proportion of homosexual women
within the German women's rights movement.

The subjectivities described by Rüling, Elberskirchen, and Mayreder transgressed the existing sexual binary, and in so doing evaded
the strictures of women's public and private roles. They were represented as possessing innate rights to access education and the
professions, and as requiring freedom from marriage and motherhood. Frequently, they were represented as exemplary feminists,
and even as superior to normal women. As such, they offered a
range of new existential possibilities for female-identified individuals. However, these subjectivities were enmeshed in complex
gender politics. While they profoundly challenged a social order
premised on dualistic sexual difference, these subjects were not
meant to fundamentally revolutionize existing modes of sexual
governance. The aim of articulating these new subjectivities was
not to undo patriarchal structures, but rather to claim a greater
share of patriarchy's powers and privileges for those who did not
envision a life course defined by marriage and motherhood. In fact,
all three authors made rights claims at the expense of the "normal" woman, whom they portrayed as incapable of the rights and
freedoms the women's movement demanded for her. Yet even the
supposedly superior "unwomanly women" championed by Rüling
and the others were themselves limited by their authors' investments in sexology's eugenic rationale. Rüling and Elberskirchen
reinforced demands made on behalf of their subjects by stressing

the negative hereditary consequences of forcing these nonnormative individuals to physically reproduce. Their deployment of eugenics not only destabilized their positive representations, but also entrenched existing associations of homosexual men and women with racial degeneracy.

Inverts, Intermediaries, and Instigators: Female Homosexuality and Feminism in Sexual Science

Sexual scientific theories of female homosexuality emerged at a cultural moment marked by rising antifeminist reaction and fears of sexual anarchy. These intersecting anxieties contributed to the conflation of the feminist and the female homosexual as figures that threatened the social and sexual orders. By demanding—and demonstrating—women's independence from men, both feminists and female homosexuals undermined existing ideas regarding naturally ordained sexual roles and relations. They posed a significant challenge to the system of unequal powers and privileges accorded to the sexes—powers and privileges legitimized by a belief in biological binary sexual difference.

The conjunction of the feminist and the female homosexual should not be viewed as merely strategic or developed with the exclusive intent of undermining women's rights: it must also be understood as a consequence of the existing scientific understanding of sex. During the period under study, most commentators, scientific and nonscientific alike, treated sex as a holistic category that connoted one's gender *and* denoted the nature and direction of one's sexual desires. This understanding of sex posited a unity between sexed physiology, gendered performance, and sexual orientation. Above all, sexual scientists insisted that masculinity and femininity, as physiological properties of men and women, were responsible for determining an individual's behavior, appearance, and erotic inclination. As Iwan Bloch asserted, "The difference between the sexes is an original fact of human sexual life. . . . It manifests itself physically and psychologically in the elementary phenomenon of human love, where it appears most prominently, because here the relationship is simple and uncomplicated."[10] For most male sexual scientists, sexual difference naturally defined the direction of sexual drives. Even Magnus Hirschfeld, a prominent promoter of gay rights, declared in *The Uranian Being* (1903) that "the sex drive possesses a masculine form, that is directed toward the female, and a feminine, that is inclined to the man."[11] The women whose ideas are examined in this chapter both played within and profoundly disrupted these conceptual and discursive parameters. On the one hand, they reiterated the link between sexual orientation and gender performance; on the other hand, they decoupled gender and sexuality from specifically sexed bodies.

Because of their belief in a fundamental heterosexual unity of sexual desire, sexed physiology, and gendered performance, most male sexologists maintained that any rupture in this chain was evidence of underlying sexual "abnormality," specifically homosexuality. During the period under study, three interdependent theories for understanding homosexuality prevailed within sexology: sexual inversion, the third sex, and sexual intermediaries. The first two emerged in the decades before the turn of the century, whereas the theory of sexual intermediacy was developed in the early twentieth century. All coexisted and were used rather interchangeably. In what follows, I use male-authored texts to exemplify the key features of these theories. In so doing, I do not want to suggest that male sexologists were solely responsible for creating these theories of homosexuality, or that women's work was merely derivative: as I have argued, the creation of sexological knowledge involved many actors, and was a highly interactional process. Rather, highlighting male perspectives allows us to identify and evaluate the degree to which Rüling, Elberskirchen, and Mayreder's ideas corresponded with and deviated from those of their male peers. It further enables me to carve out a space for them within the sexological field as participants who were simultaneously complicit with and subversive of ideas gaining prominence. All three women engaged, challenged, and extended these theories in different ways.

---

10. Bloch, *Das Sexualleben unserer Zeit*, 59.
11. Magnus Hirschfeld, *Der urnische Mensch* (Leipzig: Max Spohr, 1903), 129.

Before briefly describing each fin-de-siècle theory of homosexuality, I want to highlight three analytic features they shared. First, all three theories represented the homosexual subject as one who repudiated heterosexuality by subverting gender norms and/or desiring someone of the same sex. Significantly, at the turn of the century the latter need not necessarily be present to diagnose homosexuality. In all theories, gender performance, and not sexual orientation, constituted the crucial criterion for deducing homosexuality.[12] As Magnus Hirschfeld wrote, "The homosexual should be understood and researched not only in regards to his sexuality, but also in regards to his total individuality. His sexual likes and dislikes are only symptoms, secondary consequences; the primary is his psyche and his habits in their entirety."[13] The focus on gender was particularly prevalent within theories of female homosexuality, arguably in part because male scientists found it very difficult to induce their female subjects—often brought to scientific attention against their will—to discuss their sex lives and sexual desires.[14]

---

12. Both Bauer and Gert Hekma make this point strongly. See Bauer, "Theorizing Female Inversion," 84–102; and Gert Hekma, "'A Female Soul in a Male Body': Sexual Inversion as Gender Inversion in Nineteenth-Century Sexology," in *Third Sex, Third Gender: Beyond Sexual Dimorphism in Culture and History,* ed. Gilbert Herdt (New York: Zone Books, 1994), 213–239.

13. Magnus Hirschfeld, "Die objective Diagnose der Homosexualität," *Jahrbuch für sexuelle Zwischenstufen* 1 (1899): 4. In this same text, Hirschfeld provides a ten-page questionnaire for diagnosing homosexuality, including anatomical and psychological features that would distinguish the homosexual man or woman from the "normal."

14. Some sexual scientists opined that part of the problem was due to women's own sexual ignorance. Havelock Ellis asserted that women were highly ignorant of the fact that their attraction to other women is sexual and, in his view, abnormal. Curiously, though, Ellis believed that "a slight degree of homosexuality is commoner in women than in men." See Havelock Ellis and John Addington Symonds, *Sexual Inversion: A Critical Edition,* ed. Ivan Crozier (London: Palgrave Macmillan, 2009), 61. This ignorance regarding women's sexuality was not limited to women themselves, however. As Tracie Matysik has demonstrated, sexual scientists found it exceedingly difficult not only to distinguish between normal and abnormal manifestations of sexuality, but also to define "the sexual" itself in women's behavior and desires. See Matysik, *Reforming the Moral Subject,* 152–172. Moreover, sexual scientific theories of female homosexuality were based on a small number of cases, as very few women sought medical guidance regarding their sexual "abnormality" at the turn of the century. Sexual scientists therefore

Second, all three theories sought underlying psychosomatic causes of homosexuality. Though researchers initially framed this quest as a search for the roots of pathology, by the turn of the century the etiological pursuit was represented in more neutral terms. Most leading sexologists at the time treated "true" homosexuality as a congenital phenomenon, that is, something innate and present at birth. Such representations ultimately helped decrease the power and legitimacy of assertions that homosexuality marked a form of degeneration or atavism, claims that were particularly prominent during the 1880s and 1890s. Richard von Krafft-Ebing, an early proponent of the claim that homosexuality was a product of degeneration, ultimately came to the conclusion shortly before his death in 1902 that "contrary sexuality" was a natural phenomenon that arose through no "fault" of one's own, and one that he claimed deserved "pity" rather than scorn.[15]

Third, despite the increasing neutrality of etiology, congenital theories of homosexuality were nonetheless imbued with eugenic beliefs regarding the hereditary dangers of homosexual parentage. This was particularly true in the early twentieth century. Although theorists moved away from the claim that homosexuality was the product or manifestation of degeneration, they still held that physical reproduction by homosexual men and women tended to produce "sickly" offspring. Sympathetic researchers like Hirschfeld gave such views a different valence, arguing instead that homosexual men and women had no interest in establishing a family, as it would confine them to inauthentic gender roles and involve them in undesirable sexual practices. Hirschfeld even claimed that many married homosexual women who become pregnant entertain thoughts of suicide.[16] It is possible that such eugenic assertions, particularly

---

based their theories upon three sources: first, hypotheses regarding male homosexuality; second, subjective observations of sociocultural phenomena such as the rise of the women's movement and New Woman; and third, voluntarily provided testimony by individuals who saw themselves reflected in the new identity category of the homosexual.

15. Richard von Krafft-Ebing, "Neuen Studien auf dem Gebiete der Homosexualität," *Jahrbuch für sexuelle Zwischenstufen* 3 (1901): 7.

16. Hirschfeld, *Der urnische Mensch*, 86–87.

on the part of sympathetic researchers, were advanced for strategic reasons, namely, to free self-understood homosexual subjects from marriage and heterosexual intercourse. However, other beliefs were also at play. Hirschfeld and British socialist and sex reformer Edward Carpenter both stressed that homosexual men and women were meant by nature to perform the humanitarian work of cultural reproduction, and that their sex drives were geared primarily toward love, not physical sex.[17] Such arguments led some theorists to claim that homosexual men and women were more spiritual beings, therefore superior to their heterosexual counterparts. Nevertheless, assertions regarding the negative effects of homosexual reproduction reiterated associations between homosexuality and degeneration. As we will see, women made similar arguments for their own ends, with equally ambivalent implications.

The earliest and most popular understanding of congenital homosexuality was the theory of sexual inversion, which attributed homosexuality to a failed correspondence between one's physiological sex and one's gender performance. It is perhaps best encapsulated in the maxim formulated by its earliest theorist, German lawyer Karl Heinrich Ulrichs, to account for male homosexuality: "Anima muliebris in corpore virile inclusa," which literally translates to "a female spirit in a masculine body." According to Ulrichs, the equivalent for female homosexuality was "a male soul confined to the female body," although Heike Bauer has noted that Ulrichs treated female homosexuality "largely as a logical exercise than as reality."[18] According to Bauer, Ulrichs's theorization of female homosexuality was "something of an afterthought": writing in the 1860s and early 1870s, Ulrichs was primarily concerned with the legal fate of male "inverts" under the Criminal Code of a unified Germany, which would ultimately criminalize same-sex

---

17. Curiously, Hirschfeld is particularly insistent upon the inappropriateness of physical reproduction for the Uranian of either sex, and instead insists upon his/her role in cultural reproduction. See Hirschfeld, *Der urnische Mensch*, 5, 87, 93, 157. Edward Carpenter made similar arguments in *The Intermediate Sex: A Study of Some Transitional Types of Men and Women* (London: Swan Sonnenschein, 1908), 70, 122.
18. Bauer, "Theorizing Female Inversion," 90.

acts between men under Paragraph 175.[19] In the following decades, however, scientists and physicians would develop a taxonomy of traits to characterize the sexually inverted woman. In *Sexual Inversion* (1897), Havelock Ellis identified the female invert by her deep voice, firm muscles, absent soft connective tissue, predilections for male attire, athleticism, smoking, and "disdain" for domestic work.[20] Krafft-Ebing similarly associated female homosexuality with sartorial and psychological masculinity, along with features such as a masculine physique (a muscular body, narrow hips, and short hair), masculine behavior (smoking and drinking), and a preference for same-sex companionship (exclusive involvement in "female society").[21] Although claims that homosexuality was caused by physical hermaphroditism had largely been abandoned by the fin de siècle, as late as 1912 figures such as Havelock Ellis and Albert Moll continued to suggest that one could find evidence of masculine physical traits such as hypertrichosis, or excessive hair growth, among female homosexuals.[22]

Above all other signifiers, psychological features, namely, higher degrees of intelligence and rationality, were considered the most consistent evidence of female homosexuality within sexual inversion theory.[23] According to Edward Carpenter, the mind of the female homosexual was "more logical, scientific, and precise than usual with the normal woman."[24] Such assertions led Austrian phi-

19. Ibid., 92.

20. See Ellis and Symonds, *Sexual Inversion*, 173–176.

21. Richard von Krafft-Ebing, "Neuen Studien auf dem Gebiete der Homosexualität," *Jahrbuch für sexuelle Zwischenstufen* 3 (1901): 25–26. See also August Forel, *Die sexuelle Frage: Eine naturwissenschaftliche, psychologische, hygienische und soziologische Studie für Gebildete* (Munich: Ernst Reinhardt, 1905), 256–259; Hammer, "Über gleichgeschlechtliche Frauenliebe," 396–400.

22. Albert Moll, *Handbuch der Sexualwissenschaft, mit besonderer Berücksichtigung der kulturgeschichtlichen Beziehungen* (Leipzig: F. C. W. Vogel, 1912), 654.

23. See Ellis and Symonds, *Sexual Inversion*, 178; Dr. [Christopher] Hartung, *Homosexualität und Frauenemanzipation: Ein Beitrag zur Lösung der Frage* (Leipzig: Max Spohr Verlag, 1910), 23. See also Margaret Gibson, "The Masculine Degenerate: American Doctors' Portrayals of the Lesbian Intellect, 1880–1949," *Journal of Women's History* 9 (Winter 1998): 78–103.

24. Carpenter, *Intermediate Sex*, 27.

losopher Otto Weininger and German dermatologist Albert Moll to claim that all women's intellectual and artistic achievements had been realized by "extremely virile specimens of their sex."[25] It was simply unthinkable to them that femininity or femaleness could be capable of anything other than inspiring greatness. Despite the inherent misogyny of such views, the link between higher intelligence, intellectualism, and female sexual abnormality can also be found in Rüling, Elberskirchen, and Mayreder's envisioned alternative sexual subjectivities.

Associated with the idea of sexual inversion was the claim that congenitally inverted individuals constituted a distinct third sex between man and woman. Though the term "third sex" referred in general to both male and female homosexuals, it is a bit of a misnomer, as "third sex" theorists actually recognized four sexes. Karl-Heinrich Ulrichs referred to all members of the third (and fourth) sex as Uranians, a classification that persisted until the First World War. Males were referred to as Urnings and females as Urninde.[26] Magnus Hirschfeld asserted that Uranism is evident even in early childhood, often apprehended by onlookers before the individual him- or herself.[27] The concept of a third sex is significant because it enabled individuals to imagine sexual subjectivities beyond the sexual binary, and suggested the need to expand available sexual categories. It would prove indispensable to feminist thinkers like Rüling and Elberskirchen.

---

25. Otto Weininger, *Sex and Character: An Investigation of Fundamental Principles,* trans. Ladislaus Löb (Indianapolis: Indiana University Press, 2005), 58; Moll, *Handbuch,* 316.

26. Ulrichs derived the term "Uranian" from Plato's *Symposium.* In the *Symposium,* Plato describes two different loves, and claims that they are ruled by two different goddesses of love—Aphrodite, daughter of Uranus, and Aphrodite, daughter of Zeus and Dione. The second Aphrodite rules opposite-sex love, while the daughter of Uranus rules same-sex love. Thus, Ulrichs named those who loved members of the opposite sex "Dionings," and those who loved members of the same sex "Uranians." Those who loved both males and females were called "Uranodionings," a precursor to "bisexual." See Karl Heinrich Ulrichs, *The Riddle of "Man-Manly" Love: The Pioneering Work on Male Homosexuality I,* trans. Michael A. Lombardi-Nash (Buffalo: Prometheus Books, 1994), 34–35.

27. Hirschfeld, *Der urnische Mensch,* 48.

Eventually, theorists came to believe that sexual variety could not be contained even within four sexes. Sexual science's increasing recognition of diverse combinations of sexual preferences and performances gave rise in the early twentieth century to the theory of sexual intermediaries (*Zwischenstufen*), associated today primarily with Magnus Hirschfeld, Otto Weininger, and Edward Carpenter. This theory held that one's sexual identity existed on a continuum between the ideal types of (heterosexual) Male and (heterosexual) Female. In Weininger's words, between these ideal types, "*there are innumerable gradations, or 'intermediate sexual forms.'*"[28] According to the theory of sexual intermediaries, homosexuality was the product of a fundamental physiological bisexuality; that is, all humans possessed both feminine and masculine physical and psychological traits, developed to varying degrees. Hirschfeld and Carpenter understood gender diversity to be a product of embryonic development,[29] while Weininger asserted that both male and female characteristics could be found at the level of the cell. Such theories ultimately led to the radical claim that absolute manhood and womanhood were physiological impossibilities.[30]

It is important to note that sexologists' embrace of sexual variation did not include acceptance of sexual fluidity. Ultimately, these theories made it difficult for scientists to understand "normal" women as anything but feminine and predestined by nature to become wives and mothers. Likewise, these theories made it difficult for scientists to view feminists as anything but masculinized and sexually inverted. Even feminist supporters such as Edward Carpenter asserted that the emergence of the women's movement could be attributed to a new sex, "like the feminine neuters of Ants and Bees—not adapted for child-bearing, but with a marvellous and perfect instinct of social service, indispensable for the maintenance

---

28. Weininger, *Sex and Character*, 13; emphasis in original. See also Carpenter, *Intermediate Sex*, 10.

29. Carpenter, *Intermediate Sex*, 66–67.

30. Hirschfeld, *Der urnische Mensch*, 127. See also Bloch, *Das Sexualeben unsere Zeit*, 44.

of the common life."[31] For Wilhelm Hammer, the women's movement constituted "a true treasure trove for researchers of female
homosexuals and homosexuality."[32] Curiously, virtually no mention was made of the fact that many leaders and members of the
German feminist movement lived with other women and maintained intimate relationships with them throughout their lives. Scientists' elision of this lived reality within the feminist movement
indicates that it was the challenge feminists and female homosexuals posed to binary sexual difference and women's dependence
upon men that was most threatening.

In the eyes of many male sexologists, feminism was not just
attributable to homosexuality, but was actually responsible for
inciting homosexuality. According to Havelock Ellis, feminism
provoked underlying hereditary tendencies toward inversion and
inspired "spurious" imitations.[33] Albert Moll similarly accused the
women's movement of provoking a "virilisation" of the female sex
by diverting women from their supposed destinies as wives and
mothers. In his 1912 handbook, Moll cited the 1904 International
Women's Congress in Berlin to prove that this "fact" was evident
in feminists' appearance. "That the women's movement cannot
be separated entirely from the masculinization of women is manifested through pictures," he wrote. "In any case more virile types
can be found in the women's movement than in the rest of the
female population."[34] Such attitudes led some sexologists to declare that the woman question was itself, in Iwan Bloch's words,
"actually the question of the fate of virile homosexual beings."[35]
Although Magnus Hirschfeld repudiated the notion that feminism

31. Edward Carpenter, *Love's Coming of Age: A Series of Papers on the Relations of the Sexes* (Manchester: The Labour Press, 1896), 87–88.
32. Hammer, "Über gleichgeschlechtliche Frauenliebe," 440.
33. Ellis and Symonds, *Sexual Inversion*, 178.
34. Moll, *Handbuch*, 316, 345. Albert Moll was especially alarmist not only
in his representations of the connection between homosexuality and the women's
movement, but also in his condemnation of the women's movement itself. Moll
dedicated at least two chapters of his *Handbuch* to feminism and its future consequences, and additional chapters to the phenomenon of female homosexuality. See
Moll, sec. 4, chaps. 2 and 3, and sec. 7, chap. 4.
35. Bloch, *Das Sexualeben unsere Zeit*, 580.

caused homosexuality, he nonetheless maintained that homosexual women were attracted to the movement because of the opportunity it offered them to realize their true selves.[36]

One of the most sustained examinations of the supposed relationship between feminism and homosexuality can be found in the article "The Woman Question and Sexual Intermediaries," published in the *Yearbook for Sexual Intermediaries* in 1900. Like other sexologists, the article's author, a Dr. Arduin, asserted that homosexual women led the women's movement; however, he also argued that this relationship was natural because the expected life course of "full womanhood"—that is, marriage and motherhood—would not constitute a complete life for these individuals.[37] According to Arduin, "masculine" work was an innate requirement for homosexual women, given their particular constitution. He insisted that they deserved occupations in line with their nature, and that to bar them from such occupations would constitute an injustice.[38] Yet this position also led him to assert that rights to masculine work should be denied to normal women fated to become wives and mothers.[39]

As suggested by Arduin's arguments, male sexologists viewed marriage and especially maternity as the fault lines that distinguished heterosexual and homosexual women's destinies and determined the legitimacy of demands for access to masculine prerogatives. Part of the reason seemingly sympathetic writers like Arduin accorded rights to the homosexual woman stemmed from their belief that this figure's greater masculinity made her unfit for motherhood. Women's rights were consequently framed as only necessary for those women who would not or could not (and should not) fulfill their reproductive duties.

According to many sexologists, motherhood was incommensurate with an expansion of women's public roles; however, such claims were made precisely at a time when many German feminists across

---

36. Hirschfeld, *Der urnische Mensch*, 124.

37. Dr. phil. Arduin, "Die Frauenfrage und die sexuellen Zwischenstufen," *Jahrbuch für sexuelle Zwischenstufen* 2 (1900): 215, 220.

38. Ibid.

39. Ibid., 223.

the political spectrum asserted that women's capacity for motherhood necessitated an expansion of women's public roles, rights, and freedoms. Such claims, foundational to an ideology often referred to as maternalism, took shape across western Europe and the United States around the turn of the century as motherhood and the quantity and "quality" of populations became widely discussed subjects of public concern. A versatile ideology mobilized to support demands ranging from increased welfare provisions for mothers and children to greater reproductive rights and freedoms, maternalist discourses are described by Seth Koven and Sonya Michel as "exalt[ing] women's capacity to mother and extend[ing] to society as a whole the values of care, nurturance, and morality."[40] For some maternalists, motherhood was a service to the state analogous to military service, and thus in itself a qualification for women's citizenship.[41] Koven and Michel note that maternalism "extolled the private virtues of domesticity while simultaneously legitimating women's public relationship to politics and the state, to community, workplace, and marketplace."[42] Consequently, as they observe along with Ann Taylor Allen, maternalists challenged the division between the public and private sphere that undergirded bourgeois nineteenth-century culture.[43]

Maternalist feminists claimed that the spiritual qualities of motherhood that women would bring to their public roles would contribute a much-needed counterbalance to men's inclinations toward destructive and aggressive behavior. According to Karen Offen, maternalist feminists stressed women's differences from men, which they "grounded in their motherly nature (even if they had no children of their own)," as "their central qualification for full participation in sociopolitical decision making."[44] However,

40. Seth Koven and Sonya Michel, "Womanly Duties: Maternalist Politics and the Origins of the Welfare States in France, Germany, Great Britain, and the United States, 1880–1920," *American Historical Review* 95, no. 4 (Oct. 1990): 1079.

41. Ann Taylor Allen, *Feminism and Motherhood in Western Europe, 1890–1970: The Maternal Dilemma* (London: Palgrave Macmillan, 2005), 2, 5.

42. Koven and Michel, "Womanly Duties," 1079.

43. Ibid.; Allen, *Feminism and Motherhood in Western Europe*, 3.

44. Karen Offen, *European Feminisms, 1700–1950: A Political History* (Palo Alto, CA: Stanford University Press, 2000), 236.

turn-of-the-century maternalists did not simply celebrate a "traditional" understanding of motherhood; rather, they sought to remake motherhood in ways that would not "restrict, but enhance, [women's] development as individuals."[45] Allen points out that "feminists who extolled motherhood as woman's distinctive contribution to society . . . had no intention of confining mothers to their conventional roles of dependent wife, domestic drudge, and sexual slave. Indeed, along with Ibsen's Nora, they aspired to be both mothers and human beings. Their aspirations included not only political rights and legal equality, but also economic self-sufficiency . . . and above all control over their reproductive lives."[46] Maternalists believed motherly qualities were commensurate with active roles as "electors, policymakers, bureaucrats, and workers, within and outside the home."[47] Indeed, the question of exactly how to combine motherhood and public involvement was a preoccupation of many German feminists at the time, as evidenced by influential studies such as Adele Gerhard and Helene Simon's *Motherhood and Intellectual Labor* (1901), which investigated how women combined motherhood with professional work and public activism.[48]

Maternalists thus viewed women's capacity for motherhood not as a liability, but as a source of strength and agency.[49] Yet by treating motherhood, or rather the potential for motherhood, as the

45. *Feminism and Motherhood in Western Europe*, 2; see also Offen, *European Feminisms*, 236.

46. Allen, *Feminism and Motherhood in Western Europe*, 13.

47. Koven and Michel, "Womanly Duties," 1077.

48. See Adele Gerhard and Helene Simon, *Mutterschaft und geistige Arbeit* (Berlin: G. Reimer, 1901). As Ann Taylor Allen notes, Gerhard and Simon were pessimistic regarding the ability of most (middle-class) women to combine motherhood and a career because of the psychological and emotional demands of motherhood. They therefore concluded that "only women with exceptional talent were justified in overcoming this conflict in order to make a uniquely valuable contribution to culture. In all other cases, motherhood itself, when rightly understood and practiced, was a sufficiently complex and valuable function to occupy a woman's total intellectual energy." Nonetheless, they supported other forms of women's public involvement, and became early supporters of women's suffrage. See Allen, *Feminism and Motherhood in Germany*, 165.

49. Koven and Michel, "Womanly Duties," 1084.

132 Sexual Politics and Feminist Science

primary justification for women's empowerment and public inclusion, maternalist feminists reified the notion that true womanhood was defined by maternity, and that motherhood, in the words of Swedish feminist Ellen Key, was "the most perfect realization of human potential that the species has reached."[50] Where did maternalism leave women who did not want to become, or did not identify as, mothers? Where did it leave those who did not accept maternity as the essence of femaleness, yet still wanted to be involved and active in public life? Although Karen Offen notes the long-standing existence of an "individualist" tendency within feminism alongside what she calls a "relationist" position (within which maternalism falls), she also points out that individualist feminism constituted not just a minority position, but an unpopular position, at the very least in turn-of-the-century Continental Europe. Significantly, she cites the contemporary "failure" of French feminist Madeline Pelletier, "a woman doctor who dressed in mannish clothing, cropped her hair . . . and openly disparaged 'femininity' as it was then constructed," as evidence.[51]

Perhaps not surprisingly given the stigma surrounding homosexuality at the time, most feminists reacted negatively to imputations of abnormality because they believed that such associations would delegitimize their goals and demands. The conflation of feminism and homosexuality became a particularly fraught topic in Germany after 1909, when legislators proposed to criminalize female homosexuality as part of broader reforms to the Criminal Code.[52] German-speaking feminists recognized that this conflation threatened to undermine their respectability—an invaluable commodity for actors lacking significant legal rights and political resources. Consequently, many attempted to distance themselves from homosexuality or make vehement denials bolstered by expressions of disgust. As

---

50. Ellen Key, *Über Liebe und Ehe*, trans. Frances Maro (Berlin: Fischer, 1906), 222; cited in Allen, *Feminism and Motherhood in Western Europe*, 2.

51. Karen Offen, "Defining Feminism: A Comparative Historical Approach," *Signs* 14, no. 1 (Autumn 1988): 144–145.

52. See Matysik, *Reforming the Moral Subject*, 152–172; Margit Göttert, "Zwischen Betroffenheit, Abscheu und Sympathie: Die alte Frauenbewegung und das 'heikles Thema' Homosexualität," *Ariadne: Almanach des Archivs der deutschen Frauenbewegung* 29 (May 1996): 14–21.

Margit Göttert points out, one can find a "violent reaction" (*heftigere Reaktion*) to Rüling's speech in the *Central Paper of the Federation of German Women's Associations* under the title "Shamelessly Cheeky Agitations." The notice, which Göttert argues was written by the journal's editor Marie Stritt, took particular exception to the connection made between the women's movement and homosexuality.[53] Similarly, Ella Mensch, an opponent of Johanna Elberskirchen, asserted in her tract *Iconoclasts in the Berlin Women's Movement* (1906) that only "normal-feeling" women could be leaders of the feminist movement because of the "passivity" of members of the third sex, as well as their "tendency to loneliness," their nervousness, and their disinclination to be part of collective life.[54] Others, like Ruth Bré, argued that homosexuality was a consequence of the denial of women's social rights and sexual freedoms.[55]

Although the majority of feminists either shrank from engagement with imputations of homosexuality or confronted them only to aggressively deny any such connection, not all women with feminist desires disavowed this link. For theorists and activists like Rüling, Elberskirchen, and Mayreder, scientific theories of female homosexuality helpfully unmoored sex from a strict binary, and in so doing naturalized sexual variety. These scientific theories also held out the possibility of a fate beyond motherhood. Sexual science thus offered female sexual theorists conceptual resources and a lexicon with which to imagine and articulate new models of sexual subjectivity. Like campaigners in the Scientific Humanitarian Committee who demanded the decriminalization of same-sex acts between men, these authors mobilized congenital theories of homosexuality for political purposes. With members of the committee, these authors believed science revealed that particular subjects had "certain human rights, duties, and special interests" that sprang from their "inborn natures."[56]

53. Göttert, "Zwischen Betroffenheit, Abscheu und Sympathie," 16.
54. Ella Mensch, *Bilderstürmer in der Berliner Frauenbewegung* (Berlin: Hermann Seemann, 1906), 75.
55. See, for example, Ruth Bré, *Das Recht auf die Mutterschutz: Eine Forderung zur Bekämpfung der Prostitution der Frauen- und Geschlechtskrankheiten* (Leipzig: Verlag der Frauen-Rundschau, 1903), 57.
56. Magnus Hirschfeld, "Vorwort," *Jahrbuch für sexuelle Zwischenstufen* 1 (1899): 2.

Anna Rüling's Urninde: The Masculine Woman as Both "Noble and Fine"

Anna Rüling was a pseudonym used by the German journalist Theo Anna Sprüngli, who was active within feminist causes before the First World War. In addition to her journalistic work and her now-famous speech on the women's movement and the "homosexual problem," she authored a short story collection entitled *Who amongst You Is Free from Sin . . . Books from the Shady Side* (1906). Unlike most fiction featuring same-sex relationships at this time, at least two of these stories had happy endings. In 1911 she became one of the few female chairs of the Scientific Humanitarian Committee.[57] Curiously, around the time of the outbreak of the First World War, Rüling's politics shifted to the right, and she became involved in nationalist organizations like the Naval Association of German Women (Flottenbund deutscher Frauen).

Rüling's speech of 9 October 1904 at the annual meeting of the Scientific Humanitarian Committee in Berlin has received considerable scholarly attention in recent years.[58] Rüling delivered her speech before an audience of 300 people, including progressive feminists Minna Cauer and Dr. Agnes Hacker.[59] Within this speech, Rüling not only tackled the relationship between feminism and homosexuality but also gave voice to a new sexual subject, the Urninde, who embodied the ennobling and empowering possibilities of sexual inversion.[60]

---

57. See Christiane Leidinger, "Theo A[nna] Sprüngli (1880–1953) alias Anna Rüling/Th. Rüling/Th. A. Rüling—erste biographische Mosaiksteine zu einer zwiespältigen Ahnin lesbischer herstory," *Mitteilungen der Magnus Hirschfeld Gesellschaft* 35/36 (2003): 28–39; Leidinger, "'Anna Rüling': A Problematic Foremother of Lesbian Herstory," *Journal of the History of Sexuality* 13, no. 4 (October 2004): 477–499.

58. See Biddy Martin, "Extraordinary Homosexuals and the Fear of Being Ordinary," *differences* 6 (1994): 101–125; Bauer, "Theorizing Female Inversion," 84–102.

59. Leidinger, "Theo A[nna] Sprüngli," 39.

60. Rüling's speech was reprinted in the *Jahrbuch für sexuelle Zwischenstufen* in 1905. See Anna Rüling, "Welches Interesse hat die Frauenbewegung an der Lösung des homosexuellen Problems?," *Jahrbuch für sexuelle Zwischenstufen* 7 (1905): 131–151. The English translations of Rüling's article come from Anna

In her articulation of female homosexual subjectivity, Rüling drew upon all three of the aforementioned theories of homosexuality. While stressing that there exist "innumerable gradations of the sexed personality," she nonetheless asserted that the female homosexual constitutes a distinct sex, "the natural and obvious link between men and women" (143). Rüling's indebtedness to third sex theory is apparent in her use of Ulrichs's term "Urninde" to designate the female homosexual as a third sex. Meanwhile, her engagement with the concept of sexual inversion is evident in her characterization of the Urninde as a subject who is "inherently similar" to the "average man" (144). According to Rüling, the Urninde's inherent similarity to man could manifest itself in behavior and appearance. She observed that in many cases "homosexual proclivities express themselves often unconsciously and unintentionally in appearance, speech, deportment, movement, dress, etc." and are visible to a degree that is "obvious to all onlookers" (148). Above all, she stressed the Urninde's mental masculinity, arguably because, as Rüling herself noted, superficial signifiers of inversion were not always present. She pointed out that "not all homosexual women show masculine exteriors that harmonize with their inner selves. There are many Uranian women with completely feminine appearance which they accentuate with very feminine behavior in order to escape being detected as homosexuals" (148). Rüling maintained that despite a shared corporeality with woman and the potential confusion it could engender, the Urninde's psyche would ultimately betray her true sexual subjectivity.

Rüling's anxiety that the Urninde not be mistaken for the feminine heterosexual woman is evident in her persistent contrasting of the two figures. She argued that whereas the "predominant and deciding trait" of the heterosexual woman is emotionality, "clear reason" rules the Urninde (144). Like the "average man," she insisted, the Urninde is "more objective, energetic, and goal oriented

---

Rüling, "What Interest Does the Women's Movement Have in the Homosexual Question?," in *We Are Everywhere: A Historical Sourcebook of Gay and Lesbian Politics*, ed. Mark Blasius and Shane Phelan (London: Routledge, 1997), 143–50. Subsequent citations of this translation of Rüling's work appear parenthetically in the text.

than the feminine Woman" (144). Rüling further described the Urninde as "physically more suited for a rugged life's struggle than a Woman," much like the "completely virile man" (146). It was important for Rüling to insist on the Urninde's masculinity, as it was this particular quality that she believed made the Urninde a worthy, legitimate, and capable candidate for greater social and civic rights and access to education and the professions. Tellingly, Rüling asserted that the Urninde is especially suited to the study of the sciences and other "manly" professions, such as "medicine, law, agricultural professions, and the creative arts" because of her "possession of those qualities lacking in feminine women: greater objectivity, energy, and perseverance" (146, 147). Conversely, Rüling insisted that "the feminine woman has been designed by nature to become first of all wife and mother" (146). If given access to education, feminine women would pursue studies suited to their duties as wives and mothers. According to her, "Under favorable conditions most heterosexual women choose marriage. They seek a broader, more comprehensive education in order to become esteemed companions for their husbands, not just sensual love objects, and to be wives who are respected by their husbands as intellectual equals, and accordingly granted equal rights and responsibilities in marriage" (147). Such statements recall Weininger's assertion that providing women with access to education would be a mistake because women would treat studying as a "fashion" and as an opportunity to "ensnare a man."[61] They also reflect the fact that although access to higher education and the professions was a fundamental goal of the German women's movement, many of the most sexually radical feminists were invested in women's liberation as mothers.[62]

Motherhood was certainly not a destiny Rüling envisioned for the Urninde. In her view that potential fate was nightmarish, not only for the Urninde but also for humanity itself. Rüling drew directly upon the eugenic anxieties embedded in scientific theories

---

61. Weininger, *Sex and Character*, 58.
62. Edward Ross Dickinson, "Reflections on Feminism and Monism in the Kaiserreich, 1900–1913," *Central European History* 34, no. 2 (2001): 198.

of homosexuality to argue for the Urninde's freedom from marriage and motherhood. After claiming that the Urninde could only fulfill "marital duties" in a heterosexual partnership "with aversion, or, at best, indifference," she portentously declared that "the marriage of homosexuals is a triple crime; it is a crime against the state, against society itself, and against an unborn generation, for experience teaches us that the offspring of Uranians are seldom healthy and strong" ("What Interest?," 145). Rüling went so far as to assert that homosexuals' "procreation against their nature" was the cause of "a large percentage of the mentally disturbed, retarded, epileptics, tuberculars, and degenerates of all kinds" (145). In her view, enabling the Urninde to be single and self-sufficient would have the added benefit of leaving more husbands "for those women whose natural inclinations are satisfied by the role of wife, housekeeper, and mother" (145). Rüling thus made her demand for the Urninde's freedom from reproductive imperatives by stressing the "racial" benefits of this subject's exclusion from maternity; however, doing so meant accepting the framework of pathology.

Given her belief in the superior capacities and rights-worthiness of the Urninde over the normal woman, how did Rüling envision the Urninde's relationship to the feminist movement? In her view, the female homosexual served as a bridge not only between the women's movement and the homosexual movement but also between the normal woman and the goal of emancipation (143). Rüling explicitly asserted in her speech that "contrary to the belief of the antifeminists that women are inferior and that only those with strong masculine characteristics are to be valued, I believe that women in general are equal to men"; however, what she exactly meant by equality in this instance, especially in light of her persistent contrasts between the Urninde and other women, is unclear (148). Her statement is further complicated by the fact that, in the very next sentence, Rüling echoed the views of figures such as Arduin and Hirschfeld by declaring, "I am convinced . . . that the homosexual Woman is particularly capable of playing a leading role in the international women's movement for equality" (148). According to Rüling, "without the active support of the Uranian

woman, the women's movement would not be where it is today—
this is an undisputable fact" (150). It was often the Urninde, she
insisted, "with her androgynous characteristics," who "initiated
action because she felt most strongly the many, many injustices
and hardships with which laws, society, and archaic customs treat
women" (150). As proof of the Urninde's leading role within the
feminist movement, Rüling claimed that "anyone with the slightest
bit of familiarity with homosexual traits who has been following
the women's movement at all or who knows any of its leading
women personally or by pictures, will find the Uranians among
the suffragettes and recognize that Uranians are often noble and
fine" (148). According to her, the Urninde's leadership was indispensable because she had the unique capacity to awaken "naturally indifferent and submissive average women to an awareness
of their human dignity and rights" (149–150). In her assessment of
the relationship between the Urninde and the women's movement,
Rüling ultimately reinforced existing sexological claims and provided fodder for future assertions made by Iwan Bloch and Albert
Moll regarding the confluence of feminism and homosexuality—in
fact, Moll's aforementioned assertion regarding the prevalence of
"virile" women at the 1904 International Women's Congress was
explicitly inspired by Rüling's comments. Rüling's views resemble those of Otto Weininger, who insisted that "all those women
who really strive for emancipation . . . always display many male
properties."[63] They also echo Arduin's assertion that the woman
question was fundamentally a homosexual woman question. Ultimately, then, Rüling's demands for rights on behalf of the Urninde
come at the expense of the normal woman, who is represented in
her speech exactly as many antifeminists would have her: as incapable of freedom and biologically predestined to marriage and
motherhood.

Clearly, sexual science played a critical role in Rüling's representation of the Urninde as a subject legitimately in need of
social rights and specific kinds of sexual freedom. By stressing
this subject's masculinity, Rüling justified her demands for access

---

63. Weininger, *Sex and Character*, 58.

to education and the professions and freedom from the strictures of marriage and motherhood. She sought recognition for the Urninde, along with a social niche that would correspond to her purportedly innate traits and abilities. Rüling sought the privileges and powers of patriarchy by asserting her subject's greater aptitude for them, and did so at the expense of supposedly average heterosexual women. Upon reflection, it is evident that in all instances where Rüling identified common cause between the women's movement and the homosexual rights movement, she did so to argue on behalf of the Urninde's liberation from the strictures of the category of woman itself. She legitimized this move through recourse to the claim, first pioneered by Ulrichs and later echoed by Hirschfeld and Arduin, that all humans should have a right to live according to their natures. In her attempt to abandon the heterosexual woman and the limits imposed by her reproductive sexuality, Rüling's speech represents an intriguing reversal of feminists' attempts to distance themselves from homosexuality.

"Woman-Identified Woman" avant la lettre: Johanna Elberskirchen's Feminine Homosexual

Like Rüling, Johanna Elberskirchen was one of the few female members of the Scientific Humanitarian Committee. In the 1920s she also joined the World League for Sexual Reform.[64] In *The Love of the Third Sex* and *Revolution!* Elberskirchen articulated a model of female homosexuality that diverged significantly from Rüling's. Elberskirchen did not view female homosexuality as a masculine subjectivity; instead, she insisted that the homosexual woman was more feminine than the average heterosexual woman. She maintained that the homosexual woman's greater femininity was revealed by her attraction to women, as well as her greater capacity and stronger desire for spiritual rather than sexual union. Elberskirchen also viewed the female homosexual as a more feminist

---

64. See Christiane Leidinger, *Keine Tochter aus gutem Hause: Johanna Elberskirchen (1864–1943)* (Konstanz: UVK Verlagsgesellschaft, 2008).

identity, albeit for complex reasons. In her view, homosexual love constituted a purer, elevated form of love, particularly when compared with the excesses and failings of heterosexuality.

In both *The Love of the Third Sex* and *Revolution!* Elberskirchen invoked scientific theories and evidence to represent female homosexuality as denoting a distinctive, superior subjectivity.[65] After pointing out evidence of homosexuality's existence in all times among all peoples, in *The Love of the Third Sex* Elberskirchen invoked theories of sexual intermediaries to argue that homosexuality constituted a "transitional form between female and male" resulting from humanity's fundamental physiological bisexuality.[66] According to her, "Embryology, anatomy and physiology . . . have taught us that the types Man and Woman (*Weib*) are deeply connected with one another" (9). Elberskirchen stressed that the female and male sexes developed biologically from organs they both shared in common (9–18). Drawing on the work of biologist Ernst Haeckel, Elberskirchen pointed out that sex differentiation only began in the ninth week of embryonic development (9).

Elberskirchen maintained that humanity's original biological bisexuality created variegated subjective possibilities between the two poles of heterosexual man and woman. She claimed that an individual's gender and sexuality ultimately depended upon the influence of certain "physiological stimuli" (*physiologische Reiz*): "According to stimuli this or that bisexual variety develops itself, the so-called man or the so-called female or the so-called homosexual or some interstitial degree (*dazwischenliegender Grad*)" (19). For this reason, Elberskirchen insisted, sexual variation and not sexual dimorphism reflected the true state of nature. Like theorists of sexual intermediaries such as Hirschfeld and Weininger, Elberskirchen declared that "the absolute man and the absolute woman are chimera, are errors. There is no absolute man. There is no absolute woman. There are only bisexual varieties" (18). In

---

65. Translations of Elberskirchen's texts are my own.

66. Johanna Elberskirchen, *Die Liebe des dritten Geschlechts: Homosexualität, eine bisexuelle Varietät keine Entartung—keine Schuld* (Leipzig: Verlag von Max Spohr, 1904), 8. Subsequent citations of this work appear parenthetically in the text.

Elberskirchen's view, biological bisexuality produced natural variation not only in gender expression but also in sexual desires. She
went so far as to declare that "in the end we are all, closely examined, homosexual—the one more, the other less. . . . Or more accurately: we are all bisexual . . . and according to our development
capable of liking and loving the two sexes, the one more, the other
less—the one in a form of platonic friendship—the other in the
form more or less of platonic love" (19).

Intriguingly, although Elberskirchen began from the premise of
sexual variety, like Rüling she ultimately treated homosexuality as
constitutive of a unique subjectivity. As suggested by the title of one
of her tracts, she clearly thought that homosexuals constituted a
third sex. In *The Love of the Third Sex*, Elberskirchen characterized
the "homosexual person" as "a person of soulful love, a person of
spiritualized love . . . of strong passion . . . of highest spirituality"
(27). To her, the homosexual constituted "nature's finest expression
of life" (34). Unlike Rüling, Elberskirchen's belief that homosexuals
constituted a third sex did not coincide with an embrace of sexual
inversion theory. She vigorously denied that masculinity played any
role in defining female homosexuality and even intimated that sexual inversion theory, when applied to women, marked an attempt
to undermine women's demands for emancipation.[67]

Instead, Elberskirchen stressed the relational element of homosexuality and defined it as the love of one's own sex. While
identifying biology as the cause of homosexuality, she nonetheless
insisted that it must be understood as an interpersonal phenomenon that occurred between (at least) two people. Strategically rely-
ing on the sexual binary, Elberskirchen further asserted that female
homosexuality constituted a fundamentally feminine subjectivity.
As she astutely pointed out, neither woman in a same-sex couple is
"impelled towards man"; rather, "both love in the other the same
sex—the feminine, not the masculine."[68] If this was the case, she

---

67. Johanna Elberskirchen, *Was hat der Mann aus Weib, Kind und sich gemacht?
Revolution und Erlösung des Weibes: Eine Abrechnung mit dem Mann—ein Wegweiser in die Zukunft!* 3rd ed. (N.p.: Magazin-Verlag, 1904), 4, 8–9.
68. Ibid., 4; see also Elberskirchen, *Die Liebe des dritten Geschlechts*, 5.

asked, how could sexologists justify their claims that the female homosexual was innately masculine?

Beyond interpersonal dynamics, Elberskirchen located the essence of homosexuality in the nature and orientation of same-sex love. Citing authorities including Plato and Hirschfeld, Elberskirchen declared that homosexual love was always spiritual in the first instance. Physical love, she insisted, was only a side effect.[69] For such reasons, Elberskirchen believed that "homosexuality and the love of homosexuals is no degeneration, is no psychopathy, and—it is not a source of guilt or shame" (34). In Elberskirchen's eyes it was heterosexuality that was truly shameful and degenerate, primarily because of its treatment of women. "The tragedy of the female in the realm of normal-sex love," she wrote, "is the most damaging, the most atrocious," that has ever been recorded in culture (23). Heterosexuality's history is marked by "thorns, blood and wounds" and constitutes the site of the "eternal rebirth of . . . human bestial depravity" (23–24). According to Elberskirchen, heterosexuality is nothing but "excess," "terrible sickness," and "dehumanization," all of which stood in marked contrast to homosexual love (24). She asserted that whereas "the homosexual loves above all things the soul of the other," for the heterosexual "all is sex" (26).

Despite this strong statement, at certain points in her texts Elberskirchen seems to forget the degeneracy of heterosexuality, because, like Rüling, she too invoked eugenic fears to insist that homosexual women had a "physiological-psychological right" to be free of marriage and motherhood and allowed to pursue education and other occupations instead.[70] In *The Love of the Third Sex*, Elberskirchen questioned whether everyone needs to or should have children and declared that, as a rule, homosexuals are not very good at physical reproduction (30, 32). She even claimed that "nearly all of them [homosexuals] made a mess in the field of physical reproduction" (33). Much like Hirschfeld and Carpenter,

---

69. Elberskirchen, *Die Liebe des dritten Geschlechts*, 26. Subsequent citations of this work appear parenthetically in the text.

70. Elberskirchen, *Revolution*, 9.

Elberskirchen maintained that homosexuals properly constituted humanity's spiritual and intellectual regenerators and were responsible for cultural achievements and refinement (31–32). Homosexuals fulfilled this role, she insisted, as a result of the fundamentally spiritual nature of their love, as well as their ability to sublimate their sexual and reproductive drives (31–32). Elberskirchen further asserted that homosexual men and women served as the "safety-valve of nature" and helped prevent overpopulation (31). On the basis of such claims, Elberskirchen proposed a division of reproductive labor, with homosexuals responsible for spiritual and intellectual reproduction and heterosexuals responsible for physical reproduction. She further rationalized this division of labor by asserting that heterosexuals do not often exceed average intelligence, usually as a result of dementia induced by sexual excess (32–33).

Elberskirchen's hypothesized division of labor would liberate homosexual women from the pressure to marry and bear children and enable them to be active "in areas other than the sexual," including "so-called masculine occupations."[71] For this reason, Elberskirchen implied, many homosexual women were involved in the women's emancipation movement. Although she vehemently denied a causal relationship between homosexuality and feminism and rejected the idea that the leaders of the feminist movement were masculinized, she nonetheless declared, "If we women of the emancipation are homosexual—well, then let us be! We are with good reason."[72] She insisted that if women's strivings toward emancipation were caused by homosexuality, science would have no right to denigrate the women's movement or represent it as the result of a degenerate condition, because it actually reflected humanity's biological bisexuality.[73] Finally, Elberskirchen sarcastically asked her reader, "If woman's strivings for emancipation . . . are attributable to a sexual abnormality—why fight it?"[74] If this were the case, she claimed, normal women would be excluded

---

71. Elberskirchen, *Revolution,* 9.
72. Ibid.
73. Ibid., 10.
74. Ibid., 9.

from emancipation anyway and would preoccupy themselves with marriage and motherhood.

In making such claims, Elberskirchen, like Rüling, implied that reproductive sexuality marked a fundamental difference in the subjectivity and life courses of homosexual and heterosexual women, and that only the former was truly in need of greater rights and freedoms. Thus, while Elberskirchen's representation of female homosexuality challenged the evaluative priorities of patriarchal thought by celebrating women's same-sex love and spiritual intimacy, she nonetheless created distinctions of value between heterosexual and homosexual women premised on proximity to reproduction. Here, too, the prospect of maternity seemed to place limits on women's potential emancipation. And like Rüling's Urninde, Elberskirchen's feminine homosexual woman sought greater access to patriarchal rights and privileges as a matter of "natural" right and necessity that precluded the so-called normal woman.

Idealizing the Individual: Rosa Mayreder's Synthetic Human

Perhaps the most high-profile of the three authors examined here, Rosa Mayreder was a pioneering feminist activist and intellectual whose philosophical and literary work was celebrated in her own time. Mayreder was a founding member of the General Austrian Women's Organization (Allgemeine Österreichischer Frauenverein), created in 1902 as the central organizing body of the Austrian women's movement; she also helped establish *Documents of Woman*, a key Austrian feminist journal. Mayreder was involved in feminist campaigns against the state regulation of prostitution, and was a member of the Austrian branch of the League for the Protection of Mothers and Sexual Reform. Upon the outbreak of the First World War, she became heavily involved in the peace movement, particularly the International Women's League for Peace and Freedom. Her treatise *Toward a Critique of Femininity* was highly respected and influential: following its initial publication in 1905, it was translated into numerous languages, including an English version entitled *A Survey of the Woman Problem* (1912).

Rosa Mayreder is not usually considered a theorist of nonnormative gender and sexuality. However, unpublished autobiographical notes and essays in *Toward a Critique of Femininity* suggest that sexological theories of homosexuality played an important role in her rethinking of female subjectivity. Specifically, I argue that they informed her ideal of the synthetic human, a subject that embraced both male and female traits and stood at the pinnacle of sexual evolution. Mayreder represented the synthetic human being as a truly individual subject who escaped the limitations of binary sexuality; nevertheless, it is clear that this subject had an affinity for one end of the sexual spectrum, namely, the masculine. Like Rüling, Mayreder prized masculine qualities above feminine qualities because of their supposedly greater disconnection from physiological limitations, above all those imposed upon women by motherhood. Mayreder argued that women's evolution toward the ideal of the synthetic human being would enable them to transcend the limits of their reproductive sexuality.

Autobiographical material suggests that for Mayreder, rethinking sexual subjectivity began as a personal project rather than a political one. A collection of notes titled "Memories of Youth from Rosa Mayreder, Part II: The Internal World" indicate that, as an intellectual young woman, Mayreder struggled with what she perceived to be a discrepancy between her physical and mental sexes. As she noted in her autobiographical sketch, family members called her a bluestocking because of her love of philosophy, and thereby taught her that being an intellectual was antithetical to femininity.[75] Consequently, she lamented the limitations imposed by her gender, writing in her diary, "Nature, you have given me talents, manifold and many;—but you made me a woman—and I know what a woman's job entails. If I would be a man, I would

---

75. Rosa Mayreder, "Jugenderinnerungen von Rosa Mayreder, II: Teil; Die innere Welt," Manuscript, n.d., 53c, Teilnachlass Rosa Mayreders, Ser. N. 24556, Österreichische Nationalbibliothek. Quotations and material in the following paragraphs derive from this source.

have probably become the most important person in my Father-land with these talents."

Mayreder eventually questioned whether she was psychologi-cally male, and recalled that

> a critical analysis of my own being finally raises the question—how to explain the fact that my drives and tendencies correspond more to the male than to the female ideal of life. That the concept of individuality comprised a multitude of various characteristics which are not linked to a sex was the result of my thinking. So I created the hypothesis in order to explain the way I am—that nature has planted in me a man in the physical appearance of a woman. With that I thought to have found the solution to the puzzle, why my inner life was aiming in a quite different direction than that of all other females in my social circle.

Mayreder eventually learned that she was not the first person to have arrived at this hypothesis. Thanks to a male friend, she came into contact with the ideas of the "Assessor Karl Heinrich Ulrichs," who she believed had aptly addressed "the problem of spiritual sex differentiation" through his theory of sexual inversion. Mayre-der recalled being encouraged by Ulrichs's theory and attempted to discover more about this "extraordinary" man and how he devel-oped his ideas. However, reading Krafft-Ebing's *Psychopathia Sex-ualis* (1886) ultimately dashed Mayreder's enthusiasm for Ulrichs's ideas. Though she disagreed with Krafft-Ebing's refutation of Ul-richs's theories, she accepted Krafft-Ebing's assertion that Ulrichs's schema applied only to individuals attracted to members of their own sex. Because she did not feel that her psychosexual inversion included a sexual attraction to women, she concluded that the ap-plication of Ulrichs's ideas to her situation was inaccurate. Mayre-der insisted that, physically and intellectually, "the female sex did not attract me in the least." She later claimed that she had always rejected the "unreasonable demand" of sisterhood that prevailed within the women's movement because she "regarded sex as such as something very minor and unimportant."

Yet as Mayreder herself noted, despite her renunciation of Ulrichs's theories, she only slowly and unhappily separated her-self from the ideas undergirding them. I maintain that her early engagement with Ulrichs influenced her later theoretical musings on ideal sexual subjectivities. According to her autobiographical notes, her reading of Ulrichs informed her conviction that psychic sexual inversion was symptomatic of an evolutionarily superior type, a type she believed was prefigured in Goethe—and that she believed herself to embody. Crucially, Mayreder believed that psychic sexual inversion did not constitute an exceptional condition but rather an "announcement of nature" about the future. "The exception of today must become tomorrow's rule," she declared, "otherwise my life had no sense." Mayreder ultimately adopted the view that "the higher development of humanity aims for the center of sex, and not for the end poles."

With her entry into the women's movement, Mayreder's personal investment in reformulating sexual subjectivity became political, and would find theoretical expression in the figure of the synthetic human being, which she developed in *Toward a Critique of Femininity*.[76] For Mayreder, the synthetic human being constituted the apotheosis of sexual subjectivity. She identified "the distinguishing mark of synthetic people" as their "outlook over the barriers of sex," which enabled them "to reach a mental sphere common to both sexes of the human species." Synthetic humans are able to "raise themselves to a universality of perception. . . . To them the life of the other sex does not appear as something strange and unaccountable but as something closely related, originally a part of their own life and now the complement of their special individual existence advancing to meet them from without" (266–267) The synthetic human being had the capacity to overcome the barriers of binary sexuality and could help ameliorate the relationship between the sexes, much in the way Edward Carpenter's hypothesized the role of the intermediate sex (263–264).

According to Mayreder, the synthetic human being would only become an evolutionary possibility if humans were defined by their

---

76. Rosa Mayreder, *Zur Kritik der Weiblichkeit* (Jena: Eugen Diedrichs, 1905). The passages that follow are from the English translation: Rosa Mayreder, *A Survey of the Woman Problem*, trans. Herman Scheffauer (London: Heinemann, 1913). Subsequent citations of this translation of Mayreder's work appear parenthetically in the text.

intellect as opposed to their biological properties and processes. She maintained that the mind was not sexually differentiated to the same degree as the body, since the intellect, unlike the body, did not serve evolutionary—that is, reproductive—purposes through sex. Intriguingly, she asserted that the origin of the intellect lay in "religious strivings in which the highest aim was the overcoming of sexuality" (270). By embracing the "innumerable gradations" between the male and female psyches, the synthetic human being had a better grasp of the "meaning of individuality and its importance to human society" (269). This formulation again makes clear Mayreder's belief that the psyche, and more specifically the intellect, constituted the true site of subjectivity.

As an individualized sexual subjectivity that transcends the barriers of binary sexuality, the synthetic human is, theoretically, a subject position that could be realized by men and women. Yet as other essays in *Critique* make clear, Mayreder was particularly eager that women evolve to this state. For Mayreder, the synthetic human being represented for women the chance to truly become individuals by escaping what she called the "teleological limitations of the sex": namely, motherhood (62–63). In her view, "The compulsion of woman to perform the duties of propagation places her under a natural disadvantage" (40). Specifically, she believed that the all-consuming demands of reproduction placed a barrier on women's development (49). According to Mayreder, the price a woman pays for her maternity "is nothing less than spiritual freedom and equality" (46). Consequently, she believed that "the farther humanity advances towards higher forms, just so much farther must the female sex, for the sake of motherhood, remain behind the male" (46). Mayreder insisted that the task of the women's movement and its "exceptional" leaders involved "adapt[ing] social conditions to their nature and needs, and to transform the prevailing idea of what women should be in the interests of those women who vary from the norm—the accepted type" (75). She believed that the battle of the "deviating individual" against the "normal majority" was necessary for the "organic evolution of civilization" (75). Moreover, she held that the success of the women's movement lay in "the degree to which the sex in general can be won over to it" (75).

But who were these "exceptional leaders" of the women's movement? According to Mayreder, these were women who had freed themselves from the teleological fate of their sex. She described these women as "the 'unwomanly' ones—no doubt less useful for man and the elemental sex purpose, and yet indispensable factors of the advancing processes of civilization" (63). As such, these women resemble the intellectual and cultural reproducers described in Elberskirchen's characterization of female homosexuality. As unwomanly women, they also suggest Rüling's rational female masculinity. Mayreder insisted that exceptional women, and women of genius, "more often approximate to the male type" (256). In her view, exceptional, unwomanly women will be responsible for establishing the "future order of things" that will ultimately "redound to the benefit" of the "general mass of women" (63).

Unlike Rüling, Mayreder did not believe that the exceptional women of the feminist movement were homosexual or masculinized in their external appearance. Indeed, she insisted that synthetic humans exhibited no signs of "latent bodily bi-sexuality" (258). Mayreder viewed physiological hermaphroditism as a kind of degeneration, claiming that "every deviation from normal physiological sex characteristics renders the individual an imperfect being; bodily hybridism is repulsive because it indicates incompleteness, a defective and faulty structure" (258). Explicitly contra Weininger, she maintained that "the approximation of the manly to the womanly" in no way "necessitates the man being less manly or the womanly being less womanly" (270). Mayreder asserted that exceptional women were feminine; however, their femininity was divorced from their reproductive sexuality, and manifested itself *exclusively* in their external appearance. She further claimed that this alienated, performative femininity was only available to women who had realized themselves intellectually as individuals (34–36). For Mayreder, then, sexual hybridity at the level of the mind—and a stylized performance of gender on the body—constituted the desirable evolutionary ideal, particularly for women.

All of the authors examined in this chapter suggested that greater possibilities for women inhered in a subjectivity that relied less on reproduction for its definition; according to them, reproductive (hetero)sexuality constituted a limit on women's existential potential. The alternatives they proposed consequently reiterated patriarchal views of the lesser social value and capabilities of maternal women, and reinforced a belief that feminism was only relevant for a limited number of "abnormal" women. Yet the alternatives offered by Rüling, Elberskirchen, and Mayreder were themselves inherently limited. They foreclosed other possible female subjectivities, such as the maternal masculine woman, and evaded the question of erotic queer desire. Perhaps most damningly, Rüling and Elberskirchen's invocation of eugenics bolstered associations of homosexuality with pathology and degeneration.

While these nonnormative subjectivities clearly had their flaws, the intellectual creativity demonstrated by Rüling, Elberskirchen, and Mayreder nonetheless illuminates the productivity of sexual science for feminist ends. Despite the ambivalence and problematic conclusions it fostered, science nonetheless provided these writers with intellectual resources to envision ways of being beyond compulsory heterosexuality and binary gender roles. Science also facilitated these writers' dissent from the maternalist paradigm that increasingly dominated early twentieth-century feminism. Examining the ideas put forward by Rüling, Elberskirchen, and Mayreder reveals the incredible intellectual ferment and controversy surrounding gender and sexuality that existed at the beginning of the twentieth century.

The ideas examined here also exercised an unacknowledged influence on subsequent discussions. Male scientists such as Albert Moll, Iwan Bloch, Magnus Hirschfeld, and Wilhelm Hammer drew upon the work of these women sexologists to elaborate their own understandings of female homosexuality and its connection to feminism—albeit not entirely in complimentary ways.[77] German lesbian movements of the 1920s also treated their work as authoritative, as evidenced by the serialization of Johanna Elberskirchen's *The Love of the Third Sex* in the Weimar-era lesbian newspaper

---

77. See Bloch, *Das Sexualeben unsere Zeit*, 580; Hammer, "Über gleichgeschlechtliche Frauenliebe," 439; Magnus Hirschfeld, *Die Homosexualität des Mannes und Weibes* (Berlin: L. Marcus, 1914), 500.

The Girlfriend in 1929.[78] Similarly, Charlotte Wolff referenced "Dr. Elberskirchen's" theories of homosexuality in her 1986 biography of Magnus Hirschfeld, and even described her writing as "of fundamental importance because her original approach throws new light on the subject."[79] Surprisingly, Anna Rüling even appears in one of the key texts of twentieth-century feminist theory, Simone de Beauvoir's *The Second Sex* (1949), as an authority on the rate of homosexuality among prostitutes (Beauvoir cited Rüling as estimating a rate of "about 20 percent").[80]

Although female sexual theorists dedicated considerable attention to female sexuality, women sexologists did not exclusively focus on issues pertaining to women. Before the First World War, they were also keenly concerned with understanding—and criticizing—male sexuality, specifically male heterosexuality. Importantly, they identified male sexuality as a problem not just for women's freedom, but also for human evolution. In the next chapter, I examine how women sexologists analyzed male sexuality, and how their use of particular scientific resources shaped their perspectives on the possibility of its rehabilitation.

---

78. Johanna Elberskirchen, "Was ist Homosexualität?" *Die Freundin: Wochenschrift für ideale Frauenfreundschaft*, 10, 17, 24 July 1929.

79. Charlotte Wolff, *Magnus Hirschfeld: A Portrait of a Pioneer in Sexology* (London: Quartet Books, 1986), 149. On that same page, Wolff declared that Elberskirchen "proved scientifically the idiocy of male and female stereotypy, and she did it with the brilliance of a mind which dissects an ideological illness with the sharpness of a surgeon's knife." Wolff also identifies Elberskirchen as "a physician and a scientist" (150).

80. Simone de Beauvoir, *The Second Sex*, trans. Constance Borde and Sheila Malovany-Chevallier (New York: Vintage Books, 2010), 619.

4

TROUBLING NORMAL, TAKING ON PATRIARCHY

Criticizing Male (Hetero)Sexuality

On 16 February 1914, former president of the League of German Women's Associations, Marie Stritt, wrote a letter to Dr. Max Hirsch regarding his invitation to contribute to his new journal, the *Archive for Women's Studies (Frauenkunde) and Eugenics*. A pioneer in the fledgling field of *Frauenkunde*, which sought to comprehensively study Woman beyond gynecology,[1] Hirsch aimed to publish cutting-edge scientific research on all matters pertaining to women in order to establish objective—and, as suggested by his journal's title, eugenic—answers to the woman question that preoccupied many Europeans at the beginning of the twentieth century.

---

1. Hirsch viewed *Frauenkunde* as an "inter-disciplinary study combining the expertise of biologists, medical scientists and social scientists. But physicians and especially gynaecologists were meant to have the major responsibility in this enterprise, for they supervised all aspects of life from the cradle to old age." Paul Weindling, *Health, Race, and German Politics between National Unification and Nazism, 1870–1945* (Cambridge: Cambridge University Press, 1993), 257.

In her letter, Stritt not only declined Hirsch's offer, but also called for the establishment of a new journal, the *Archive of Men's Studies* (*Archiv der Männerkunde*).[2] Such a journal, she asserted, would address the fact that while "much thought and talk have been dedicated to the subject of man as a species and concept . . . very little has been written about it and so far there has been no mention of an appropriate study and comprehensive science of man."[3]

Stritt was not alone in her desire for a comprehensive scientific treatment of masculinity, and above all male heterosexuality, that would shift the critical focus from Woman to Man. As moderate feminist leader Helene Lange lamented, "It is never the man, always the woman who is assumed to be the object of observation. Man is the human being par excellence. . . . He establishes the norm against which woman is measured."[4] In making men the "objects of observation," women hoped to create knowledge that could possibly undermine men's legally and socially sanctioned privileges, including in the sexual realm. After all, as Grete Meisel-Hess argued, "as we learn from every-day experience, man, far more often than women, is the primal source of the sorrows, disillusionments, and unending troubles of love."[5]

Such desires for transformative knowledge arguably stemmed from decades' worth of political frustration. Since the mid-nineteenth century, feminists in many European polities had advanced critical analyses of male sexual behavior ranging from the consumption of prostitution to marital rape. Although the aforementioned acts were deplored as immoral and undesirable, feminists nonetheless encountered resistance to their critiques and demands

---

2. As Paul Weindling notes, Hirsch was more successful in marshaling the support of prominent scientific figures such as Havelock Ellis, Alfred Grotjahn, Alfred Hegar, and Wilhelm Schallmeyer. See Weindling, *Health, Race, and German Politics*, 257.

3. Marie Stritt to Max Hirsch, 16.02.1914, Hirsch Nachlaß, Handschriftabteilung, Staatsbibliothek zu Berlin—Preußischer Kulturbesitz.

4. Helene Lange, *Intellektuelle Grenzlinien zwischen Mann und Frau*, 2nd ed. (Berlin: W. Moeser Hofbuchdruckerei, n.d. [est. 1897]), 1.

5. Grete Meisel-Hess, *The Sexual Crisis: A Critique of Our Sexual Life*, trans. Eden Paul and Cedar Paul (New York: Critic and Guide, 1917), 291. Subsequent citations of this work appear parenthetically in the text.

for reform, in large part because men's behavior was naturalized and normalized through medical claims that men required regular sexual activity to maintain good health. In the nineteenth century this medicalized norm of male sexuality, along with that of passive female sexuality, helped underwrite the so-called double standard of sexual morality that differentially evaluated what constituted acceptable sexual behavior for men and women. The sexual double standard espoused and rationalized differential codes of sexual conduct for men and women. While tacitly condoning extramarital sexual behavior among men, it heavily penalized the same behavior among women.

By the turn of the century, however, a number of social, cultural, and economic factors converged to put pressure on prevailing norms of male sexuality and render masculinity and male sexuality objects of social concern. In particular, growing public anxiety regarding the spread of venereal diseases in expanding urban centers like Berlin shifted attention from female prostitutes to their male clientele as the primary vectors of disease. Men's sexual practices became linked to the degeneration of the body politic, and helped to frame male sexuality as racially threatening.

Emboldened by these developments, at the turn of the century some female sexual theorists began engaging science to challenge not only the sexual double standard, but also hegemonic forms of male sexuality. In so doing, they questioned the wisdom of using male sexuality as the basis for the rules of sexual governance. In this chapter, I examine critiques of masculinity and male sexuality from three by now familiar figures: Johanna Elberskirchen, Rosa Mayreder, and Grete Meisel-Hess. In their monographs, these authors drew upon evolutionary theories and even Freudian psychoanalysis to argue that men's existing sexual practices contravened and exceeded nature, with negative implications for the future of humanity. Elberskirchen went further and also referenced sexual biology and anthropological theories of a universal, primordial matriarchy to account for the origins of men's sexual behavior. The kinds of scientific evidence these theorists used had implications for the reforms they proposed to regulate and ameliorate male sexuality.

Masculinity and Its Discontents: Fin-de-Siècle
Discourses on Male Sexuality, Disease,
and Degeneration

Women's sexological critiques of male sexuality emerged at a time
when many middle-class social reformers, commentators, artists,
and intellectuals feared that masculinity itself was in a state of crisis.[6] This sense of crisis was largely inspired by the perceived destabilization of middle-class masculinity. Over the course of the
nineteenth century, an idealized norm of bourgeois masculinity
had developed across Europe that was "at once self-assertive and
self-controlled," defined by its "productivity, economic usefulness,
self-discipline and moderation."[7] According to George Mosse, this
"manly ideal" embodied modern society's "felt need for order and
progress."[8] A corresponding feminine ideal, defined by passivity,
greater emotional expressiveness, and nurturance, provided helpful contrast. However, by the 1890s, contemporaries increasingly
believed that new political, economic, and cultural realities, ranging from feminism to the desegregation of the white-collar workforce to the rise of new, predominantly urban subjects such as the
dandy, were threatening masculinity and patriarchal power itself.[9]

---

6. On the "crisis of masculinity," see Peter Davies, "Introduction: 'Crisis' or
'Hegemony'? Approaches to Masculinity," in *Edinburgh German Yearbook*, vol.
2, *Masculinities in German Culture*, ed. Sarah Colvin and Peter Davies (Rochester: Camden House, 2008), 3–12; Gerald N. Izenberg, *Modernism and Masculinity: Mann, Wedekind, Kandinsky through World War I* (Chicago: University of
Chicago Press, 2000), 5, 7–9; Claudia Opitz-Belakhal, "'Krise der Männlichkeit'—
ein nützliches Konzept der Geschlechtergeschichte?," *L'Homme* 19 (2008): 31–50.
7. Izenberg, *Modernism and Masculinity*, 6. Conditions in turn-of-the-century
Britain offer an insightful parallel to those prevailing in Germany, and are helpfully illuminated in Andrew Smith, *Victorian Demons: Medicine, Masculinity, and
the Gothic at the Fin-de-Siècle* (Manchester: Manchester University Press, 2004),
19–23.
8. George Mosse, *The Image of Man: The Creation of Modern Masculinity*
(Oxford: Oxford University Press, 1996), 77.
9. See Izenberg, *Modernism and Masculinity*, 7–9; Angus Maclaren, *Trials of
Masculinity: Policing Sexual Boundaries, 1870–1930* (Chicago: University of Chicago Press, 1997), 1–2; Judith Allen, "Men Interminably in Crisis? Historians on
Masculinity, Sexual Boundaries, and Manhood," *Radical History Review* 82 (Winter 2002): 200; Edward Ross Dickinson, "'A Dark, Impenetrable Wall of Complete

For many, the growing visibility of male homosexuality, dramatically signified by the scandalous trials of Oscar Wilde, provided the most troubling evidence of masculinity's decline. Conservative social commentators believed that these developments were not only undermining the martial masculinity required for imperial and domestic governance, but also precipitating the feminization of man and the coming of "sexual anarchy."[10] As Mosse observed, "The corruption of the purity and chastity of manhood stood for the sickness and dissolution of society."[11] The "sickness" of masculinity was a widespread preoccupation at the turn of the century, as physicians and social commentators noted increasing rates of nervousness—a trait usually associated with women—among men.[12]

The perceived failings of masculinity were fueled by and contributed to the pervasive discourse on degeneration. Though disease and vice, and health and virtue, had been coupled at least since the beginning of the 1800s,[13] by the end of the nineteenth century these associations coalesced into a medico-scientific and cultural discourse that acquired a name and a diagnostic framework, thanks to studies such as Bénédict Augustin Morel's *Physical, Intellectual, and Moral Traits of Degeneration in the Human Species* (1857), Cesare Lombroso's *Criminal Man* (1876), Ray Lankester's *Degeneration* (1880), and Max Nordau's *Degeneration* (1892).[14] Although the reception and deployment of degeneration discourses

---

Incomprehension': The Impossibility of Heterosexual Love in Imperial Germany," *Central European History* 40 (2007): 487–490.

10. Fin-de-siècle anxieties surrounding sexual anarchy were also international at this time. For an exploration of conditions in the United States and United Kingdom, see Elaine Showalter, *Sexual Anarchy: Gender and Culture at the Fin de Siècle* (New York: Viking, 1990), 9–12. See also Andrew Smith's discussion of Max Nordau's analysis of fin-de-siècle masculinities as degenerative phenomenon, in *Victorian Demons*, especially his chapter entitled "Degeneration, Masculinity, Nationhood and the Gothic."

11. Mosse, *Image of Man*, 80.

12. Ibid., 83–85.

13. Ibid., 79.

14. For a discussion of why the period 1880–1914 is particularly important in understandings of degeneration, see Daniel Pick, *Faces of Degeneration: A European Disorder, c. 1848–c. 1918* (Cambridge: Cambridge University Press, 1989), 20–21.

varied across national contexts, their popularity throughout western Europe fed off anxieties surrounding social, political, and economic instability.[15] Degeneration discourses treated forms of embodiment that indicated a "morbid deviation from an original type" as symptoms of decline and decay.[16] Particularly disconcerting to degeneration theorists was the supposed effeminacy and weakness of modern, urban, middle-class men.

Perhaps the most important catalyst inspiring critical investigations into male sexual behavior and norms of masculinity was the growing anxiety surrounding the spread of venereal diseases in major metropolitan centers at the turn of the century. Alfred Blaschko, a chairman of the German Society for the Fight against Venereal Diseases, estimated in 1892 that 10 percent of Berlin's population was syphilitic.[17] In 1900 he asserted that in Prussia, 3 out of every 1,000 people became sick with an infectious venereal disease daily; he further extrapolated that, out of a population of 56 million, 174,000 were infected with venereal diseases.[18] Meanwhile, Berlin gynecologist Ernst Bumm estimated that 20–30 percent of sterile marriages were due to gonorrheal infections.[19] Venereal diseases were held responsible for causing miscarriages, stillbirths, congenital illnesses, and sterility. They therefore threatened not only those infected, but also their offspring. Beyond their devastating health consequences, venereal diseases and their transmission were subjects of concern among social reformers on moral grounds.

---

15. Ibid., 7–10.

16. Bénédict Augustin Morel, *Traité des dégénérescences physiques, intellectuelles et morales de l'espèce humaine* (1857); quoted in Max Nordau, *Degeneration*, 9th ed. (London: William Heinemann, 1896), 16.

17. Weindling, *Health, Race, and German Politics*, 174.

18. See Siegfried Borelli, Hermann-Joseph Vogt, and Michael Kreis, eds., *Geschichte der deutschen Gesellschaft zur Bekämpfung der Geschlechtskrankheiten* (Berlin: Blackwell, 1992), 25. See also Lutz Sauerteig, "'The Fatherland Is in Danger, Save the Fatherland!' Venereal Disease, Sexuality, and Gender in Imperial and Weimar Germany," in *Sex, Sin, and Suffering: Venereal Disease and European Society since 1870*, ed. Roger Davidson and Lesley A. Hall (London: Routledge, 2001), 76.

19. Weindling, *Health, Race, and German Politics*, 174.

For many, the spread of venereal diseases like syphilis and gonorrhea symbolized the larger crisis of sexual morality they believed
was afflicting society as a whole.[20] Even socialists viewed venereal
disease metaphorically: in his widely influential text *Woman and
Socialism*, leader of the Social Democratic Party August Bebel declared that venereal disease was the result of the repressive nature
of the bourgeois family, and especially the suppression of women's
sexuality.[21] In many ways, public concern with venereal diseases
marked the extension of long-standing anxieties surrounding prostitution; however, preexisting anxieties were now amplified by new
developments. Intensive urbanization, particularly in Germany,
created greater awareness and visibility of the disease, while scientific advances in the later nineteenth and early twentieth century led
to the discovery of the bacteriological origins of venereal disease.[22]
Furthermore, increasing scientific and public interest in eugenics
at the turn of the century drew attention to the role of syphilis
and gonorrhea in causing hereditarily transmitted illnesses. Venereal diseases, alongside alcohol, were viewed as pernicious "racial
poisons" that caused an array of pathological conditions that damaged "the quality of the nation's hereditary stock."[23]

Whereas female prostitutes had been the primary object of
medico-scientific concern in the fight against venereal diseases during the ninenteenth century, in the early twentieth century attention shifted to men's role in spreading venereal disease throughout
the broader population. Blaschko asserted in 1901 that for every
10,000 adult men (over the age of fifteen) in Berlin, 83 were in
treatment for gonorrhea and 36 for syphilis.[24] In 1903, he maintained that two-thirds of all those suffering with venereal diseases

---

20. On this point, see Ann Taylor Allen, "Feminism, Venereal Disease, and the
State in Germany, 1890–1918," *Journal of the History of Sexuality* 4 (July 1993):
27–50.

21. Weindling, *Health, Race, and German Politics*, 94.

22. Albert Neisser identified *Gonococcus bacillus* as the cause of gonorrhea in
1879. F. Scahudinn and Erich Hoffmann pinpointed *Treponema pallidum* as the
cause of syphilis in 1905.

23. Weindling, *Health, Race, and German Politics*, 246.

24. Borelli, Vogt, and Kreis, *Geschichte der deutschen Gesellschaft*, 25.

were young men between the ages of twenty and thirty; indeed, he estimated that, on an annual basis, out of every 1,000 young men between twenty and thirty, almost 200 became infected with gonorrhea, and 24 with syphilis.[25] Growing scrutiny of male sexuality was consistent across northern Europe at the turn of the century, as Roger Davidson and Lesley A. Hall have noted.[26] Increasingly, normal male sexuality was represented as posing a pathological threat to the wider body politic. Contemporaneous literary works such as Henrik Ibsen's *Ghosts* (1881) dramatized the physical and psychological suffering men inflicted via venereal disease not only upon their immediate victims, but also upon hereditarily tainted next generations. Such turn-of-the-century texts represented men who cavorted with prostitutes or other extramarital partners as poisoning their sexually naive wives and unborn children, thereby imperiling racial health and progress. Diverse commentators and activists began to suggest that putatively normal male sexuality was a problem for social and racial hygiene.

Critical attention to men's roles as vectors for the spread of venereal disease also helped expose contradictions within the bourgeois ideal of masculinity.[27] Specifically, it illuminated the conflict between man's self-discipline and his sexual instincts. On the one hand, as mentioned earlier, middle-class masculinity was defined by its supposedly superior capacity for self-control and moderation, particularly over animalistic sexual desires. On the other hand, the normal man was also attributed with an instinctual need for regular sexual fulfillment that exceeded the needs of the normal woman. This latter assertion had served to legitimize prostitution as a necessary evil that prevented men from becoming "pests" to their wives. Yet given the apparent frequency with which men's sexual desires won out over their self-control—and the dangerous

---

25. Ibid., 21.

26. Roger Davidson and Lesley A. Hall, "Introduction," in Davidson and Hall, *Sex, Sin and Suffering*, 10.

27. In his reading of British self-help literature, Andrew Smith skillfully demonstrates how this tension was elemental to paradigms of middle-class masculinity since at least the mid-nineteenth century. See Smith, *Victorian Demons*, 19–23.

racial consequences of this capitulation—the tensions within the bourgeois masculine ideal were becoming increasingly clear.

Although the German state did not treat venereal disease as a matter of pressing regulatory or legislative concern until the outbreak of the First World War, between 1899 and 1914 civil society mobilized. Feminists were particularly active on this issue. For feminists, venereal diseases were disconcerting not only because of the threat they posed to public health, but also because of the dangers they posed to women, above all married women, who could be unknowingly infected by their husbands.[28] The German Abolitionist Federation, which opposed the state regulation of prostitution and was led by Anna Pappritz and Katharina Scheven, played a major role in publicizing the dangers of venereal disease infection. The activity of feminists like Pappritz and Scheven was also instrumental in shifting the focus away from prostitutes and onto average men as the loci of disease transmission. Here, they criticized men's privacy rights, including within the physician-patient relationship, that feminists claimed kept women ignorant of the risks of infection they faced. Furthermore, they sought to make women aware of the health risks they might incur upon marriage to men "with a past."

New organizations were also formed at this time specifically to try to halt the spread of venereal diseases. The First International Congress for the Fight against Venereal Diseases, held in Brussels on 19 September 1899, played a catalytic role in the formation of the German Society for the Fight against Venereal Diseases, established in 1902. According to its founding documents, the society's early goals included combating ignorance and shame by publicly discussing sexual dangers, eradicating prejudice toward people with venereal diseases through popular education, attempting to shape legislation that would help prevent and treat venereal diseases, and fighting against prostitution using "practical means."[29] Although its membership never exceeded 5,000 in the prewar

---

28. Ann Taylor Allen, "German Radical Feminism and Eugenics, 1900–1908," *German Studies Review* 11 (Feb. 1988): 44.

29. Borelli, Vogt, and Kreis, *Geschichte der deutschen Gesellschaft,* 19–21.

period,[30] the society's members included a number of high-profile figures and participants, such as the well-known medical reformers and esteemed scientists Alfred Blaschko and Albert Neisser, and leading feminists Henriette Fürth, Anna Pappritz, Katharina Scheven, Helene Stöcker, Anita Augspurg, Lida Gustava Heymann, Marie Stritt, and Rosa Mayreder. Although the society brought together a diverse group of men and women who shared a concern with venereal diseases and how to prevent them, it also served as a site of conflict among these actors regarding effective and just solutions to this problem.

The conflicts within the society regarding the regulation of venereal diseases were a microcosm of broader social struggles concerning the governance of male sexuality. Despite increasing critical attention devoted to male sexual behavior and its social effects, many male medical experts remained reluctant to advocate measures to discipline male sexuality. While anti–venereal disease activists of all stripes broadly agreed upon the desirability of certain social hygienic measures such as sexual education, treatment clinics, and legally mandated premarital health examinations, the treatment of male sexuality within anti-VD programs consistently provoked conflict.[31] Most men within the German Society for the Fight against Venereal Diseases continued to support the state regulation of prostitution, much to the consternation of their feminist colleagues, and even sought the transfer of regulatory authority from the police to public health officials.[32] They also promoted a

---

30. Ibid., 28.

31. For contemporary feminist examples of such demands, see Lida Gustava Heymann, "III. Kongreß der deutschen Gesellschaft zur Bekämpfung der Geschlechtskrankheiten," *Der Abolitionist* 3 (1904): 65–66; Maria Lischnewska, "Die geschlechtliche Belehrung der Kinder," *Mutterschutz* 1 (1905): 137–170; Henriette Fürth, "Der Aufklärungsunterricht: Ein Beitrag zur Sexualpädagogik," *Sozialistische Monatshefte* 12 (1908): 243–246; and Fürth, "Sexualpädagogik und Sexualethik," *Sozialistische Monatshefte* 12 (1908): 564–568. See also the Bund für Mutterschutz's 1906 petition to the Reichstag, "Einführung der geschlechtlichen Belehrung in den Schulunterricht," Folders 3.1 Frauenbewegung, 3.1.1 Bund für Mutterschutz, 29; Thesen, Aufrufe, Flugblätter, Petitionen und Veröffentlichungen des BfM, Schreiber Nachlass, Bundesarchiv Koblenz.

32. Allen, "Feminism, Venereal Disease, and the State in Germany," 32.

range of other measures that would safeguard the health of male clients and effectively preserve the sexual status quo, such as the distribution of prophylactics and the use of pharmaceutical treatments for venereal disease such as Salvarsan, which entered clinical use in 1910 and proved more effective than existing treatments involving mercury salts.[33] Conversely, women sexologists and feminists insisted upon new standards of sexual morality and new modes of sexual governance that would empower women to regulate male sexuality, including marriage certificates that attested to the health of marital partners[34] and, later, criminalization of venereal disease transmission.[35] In the view of many feminists, laws seeking to regulate sexual conduct should affect men and women equally.

Male scientists within and beyond the society rationalized their position by arguing that male sexual traits and behavior were products of evolutionary instinct and sexual physiology. They claimed that men possessed an aggressive, powerful sexual instinct that sought to satisfy their innate sexual needs. In Richard von Krafft-Ebing's view, a man's sexuality was guided by "a powerful natural drive" that made him "aggressive and stormy in his love-play."[36] At times this aggressive instinct could be so overpowering that it overwhelmed a man's attempts at resistance and self-discipline and even lead to sexual violence. Krafft-Ebing went as far as to claim that sadism was merely "a pathological exaggeration of the male sexual character."[37] Male scientists further asserted that the

---

33. For further details on the debate among feminists and male physicians regarding male and female sexuality and their appropriate regulation, see Dickinson, "'A Dark, Impenetrable Wall.'"

34. See Adele Schreiber, "Die Anfang neuer Sittlichkeitsbegriffe in Hinblick auf die Mutterschaft," in *Mutterschaft: Ein Sammelwerk für die Problems des Weibes als Mutter*, ed. Adele Schreiber (Munich: Langen, 1912), 163–188, as an example of feminists' advocacy of marriage certificates.

35. Norway and Denmark passed such laws in 1860 and 1906, respectively, which legally required both men and women to submit to treatment and penalty for knowingly exposing others to infection. The Norwegian law included a penalty of up to three years in prison for this offense. See Allen, "Feminism, Venereal Disease, and the State in Germany," 42.

36. Dickinson, "'A Dark Impenetrable Wall,'" 472.

37. Ibid., 476.

strength and aggression of male sexuality necessarily exceeded the boundaries of monogamy. In a curious turn of phrase, psychiatrist Paul Näcke claimed that men were "by nature polygamous and inclined to sexual 'snacking.'"[38]

Within their analyses of male sexuality, these male sexual scientists asserted that their observations were neutral, and that they arrived at their conclusions through objective study. They insisted that because male sexuality was a product of nature, it should be subject to neither moral censure nor social regulation. However, women sexologists developed their own analyses to refute such contentions, and to further argue that, for the good of men, women, and the future of the race, male sexuality ought to be subordinated to what they argued were the more altruistic impulses of female sexuality. They drew upon scientific evidence to prove that their arguments and solutions were justified not only by social needs, but also by biological realities.

Discerning the True Nature of Male Sexuality

In order to understand masculinity, female sexual theorists probed the evolution and psychology of male sexuality, drawing attention to its innate qualities and how they informed a man's total personality. They further probed how male sexuality impacted relations between the sexes, and the very constitution of the social order.

Rosa Mayreder insisted that masculinity and male sexuality must be considered in light of historical developments, specifically the rise of civilization and its effects on sexual roles and relations. Here she developed an evolutionary framework that treated gender as plastic and as fundamentally tied to and shaped by cultural and sociopolitical changes. According to Mayreder, "The conception of masculinity in modern society rules like an ancient idol which is still publicly worshipped and served with prescribed sacrifices, although it has long ceased to work miracles. The ideas connected with this are made up of remnants of bygone ages and survivals

---

38. Ibid., 474.

of relationships."[39] These "remnants" are the two types of masculinity that Mayreder maintained have been in conflict with one another since the earliest days of civilization: namely, primitive masculinity, "which is based on the utmost development of physical faculties," and what Mayreder calls "differentiated masculinity," which is "directed to the development and the increase of the intellectual faculties" (94). This conflict between "the power arising from physical superiority" and "the power arising from intellectual superiority" has long "struggl[ed] for mastery within the male sex itself," and found its oldest cultural representations in the contrast between the warrior and the priest (94).

Although Mayreder believed that turn-of-the-century masculinity was profoundly "differentiated," she nonetheless acknowledged that the further evolution of masculinity into what she viewed as a higher, more intellectually and spiritually elevated form was inhibited by the persistence of primitive masculinity. Part of this persistence, she suggested, stemmed from biology: "The warlike element in masculine nature has its origin in neuro-muscular activity. In general the male sex is brave and aggressive on account of its muscular strength, while the female sex is timid and passive because of its muscular weakness" (99). In any event, vestigial primitive masculinity inculcated a state of mind that prevented men from fully embracing their differentiated nature. Mayreder described modern man as "suffer[ing] through his intellectuality as from an illness" (108). Modern man continually sought to cling to his "primitive" strength; consequently, Mayreder claimed, "this fear of appearing unmanly, or displaying any lack of that virility attributed to the primitive ideal of the sex, serves to maintain all the preposterous atavistic prejudices, all the senseless, incompatible tendencies of which the life of the modern man is so full" (109).

This struggle was particularly true in the sexual realm. It was within the sexual realm that the conflict between men's "primitive" and "differentiated" natures was most starkly realized. According

39. Rosa Mayreder, *A Survey of the Woman Problem*, trans. Herman Scheffauer (London: Heinemann, 1913), 91. Subsequent citations of this work appear parenthetically in the text.

to Mayreder, "Civilisation makes demands on him which are at variance with his teleological nature as a male. It is the teleology of his primitive sexual instincts that determines the intractability of the impulse which asserts itself beyond all restraint in the individual soul, and shapes the personality towards its own ends" (115). The development of men's intellect does not curb or kill this "primitive instinct"; rather, Mayreder argued, "when the masculine intellect, having developed itself in the direction of abstract study and grown out of proportion by force of 'specialising' in one particular field, incurs the danger of disturbing the relation of the individual to the totality of life, then the masculine temperament disturbs its equilibrium still more by dividing the individual into a spiritual being . . . and an animal being, degraded to the lowest level of sexual existence" (116). Mayreder declared that the current arrangements of sexual life reveal that "the sexual instinct is the most dangerous enemy to self-mastery in a man. In seducing the individual into sinking below the level of his personality, it assumes the aspect of an irresistible force and destroys the consciousness of that inner liberty which springs out of the ability of the higher impulses of the will to resist the lower" (119).

Mayreder tied primitive masculinity to the sexual instincts of a male type she called the masterful lover or masterful man, a kind of man "who will have nothing in common with women, who will not suffer her to enjoy the same rights as himself" (194).[40] The masterful man was the purveyor of what she characterized as an erotic of the "strong fist," which depended not only upon aggression and violence but also upon the subordination and sexual objectification of women to achieve sexual satisfaction. In Mayreder's words, "The sexual relationship for the masterful man is bound up with the idea that woman is a lower order of being, essentially different from man but created for his purposes. The sexual relationship ministers to his sense of superiority—it gives him the sensation

---

40. To be clear, when Mayreder used the term "masterful" to describe this kind of man as lover, she—or rather, her translator—meant to suggest a domineering attitude toward sex. In the original text, Mayreder uses the phrases "Männer der herrischen Erotik" and "herrische Männlichkeit"; Rosa Mayreder, *Zur Kritik der Weiblichkeit* (Jena: Eugen Diedrichs, 1905), 211.

of power and possession" (194–195). According to Mayreder, an "element of the cruel is latent always in the masterful lover, and it discloses itself in the craving to make the woman feel the weight of the strong hand"; she insisted that when this cruelty "becomes connected with morbid instincts," it shades into sadism (216). For Mayreder, the apotheosis of the masterful man in modern life was the man who beat his wife (195).

True erotic pleasure for masterful men derived from their sense of power over women and the associated belief that they could conquer every female being if and when they wanted (201). This is why masterful men highly esteemed virginity and the sexually restrained woman: "He cherishes the idea that the woman offers herself up as a sacrifice" (197). This pleasure stemmed from a pernicious, misogynistic view of women: as Mayreder observed, "According to the masterful man, a weak, inferior creature, without individuality—such as the woman of his conception—can have no control over herself; she is bound to succumb to temptation once she comes under the power of a masculine will" (199).

For Mayreder, contemporary gender dysfunctions emerged precisely from the sexual inclinations of the masterful man: "It may be said . . . that the position of the female sex in life is established in accordance with the sexual instincts of the domineering type of man" (195). In her view, masterful men's sexuality produced a "state of terrorism" that bore "most hardly upon the higher order of cultured women" by turning a blind eye to "the existence of any other kind of woman than that of which he has need," and treating "all women [as] of a piece . . ., scarcely distinguishable one from another" (199). He therefore "prefers to designate as pathological anomalies all aspects of womanliness that do not accord with it. A woman who seeks independence, a woman of strongly-marked individuality, is in his eyes either a neurotic or else a mass of affection; and he always detects the influence of a man in anything that a woman happens to achieve in the field of the intellect" (200). It was the masterful man who conceived "love as a battle" (207). Moreover, Mayreder saw the masterful type of man and his sexuality as dangerous because he applied the strong fist not just to the female, but to all life phenomena: "The 'strong hand' which they use toward women they use in all the contingencies of life. They ride rough-shod over the world as well as over their wives, and they sacrifice their weaker fellow-men to their own ends" (196). Man's single-minded sexual selfishness and aggression thus extended itself beyond the bedroom, and may help explain man's lust for sociopolitical power and control. Although Mayreder conceded that "masterful" sexuality may have served an evolutionary purpose at an earlier moment of development—"the illusion of superiority," she suggested, may be "seen to be a device of Nature for providing the man with the necessary aggressive self-confidence required for his sexual conquest"—such behavior was reflective of a "primitive order of life in which the individual is rather a propagative unit than a personality" (203). On the "higher planes of life," such behavior appears "very ridiculous" (204).

Mayreder was not alone in viewing prevailing impulses of male sexuality as "primitive," or in arguing that men's sexual characteristics directed their actions beyond the bedroom: writers like Grete Meisel-Hess and Johanna Elberskirchen also believed that men's sexuality shaped their entire personality. Meisel-Hess adopted a psychological approach to male sexuality that endeavored to analyze the relationship between modern man's mind, drives, and cultural environment; as we will see, it drew upon and redeployed psychoanalytic concepts. In Meisel-Hess's view, the "strongest impulse of [man's] own nature [is] the impulse to the discharge of sexual tensions" (*Sexual Crisis*, 292). With respect to their sexuality men were like children: like children, men were "remarkabl[y] susceptib[le] . . . to the influence of suggestion," were "endowed with a considerable element of childish greed, the greed of acquirement, the greed of possession, so long as [their] desire is resisted," and shared "the impulse to spoil or to throw away [their] new possession when its first freshness has worn off, and when the novelty of ownership has begun to stale" (291). In her view, modern men suffer from a "peculiar form of sexual dependence," namely, upon "some special fetich": "In almost all men . . . erotic sensibilities can be aroused only by some peculiar shade of sensation" (287). Whereas Mayreder viewed male sexuality as tending toward sadism, Meisel-Hess believed it was more inclined toward a kind of spiritual masochism, evidenced in men's predilection for women who were "masterful" and "frigid" (298). "Man now seeks a severe mistress, one whose domination he will be unable to escape," she maintained (299). These women offered to men a kind of "security imposed by the proximity of strong and severe natures"—and even "by a subflavor of suggestion . . . the ideas of a mother, the sort of mother that everyone would like to have had, strong, and leading onwards" (299). Meisel-Hess's claim that men seek out a mother figure, unbeknownst to their conscious selves, reveals her familiarity with and manipulation of emerging psychoanalytic themes.

In agreement with Mayreder, Meisel-Hess observed that, as a consequence of the peculiarities of modern male sexuality, men were unable to appreciate women as personalities, and instead viewed them as belonging to a singular type: "Numerous indeed are the men who lack the very beginnings of the power to understand the individuality of women of the higher type; and rarer still are those competent to understand such women to the full, and therewith truly to enjoy them" (301). Men use and abandon women "of noble and self-sacrificing type" (292); for this reason, Meisel-Hess argued that "the so-called new women"—like herself—were the greatest victims of current conditions: "The tragedy of their lives is that they have been born too soon" (301). Meisel-Hess maintained that whereas "frigid women readily attain to marriage and to procreation," "healthier and more ardent women, those who give themselves freely and are therefore more genuinely woman, rarely succeed . . . in effecting permanent sexual associations with such men as predominate to-day" (294). For this reason, Meisel-Hess suggested that women may be better off channeling their impulses of "self-surrender" into "channels of friendship, philanthropy, and even love of pets"; in her view, "it is better to bestow this kind of tenderness upon a favorite cat or a lap-dog than to bestow it without limit upon a man" (292).

From the perspective of these writers, men seemed innately and single-mindedly interested and invested in the pursuit of their own perverse sexual satisfaction. In her assessment of the overweening importance of sex for men, Johanna Elberskirchen reversed Otto

Weininger's claim that women were nothing more than sex by asserting that sex constituted the first and deepest point of life for men. In her words, "Sexual life in its most repulsive, sickest form was the first and deepest meaning of life for men, God Priapos their highest deity!"[41] Elberskirchen even refused to characterize male sexuality as bestial because "the animal does not know sexual degeneration" (87). Based on her understanding of male heterosexuality as below bestial, in *Revolution!* Elberskirchen elaborated a grand narrative that held male sexuality directly and brutally responsible for women's subordination. Elberskirchen drew upon anthropological claims of a universally prevalent primordial matriarchate and evolutional theories to assert that men's self-serving sexuality led them to usurp women's rightful roles as centers of the social order and regulators of sexual life.[42] Based on her reading of scientific writings by Darwin, Jean-Baptiste Lamarck, and Oscar Hertwig, as well as the anthropological studies of J. J. Bachofen and Friedrich Engels, Elberskirchen argued that women's social subordination and sexual disempowerment were caused by the fall of the matriarchy and the rise of patriarchal civilization based on private property and individual rather than collective enrichment. According to Elberskirchen, women could not equally compete within or participate in systems based on individual accumulation because of the demands of pregnancy and childcare. Women's material dependency in turn enabled men to sexually dominate women and force women to service their excessive sexual lust. In Elberskirchen's words, "With the overthrow of matriarchy, the emergence of private property and of slavery, and with the onset of the degeneration of the man's sexual instinct, the woman fell into

41. Johanna Elberskirchen, *Was hat der Mann aus Weib, Kind und sich gemacht? Revolution und Erlösung des Weibes: Eine Abrechnung mit dem Mann—ein Wegweiser in die Zukunft!* 3rd ed. (N.p: Magazin-Verlag, 1904), 87. Subsequent citations of this work appear parenthetically in the text.

42. On the popularity of matriarchal theories at this time, see Ann Taylor Allen, "Feminism, Social Science, and the Meanings of Modernity: The Debate on the Origins of the Family in Europe and the United States, 1860–1914," *American Historical Review* 104 (October 1999): 1085–1113.

the sexual servitude of man. The woman was unfree, a servant, a slave" (73, 75, 77).

Men's domination of women, sexually and materially, led men's sexual instincts to become decadent, as men could force women to fulfill their sexual desires out of proportion with their sexual needs. Consequently, she asserted, men's sex drive had become unnaturally aroused, in turn requiring an unnatural satisfaction (76). As she put it, "The sex drive of the man became unnaturally aroused and required an unnatural, over-natural satisfaction. The man could achieve this satisfaction: the female was in his economic power, at least under his economic supreme authority, and not he, but rather the female, had to carry the physiological consequences of this satisfaction, the child!" (76). The unrestricted possibility of sex also caused men to lose sight of what constituted real sexual needs, and to confuse their decadent standard with a healthy one. For Elberskirchen, then, men's seizure of social and political power was bound up with their sexual desires and instincts. She implied that it was man's innate sexual selfishness, which permeated his entire being, which drove him both to accumulate private property and to sexually dominate women. Male sexuality and material dependence were represented as the interconnected causes of women's downfall.

Elberskirchen further argued that women's evolution had been hampered by patriarchal modes of sexual governance, which placed men unnaturally in charge of sexual selection. Here she drew upon Darwin's theory of sexual selection, as outlined in *The Descent of Man* (1871). Darwinian sexual selection postulated that within the mating process, males and females play distinctive yet equally important roles. Significantly for women like Elberskirchen, the theory asserted that although males were responsible for wooing the female and fighting off competitors, females exercised the final decision over mate selection. Moreover, sexual selection theory held that mate selection was based upon criteria that would contribute to the improvement of the species.

According to Elberskirchen, much in line with the principles of private property ownership, men exercised sexual selection not in the interests of racial advancement, but rather according to their own individual inclinations. Men selected women who would satisfy their sexual desires, expressing a marked preference for subservient, passive, and superficially beautiful women. Such women, Elberskirchen asserted, were "best designed to serve the degenerate sexual lust of man—[they were] without will and without the capacity to resist." With such a prevailing standard of sexual selection, Elberskirchen maintained that men could hereditarily perpetuate women's biological and psychological inferiority in order to maintain unequal relations between men and women (*Revolution*, 79–80). In her view, men had transformed woman via perverse selective practices into a sexual object, "a sad and sadness-arousing torso of human strength and beauty" (88). Importantly, Elberskirchen was not alone in lamenting the evolutionary and eugenic consequences of male sexual degeneration. Grete Meisel-Hess similarly asserted that men's "blunted [sexual] senses" not only rendered them "insufficiently stimulated in a union with his most favorable biological complement," but also ensured that they found "such a union tedious" (*Sexual Crisis*, 287).

Female sexual theorists' analyses of male sexuality offer a damning view of male sexuality and masculinity. They further suggest that women's prospects for equality and fulfillment within heterosexuality were bleak. Some theorists argued that modern male sexuality was incapable of intimacy, and had destroyed the grounds of understanding between men and women. Marking the gulf between female and male sexuality at this particular moment in time, Meisel-Hess pointedly observed, "It happens in our day the regeneration of one sex is coincident with the manifest degeneration of the other" (301). According to Meisel-Hess, the men of her generation were unable to initiate, sustain, or even recognize loving relationships with "ardent," healthy women. Men's inability to love, as well as their dependence upon sexual fetishes for the attainment of sexual enjoyment, were, she maintained, "common characteristic phenomen[a] of our time [that are] pathological in character, the outcome of a disease to which Professor Freud of Vienna has given the name of *sexual neurosis* (also *sexual psycho-neurosis* or *sexual compulsion-neurosis*)" (153; emphasis in original). This neurosis, she asserted, is characterized by the presence of "physical sexual tension, to the degree of ardent desire," alongside "psychic inadequacy for its discharge" (154). Following Freud again, she claimed that another characteristic of the "sexual compulsion neurosis" was the "exaggerated conscientiousness of the sufferers," which prevented them from acting on their sexual impulse and instead transformed them into "sexual cripples" and "masculine *demi-vierges*" (154–155). According to Meisel-Hess, male "sexual cripples are to-day in the majority"; she evocatively diagnosed them as "remain[ing] susceptible to stimuli and yet are dead within." Referencing Ibsen's *Ghosts*, she described their souls as "worm-eaten" (155). Meisel-Hess further argued that men's sexual neurosis helped create the "dread of woman" that she perceived as "so characteristic of contemporary males." "From the sexual excitement produced by woman arises," she declared, "the conflict which is the very essence of this disease" (154). The fundamental problem was that men want to have sex with women, but feared becoming entangled with them, particularly women who may be their equals. Quoting herself from an earlier text, she argued that modern men were

> unable to surmount the ultimate obstacles between I and Thou. . . . Their amatory intimacies are never fully consummated. They get through the preliminaries of love and the first preludes; but that which comes afterwards, the most beautiful and also the most difficult part, remains unenjoyed, unmastered, unconsummated. I am not referring here to what is ordinarily termed impotence. This sentimental impotence has nothing to do with mere physical weakness, but is far more disastrous, since it forever debars those affected with it from an entry into the deepest experiences of love. (155)

Meisel-Hess concluded that men's pathological inability to love, particularly to love women who may be their equals, predisposed her male contemporaries to vacillate between the extremes of sexual renunciation and sexual excess.

According to female sexual theorists such as Elberskirchen, Mayreder, and Meisel-Hess, men's degenerated sexuality had transformed heterosexuality into a toxic institution. As Edward Ross Dickinson has observed, by positing fundamental differences between male and female sexuality, women writers like these three, alongside many of their male sexual scientific counterparts, suggested a fundamental incommensurability between modern men and women.[43] Elberskirchen and Meisel-Hess further maintained that men's pathological sexuality had broader consequences beyond the possibilities of individual heterosexual intimacies, and implicated the fate of humanity. In light of such conclusions, what kinds of reforms were possible?

Competing Visions of Sexual Reform: Equality, Matriarchy, Asexuality

Despite sharing a dim view of male sexuality, women sexologists advanced different visions for the reform of sexual life. Mayreder and Meisel-Hess believed that male sexuality could be remade and improved by creating conditions of greater equality in social and sexual life via changes to law and sexual ethics. Conversely, Elberskirchen insisted that, given the innate incommensurability between male and female sexuality and the degenerative effects of male sexuality, radical change was needed that would return women to the center of social and sexual life. Their divergent attitudes toward sexual reform can in part be explained by the kinds of scientific ideas and evidence they invoked.

For Mayreder and Meisel-Hess, the reform of male sexuality—and heterosexuality itself—was possible, but depended upon profound social reforms and a transformation of gender ideologies. They insisted that true love and partnership, both social and sexual, were possible only when conditions of equality existed between the sexes. As part of this equality, they demanded that men begin to recognize women as individuals with different, fully developed personalities and dreams and life goals of their own. Part of the reason that Mayreder and Meisel-Hess were optimistic about the prospects of reforming male sexuality lay in the fact that they believed that male and female sexualities and subjectivities were the products of evolution and its mechanisms, such as sexual selection.

---

43. On this point, see Dickinson, "'A Dark Impenetrable Wall.'"

Importantly, evolutionary theory does not relate a linear narrative of either progress or decline: rather, it is premised upon the possibility of change and adaptation.[44] As Rosa Mayreder asked of her fellow feminists, "Inasmuch as sexuality has, during the evolution of civilisation, become sublimated into love, why should a biological change, destined to influence still further the psychosexual disposition of the sexes, be regarded as a mere Utopian assumption?" (*Survey of the Woman Problem*, 221).

Mayreder for one was confident that "the increasing intellectualisation of humanity," which she believed characterized the trajectory of Western civilization, would eventually produce a better kind of man. For her, part of the problem with contemporary manhood was that men were living in a time of evolutionary change and transition, one that exacerbated the strain between their "primitive" instincts and their strivings for progress. The tensions in the male condition were further highlighted by the fact that, thanks in part to the feminist movement, women's roles were changing and becoming more "like men." Mayreder insisted that contemporary life showed "how liable to modification are the characteristics which we are inclined to label once and for all as masculine or feminine" (105). The solution to the problem of male sexuality lay for Mayreder in men's full embrace of the trajectory of evolution. Men must embrace the evolution of their being toward the "differentiated" model of masculinity, and allow their intellectual refinement to "extend to the sexual side of [their] nature." "To be reborn in a new masculinity," Mayreder declared, men "must do away with all the prejudices and weaknesses which belong to the primitive manhood, retaining only those elements which are inseparable from [their] nature as [men]" (123).

Mayreder believed that men would only be able to fully embrace their differentiated masculinity and triumph over the "temptations of sex" through a "higher determination of the will," which would

---

44. For this reason, present-day feminists such as Elizabeth Grosz continue to view evolutionary theory as a serviceable narrative for feminists. See Elizabeth Grosz, *Time Travels: Feminism, Nature, Power* (Durham, NC: Duke University Press, 2005), 13–53.

prevail if "the conditions of the individual's life [were] favorable." However, she pointed out that modern life was characterized by conditions that everywhere "expose [men] and the claims of [their] sexuality to the worst conditions," which ensured that "debasement is unavoidable from the moment that personality and sexual impulse are in conflict" (121). The conditions producing this conflict stemmed from what Mayreder saw as the unnatural channeling of sex life into either marriage or prostitution. Upholding marriage as the only legitimate outlet for sexuality means that boys are improperly educated not only about sexuality but also about love: "At the age when their organism is beginning to tremble under the shocks of approaching manhood, they are treated like sexless machines, condemned to the tedium of dull lessons and the unwholesomeness of a sedentary life. . . . They are thus in their most impressionable years allowed to blunt their sensibility . . . and to become deaf to the warnings of Nature" (120). Mayreder maintained that this insufficient education virtually ensured that young men would become inhibited from realizing "the right to love during the very period in which Nature most strongly urges it" (117). Consequently, she observed, young men were "condemn[ed] . . . in the prime of [their] youth to have sexual relations with the lowest order of woman—those who earn their livelihood by prostitution" (117). Notably, Mayreder did not deny here that men may have instinctive sexual urges, but believed they must be trained and properly channeled to reflect and correlate with the current state of civilization. Moreover, male sexuality must be directed toward appropriate gender *and class* objects.

Clearly, in Mayreder's view a new sexual-ethical order was required, one that was more in touch with the realities of evolution. Although Mayreder did not explicitly call for recognition of free-love unions as Meisel-Hess did by championing "erotic friendships" (discussed further in chapter 5), she did believe that the two conflicting sides of men's nature could be reconciled through love. Love could serve as the bridge between the mind and the body, and could help men gain mastery over their sexual impulse, for "love permits of the sexual relation being transfused with a content of personality" (117). Mayreder defined love as "the emotion which permits of the fulfilling of the task of generation in a spirit of self-respect, as distinguished from lust, which is limited to a purely physical desire for sexual intercourse" (208). A precondition of love, in her view, was "[a] real communication of souls between individuals of opposite sex"—a skill only possible in the present between women and men who had attained "a high development in the sphere of psycho-sexuality" (208). The "man with a genius for love," Mayreder maintained, was able to treat women "with intuitive understanding," and was "capable of completely assimilating himself with them" (209). He did not experience sexual and loving intimacy with women as a kind of loss of either personal integrity or self-respect, but rather as a form of spiritual enrichment. Moreover, he was capable of union with a woman who was a fully realized, complex, and individual personality, and was not merely a projection of his own "domineering" erotic tastes. Between these two equals, Mayreder noted, bonds of "unextinguishable friendship" were forged that did "not end when the phase of rapture has passed" (210). Ultimately, in Mayreder's view this "unextinguishable friendship" between two equal personalities, accomplished through the subordination of lust to love, the intellectual domination of sexual impulses, the eradication of fantastical projections of gender norms, and the full inclusion of women in public life, would provide the foundation for the regeneration of heterosexuality.

Mayreder maintained that women, currently men's sexual and ethical superiors, could serve not only as models toward which men could aspire, but also uplifting influences on masculinity and male sexuality. According to her, the consequence of centuries of demanding sexual purity and monogamic loyalty from women meant that they had developed a superior sexual consciousness and self-mastery that made them well equipped to regulate sexual life. "Whether or not sexuality bears a different ratio to the totality of a woman's nature, or whether the sexual differentiation be only the outcome of the demands on women made by men," she asserted, "certain it is that woman's strenuous striving after sexual purity and her exclusive self-surrender to the one man of her choice have resulted in the refining and ennobling of sexual consciousness among women. The heroism of self-mastery which women display in thus insisting upon the sexual integrity of the personality is a form of superiority which cannot but make itself felt as soon as the recognized restrictions of their social position shall have been done away with. It already places them above the newer form of manhood" (122–123). Mayreder suggested that women's greater involvement in public life "as a social fellow-worker" might help to achieve a change in sexual life, "that field where one-sided masculine civilisation has failed" (123). On this basis, she confidently asserted that "the part taken by women in modern ideals of culture, in the liberation of the individual for the purpose of his unfettered spiritual development, in the battle for the rights of a free personality, will not, in the long run, pass without leaving its definite stamp upon the organisation of society" (222).

Like Mayreder, Grete Meisel-Hess believed that male sexuality was malleable. Throughout her discussions of male sexuality, she was careful to qualify that her comments pertained to men of "today," or to "modern men." According to Meisel-Hess, "the sensual impotence of our contemporaries, their incapacity to react to stimuli, their 'love-loathing,' are the outcome of the corruption and weakening of their physical energies, of their deficient powers of nervous resistance, and their general confusion of mind" (*Sexual Crisis*, 152). "Cerebral" and physical "exhaustion," as well as nervous conditions such as neurasthenia, were major contributing factors to the degeneration of male sexuality. To this end, many of the problems of male sexuality stemmed from the conditions of modern life: in Meisel-Hess's view, "The struggle for existence, whose intensity in modern social life exceeds all normal dimensions, renders the evil acute" (152). Taking an evolutionary and eugenic perspective, she also maintained that the problems of modern manhood were the cumulative consequence of "the impairment of the selective process"—that is, faulty sexual selection. Like Elberskirchen, Meisel-Hess believed that sexual selection under patriarchy had degraded women and perverted men: "Inheritance from a bad stock creates the predisposition; the conventional code of sexual morals which permits to the male every possible sexual excess is an accessory factor" (152). Because the "pathological" condition of male sexuality was the result of environmental conditions and faulty evolutionary mechanisms, Meisel-Hess maintained that masculinity could be recuperated. Although she acknowledged that there existed a "sub-group" of men "in whom the stigma of this inadequacy is inborn and therefore irremediable," she insisted that other "sexual cripples" had "acquired it in the steeplechase of the struggle for existence." This latter group, she maintained, "may be cured when the conditions of life become favorable," with the cure signified by the "capacity to enjoy love" (154).

Meisel-Hess, like Mayreder, held sexual ethical reform to be critical to the rehabilitation of masculinity and male sexuality. Meisel-Hess clarified that a new sexual morality was desperately needed, but specified that it must be accompanied by women's economic emancipation (155). She maintained that women ought to guide men, who would be saved by the "limitless power of self-sacrifice in the loving hearts of women" (155). Meisel-Hess defined love more metaphysically than Mayreder: drawing on the writings of Wagner and Maeterlinck, she described love as mutual sympathy, and as the process of "acquir[ing] knowledge of another soul . . . rejoic[ing] over each new discovery . . . grow[ing] more intimate through ever fresh confidences . . . [and] be[ing] aware of every stage at which the inner impulsive energy of either has rushed to meet and to mingle with the like energy in the other" (156). This definition of love, like Mayreder's, presumed equality between men and women—not just formal, civic equality, but existential equality, the ability of each party to realize themselves fully as independent, complex human beings.[45] Meisel-Hess went so far as to declare misogyny a "morbid manifestation of the sexual life" that had become instinctual in men (as opposed to accusations of misandry hurled toward women, which she believed stemmed from women's "unwilling[ness] to pervert the truth in man's favor") (289).

Whereas writers like Mayreder and Meisel-Hess believed male sexuality, and thus heterosexuality, could be rehabilitated through ethical and social reforms and through women's empowerment,

---

45. During her own time, Meisel-Hess believed that such a "natural and healthy human relationship, one in which both partners are equally tender and equally ardent," was "rarely encounter[ed]." Meisel-Hess, *Sexual Crisis*, 300.

others like Johanna Elberskirchen were pessimistic. Arguably, Elberkirchen's pessimism stemmed from her belief that true sexual equality did not exist in nature. Although she drew upon evolutionary ideas like her optimistic counterparts, Elberskirchen also relied upon evidence from sexual biology, which suggested that sexual traits were innate and, more importantly, unchanging. Her analysis therefore led her to conclude that social and ethical reforms could not affect sexual equality because the sexes were unequal at the most basic biological level. Put simply, Elberskirchen believed that men were intrinsically inferior to women. For this reason, she maintained that the existing social order was based on a perversion of nature that could only be rescued by placing women in charge of sexual life.

Elberskirchen believed that maleness itself was less biologically valuable than femaleness. She found the most material evidence of man's inferiority (and women's superiority) in the sperm and the ovum. In Elberskirchen's view, the sperm was but "an appendage of the ovum," completely dependent upon the ovum for its existence. Unlike the ovum, the sperm lacked protoplasmic nutrients with which to nourish itself; if it wanted to develop itself, Elberskirchen pointed out, it must bind itself to the ovum and allow itself to be fed. Elberskirchen even advanced the peculiar metaphoric claim that the sperm was a "natural-born proletariat, dependent upon the ovum, dependent upon the woman in his entire development and existence" (*Revolution*, 71). Contrary to the sperm, Elberskirchen maintained that the ovum, "the mother-cell," was the original source of all being. According to her, the superiority of the ovum is apparent in its rich abundance of plasma, which nourishes and sustains life (69). It is the ovum, she declared, in which "all strength is saved—not in the masculine semen cell" (68). Indeed, in Elberskirchen's view, "the sperm is destitute!" (69–70). Contrary to Mayreder, Elberskirchen declared that women's capacity to create life is what makes them superior: "Motherhood makes the female strong—in natural, healthy circumstances, the female is powerful, superior, the ruler" (61).

In asserting the biological superiority of females, Elberskirchen echoed Havelock Ellis's conclusion in *Man and Woman* (1894) that "[Woman] is thus of greater importance than the male from nature's point of view."[46] As Elberskirchen phrased it, "The female is rich, the female has nourishment, not the man. The man is incapable of producing a surplus of nourishment. Everything that he produces he uses for himself. . . . The man can in no direct way be creatively active, like the female, [for] the man is destitute!" (*Revolution*, 70). Elberskirchen attributed the problems of patriarchal social order to the discrepancy between man's biological responsibilities and his social privileges and power:

> The expansion of life, the biological performance and the biological obligation and responsibility of man is much less than that of the woman—but his rights are much greater, outrageously much greater. . . . From this a monstrous decadence must naturally develop with iron regularity. For . . . where the law of equivalence does not govern, a decline must necessarily enter. The fact is that patriarchy has caused only unnaturalness, sickness, prostitution, physical, spiritual, and economic degeneration, in short individual and social degeneration. (109–110)

Given what she believed to be the demonstrable and innate biological superiority of the female over the male, Elberskirchen insisted upon a radical overhaul of existing modes of social organization and sexual governance that would place the preponderance of power in women's hands. In the first instance, she insisted on women's need for economic security and their right to work. Elberskirchen framed this demand in evolutionary terms, proclaiming women's need to reenter the "struggle for existence" (89). According to Elberskirchen, "Nature wants the female to work . . . [to be] independent and self-sufficient and in every relationship capable to provide for nourishment, because she is a mother, and thereby she can support herself and her child" (71). Becoming self-reliant, she claimed, would improve woman and womanhood both physically and psychologically. It would restore to woman "her property, her freedom, her health, her good fortune," which "man robbed from her through his degenerate sexual impulse" (99). For Elberskirchen,

---

46. Havelock Ellis, *Man and Woman: A Study of Human Secondary Sexual Characteristics* (London: Walter Scott, 1894), 384.

all of the "so-called 'specifically masculine' characteristics . . . and occupations of man are nothing other than stolen goods" (114, 99). Yet Elberskirchen's ultimate vision was much more radical than demanding economic independence and the right to work: she insisted on the creation of a social order wherein the sexes' powers corresponded with their innate biological value and degree of responsibility for reproduction of the species. Elberskirchen advocated the establishment of what she called a new-style matriarchate that recentered woman, the "original social cell," as the "biological fulcrum and crux of the world" (100–101). A "female dictatorship" (*Weiberherrschaft*), in Elberskirchen's view, would reflect the natural order based upon woman's central role in generating and sustaining life (108–110). Returning to a matriarchal order would regenerate the race by returning to women their supposed right of final choice in sexual selection. Just as they had during the time of the ancient matriarchate, women would exercise their sexual choice with a view to improving the race, and would choose their mates according to "intelligence, strength, and beauty" (89).

At the same time, Elberskirchen maintained that women's freedom was only possible via an abandonment of sexual dissipation; for her, this meant an abandonment of heterosexuality and men. A release from what she referred to as "Sexus" would free women to develop their personalities and realize their full existential potential. An abandonment of men and heterosexuality would constitute a protest against women's assigned sexual inferiority. In the name of women's emancipation Elberskirchen demanded that women break "away from sex, away from inferiority—back to freedom and health, back to spiritual and physical superiority! Back to the mighty, holy, natural law of the mother—back to matriarchy. That is the real, the innermost slogan of the emancipation of women— that is their innermost necessity" (115).

Women's theories of masculinity and male sexuality offered not only potent criticisms of existing male sexual practices, but also powerful and even radical means of arguing for new modes of sexual governance that empowered and liberated women. Despite sharing some similar views about the nature of male sexuality, Mayreder,

Meisel-Hess, and Elberskirchen did not agree on the kinds of reforms that were needed to improve existing conditions. Their differing proposals arguably stemmed from their engagement with particular forms of scientific knowledge. Because Mayreder and Meisel-Hess drew primarily upon evolutionary ideas and arguments, they tended to be more optimistic regarding the possibility of changing male sexual behavior and improving the status quo. Conversely, Elberskirchen's reliance on biological arguments that held sexual traits to be innate and unchanging made her less hopeful about the possibility of change, and rendered her more likely to propose radical solutions

It would be easy to dismiss the ideas examined in this chapter; however, I maintain that these texts and the ideas contained within them are worthy of investigation for a number of reasons. First, they demonstrate the ways women were able to work with science to articulate visions of an alternative social order wherein male needs and experience did not anchor and orient sexual and social life. Science enabled women to envision futures as equals or superiors to men, and even futures without men. The fact that their analyses were in some cases expressed in absolutist terms can further be read as evidence of women's frustration with men's seeming unwillingness to change in the face of fifty years of sustained activism. We must remember that, as noncitizens with no recourse to political or economic power, whose previous appeals to justice and ethics had seemingly fallen on deaf ears, women had very few legal or political tools at their disposal. We may therefore want to ask ourselves what other means they had available to have their voices legitimized—and why these writers should have necessarily felt magnanimous toward men.

Second, these critiques of masculinity and male sexuality provide further evidence of how women were able to appeal to the scientific revelations of nature in order to criticize the sexual status quo. By showing existing conditions were unnatural, hence abnormal and injurious to the health of individuals and the body politic, women could demand that sexual life no longer privilege male sexual preferences and prerogatives.

Third, the ideas examined here hint at the ways some women sexologists connected women's sexual oppression to racial degeneration—and, conversely, women's sexual emancipation to racial regeneration. We have encountered such rhetorical moves already in the discourses on the female sex drive and on nonnormative female subjectivities. Here, both Grete Meisel-Hess and Johanna Elberskirchen invoked the theory of sexual selection to criticize men's unnatural, self-interested mate choices, which purportedly contributed to racial degeneration, and to highlight women's altruistic selection, which contributed to the elevation of the species. By tying women's emancipation to racial imperatives, these women suggested that they did not seek sexual reform solely (or even primarily) for women's benefit. Was this move sincere or purely strategic? In the next chapter, I consider in greater depth how one of these women sexologists, Grete Meisel-Hess, theorized the relationship between sexuality and race, and explore reasons why racial thinking appealed to women like her. I further demonstrate how racial appeals could be deployed to support demands for women's freedom to engage in pleasurable (hetero)sexual experiences.

5

THE EROTICS OF RACIAL REGENERATION

Eugenics, Maternity, and Sexual Agency

Race and calls for its regeneration were cornerstones of women sexologists' analyses and constituted key rationales for their demanded sexual reforms. Their invocations of race, specifically in connection to sex, mark out their ontological and political investments in eugenics, an integral aspect of early twentieth-century sexology and sex reform politics. Simultaneously a self-proclaimed science of human heredity, a code of sexual ethics, and a social movement, eugenics was dedicated to the enhancement of "racial quality." Eugenics offered a worldview that framed social improvement as a racial project and viewed sex as its point of intervention.[1] In Germany, the supposedly more scientific field that dealt with such questions and was closely allied to eugenics was referred to

---

1. See Weindling, *Health, Race, and German Politics between National Unification and Nazism, 1870–1945* (Cambridge: Cambridge University Press, 1993), 141, 151–152.

as racial hygiene. Racial hygiene expanded somewhat on eugenics by considering both heredity and environment as factors that influenced evolutionary processes. Eugenics and racial hygiene were allied fields that were often treated interchangeably. Common to both was an evaluative impetus, that is, a desire to classify humans as either "fit" or "unfit" according to a range of purportedly heritable traits. German-speaking women sexologists were not exceptional in their enthusiasm for eugenics; in recent years, numerous historians have pointed out that a range of progressive social and political activists were highly committed to eugenics in Germany and elsewhere. Eugenics arguably amounted to an international obsession in the early twentieth century.[2]

At first blush, eugenics' appeal for female sexual theorists is not obvious. Many eugenicists insisted that nature intended for women to serve only as the reproducers and caretakers of the race; therefore, women ought to forsake any activity that interfered with their reproductive ability. The man credited with coining the term "eugenics," Francis Galton, envisaged and idealized women, in Richard Soloway's words, as "submissive vessels for conveying and nurturing the vital germ plasm provided by their mates."[3] Nevertheless, eugenics appealed to the female sexual theorists studied here for a number of reasons, of which I will mention three. First, as Lucy Bland has observed of the situation in Britain, racial discourses offered women social esteem and political capital through the subject position of the "race mother," which was framed as both morally and evolutionarily superior to men (and, presumably, childless women), and which positioned women as the "link

2. For a comprehensive global history of eugenics, see Alison Bashford and Philippa Levine, eds., *The Oxford Handbook of the History of Eugenics* (Oxford: Oxford University Press, 2010).

3. Richard Soloway, *Demography and Degeneration: Eugenics and the Declining Birthrate in Twentieth-Century Britain* (Chapel Hill: University of North Carolina Press, 1990), 114. In his reading of Galton's antifeminist attitudes, Soloway insightfully muses that "underlying much of this sort of rhetoric was an almost palpable fear of the loss of power and control on the part of men if women did not need or want them and declined to fulfill their biological destiny" (129).

to the future."[4] Second and somewhat relatedly, it offered women the chance to infuse agency into their maternal role by asserting final decision-making power over the terms and conditions of reproduction and claiming a larger role in public life. Writers like Johanna Elberskirchen argued that, as bearers and nurturers of children, women played a more important role in human evolution than men; consequently, they should play a greater role in shaping the social conditions confronting future generations. Eugenics gave women a basis upon which to claim that they had the right to reject unfit male partners, challenge husbands' assumed right of unrestricted sexual access to their wives (and even reject the institution of patriarchal marriage itself), insist upon social, legal, and economic equality with men as a foundation for sound sexual decision-making, and demand financial support from the state in the form of maternal welfare. All such reforms, women argued, would help them successfully realize their responsibilities as "race mothers." Such claims resonated at a time when the health of national populations was emerging as a political and social issue, and when physical and cognitive disabilities, understood as the result of hereditary "taint," increasingly constituted sources of familial shame and occasions for secrecy.[5] Third, eugenics politicized and publicized sexual ethics and sexual governance. Race thinking profoundly shaped many women sexologists' views on sex as something that did not take place in isolation, but rather within the context of a broader interdependent community. These women sexologists were attuned to the consequences of pursuing sexual desire, and this consciousness shaped the kinds of demands they were willing to make on women's behalf.

Nevertheless, eugenics produced no singular or shared sexual politics among female sexual theorists. While they generally agreed that sexual independence and empowerment would improve both

---

4. Lucy Bland, *Banishing the Beast: Feminism, Sex, and Morality* (London: I. B. Tauris, 2001), 230. Bland convincingly argues that eugenics' "praise and sacralization" of women's maternal role endowed them with great responsibility for "racial regeneration," in turn strengthening their demands for social reform.

5. On this point see Deborah Cohen, *Family Secrets: Shame and Privacy in Modern Britain* (New York: Oxford University Press, 2013), esp. chap. 3.

individual women's lives and "the race" itself, they disagreed on what women's sexual independence and empowerment looked like. This disagreement resulted from their divergent understandings of the purpose of sex and the nature of women's sexuality, which had consequences for the kinds of reforms they advocated. Intriguingly, these disagreements among women mirrored debates among eugenicists regarding the relationship between sexual freedom and racial regeneration. George Robb has noted a helpful ideological division between what he termed moral eugenicists, who believed sex was exclusively reproductive and inferior to spiritual love unions, and progressive eugenicists, who attributed racial degeneration to sexual repression, particularly women's sexual repression.[6]

Although Robb's analysis focused on British eugenicists, his insights characterize cleavages among eugenicists and racial hygienists in Germany as well. Whereas the ideas of women sexologists like Johanna Elberskirchen represent a form of moral eugenics, this chapter examines those consistent with progressive eugenics. Specifically, it examines how eugenics underwrote a vision of sexual reform that treated women's greater sexual freedom and autonomy as commensurate with—in fact, fundamental to—racial regeneration. Here, sexual freedom was understood as a "positive liberty," that is, as a "freedom to" engage in heterosex on the same terms as men, and experience sexual pleasure in heterosexual intercourse. My analysis draws upon the historiographic foundation laid by scholars whose work has shown that many female sexual theorists in German-speaking Europe and beyond believed racial regeneration provided the foundation for arguments against sexual conservatism, particularly for women.[7]

---

6. George Robb, "Race Motherhood: Moral Eugenics vs. Progressive Eugenics, 1880–1920," in *Maternal Instincts: Visions of Motherhood and Sexuality in Britain, 1875–1925*, ed. Claudia Nelson and Ann Sumner Holmes (London: Macmillan, 1997), 57–71.

7. See, for example, Ann Taylor Allen, "German Radical Feminism and Eugenics, 1900–1908," *German Studies Review* 11, no. 1 (February 1988): 31–56; Bland, *Banishing the Beast*; Ann Taylor Allen, "Feminism and Eugenics in Germany and Britain: A Comparative Perspective," *German Studies Review* 23, no. 3 (October 2000): 477–505; Edward Ross Dickinson, "Reflections on Feminism

In what follows, I focus on the ideas of one writer, Grete Meisel-Hess, and offer a synthetic reading of texts she published before the First World War. Meisel-Hess's ideas have appeared elsewhere in this book, but here receive sustained attention for a number of reasons. Meisel-Hess's prolific output, which included novels, monographs, lectures, articles, and pamphlets, articulated a multi-faceted analysis of contemporary social and sexual problems. She offered new interpretations of female and male sexuality and put forward a comprehensive set of sexual reform demands. Meisel-Hess's work also exercised a remarkable international influence in the early twentieth century, and was fairly well-received by her male sexological colleagues. From a twenty-first-century perspective, her work is highly challenging. On the one hand, she was a fierce champion of women's (hetero)sexual autonomy, extramarital monogamy, and what we might call alternative family forms. She also brought an explicitly materialist analysis to bear on her examinations of sexual and social problems: for her, capitalism and patriarchy are intertwined forces of destruction and degeneration that propelled sexual and "racial" crises. On the other, she was a staunch maternalist, ambivalent about birth control, and deeply invested in eugenics and the politics of racial improvement.

It is precisely this confounding blend of feminist sexual radicalism and racialism that call out for analysis. Like the work of many of her male peers in the early twentieth century, particularly in the years immediately preceding the First World War, Meisel-Hess's sexological contributions were thoroughly saturated by eugenic precepts and preoccupied with the fate and fortunes of the race. However, unlike male sexologists, Meisel-Hess insisted that the liberation of female sexuality, marked above all by women's ability to select their sexual partners, initiate sexual encounters outside of marriage, and determine the conditions of their maternity, would solve both sexual and racial problems. Meisel-Hess's work demonstrates the ways that racial thinking not only bolstered new understandings of female and male sexualities, but also helped

---

and Monism in the Kaiserreich, 1900–1913," *Central European History* 34, no. 2 (2001): 191–230.

underwrite a sexually radical worldview that placed women, their desires, and their sexual agency at its center. Thinking in terms of race provided Meisel-Hess a way to conceptualize and articulate women's erotic power.

At the same time, an analysis of Meisel-Hess's writings illuminates how racial discourses and eugenic logics, when combined with feminist insights and new scientific ideas about female sexuality, gave rise to demands for greater restrictions on and regulation of certain women's and men's sexuality. Within Meisel-Hess's work, the reader encounters unequal evaluations of human life, and a great stress on "health" as a criterion for sexual rights and freedoms. A critical examination of Meisel-Hess's ideas illuminates the social, subjective, and selective character of supposedly natural rights claims, above all the "biological right" to sexual freedom articulated by many women sexologists. It also illustrates the challenges female sexual theorists faced when confronting the ethics of women's sexual liberation; that is to say, it shows how they struggled to balance women's sexual freedom and autonomy with a sense of responsibility for social consequences, specifically potential reproductive consequences—an important consideration in an era when women lacked easy access to reliable contraceptive knowledge and technologies.

Before proceeding further, a quick note regarding language. Throughout the chapter, I deploy "race" as a noun and as a modifier (as in "racial regeneration," for example). In the early twentieth century, "race" was a particularly slippery term with many possible meanings.[8] As noted earlier, "race" could connote humanity itself; it could also signify nationality, continental identity, ethnicity, or skin color. In what follows, I also use terms in currency at the

---

8. Although race was a polysemic concept during the nineteenth and early twentieth centuries, in this chapter I do not examine the theories of race associated with Count Arthur Gobineau and Houston Stewart Chamberlain. Such theories of race stressed the importance of blood, rather than physiology, in defining racial difference, and concerned themselves primarily with questions of purity, unity, and aesthetics. Gobineau posited an "aristocracy of blood" that depended upon a rather stark separation between the races, and an insistence upon the superiority of the white race. See Weindling, *Health, Race, and German Politics*, 51–52.

time, such as "fitness" when discussing eugenicists' and women sex-ologists' ideas. These terms, while still in use today, meant something different in the past than they do in the twenty-first century. "Fit-ness," for example, connoted innate, inherited, and superior men-tal and physical ability, and not an exclusively physical condition an individual could attain through exercise and diet. I make these points about language here to indicate my awareness of, and dis-tance from, early twentieth-century uses of these terms, and thereby avoid the use of scare quotes serving this purpose.

Race, Sex, and Science in the Early Twentieth Century

Over the course of the nineteenth century and well into the twen-tieth, an array of social actors including scientists, politicians, and social reformers became increasingly interested in, and anxious about, race. For these groups, race provided a language and epis-teme for discussing and analyzing populations, specifically their "quality" and quantity. Race thinking signaled a new way of con-ceptualizing collective human life as organically interconnected, interdependent, and sharing a common fate. This view of human-ity owed much to the then-fashionable doctrine of monism, which rejected the separation of spirit and matter and held that society ought to be governed by the same laws as the natural world.[9]

In Germany, racial panics primarily stemmed from anxieties surrounding the future of the newly unified nation. Emerging in the decades before the turn of the century as a major economic, military, and imperial power, Germany experienced changes that were unprecedented in their speed and scope. Domestically, the na-tion rapidly transformed from a largely agrarian to an industrial economy, with cities like Berlin exploding thanks to new economic migrants. This development may have represented progress in the eyes of some commentators, but it came at a cost, as evidenced by the ill health and poor living conditions of the urban laboring poor. Indeed, in pre–World War I Germany, the populations that often

---

9. See Dickinson, "Reflections on Feminism and Monism in the Kaiserreich," 206.

provoked racial panic were "not racial outsiders, but marginalized insiders whose very existence threatened national and class ideals," as Alison Bashford and Philippa Levine have noted of Britain. Of particular concern were the "massed and urban poor," the so-called problem populations of industrialization.[10]

In the early decades of the Wilhelmine era, the German state attempted to mitigate the damages of industrial capitalism—as well as the threat of workers' radicalism—by enacting a pioneering array of social legislation, including workers' insurance and pension programs. By the turn of the century, however, reformers and scientists began to argue that the solutions to Germany's so-called social question lay not only in prudent welfare policy but also in biology. They began to look inward, to heredity and reproduction, as the keys to humanity's improvement, and became especially drawn to eugenics, the supposed science of good breeding, which maintained that individuals' life chances were primarily determined not by material conditions, but by the genetic inheritance they received at birth. Developed by Darwin's cousin Francis Galton, eugenics treated heredity as the key to racial improvement, and examined how reproductive choices affected hereditary outcomes. According to eugenicists, traits such as intelligence, self-control, and diligence were essential for human survival and improvement.[11] Eugenicists insisted that men and women in possession of these desired (yet highly subjective) qualities ought to seek them out in their potential reproductive partners, to the exclusion of all other considerations. Galton for one viewed his science as a new secular religion aimed at inculcating a "sentiment of caste among those who are naturally gifted." He wanted the elite members of his envisioned "natural aristocracy of talent" to breed exclusively with each other and effect racial regeneration through the purification of genetic lines.[12] Eugenicists understood sex as ideally an act of

10. Alison Bashford and Philippa Levine, "Introduction: Eugenics and the Modern World," in Bashford and Levine, *Oxford Handbook of the History of Eugenics*(Oxford: Oxford University Press, 2010), 6.

11. Soloway, *Demography and Degeneration*, 23.

12. Intriguingly, as Richard Soloway notes, in Galton's unpublished novel *Kantsaywhere*, the racially blessed inhabitants of this fictional eugenic utopia "worshipped a sort of fuzzy, omnipresent life force represented by judgmental

reason, not passion, and insisted that a fundamental precondition for racial regeneration was the reform of reproductive practices and sexual ethics along these lines.

Eugenics as a science built upon numerous intellectual foundations, including scientific theories of heredity dating back to the late eighteenth century, as well as Malthus's theory of population and stirpiculture, or animal husbandry. However, in its sense of urgency and dire consequences, eugenics was especially indebted to theories of degeneration and Darwin's theory of evolution via natural selection, which emerged in the late 1850s.[13] Both degeneration theory and natural selection stressed the decisive importance of inherited traits not only for individual health and well-being but also for the survival and improvement of the species. Psychiatric theories of degeneration, first outlined in Bénédict Augustin Morel's *Physical, Intellectual, and Moral Traits of Degeneration* (1857), deployed Lamarckian theories regarding the transmission of acquired traits to suggest that psychopathology was the product of biological inheritance. Degeneration theory further insisted that psychological abnormalities were atavistic, that is, reflective of a more primitive evolutionary state. Darwin's theory of evolution via natural selection, as outlined in *On the Origin of Species* (1859), held that creatures best adapted to their environments are more likely to survive, reproduce, and transmit their traits to future generations. Conversely, traits that did not aid survival would eventually become extinct.[14]

Eugenic ideas became extremely popular with middle-class intellectuals and social reformers at the turn of the century as these groups became disenchanted with the failings of liberal capitalism

---

ancestral spirits who closely watched the progress of selective breeding." See Soloway, *Demography and Degeneration*, 81.

13. Bashford and Levine, "Introduction," 4–5.

14. Darwin's theory of natural selection incited an intellectual tendency commonly referred to as Social Darwinism, which advocated unmitigated social competition to ensure the survival only of "the fittest." Social Darwinism is markedly distinct from eugenics, although the two are often confused: eugenicists disliked the randomness and anarchic competitiveness of the Social Darwinist vision, and believed that the extinction of "useless" traits should be made certain. Contrary to Social Darwinism, eugenicists believed that regulating and rationalizing natural selection was key to racial improvement.

and more favorably disposed to collective, interventionist solutions. They were particularly attracted to the idea that identifying supposedly meaningful and unchanging differences between humans could help establish a natural order over the chaotic and contested transformations of social and political life. As British sexologist Havelock Ellis claimed in *The Problem of Race-Regeneration* (1911), studying and regulating the transmission of racial traits offered the chance for people to take control of their collective fate. Whereas environmentalist approaches to social problems assumed that "we [humans] have no control over human life and no responsibility for its production," Ellis insisted that individuals "possess the power, if we will, deliberately and consciously to create a new race, to mould the world of the future."[15] The appeal of eugenics—and of racial discourses more generally—lay in its proclaimed ability to definitively resolve moral and political questions by establishing and evaluating innate differences between and within human groups.[16]

In spite of eugenics' claim to scientific status, early twentieth-century eugenicists actually understood very little about the mechanisms of inheritance and genetic transmission: most of their ideas were based on statistical extrapolations of probability from patterns with family trees and crude derivations of Mendelian genetics. Nevertheless, eugenics quickly infiltrated sexology. Sexologists' strong embrace of eugenics is signified rather explicitly by the name of the first professional sexological society, the Medical Society for Sexual Science and Eugenics, established by Magnus Hirschfeld and Iwan Bloch in 1913. That sexologists were simultaneously eugenicists is perhaps not surprising in light of the field's development and envisioned mandate. As many scholars have pointed out, many sexual researchers, in particular psychiatrists like Richard von Krafft-Ebing, were concerned with degeneration, and sought to root out pathologies that contributed to individual and social

---

15. Havelock Ellis, *The Problem of Racial Regeneration* (London: Cassells, 1911), 26, 54.

16. See Nancy Stepan, *The Idea of Race in Science: Great Britain 1800–1960* (Hamden, CT: Archon Books, 1982), xiii, xx–xxi.

decline. Sexologists' interest in eugenics also makes sense in light of the field's mission to create knowledge that would shape sexual behavior. For sexologists like Max Marcuse, sexology's mission encompassed the goal of protecting the state and society by inhibiting the reproduction of the unfit and maximizing the fertility of those whose lives were deemed valuable.[17] As Volkmar Sigusch has observed, sexology and eugenics shared the same nightmares and fantasies: namely, "that misery . . . in the form of unemployment, poverty, alcoholism, sexually transmitted diseases, deformity, criminality, etc. . . . could be reduced until eradicated through a focused intervention into reproduction and through biologically based measures."[18]

Most of the sexologists mentioned in this book were not proponents of "negative" eugenic measures such as involuntary sterilization; instead, they championed positive measures like robust welfare provisions that would support children and families. Beyond such state-based measures, they supported reforms to prevailing sexual ethics, norms, and values that they hoped would guide individual behavior and decision making. Progressive eugenicists maintained that individuals had to internalize their responsibility "not only to generate life, but . . . to regenerate life," as Havelock Ellis put it, by either reproducing or refraining from reproducing.[19] Although such an ethical stance could be viewed as provoking a tension between an individual's sexual liberties and his or her reproductive "responsibility," eugenicists like Ellis argued that sexual freedom was rooted not in license, but in self-governance, specifically in "order, self-control, sympathy, [and] intelligent regulation."[20]

Many female sexual theorists shared progressive eugenicists' sexual-ethical vision. They stressed the relationship between individual sexual choices and their broader collective consequences, often citing the spread of venereal diseases and their hereditary

---

17. Max Marcuse, "Ein Wort zur Einführung," *Sexual-Probleme* 4 (January 1908): 3.

18. Volkmar Sigusch, *Geschichte der Sexualwissenschaft* (Frankfurt am Main: Campus Verlag, 2008), 325.

19. Ellis, *Problem of Racial Regeneration*, 54, 50.

20. Ibid., 71.

effects as a devastating example. However, female sexual theorists also drew critical attention to the moral, legal, and social contexts within which individuals—particularly women—made, or could make, decisions about their sex lives. As Grete Meisel-Hess's work demonstrates, the bulk of feminist sexual theorizing at the turn of the century questioned what kinds of sexual rights and freedoms could be biologically and socially justified in view of the individual's inextricable, organic ties to his or her larger community.

Female sexual theorists also agreed with male eugenicists' emphases on women's critical role in effecting racial regeneration and the importance of maternal well-being in determining the "quality" of her offspring. In *The Task of Social Hygiene* (1912), Havelock Ellis went as far as to declare the "question of eugenics" to be at one with the "woman question," as "the breeding of men lies largely in the hands of women."[21] While many women sexologists agreed with eugenicists' claim that racially fit women had a duty to bear children, they did not believe that women's roles ought to be limited to mothering and caretaking. Moreover, they insisted that racial regeneration required that women be empowered to make autonomous sexual decisions, including about the timing and number of children. At the turn of the century, German-speaking women not only articulated these arguments in books, public talks, pamphlets, and journal articles, but also organized (with like-minded men) to demand their realization. In prewar Germany one organization stood out in its encouragement of women's sexological analyses of sex, race, and women's empowerment: the League for the Protection of Mothers and Sexual Reform.

"Procreate, Not to Multiply, but to Advance!" The League for the Protection of Mothers and Sexual Reform

The League for the Protection of Mothers and Sexual Reform was certainly not alone in its concerns with race and its mobilization

---

21. Havelock Ellis, *The Task of Social Hygiene* (London: Constable, 1912), 46.

of a eugenic rationale in the service of social reform. In the later nineteenth and early twentieth centuries, eugenic ideas inspired a range of social movements around the world. The wide-ranging and flexible appeal of eugenics is evidenced by the fact that it was adopted not only by white social reformers who feared threats to "racial purity," but also, for example, by African Americans and German Jews as defense mechanisms against hostile white majorities.[22] Within these movements, women often played a key role. For example, Britain's first eugenic organization dedicated to publicly disseminating and popularizing eugenics, the Eugenics Education Society, was founded by Sybil Gotto in 1907. Although men formally led the society, women did most of the work, as Ann Taylor Allen has noted. In fact, the society's membership was approximately 40 percent female.[23]

In Germany, women constituted only about a fourth of the membership of the nation's primary eugenic organization, the Society for Racial Hygiene. Its founder, physician Alfred Ploetz, envisioned the society as a vehicle for the promotion of race hygiene. Though Ploetz was interested in recruiting female members, he was extremely hostile toward the involvement of feminist sex reformers or supporters of "modern sexual ethics." Paul Weindling notes that the women involved in the society were specifically tasked with challenging radical sex reform ideas. According to Weindling, Ploetz initially conceived of the society as forming "an elite breeding group," wherein women could receive professional education insofar as they obeyed their "'higher' duty to the race."[24] By 1913, the society had the support of seven female doctors; only one of them, the gynecologist Agnes Bluhm, had prominent ties to the "moderate" German women's movement. Most of the women

22. See, for example, Sharon Gillerman, *Germans into Jews: Remaking the Jewish Social Body in the Weimar Republic* (Stanford, CA: Stanford University Press, 2009); and Michele Mitchell, *Righteous Propagation: African Americans and the Politics of Racial Destiny after Reconstruction* (Chapel Hill: University of North Carolina Press, 2004).

23. Allen, "Feminism and Eugenics in Germany and Britain," 480.

24. Weindling, *Health, Race, and German Politics*, 146.

involved in the society were not professionals, and were described only as wives and daughters.[25]

Contrary to the Society for Racial Hygiene, the League for the Protection of Mothers and Sexual Reform championed a progressive, feminist eugenics. Almost all of the women sexologists studied in this book were members or active supporters of the league, which provided a crucial platform for the expression and dissemination of their work through its journals *The Protection of Mothers* and *The New Generation*. By 1908, the league could boast 3,800 male and female members, a number quite large for a radical sex reform group, as Ann Taylor Allen has pointed out.[26] Indeed, according to Edward Ross Dickinson, the league was the largest and most active sex reform organization in Germany before the First World War.[27] In contrast, the Society for Racial Hygiene had 150 members in 1908, and by 1914 reached only 425 members.[28]

Competing claims exist surrounding the formation of the league. Most scholars maintain that although it was the brainchild of Ruth Bré, who took tentative steps to establish the group in 1904, it was founded in Berlin in 1905 by an eclectic mix of radical and left-leaning feminists, socialists, physicians, racial hygienists, and political economists.[29] This diverse group included feminists

---

25. Ibid.

26. Allen, "Feminism and Eugenics in Germany and Britain," 480.

27. Dickinson, "Reflections on Feminism and Monism in the Kaiserreich," 191.

28. Allen, "Feminism and Eugenics in Germany and Britain," 480.

29. The poet and teacher Elisabeth Bouness, a.k.a Ruth Bré, claimed the league as her creation long after its formation. After falling out with the other members of the organization, she alleged that money meant for settlements for unmarried mothers was stolen from her. Helene Stöcker also asserted ownership over the league's origins, and insisted that she founded the league with fellow feminist Marie Lischnewska out of frustration with her feminist colleagues' failure to explicitly demand radical sexual reforms. Most of the scholarly literature engages both claims, while siding in favor of Stöcker. The league would be rocked by controversy again in 1910, after a falling out between Stöcker and Adele Schreiber over the direction of the league and the fate of funds earmarked for the building of homes for mothers. Schreiber's Nachlass in the Bundesarchiv Koblenz provides a rich source of documentation regarding both controversies. See Folders 2.15, 2.17, 2.19, 3.1.1–41, Nachlass Adele Schreiber, Bestand N1173, Bundesarchiv Koblenz. For a general history of the league's early years, see Bernd

Helene Stöcker, Adele Schreiber, Henriette Fürth, Maria Lischnewska, and Marie Stritt (later joined by Grete Meisel-Hess);
sexologists Iwan Bloch, August Forel, Magnus Hirschfeld, and
Max Marcuse (who was kicked out by 1908); Social Democratic
Party leader August Bebel; and sociologists Max Weber and Werner Sombart.[30] The league sustained its diversity by rhetorically
synthesizing its members' concerns with women's rights, racial regeneration, sexual ethics, and motherhood by stressing the interconnections between individual sexual liberties and perceived racial
duties to the community. League members endeavored to develop
what Edward Ross Dickinson has described as "an explicitly feminist and democratic vision of the relationship between the sexes, and
of the human condition, centered on the dominant scientific dogma
of the day: the theory of evolution." Beyond evolution, the league's
platform also drew upon "philosophical materialism and an anti-
Christian stance."[31] As part of its program, the league sought to
reform the laws, norms, and values governing sexual life. Its members demanded equal rights for children born out of wedlock; an
end to the sexual double standard; equal rights for women within
marriage; sexual education in schools; the legalization of contraceptives and abortion; the recognition of extramarital relationships
(akin to what today would be called common-law relationships);
an end to the state regulation of prostitution; and financial support
for all mothers, regardless of whether they were married or not.[32]
After 1910, they also fought against the attempt to criminalize sex
acts between women. Though estranged from the broader wom-
en's movement because of its radical positions—its application to
join the League of German Women's Associations was rejected in
1909—the league was feminist in its orientation and its leadership.
In fact, the league's explicit and uncompromising feminism would

Nowacki, *Der Bund für Mutterschutz (1905–1933)* (Husum: Matthiesen Verlag,
1983), 11–30.
    30. Rosa Mayreder and Sigmund Freud belonged to the Austrian branch of the
league.
    31. Dickinson, "Reflections on Feminism and Monism in the Kaiserreich,"
191–192.
    32. Ibid, 195.

ultimately alienate many early male supporters, including Alfred Ploetz. At times the league proved too radical even for its feminist members, as evidenced by Henriette Fürth's departure from the league because of its "sexual-anarchist propaganda."[33]

The league's intersecting concerns are best demonstrated by its portrayal of the plight of the unwed mother.[34] The league represented the unwed mother as a victim of society's unscientific, patriarchal attitudes toward sexuality, which denied women's physiological need for sexual activity. Though not all league members believed that sex must lead to reproduction, most agreed that women's destiny was motherhood. The league therefore demanded sweeping reforms to sexual ethics that would enable the recognition and support of unmarried mothers and their children. It also proposed pragmatic social reforms that would provide state support for unwed mothers and their children, ranging from infant homes to maternal welfare. Importantly, these arguments and claims were premised not only upon women's physiological needs, but also upon what were described as racial needs. In its 1905 petition to the German parliament, for example, the league lamented the loss of high-quality life as a result of the perverse and unnatural sexual ethics that penalized reproduction among young, racially healthy parents.[35] Likewise, as various drafts of the league's 1908 Constitution reveal, it considered mothers to be at the very heart of national futures—and thus women's well-being and development as crucial to racial improvement.[36]

---

33. Ibid., 193.

34. See, for example, Ruth Bré, *Das Recht auf die Mutterschaft: Eine Forderung zur Bekämpfung der Prostitution der Frauen- und Geschlechtskrankheiten* (Leipzig: Verlag der Frauen-Rundschau, 1903); Helene Stöcker, Lily Braun, Ellen Key, et al., *Bund für Mutterschutz* (Berlin: Pan-Verlag, 1905); Adele Schreiber, "Ehereform," *Die Umschau* 12 (7 March 1908): 181–185; Schreiber, *Der Bund für Mutterschutz und seine Gegner* (Leipzig: Felix Dietrich, 1909). See also Ann Taylor Allen, "Mothers of the New Generation: Adele Schreiber, Helene Stöcker, and the Evolution of a New German Idea of Motherhood, 1900–1914," *Signs* 10, no. 3 (Spring 1985): 418–438.

35. "Aufruf Januar 1905," Folder 3.1, Nachlass Adele Schreiber, Bestand N 1173, Bundesarchiv Koblenz.

36. See "Entwicklung von Satzung und Programm des BfM," Folder 3.1, Nachlass Adele Schreiber, Bestand N 1173, Bundesarchiv Koblenz.

In addition to stressing reforms that would enable more women in various conditions to become mothers, many league members also provocatively connected women's reproductive rights and freedoms—that is, their right *not* to become mothers involuntarily—to the project of racial regeneration. However, the question of contraception and abortion was a fraught one among league members, despite the fact that the league officially supported and maintained institutional ties with German and international neo-Malthusian organizations such as Social Harmony and the British Malthusian League. While insisting that women should have the right to control their fertility, many members of the league, including feminists, nonetheless insisted that racially fit women have a duty to become mothers, and that their failure to reproduce would have dire racial consequences.

Beyond its practical work of advocating for legal reforms and social welfare measures, the league engaged in an ongoing ideological struggle aimed at changing the ways their contemporaries thought about female sexuality and heterosexual relations of power. Its members raised powerful questions and advanced provocative arguments regarding the meaning of sex itself and the individual and social implications of reproduction. Arguably, this intellectual labor constituted the league's most important and enduring historical contribution. As part of its efforts to champion women's sexual agency and voluntary motherhood, the league interrogated the justice and consequences of existing sexual ethics and governance, and was highly critical of the hypocrisy and "superstition" that it believed inhered within Christian sexual morality. Thanks to the guiding influence of its erstwhile president Helene Stöcker, the league was primarily dedicated to advancing a feminist "New Ethic" to reform sexual life through a "re-evaluation of values." The New Ethic was inspired by a range of intellectual and political influences including sexual science, eugenics, socialism, and even Nietzschean philosophy. Edward Ross Dickinson has characterized the central demands of the New Ethic as the liberation of sexual relationships from the "institutional and ideological constraints imposed by Christianity," an acceptance of the central importance of sex as a "natural" feature of individual and social life, and an

embrace of relationships between men and women based on mutual love, respect, and shared responsibility for the happiness of
both partners and children, "regardless of civil or sacramental
forms."[37] Through the New Ethic, Stöcker sought to fight what
she saw as the damaging asceticism of the "old morality," which
viewed sex as evil, insisted on a separation between spiritual and
physical existence (to the denigration of the latter), and ultimately
produced cultural attitudes and values that deplored and disparaged earthbound pleasures.[38] Above all, in crafting the New Ethic
Stöcker sought to "establish this life, our life, as if it were valuable." Following Nietzsche, she wanted to craft an ethic that said
yes to life, and above all to treat the sex drive as a positive aspect
of existence, especially for women.[39] In Stöcker's words, "Realizing the ideal of human beings whose bodies are strong, happy, and
healthy, whose minds are noble and mature and whose souls are
caring, seems to be the highest goal for all of us."[40]

Stöcker's New Ethic involved a complex temporality: it not only
addressed present-day problems within heterosexual relationships,
but also considered the future implications of sexual decisions and
behaviors. As she noted in her 1905 article "Toward the Reform
of Sexual Ethics," "the greatest difficulty of the sexual problem
does not lie in the relationship between man and woman alone; it
becomes very complicated when a child is involved." Here is where
eugenics entered into the New Ethic. As part of this new program,
Stöcker insisted that "we do not want to become hypocritical and
state that intercourse is only moral when it serves procreation. As
man has subjected all other things to his reasonable understanding,
so he has to become master even more of one of the most important
matters of mankind: the creation of a new human being. One will
have to find ways to prevent terminally sick or deranged people

---

37. Dickinson, "Reflections on Feminism and Monism in the Kaiserreich," 194.
38. Tracie Matysik "Beyond Freedom: A Return to Subjectivity in the History
of Sexuality," in *After the History of Sexuality: German Genealogies with and beyond Foucault*, ed. Scott Spector, Helmut Puff, and Dagmar Herzog (New York:
Berghahn Books, 2012), 188.
39. Ibid.
40. Helene Stöcker, "Zur Reform der sexuellen Ethik," *Mutterschutz* 1 (1905): 4.

from procreation."[41] Stöcker later argued that there were certain "cases in which a child would be a crime: for example among the chronically ill, or third-degree neurasthenics." In 1913, she even called for the introduction of laws preventing the reproduction of "criminals and the mentally ill," and in 1914 declared that "if the mere existence of the defective . . . is a danger and impediment to the state," it was a social right and duty to prevent their birth "with all the methods of science."[42] Clearly, for Stöcker this life-affirming New Ethic was meant to affirm particular lives, namely, those identified through their "strong, happy, and healthy" bodies and "noble and mature" minds.

The "Modern Worldview" of Grete Meisel-Hess

While the New Ethic was Stöcker's creation, it clearly shares ideas in common with theories and arguments put forward by many of the women sexologists featured in this book—especially Grete Meisel-Hess. Meisel-Hess joined the league in 1908 following a move from Vienna to Berlin. She not only gave numerous public talks on the league's behalf, but also published frequently in its journal, *The New Generation*. In addition to her articles for *The New Generation*, Meisel-Hess explored the relationship between race, sexuality, women's rights, and sexual reform in novels such as *The Intellectuals* (1911) and nonfiction treatises such as *In the Modern Worldview* (1901) and *The Sexual Crisis* (1909). Meisel-Hess's most famous work, *The Sexual Crisis*, was hugely influential and attracted an international readership. Among her fans were Havelock Ellis, British feminist and sex reformer Stella Browne, and the socialist publisher and translator Eden Paul.[43] In *The Task of Social Hygiene*, Havelock Ellis insisted that *The Sexual Crisis*

---

41. Ibid., 9.

42. Quoted in Dickinson, "Reflections on Feminism and Monism in the Kaiserreich," 205.

43. See, for example, Ellis, *Task of Social Hygiene*, 130; Stella Browne to Havelock Ellis, 25.12.22, Ellis Add. MS 70539, Havelock Ellis Papers, British Library Manuscripts and Archives. See also Lesley A. Hall, "Stella Browne and the German

deserved study, as he believed that Meisel-Hess had demonstrated, "in her femininely clever and frank discussion of present-day conditions," that the women of the future "will be full, strong, elementary natures." Her work offered a vision of "the future world, fostered by the finer selection of a conscious eugenics, and a new reverence and care for motherhood," wherein "we may reasonably hope for a truly efficient humanity, the bearers and conservers of the highest human emotions."[44]

Meisel-Hess's work combined a range of intellectual influences. Beyond progressive feminist analyses and demands emanating from sex reform movements (above all the league's claims on behalf of voluntary motherhood), her writing brought together new scientific theories and research on sex and sexuality, monism, eugenics, and racial hygiene. Like many of her feminist colleagues in the league, Meisel-Hess was also inspired by Nietzschean philosophy. She was even an early adopter of Freudian psychoanalysis. This diverse blend of influences contributed to Meisel-Hess's status as a unique voice in the sexological field. Arguably, her ability to assimilate feminism, maternalism, sexual science, and eugenics contributed to her more favorable reception among male sexologists like Havelock Ellis, and to the promotion and discussion of her lectures in journals like *Sexual Problems*. *The Sexual Crisis* was reviewed widely in journals, including predictable journals like *The New Generation* and *Sexual Problems*, as well as the *Political-Anthropological Review*, the sex reform journal *Sex and Society*, and *Journal for the Fight against Venereal Diseases*. In the English edition of *The Sexual Crisis*, American eugenicist Dr. William J. Robinson went so far as to endow Meisel-Hess with the title of "Doctor," writing that, "as a stimulus to thought, Dr. Meisel-Hess' book has few equals."[45] Likewise, in his review for *The Free Words*, Friedrich Alafberg described *The Sexual Crisis* as a "ruthless yet

Radical Sex Reform Tradition," in *Sisters of Subversion: Histories of Women, Tales of Gender*, ed. Willem de Blécourt (Amsterdam: AMB, 2008), 152–161.

44. Ellis, *Task of Social Hygiene*, 109, 130.

45. Dr. William J. Robinson, "Introduction," in Grete Meisel-Hess, *The Sexual Crisis: A Critique of Our Sexual Life*, trans. Eden Paul and Cedar Paul (New York: Critic and Guide, 1917), 10.

sensible study" of contemporary sexual life that offered a courageous, penetrating, and thoroughgoing revelation and understanding of existing sexual relationships—though he bristled at her
critique of modern man.[46] Yet some male reviewers of *The Sexual
Crisis* remained wary of the text because of what they characterized as its distinctly feminine standpoint. *Sexual Problems* featured
a review of *The Sexual Crisis* that stressed at the outset that it was
a "serious" book from which men and women alike could learn a
lot; at the same time, it complained that "Mrs. Meisel-Hess sees
everything through the eyes of a woman," making it "difficult for
a man to follow her at all times." This was particularly true of
Meisel-Hess's insistence on women's sexual freedom and pleasure
as the solution to sexual and racial problems, which the author
rejected as thoroughly individualistic and irresponsible.[47]

Whether *The Sexual Crisis* reflected a "woman's point of view"
or not, Meisel-Hess's analysis of the problems of race and sex did
depart from those offered by her eugenically informed male peers
in significant ways. Contrary to some male eugenicists, racial hygienists, and sexologists, who viewed women as instruments for
racial improvement and who maintained that feminism was causing racial degeneration by luring women, specifically middle-class
women, away from their "duty" to mother by encouraging them
to pursue educational and professional opportunities, Meisel-Hess
argued that racial degeneration was the result of existing patriarchal arrangements of sexual life that suppressed women's sexuality.
Within her texts, both racial degeneration and what she termed the
"sexual crisis" were interdependent and inextricable phenomena,
and stemmed from the harms caused by restrictions on women's
free exercise of their sex drive. Perhaps Grete Meisel-Hess's most
succinct and impassioned expression of this argument can be found
in her contribution to the radical feminist volume *Marriage? Toward the Reform of Sexual Morals* (1911). In an essay entitled

---

46. Friedrich Alafberg, "Büchertisch: Grete Meisel-Heß, Die sexuelle Krise,"
Das freie Worte 9 (1909): 528.

47. Baars, "Grete Meisel-Hess. *Die sexuelle Krise,*" *Sexual-Probleme* 6 (1910):
73–76.

"The Sexual Morality of Woman—of Today and Later," she declared that "the thing that we complain about and in which we recognize a crisis condition in the sexual life of civilized peoples" is the fact that "women are denied the normal measure of life's happiness, sexual happiness as well as love and fertility, [and] that they are separated from them as a result of unnatural social causes." In Meisel-Hess's view, the repression of women's sexuality could no longer be supported thanks to women's growing demands to develop as well-rounded individuals, and to "the ever growing and improving consciousness of society of its true reproductive interests."[48] The following analysis of Meisel-Hess's ideas draws from texts she published before the First World War. While drawing primarily from *The Sexual* Crisis (1909), it also includes her monograph *In the Modern Worldview* (1901) and her articles "The Sexual Morality of Woman—of Today and Later" (1911) and "Sexual Rights" (1912).

For Meisel-Hess, the single underlying cause of the sexual crisis and racial degeneration was capitalist patriarchy. As we will soon discover, she viewed the social and economic orders as inextricably intertwined, and maintained that their particular constitution held profound implications for the future and welfare of the race. Within Meisel-Hess's analyses of the sexual status quo, capitalist patriarchy was held responsible for producing the unnatural social conditions that inhibited women's sexual fulfillment and autonomy. The conjoined forces of male domination and free market economics restricted women's expression and exploration of their sexuality (as well as their economic security) to monogamic marriage—which Meisel-Hess referred to as a "fenced precinct"—and to prostitution.[49] Women who did not occupy the role of either wife or prostitute were consequently excluded from sexual life altogether and rendered economically insecure. This denial of women's "right of free choice of sexual partner," which Meisel-Hess

---

48. Grete Meisel-Hess, "Die Sexualmoral der Frau—von heute und spaeter," in *Ehe? Zur Reform der sexuellen Moral*, ed. Hedwig Dohm (Berlin: Internationale Verlag, 1911), 98.

49. Meisel-Hess, *Sexual Crisis*, 35, 39. Subsequent citations of this work appear parenthetically in the text.

maintained constituted one of woman's "most elementary human rights," had dire racial consequences (98). Specifically, it perverted the natural order by placing sexual selection exclusively in male hands, as women were dependent upon men financially and sexually. Here again we can hear echoes of arguments premised upon sexual selection theory encountered elsewhere. Meisel-Hess maintained that male-dominated sexual selection represented a "grossly unnatural state of affairs" that "conflict[ed] sharply with the selective process by which the excellence of the species is maintained" (22). A natural selective process, she asserted, relied upon the "freedom of [sexual] choice on the part of women (and, of course, also of men)" (22).

Noteworthy is the fact that, in the previous statement, the inclusion of men appears almost as an afterthought: indeed, in Meisel-Hess's view, women's selection was of primary importance. Meisel-Hess maintained that male-dominated sexual selection was not only unnatural but also based on selfish criteria, whereas female-dominated selection was altruistic and aimed at racial improvement.[50] Here, Meisel-Hess's arguments especially resemble those of Johanna Elberskirchen. Meisel-Hess stressed that male-dominated sexual selection excluded "superior" women from marriage because most men deemed these women undesirable due to their independence of mind and will. This situation not only created a particular sexual misery for these individual women, but also prevented the "further evolution of the species" by inhibiting "highly evolved individualities" from reproducing (62). Meisel-Hess noted that "men who find themselves unable to enter into satisfactory relationships with women of the newer types can still find plenty of available women exhibiting the characteristics of the old order. But women of the new time will not accept the old type of family relationship, based upon woman's unconditional spiritual subordination, and involving the denial of all woman's developmental possibilities" (316).

---

50. "Woman's love," Meisel-Hess asserted," is general rather than individual. Woman, far more than man, is an instrument in the hands of the species. Man wills, desires to assert his own ego, deliberately and defiantly pursues his own ends." Meisel-Hess, *Sexual Crisis*, 124.

Meisel-Hess repeatedly stressed the effects of economics upon women's sexuality, and especially their sexual freedoms. When it came to contemporary marriage and reproduction, she pointed out that patriarchal arrangements of sexual life subverted women's selection by requiring that women "give themselves to the men best able to buy, to those who in existing circumstances are often damaged articles and from the biological standpoint of inferior quality" (22). The monetary motivations for marriage depressed racial quality because money gave racially unfit men an illegitimate advantage as potential mates. Meisel-Hess insisted that the economic constraints surrounding marriage encouraged the propagation of the most adaptable men and women (as opposed to the most racially fit), who accommodated themselves—via a process of degradation—to the existing, undesirable status quo created by competitive capitalism. Meisel-Hess thus insisted that patriarchal marriage contributed to the propagation of "the ugliness and stupidity everywhere manifest" (35). When women did marry, they frequently had to do so for money rather than love; however, love, she claimed, produced the most racially fit children (279).

Even more radically, Meisel-Hess argued that marriage's stranglehold on sexual legitimacy prevented individuals from discovering their optimal sexual partner, and ensured that all children born of extramarital unions, regardless of their racial fitness, would be doomed to failure.[51] Like other modern sexual "revolutionists" she objected to the "fetters and shackles" imposed on individuals' sexual choices, and insisted that "it is wrong that the possibility of reproduction and consequently of selection should be exclusively dependent upon this single form of sexual association" (*Sexual Crisis*, 32). Although Meisel-Hess was a strict monogamist and insisted that "a permanent sexual and social union with a single member of the opposite sex . . . is the one whose attainment both sexes will and should forever strive," she declared that this goal "can be attained only by traversing manifold phases of life. An eternal pledge must not be enforced by coercion" (32).

---

51. Meisel-Hess, "Die Sexualmoral der Frau," 103.

Because of the dangerous racial implications of existing sexual arrangements, Meisel-Hess called for the reordering of sexual and social life. Specifically, she argued for reforms that were directed "at complete freedom for all those forms of the erotic life which promote racial progress; freedom, above all, for the work of reproduction in so far as this is the outcome of unrestricted natural selection" (32–33). She took care to stress that she did not seek complete sexual freedom, or a "wild" sexuality; indeed, she insisted that "did such freedom exist, it would still in all cases be the individual's ultimate aim to secure a permanent association with the most suitable mate." Nonetheless, she maintained that "only under the aegis of freedom can this mate be found" (33).

In her view, an ideal sexual arrangement would "effect a harmonious compromise between the rights and duties of the individual and the rights of the community" (207). Achieving a balance between the individual and the collective was imperative for Meisel-Hess in light of her conceptualization of race. Drawing on Alfred Ploetz, Meisel-Hess conceived of race as an "organic whole" composed of "all the individual organisms that arise out of and transmit this enduring vital unity" (248). According to her, "In every one of us, through the complicated tissue of individuality, there runs an ultimate secret thread of connection with the outer world, restricting the power of self-determination" (102). Whereas the "individual life is transient," she mused, "the race endures" (248). Meisel-Hess further maintained that achieving a balance between individual rights and duties to the race was necessary in order to make sure that "the economic misuse of valuable human energies [would] be brought to an end . . . above all as regards the energies of women" (207).

Meisel-Hess explicitly declared that the reorganization of social life she envisioned should be guided by science. New achievements in scientific and medical research made possible "a sensible social order." New knowledge was illuminating "the natural causes of things," which had previously been obscured by "superstitions of all kinds" that were "collaps[ing] one after another."[52]

---

52. Grete Meisel-Hess, *In der modernen Weltanschauung* (Leipzig: Hermann Seemann Nachfolger, 1901), 108–109.

Meisel-Hess believed that science was in the process of revealing the true nature of "species needs," which she insisted ought to provide the bases for morality. "Morality is based upon the interest of the species alone," she declared, "and the only true sexual morality is that which leads to the procreation of healthy and beautiful human beings, that which condemns no individual and no class to misery and misuse, and that which neither suppresses nor artificially corrupts the energies of the heart and of the senses" (*Sexual Crisis*, 101).[53] Scientifically guided social reform would therefore allow for the simultaneous and reciprocal development of the individual and society.

For Meisel-Hess, "species needs" implied not only reproduction and racial renewal but also sexual experience. Meisel-Hess believed that sex itself constituted a vital physiological and psychological need for women. She declared sex the "focal point of every healthy being whose instincts have not undergone partial or complete atrophy," and believed that "upon the full satisfaction of the sexual needs depends the attainment of a true equilibrium of the mental no less than the physical personality" (117). Meisel-Hess maintained that the experience of sexual passion heightened one's creative capacities, and viewed sex itself as an aid to women's development as individuals (120). According to her, "It seems that a life in which sexual fulfillment is denied is incompatible with fine creative work, at any rate in a healthy woman in whom the instinctive life is normally developed. . . . How should one whose womanly destiny confines her to the desert of sexual renunciation find in that void the energy essential to any kind of active work?" (230–231). Because she believed that women had as strong a need for sex as men, the desire for a satisfying sexual life was universal (117). Writing specifically of women, she argued that "the need for further sexual rights is therefore required not only for a small group."[54] She therefore demanded that it should be made "socially possible for everyone to satisfy [sexual] desire as may best commend itself to individual judgment"—as long as so doing did not

---

53. See also Meisel-Hess, *In der modernen Weltanschauung*, 52, 112.
54. Grete Meisel-Hess, "Sexuelle Rechte," *Die neue Generation* 8 (1912): 183.

harm others or the race (*Sexual Crisis*, 117). This caveat is significant, and will be further explored below.

To achieve her desired vision of social reform, Meisel-Hess asserted that women and their sexual needs should be placed at the
center of social life; however, because Meisel-Hess believed that
women have an "organic" need to become mothers, she stressed
above all that women's "child-bearing function" should constitute
"the nodal point of social organization" (246).[55] Indeed, she held
that the mother and child formed the "natural central unity of all
social structures."[56] Meisel-Hess argued that women were particularly important from a biological perspective, as contemporary science had shown that women transmitted a significant share of their
genetic properties to their offspring. Proceeding from the work of
Robert Müller, Meisel-Hess noted that "in the case of men of note,
as we learn from their biographies, talent, genius and faculty are
most often inherited from the mother" (*Sexual Crisis*, 210).

For Meisel-Hess, then, the path to racial regeneration lay in fundamental reforms that would "facilitate the reproductive activity
of 'fit' women," that is, "intellectually and morally independent"
women (209). This demand applied to all fit women, regardless
of whether they intended to marry. In a passage worth quoting at
length, she insisted that reproduction

> must be freed from its dependence upon any prescribed form of sexual
> association, for the procreation of the coming generation must be ef-
> fected during those years in which the energy and beauty of the indi-
> vidual and of the germ-plasm are at their maximum, whether the union
> between the parents is or is not destined to endure, and without depriv-
> ing these parents, by social censure, of the possibility of other and so-
> cially perhaps more valuable sexual experiences. The way must lie open
> for the birth of the children of vigor, youth, and free sexual selection, re-
> gardless of whether the parents are socially ripe and fit for marriage, or
> whether they intend to marry. (61–62)

---

55. See also Meisel-Hess, *In der modernen Weltanschauung*, 90. As Meisel-
Hess wrote in "Sexuelle Rechte," "Recognition of women's right to motherhood
outside of marriage,—that is what the best and most independent intellectuals demand today (190).

56. Meisel-Hess, "Die Sexualmoral der Frau," 105.

For these reasons, Meisel-Hess insisted on the need to profoundly transform marriage, intimate relations, and sexual morality generally. In her view, "The welfare of the race and the regulation of the sexual life of mankind are inseparable correlates. The quality of the race is the direct outcome of the existing sexual morality" (282–283). She went so far as to accuse male eugenicists and racial hygienists of failing to consider the dysgenic effects of existing standards of sexual morality and arrangements of sexual life; as she noted, "in the writer's opinion, those now engaged in the study of racial hygiene have hitherto failed to pay sufficient attention to the fact that the *normal* sexual system of the civilized world is responsible for the operation of numerous non-selective and even anti-selective factors." Taking aim at leading racial hygienists, she observed, "In Plötz's enumeration of non-selective factors there is no mention of this aspect of our normal sexual life, nor have I met with any references to the matter elsewhere" (262).

According to Meisel-Hess, all racially fit women ought to exercise their sexual autonomy and racial responsibility by finding erotically compatible and eugenically fit partners and becoming mothers of a new, healthier, superior generation. In her view, only "where women are able to exercise a preference, where they can choose to accept the embraces of the strongest, the fittest, among the men, and to be impregnated by these, there the selective factor is at work" (22). To this end, she called for the liberation of women's sexuality and fertility from the exclusivity of contractual marriage, and demanded the recognition of new forms of intimacy through which women could find their "optimal" sexual and reproductive partners. These new forms were particularly important for the young, and would be "inevitably transient in duration" (44). In her view, "Nothing can be more natural than that a truly satisfying sexual partnership should be attained, if at all, only after repeated experiments. . . . A man and a woman cannot really learn to know one another except by living together (or at any rate cannot possibly know one another until after the act of physical union has been effected), . . . it is surely unreasonable to expect that the right sexual partner should be found at the very first attempt" (44–45). She supported cohabitation and sex before marriage to enable couples to ascertain whether they made a good match, from both a romantic and a eugenic perspective. "During the years prior to the attainment of complete mental and physical maturity and prior to the acquirement of the social conditions suitable for permanent marriage," she insisted, "there must be provided, for women no less than for men, free opportunity to form temporary sexual unions. In both sexes it is essential that the social as well as the erotic powers should attain their fullest development before the formation of a permanent sexual association, for then only does it become possible to choose the partner best adapted for a life-companionship" (61).[57] Indeed, Meisel-Hess maintained that "a union easily dissolved, but one entered into under official sanction, would seem to be the form best adopted to satisfy the mental requirements of our own and ensuing generations" (44).

To this end, she proposed a range of options of varying duration and permanency, including "erotic friendships,"[58] and "provisional"

---

57. Intriguingly, Meisel-Hess also celebrated "new opportunities for comradeship among women," including the "bachelor woman" who cohabited with another woman and may even adopt a child. According to her, this "positive development" indicated that women would have more possibilities for fulfillment and joy outside of marriage; *Sexual Crisis*, 229.

58. Whether Meisel-Hess meant "erotic" to be synonymous with "sexual" here is unclear. She described the erotic friendship as follows: "The present generation is still untrained for the enjoyment of those forms of erotic life derivable simply from comradeship—forms that will come to fruition only in a more refined and elaborate civilization than our own. The sole love that our generation understands is that which is intended to involve an immediate and permanent association of all the interests of the two lovers. The idea that upon friendship can be based an erotic life at once delicate and satisfying is remote from the contemporary understanding. Erotic friendship—how great are the possibilities of happiness, to-day unutilized and running to waste, derivable from this source! Should any now endeavor to base their amatory life upon such a friendship, how they would be overwhelmed by the forces of social disapproval; and yet not until erotic friendship is tolerated can human beings be freed from their present dilemma, which imposes the choice between coercive marriage (for those to whom marriage is economically possible) and erotic starvation." Meisel-Hess may have meant "erotic" to denote "sensuality," similar to feminist poet and theorist Audre Lorde's deployment of the term in her famous essay, "The Uses of the Erotic." However, Meisel-Hess's description of the erotic friendship as a potential expression of "amatory life" and as an alternative to "coercive marriage" suggests that her use of the erotic at the very least included sex (107). For Lorde's essay, see Audre Lorde, "The Uses of the Erotic: The

wives and husbands, "able in either case to satisfy the most urgent needs of the earlier years of sexual maturity, but only during those years and not later" (44). If contractual marriage was to be retained, she asserted that it required women's economic independence to ensure that women could make their own choice of spouse and enter marriage as equals, motivated only by love (42). However, it should no longer constitute "the only permissible form of erotic life, nor the sole authorized method of reproduction" (42). Meisel-Hess further insisted that if people were to marry, they should do so earlier, so that couples could capitalize on their years of peak reproductive fitness. Late marriages, in her view, were a consequence of placing the burden of economic maintenance exclusively on men, and had the deleterious effects of forcing women into prolonged celibacy and leading men to seek out prostitutes, thereby increasing the risk of acquiring a venereal disease and infecting their future wife and children.

Meisel-Hess's advocacy of nonmarital and temporary arrangements for (hetero)sexual intimacies was incredibly radical for the early twentieth century, and placed her among the sexual avantgarde of her era. At the same time, these revolutionary changes, along with the enhanced sexual rights and freedoms she extended to women, were premised upon the enhancement of women's maternal prospects and legitimized by their potentially racially regenerative effects. Throughout her analysis of existing sexual life and within her visions of sexual reform, Meisel-Hess stressed the need to prioritize racial fitness. In this regard, her aforementioned description of childbearing as a social function is revealing. Meisel-Hess believed that because reproduction affected collective well-being, it ought to be subjected to public controls, and specifically to eugenic regulation; in her view, "the child belongs not to the individual, but to the community" (207).

Moreover, like other progressive eugenicists Meisel-Hess intriguingly maintained that greater sexual freedoms required greater self-restraint in the interests of future generations. In *The Sexual Crisis*,

Erotic as Power," in *Sister Outsider: Essays and Speeches* (1984; New York: Ten Speed Press, 2007), 53–59.

Meisel-Hess explicitly stated that "limitations must be imposed upon the gratification of the appetites so long as the individual, male or female, remains incompetent to estimate or provide for all the consequences of sexual activity or passivity, and so long as there exists incapacity to control some of the pathological manifestations of the sexual life" (101). Citing racial hygienist Alfred Ploetz, Meisel-Hess lamented that society was already "overweighted with defectives" because the "community makes no effort to prevent the overloading of the race with the less fit" (251). She thus proclaimed that "the higher development of our race should be deliberately pursued by the restriction of parenthood to those human beings best fitted for this privilege" (281).

Nevertheless, Meisel-Hess was wary of negative eugenic measures imposed by the state, such as legal prohibitions or sterilization, that would prevent the birth of the unfit. Though she flirted with the idea of marriage prohibitions, noting that "there are no marriage prohibitions for the diseased, the defective, and the degenerate," that "syphilitics are allowed without demur to disseminate the virus of this hereditary disease" and that "drunkards may use their degenerate germ-plasm for the production of the new generation," she stressed more positive eugenic measures: "the production of the 'well-born' must be made the concern of the community at large, altogether apart from the question of the marriage of the parents, which is a purely private matter" (252). According to Meisel-Hess, "The most important means to check the decline in the birth-rate and to improve the quality of the offspring would be the enfranchisement of the procreative power of woman"; to this end, she declared the following measures absolutely imperative: "first, an adequate system of motherhood protection; secondly, properly paid work for women, occupations which women can pursue in amplification of their other social functions as wives and mothers, which will make them economically independent and will enable them to enter sexual partnerships upon equal terms; thirdly, complete moral and social approval of every act of motherhood which in no way impairs the quality of the human race; fourthly, intelligently planned hygienic and educational measures for the care and upbringing of children." These changes, she believed, "would imply upon the part of the community a vigorous intervention in the sexual crisis on racial hygienic or eugenic principles, in order to restore to human beings their natural right to the fulfillment of their biological destiny, and thereby to give in addition that natural and spontaneous happiness, lacking which even the strongest and proudest natures lose elasticity and undergo partial atrophy and degeneration in enforced sexual isolation" (253).

Meisel-Hess's disinclination toward negative eugenic measures can be attributed to the fact that she believed that racial fitness cannot necessarily be determined at birth. She insisted that superior human beings could only be truly and accurately identified under a socialist system, which she characterized as a system that aimed for "the abolition of the economic order which renders possible the uncontrolled exploitation of one human being by another." In her view, "The unfalsified economic selection of the best cannot be effected until a genuine equalization of opportunities has been secured. When all have equal claims to elementary and to higher education, and when all have equal access to the means of production we shall, for the first time, learn who are the truly fit" (268). As a result of this conviction, Meisel-Hess took her compatriot Alfred Ploetz to task for attacking welfare measures and claiming they were undermining the survival of the fittest. "For my own part," Meisel-Hess wrote,

> I am unable to recognize in such protective organization any factors that inhibit the struggle for existence or interfere with the selection of the best. Are the fit more easy to recognize when the workers are exploited without check? Is not limitless exploitation a non-selective factor, and sometimes an anti-selective factor, one calculated to eliminate the stronger varieties also, inasmuch as excessive toil and insufficient nutriment wear down the stronger constitutions no less than the weaker, and ruin the possible offspring even in the germ? This does not lead to the survival of the fittest, but merely serves to make even the fit more and more wretched; and if, in virtue of the law of adaptation, the artificially degraded varieties are able to maintain themselves in the arena, the adaptation is productive of a lower instead of a higher human type. (269)

She therefore insisted that those concerned with racial regeneration ought to question whether capitalism and its exploitative practices were truly responsible for the "abundance in our midst of mental and physical cripples" (269–270). Given capitalism's impacts on racial progress, Meisel-Hess argued that society had a duty to protect its weaker members, and to create social and sexual conditions in which fitter children can be brought into the world. After all, she maintained, "the society that cares for the unfortunate, cures the sick, sustains the weakly, exhibits thereby the possession of intrinsic forces of regeneration" (272). In stressing the role of political economy in racial regeneration, Meisel-Hess demonstrated how both socialism and humanism could be reconciled to eugenic and racial hygienic ways of thinking.

Meisel-Hess believed that ideally, sexual life should be self-governing, guided by a eugenically informed sexual ethic and supported through comprehensive welfare policies and a just economic order. Yet her stress on ethics, self-governance, and fertility had particularly strong implications for women: she was adamant in her insistence that racially fit women have a *duty to* become mothers and to bear many children. Though she did not believe that it was necessary for those who bore children to also raise them, noting that there may be other people more qualified for such work, she insisted that "it is of the first importance that a woman mentally independent and possessed of a good physique should give children to the world" (208). Meisel-Hess consequently maintained a skeptical attitude toward neo-Malthusianism and its advocacy of contraception and abortion. While she believed that people should not be forced to bear more children than they could feed, she nonetheless stressed that every birth that was "annulled" through early death represented a "waste of motherly strength (*Mutterkraft*)" and national economic value.[59]

The other side of the ethical coin was Meisel-Hess's declaration that racially unfit women had a duty *not* to become mothers, even if they desired children. Meisel-Hess explicitly described "reverence for procreation" as "the religion of the future" (*Sexual Crisis*, 281). She maintained that people must approach reproduction as a "sacramental act"—and also recognize that "vast numbers of

---

59. Meisel-Hess, "Die Sexualmoral der Frau," 106.

individuals are quite unfitted for such responsibility" (281). Thus, she declared that parenthood ought to be restricted "to those human beings best fitted for the privilege" in the name of racial improvement (281). According to Meisel-Hess, "Upon the stuff of which man himself is made depends what man himself can make of the world. If he is blighted from birth, the world he creates for himself will be a blighted world. Hence his ultimate world-aim must be a delight in the creation of beautiful and fit human beings" (282). These statements held true not only for man, but also for woman.

Given the implications of individual acts for the collective fate, Meisel-Hess believed that restrictions upon the "freedom of the individual ego" were more than justified (282). She vehemently insisted that "the sexual order must make the aims of racial hygiene its own," and that individuals must internalize the precepts of this "religion" and use them to guide their own conduct (283). Meisel-Hess therefore premised and legitimized women's freedom to participate in sexual life beyond contractual marriage by restricting it to those women deemed fit enough to partake of the sacrament of reproduction, who she insisted would exercise a responsible sexual ethic informed by eugenic imperatives. While racial arguments facilitated Meisel-Hess's call for the liberation of women's sexuality, they also ultimately led her to impose a considerable ethical burden upon women's reproductive freedoms.

That women in Germany and beyond were deeply invested in eugenics during the early twentieth century is not a new insight. For the past three decades at least, historians have grappled not just with the reasons underlying women's investment in the sciences and politics of race and heredity, but also with the legacies of this investment. These questions are particularly fraught and meaningful when it comes to German history. Indeed, the extent to which eugenically committed Wilhelmine scientists and reformers were responsible for creating a discursive and ideological environment that helped make the Nazis' race-based policies possible has long been a pressing question for German historians.[60]

---

60. See Geoff Eley, "Introduction 1: Is There a History of the *Kaiserreich?*" in *Society, Culture, and the State in Germany, 1870–1930* (Ann Arbor: University of

In more recent years, historians have drawn attention to the productivity of eugenics for feminist purposes; that is, they have highlighted what eugenic rationale and arguments enabled women to imagine and demand. Here I have followed a similar tack. I have argued that eugenics, specifically progressive eugenics, appealed to sexual theorists like Grete Meisel-Hess because of its stress on women's critical role in racial regeneration, as well as its conceptualization of sexual ethics. What distinguished progressive eugenics' sexual ethics was its emphasis on individual sexual freedom and individual responsibility in the name of racial improvement. Progressive eugenicists insisted that accepting individual responsibility was a precondition of gaining not just sexual rights and freedoms, but existential agency itself. As Helene Stöcker argued in her 1906 monograph *Love and Women,* having and taking control over one's life, rather than being a passive tool of fate, endowed individuals with the ability—and the duty—to favorably shape the fate of future generations.[61] Eugenics facilitated a discourse that positioned women as autonomous sexual agents entitled to certain rights and freedoms—but also tasked with certain duties and responsibilities.

In this chapter I focused not on feminists in general, but on women sexologists, and specifically on Grete Meisel-Hess, whose work combined feminism, sexual radicalism, and eugenic insights and demands. Like those of many of her male colleagues, Grete Meisel-Hess's analyses of race and sex were inextricably interconnected; she shared their concerns, their values, and their criteria for judging desirable and undesirable physical and psychological traits. Contrary to her male peers, however, Meisel-Hess did not believe that the cause of racial problems lay in the proliferation of hard-wired traits; instead, her diagnosis focused on the inheritance of unjust, unhealthy, and notably patriarchal sexual morals that oppressed women, and on the perpetuation of an exploitative

Michigan Press, 1996), 27–31; Detlev Peukert, "The Genesis of the 'Final Solution' from the Spirit of Science," in *Reevaluating the Third Reich,* ed. Thomas Childers and Jane Caplan (New York: Holmes and Meier, 1993), 234–252.

61. Helene Stöcker, *Die Liebe und die Frauen* (Minden: J. C. C. Bruns' Verlag, 1906), 2.

economic system that made true choice impossible for everyone. For Meisel-Hess, racial salvation lay in the elevating power of female sexuality, and in the equalizing forces of socialism. As a consequence, Meisel-Hess's prescription for racial and sexual regeneration lay in the liberation of the female sex drive from the confines of marriage—and in the support of unrestricted fertility on the part of fit women, facilitated by prudent welfare policies that would ensure their economic security and independence.

Yet Meisel-Hess's analysis was not entirely empowering: although she demanded sexual liberation for all women, reproductive rights were restricted to women deemed valuable according to eugenic standards. Although she did not believe that individual fitness was readily apparent at birth and opposed state-based eugenic measures at this time, she nonetheless upheld a restrictive standard of physical and psychological health as the fundamental precondition for sexual rights and freedoms, including reproductive freedoms. Like her colleague Helene Stöcker, the only legitimate sexual subjects Meisel-Hess countenanced were those who were supposedly healthy in body and mind, and who would thus contribute to racial advancement. These subjects were the only ones deemed capable of affirming life and enjoying its earthly pleasures. This attitude toward sexuality, and especially the assumption that sexual freedom is only legitimate for those people fulfilling a certain limited standard of health, have had consequences for the development of sexually radical politics, particularly its assumed able-bodied rights bearer.

Part of the appeal of politicizing science and nature lies in the power and authority of making claims based on supposedly fundamental, unchanging essences. While recourse to scientifically revealed "natural laws" may be effective in staking claims, it offers little space to maneuver once these claims have been accepted as fact. When does the security of science become a political straitjacket? When does it restrict or foreclose new visions of subjectivity and social transformation, and inhibit experiments with new ways of being and living? These questions immediately jump to the fore once we reflect on the legacy of women sexologists' entanglements with eugenics. At the same, however, it is worth questioning the degree to which biology simply provided a new language for the differential evaluation and treatment of human beings. After all, social criteria such as class, rank, and status—attributes that were "inherited" by generation after generation and at times claimed to be preordained—had long divided humanity, and determined and rationalized different standards of value and treatment. The crucial distinction between biological and social dividing practices lies in the fact that, claims to divine preordination notwithstanding, the latter are unquestionably human creations, subject to human control. While bearing in mind Eve Kosofsky Sedgwick's admonition against viewing cultural constructs as "peculiarly malleable ones," I do maintain that lessons from the eugenic past serve as timely reminders that humans have the power to challenge and change social institutions and arrangements of their own making.[62]

---

62. Eve Kosofsky Sedgwick, *Epistemology of the Closet* (Berkeley: University of California Press, 1990), 43.

6

"NEW SOCIAL AND MORAL VALUES WILL HAVE TO PREVAIL"

Negotiating Crisis and Opportunity in the First World War

In a rare, direct editorial address to her readers, Helene Stöcker opened the 14 August 1914 edition of *The New Generation* by commenting on what was undoubtedly the most important geopolitical event of *her* generation's lifetime. Fourteen days earlier, Germany had declared war on Russia, and since then had invaded Belgium and declared war against France; in so doing, Germany became embroiled in the increasingly global conflict sparked by Austria-Hungary's declaration of war on Serbia on 28 July 1914. Stöcker's editorial served not only as a way of taking stock of the great transformations wrought by the outbreak of the war, but also as a justification for continued sexual knowledge production and sexual reform activism. In her editorial, Stöcker insisted that the work of "refining and elevating feeling and behavior" was needed now more than ever in this time of struggle for "naked Existence" among individuals and states.[1] In her view, "Even during

---

1. Helene Stöcker, "An unsere Leser!," *Die neue Generation* 8/9 (14 August 1914): 409.

222   *Sexual Politics and Feminist Science*

wartime the power of cultural work cannot be extinguished." In fact, she maintained that the opposite was true: namely, that "well-organized, peaceful, effective, and purposeful cultural work on the inside is one of the main preconditions by which the victory, which our weapons achieve on the outside, can be made truly fruitful for us."[2] Stöcker's insistence on the continued need for and relevance of the "cultural work" of sexual analysis and reform was not merely self-serving. Rather, she recognized at a very early stage the intimate interconnection between war and sex that would become increasingly apparent over the next four years.

The First World War marked an unprecedented moment in the sex lives of Europeans. Although states had long played critical roles in governing individuals' sex lives, for example, through laws surrounding marriage, prostitution, and access to contraceptive information and technology, they had rarely intervened so directly in the private sexual sphere as they did during the war. In Germany and beyond, military and civilian authorities endeavored to discipline and harness sex in gender-specific ways that could aid (or at the very least not inhibit) the realization of strategic national goals. Much of the German state's wartime interest in sexuality was driven by the so-called population question, which sought the best methods to increase the quantity and "quality" of the national population. Officials also demonstrated a growing concern with the state of sexual morality, and feared that a decline in sexual standards would inhibit the war effort, the stability of domestic and familial arrangements, and relations of power between the sexes after the war.[3]

---

2. Ibid., 410. She reiterated such claims at the beginning of 1915, declaring, "Our work to improve the living and developmental conditions for mothers and children—married and unmarried—[and] to help create purer, deeper, sincerer (*innigere*) love relationships between man and woman: it has not lost its meaning for the people (*Volksganze*) during the war." In fact, she insisted that the opposite was true, and that their work was more important than ever. See Helene Stöcker, "An unsere Leser!," *Die neue Generation* 1 (1915): 1.

3. On the population question during the war, see Cornelie Usborne, *The Politics of the Body in Weimar Germany: Women's Reproductive Rights and Duties* (Ann Arbor: University of Michigan Press, 1992), 16–30; Lisa Todd, "Sexual

From the perspective of many sexologists and sex reformers, the war had finally brought much-desired state attention to issues they had repeatedly insisted were pressing collective concerns, above all the "population question" and sexual morality. However, the war added new dimensions to reformers and sexologists' analyses of sexual matters, along with a new set of objectives for the transformation of sexual life following the war. Remarkably, in spite of worsening social, political, and economic conditions over the course of the war, reformers and sexologists continued to write and publish texts that grappled with the conflict's impacts on sex and sexuality, and to advance diverse visions for postwar reform. This chapter examines how the war impacted sexology, and specifically how women sexologists analyzed the effects of the war on sexuality and sexual relations. It offers a fascinating look at how sexologists tried to make sense of the war as it was happening. By examining sexologists' wartime texts, we can gain a sense of their prevailing anxieties at the time, along with their hopes and fears for the future. Furthermore, doing so allows us to consider a number of temporally specific questions. Did the war change the ways sexologists studied sex, and if so how? Did it provoke new analyses of sex and sexuality? And did it inspire new political demands, or even radicalize long-standing ones?

I explore these questions by analyzing texts written by Helene Stöcker, Grete Meisel-Hess, and Henriette Fürth, as well as a new author whose works began appearing in sexological journals during the war years, Mathilde Vaerting. Hailing from a large, well-off Catholic family in western Germany, Mathilde Vaerting began her career like many women of her time, as a teacher. While still working as a teacher, she earned her doctorate from the University of Bonn in 1911, after advanced study of math, physics, chemistry, philosophy, and medicine. Vaerting started working with radical educational reform movements, sex reform movements, and sexological associations including the League for the Protection of Mothers and Sexual Reform, and, unusually for a woman, the

Treason: State Surveillance of Immortality and Infidelity in World War I Germany" (PhD diss., University of Toronto, 2005), 181–226.

International Society for Sexual Research, after moving to Berlin in 1913 to take up a position as an *Oberlehrerin*, or senior primary-school teacher. In 1923, despite the strong opposition of her male colleagues, she was appointed to the newly established academic position of professor of pedagogy (*Erziehungswissenschaft*) at the University of Jena; she thus became Germany's second female university professor.

The First World War marked a significant moment in women's sexological writing, and provides another example of the ways in which gender mattered in sexological discourse. Although women writers were concerned with many of the same issues as their male peers, and even agreed with them on certain key points, they diverged in important ways and contributed a number of unique insights and arguments. The war empowered women to advance new critiques of male sexuality and patriarchy, and to theorize the evolutionary causes of the war. It also led women to take new factors into account when analyzing sexual life and its problems. Women sexologists treated the war not only as a crisis, but also as an opportunity for rethinking and transforming sexual life.[4] As Henriette Fürth argued, "New social and new moral values will arise and have to prevail if indeed this mightiest struggle is to be fruitful for us."[5] Arguably, the exigencies of the war and its uncertain resolution led women to hope that even some of their more radical moral and institutional reform demands could become realities.

The extraordinary conditions of the war proved productive both for women's sexological analyses and for their claims making on behalf of women's sexual and social empowerment. Yet as was the case before the war, women's understandings and evaluations of sex were fundamentally informed—and, I argue, constrained—by

---

4. My invocation of the duality of crisis and opportunity vis-à-vis sexual life is inspired by Birthe Kundrus's writing on the transformation of gender roles during the war; see Birthe Kundrus, "Gender Wars: The First World War and the Construction of Gender Relations in the Weimar Republic," in *Home/Front: The Military, War, and Gender in Twentieth-Century Germany*, ed. Karen Hagemann and Stefanie Schüller-Springorum (Oxford: Berg, 2002), 160.

5. Henriette Fürth, "Sexuelle Kriegsfragen," *Zeitschrift für Sexualwissenschaft* 2 (1915/1916): 137.

the eugenic principles and concerns with health and productivity that animated sexological and official discourse. These concerns were only heightened by the massive loss of life over the course of the war, and by mounting concerns regarding the health of the fighting forces and the starving civilian population on the home front. The responsibility for regenerating the population and upholding sexual morality still rested on women's shoulders, as was the case before the war; however, given the stakes involved, this burden now weighed especially heavily, and made it even harder for women sexologists to legitimize women's rights independently of larger "racial" goals, as ends in themselves.

Not Incidental: The Role of Sex during the First World War

Although sex had long been a part of warfare, the First World War marked an unprecedented moment of state regulation of the sex lives of private individuals. This phenomenon was not particular to Germany, but extended throughout Europe and into the larger imperial world.[6] Within Germany, the state introduced a range of new laws, policies, and legislative proposals between 1914 and 1918 that aimed to regulate sexuality both at the war front and on the home front. Reviewing the state's regulatory efforts during the war helps illuminate not only the perceived importance of sexuality to the war effort and even to the fate of the nation, but also the changing social, political, and legal landscapes sexologists and reformers confronted.

Although women and men both faced thoroughgoing regulation of their sexual activity during the war, the regulations themselves

---

6. See, for example, Philippa Levine, *Prostitution, Race, and Politics: Policing Venereal Disease in the British* Empire (New York: Routledge, 2003); Nicoletta Gullace, *The Blood of Our Sons: Men, Women, and the Renegotiation of British Citizenship during the Great War* (New York: Palgrave Macmillan, 2002); Susan Grayzel, *Women's Identities at War: Gender, Motherhood, and Politics in Britain and France during the First World War* (Chapel Hill: University of North Carolina Press, 1999).

were gender differentiated in ways that recapitulated and legally inscribed the sexual double standard. Fears regarding a high rate of venereal diseases among soldiers, in addition to gendered beliefs regarding the necessity of (hetero)sexual activity for men's health, led the military to facilitate and regulate prostitution at the war front. The military helped arrange soldiers' regular visits, provided them with prophylactics, and also subjected them to frequent inspections for disease. Military leaders undertook these measures not to ensure the happiness of individual soldiers, but rather in the name of military efficiency and public health. Specifically, officials believed regulated prostitution would help maintain troop morale, bolster Germany's fighting power, and prevent the spread of venereal diseases in the civilian population.[7]

On the home front the long-term and often permanent separation of husbands and wives, combined with the increased presence of unaccompanied women in public as workers, volunteers, and household providers, gave rise to new measures that placed women's sexual behavior under widespread surveillance. The state tightened its control over prostitution "at home" by broadening the definition of a prostitute to include any woman who had sex outside of marriage, regardless of whether money changed hands.[8] Lisa Todd has shown that even in the early days of the war, German police "declared, in essence, that 'acting like a prostitute' was akin to actually being one."[9] According to Elizabeth Domansky, the effect of this change was to make it "legally admissible to report women who had several male visitors in a month's time to the police as suspected prostitutes." Women who were repeatedly reported could then be forced to register as prostitutes.[10]

---

7. Elizabeth Domansky, "Militarization and Reproduction in World War One Germany," in *Society, Culture, and the State in Germany, 1870–1930*, ed. Geoff Eley (Ann Arbor: University of Michigan Press, 1997), 449.

8. Todd, "Sexual Treason," 18.

9. In May 1916, the commander of the Second Army Corps declared that "any female person infected with a venereal disease could be placed under surveillance, 'even in the event that evidence of professional prostitution is not present'"; Todd, "Sexual Treason," 108.

10. Domansky, "Militarization and Reproduction," 450.

Beyond these new measures aimed at suppressing prostitution, police also stepped up their surveillance of taverns, pubs, and hostess bars in order to control the supposedly loose and lewd women who pursued work and pleasure there. Local police departments attempted to force these establishments to prohibit registered women from entry, dismiss their female employees, and close by an appointed curfew.[11] Women were further policed in their interactions with foreign prisoners of war. Here, the penalties for fraternization were severe: women faced imprisonment for up to one year, or a fine of up to 1,500 marks, if they had intimate encounters with the enemy.[12] All of these measures aimed not just to control women's behavior in public spaces, but to suppress all expressions of extramarital, extradomestic female sexuality and, by punishing contact with POWs, to try to safeguard national and racial purity. In so doing, the state took it upon itself to defend the institution of marriage, specifically by keeping an eye on soldiers' sexual "property" at home, as Domansky points out.[13] The state took an active role in policing the boundaries of female respectability and suppressing perceived signs of female sexual disorder.

The state's unprecedented intervention into women's sex lives paralleled women's unprecedented involvement in public life. Women were mobilized in service of the total war effort through a variety of activities, including paid industrial labor, agriculture, nursing, military auxiliaries, and traditionally male civil service jobs, in addition to myriad voluntary activities. Over the course of the war, the League of German Women's Associations introduced the National Women's Service, which cooperated with the Ministry of the Interior to provide support for families of men fighting at the front, mobilize women for war work, and coordinate the food supply. The National Women's Service put the women's movement in constant contact with the government at all levels, and it advised the government on matters of welfare and women's

---

11. Todd, "Sexual Treason," 126–127.
12. Ibid., 150–152.
13. Domansky, "Militarization and Reproduction," 450.

labor.[14] Even progressive feminists such as Henriette Fürth worked in the National Women's Service and helped establish "war kitchens" (*Kriegsküche*) and other services that supported the war effort.[15] Local branches of the League for the Protection of Mothers and Sexual Reform also stepped up their provisions for unwed mothers and their children by establishing more birthing centers and advice centers and providing more beds for pregnant single mothers.[16] Meanwhile, women who opposed the war effort also took on important leadership roles in the international women's pacifist movement, a development that not only led them to articulate highly sophisticated critiques of the nation-state and visions for international governance institutions, but also served as a training ground for further political leadership positions after the war. Women involved in the suffrage movement were especially prominent in the peace movement.[17] Although historians have debated the questions of whether any of these developments had long-standing, transformative implications for women's rights and gender roles themselves, and whether the war marked a moment of emancipation for women, it seems clear that women experienced a greater degree of agency than before, even if it was constrained. As a result of their experience during the war, many women believed they had proven themselves capable of greater roles and responsibilities in the postwar polity.

In addition to measures aimed at controlling venereal disease among soldiers and policing women's sexual behavior at home— measures that often facilitated men's sexual opportunities while restricting women's—the German state proposed and introduced new measures aimed at boosting national population numbers.

---

14. Richard J. Evans, *The Feminist Movement in Germany, 1894–1933* (London: Sage Publications, 1976), 208.

15. Angelika Epple, *Henriette Fürth und die Frauenbewegung im deutschen Kaiserreich: Eine Sozialbiographie* (Pfaffenweiler: Centaurus Verlaggesellschaft, 1996), 107–108.

16. Bernd Nowacki, *Der Bund für Mutterschutz (1905–1933)* (Husum: Matthiesen Verlag, 1983), 92–94.

17. On German feminists and the peace movement, see Evans, *Feminist Movement in Germany*, 214–223.

Although Germany's birthrate had been falling since the late 1890s and had already become a subject of concern among some state officials and social reformers before the war, this issue gained in importance during the war.[18] As Cornelie Usborne has observed, "The prospect of slaughter on the battlefields and the need for national defence meant that *Volkskraft* (population strength) was more than ever equated with *Wehrkraft* (military strength)."[19] Discussion of and activism surrounding the population question markedly intensified during and after autumn 1915, following a breakthrough of German and Austrian forces in Russia that led many to think that victory on the Eastern Front was near, but that the nation was not ready for the task of postwar rebuilding and renewal.[20]

To promote the birthrate, the state proposed a range of positive and punitive measures; however, many of these measures were never realized, and among those that were put into effect, punishment trumped incentive. Usborne has noted that despite the enthusiastic support of the Kaiser, state ministries, and the army—to say nothing of the fervent support expressed by certain quarters of civil society—the comprehensive system of material incentives initially envisioned by the government, which included the construction of new infant care centers, children's hospitals, and crèches, was ultimately "reduced to small-scale measures which were often uncoordinated, contradictory, and unrealistic."[21] Some of the new welfare provisions that were introduced included midwifery reforms, the development of improved infant feeding practices, and enhanced training of pediatric nurses.[22] The state also enhanced welfare provided to soldiers' wives and families under the Law Regarding the Support of Men in Military Service (1888/1914), and

18. Usborne, *Politics of the Body*, 16–17; Todd, "Sexual Treason," 184–185.
19. Usborne, *Politics of the Body*, 16.
20. Todd, "Sexual Treason," 186.
21. Usborne, *Politics of the Body*, 19; see also Todd, "Sexual Treason," 213. According to Paul Weindling, this outcome was largely the responsibility of the Finance Ministry, which withheld necessary funds. See Paul Weindling, *Health, Race, and German Politics between National Unification and Nazism, 1870–1945* (Cambridge: Cambridge University Press, 1993), 290.
22. Todd, "Sexual Treason," 211.

even extended support to unwed mothers and their children, providing women could prove the child's father was in active service.[23] The extension of welfare to unwed mothers exemplifies how ideas that were considered "morally outrageous" before the war—in this case the League for the Protection of Mothers and Sexual Reform's decade-long campaign for rights and recognition of unwed mothers and their children—became "recognized as intrinsic to the national interest," as Paul Weindling has observed.[24] In addition to these welfare measures, venereal disease treatment clinics began appearing in major German cities, offering another example of the moral changes effected by the war. Funded by local insurance boards, these clinics offered free advice, testing, and treatment to their clients. The first clinic had actually opened before the war, in Hamburg in January 1914, and treated 932 patients in its first year. By 1917, ninety clinics had opened nationwide.[25]

Whereas the state's patchy public health and welfare measures sought to incentivize reproduction, its more thoroughgoing punitive approaches endeavored to prevent contraception. Beginning in 1915, military authorities prohibited the display, advertisement, and sale of contraceptives and abortifacients—aside from condoms, which were exempted as prophylactics and primarily facilitated men's sexual freedoms.[26] In the following years, the Prussian Medical Council and Reich Health Council articulated guidelines to restrict doctors' abortion practice: henceforth, only registered medical practitioners would be able to terminate pregnancies, and only in instances where the woman's health and life were seriously threatened.[27] Additionally, the state introduced a legal ban against the publication of the names of newlyweds to prevent contraceptive dealers from soliciting to them.[28] In 1917, the German government tabled three bills that drastically aimed to "solve" the population problem. These bills required the mandatory treatment of VD and

---

23. Ibid., 214, 218.
24. Weindling, *Health, Race, and German Politics*, 281.
25. Todd, "Sexual Treason," 193.
26. Usborne, *Politics of the Body*, 21.
27. Ibid.
28. Todd, "Sexual Treason," 204.

threatened up to three years in jail for anyone who knowingly infected others. They also prohibited the manufacture, sale, and advertising of all contraception—except, again, the condom—and outlawed abortion except under strict medical regulations. Furthermore, physicians who performed unlawful sterilizations could be sentenced to up to three years of prison time, and their patients would also be subject to criminal sanction. Although these bills passed the German parliament, they were never enacted, thanks to the November 1918 Revolution.[29]

Despite the comprehensiveness and potential reach of these laws, their success in realizing their objectives was mixed. Although these new measures, along with increased vigilance among policing authorities, led to an increase in prosecutions of male pharmacists and doctors, the informal, neighborhood-based, and predominately female networks that circulated contraceptive techniques were more difficult to regulate.[30] Moreover, public response to the suppression of abortions and contraception was divided and complicated by debates regarding the fate of children born to German mothers and foreign fathers, whether consensual or the result of force.[31] The inadequacies of the aforementioned criminal laws, along with the public ambivalence surrounding the desirability of restricting abortion and contraceptives, illuminate the complications involved in the state's efforts to regulate sexuality during wartime, and suggest some of the reasons why civilian sexual experts and activists may have felt emboldened to intervene with their own ideas for reform.

Sexology during Wartime

As the preceding section demonstrates, sex was not inconsequential or marginal to the waging of war. On the contrary, the state's multifaceted intervention into the sexual lives of soldiers and

---

29. Usborne, *Politics of the Body*, 21–23.
30. Todd, "Sexual Treason," 205–207.
31. Ibid., 222–224.

civilians illuminates the importance attached to sex as key to social order, military success, and national aggrandizement. From the
perspective of many sexologists and reformers, the state's willingness to take an active role in shaping private sexual lives, particularly surrounding reproduction, was a welcome change from its
prewar stance. The war actually appeared to confirm sexologists'
long-standing insistence that understanding and improving sexual life were matters of critical sociopolitical, national, and racial
importance.

Perusing the pages of the major sexological and sex reform journals during the First World War, the reader is immediately struck
by the continuity of themes from the prewar era. During the war,
writers continued to pursue their preoccupations with the spread
and containment of venereal diseases, prostitution, abortion and
contraception, sexual and racial hygiene, female sexuality, heterosexual unions, and sexual ethics. Yet wartime analyses of these
phenomena necessarily differed from those advanced during the
Wilhelmine era because the war exacerbated already troubling prewar sexual realities and created a new set of objectives for the reform of sexual life. The tone of sexological analyses also changed
over the course of the war, and arguably reflected not only the
unprecedented human cost of the war but also Germany's declining fortunes.

During the first years of the war, the majority of German sexologists espoused explicitly nationalist sentiments. This development
represented a break with work produced before the war, which
by and large eschewed explicit nationalism and certainly profited
from international collaboration; in fact, the envisioned audience
of much prewar sexological work was seemingly universal. Texts
written and published especially during the early years of the war
reflected their authors' desires to serve the German nation, and
many male sexologists served at the front in surgical hospitals.
They continued to write during their service, and the designation
"zur Zeit im Felde," or "at the moment in the field," accompanied
their bylines. The *Journal for Sexual Science* went so far as to ad-
vertise war loans. Notably, this early tendency toward nationalism
can be found not only in the texts of male sexologists, but also in

the work of left-leaning women sexologists like Helene Stöcker. Although Stöcker had long-standing links to the German peace movement dating back to 1892, her early war writings expressed remarkable patriotism.[32] In articles like "The War and Women" and "Love or Hate?" for example, she declared that the League for the Protection of Mothers and Sexual Reform was a distinctively "Germanic" movement that fought for the "healthy physical development of our people."[33] At the beginning of the war, she described women's lack of civilian mobilization in support of the war as "shamefully deficient," and insisted that women ought to take an active role in the war effort.[34] According to Stöcker at that time, women had distinctive roles to play as caregivers, protectors of morality, and purveyors of love in the face of nationalistic hatred.[35]

However, as the war dragged on and casualty rates soared, Stöcker's horror at the slaughter of millions and her concern for the fate of cultural progress led her to adopt a defiantly pacifist stance that subsequently influenced her analyses of the war. Her position was also reflected in the leadership roles she assumed within new, uncompromising pacifist organizations such as the League for a New Fatherland. Over the course of 1915, her attitude toward the war became unambiguously critical. In her article "Sex Psychology and War," she wrote that one of the few good side effects of the war were "the gains in psychological clarity and insight" it provided, specifically concerning the true nature of "civilized peoples" (*Kulturmenschen*).[36] Increasingly, Stöcker believed that the

32. Regina Braker, "Helene Stöcker's Pacifism in the Weimar Republic: Between Ideal and Reality," *Journal of Women's History* 13 (Autumn 2001): 71.

33. According to Stöcker, the fact that the league's practical endeavors to improve biological and social conditions were inextricably connected with an intellectual, idealistic movement was what made the league so "eminently German" and gave to it a very "Germanic character." Helene Stöcker, "Liebe oder Hassen?," *Die neue Generation* 12 (1914): 531–532.

34. Helene Stöcker, "Der Krieg und die Frauen," *Die neue Generation* 8/9 (14 August 1914): 425–426.

35. Stöcker, "Liebe oder Hassen?," 545–546.

36. Helene Stöcker, "Geschlechtspsychologie und Krieg," *Die neue Generation* 1 (1915): 287. In 1917, Stöcker asserted that "we have learned more about human psychology during the last three years than we knew thirty years ago"; Stöcker, "Gewalt oder Verständigung," *Die neue Generation* 5 (1917): 200.

so-called civilized nations had really not evolved at all, and that the evolutionary progress enjoyed by civilized people was only technical and superficial.[37] The war proved to Stöcker that "primitive" tendencies lay just under the surface, and that one had "only to scratch—and the barbarian is revealed."[38]

By 1916, Stöcker's pacifism and commitment to cosmopolitanism became unmistakable and enmeshed with her views on gender, sexuality, and civilization. She ultimately came to see the goals of the protection of mothers, sexual reform, and pacifism as interconnected. In her article "Hatred of Other Peoples and the Press," she observed, "Before the war we fought for a refinement of sexual morals, against the double standard in the relationship of the sexes. Since the war started, we have had to recognize that a double moral standard also exists beyond sexual life, that is, wherever force seeks to replace the rule of law."[39] Stöcker came to view the "double standard" as a feature not just of sexual life, but of social and even geopolitical life, and that the further evolution of culture was impossible without a fight against the ideology justifying war.[40] She was adamant in her belief that "a human being is not just a means, but an end in itself at any time."[41] Aside from such universalist principles, Stöcker's maternalist views also influenced her pacifism. Although she did not believe that women were innately pacifistic, she did maintain that women were more inclined toward peace. In her article "Sex Psychology and War," she argued that women ought to recognize how "senseless and suicidal for women" (*sinnlos und selbstmörderisch für Frauen*) it is to support a worldview that placed power and violence (*Gewalt*) above Right (*Recht*), given that such systems tended to operate against women's interests and their investments in the creation, rather than the destruction, of life.[42]

37. Stöcker, "Gewalt oder Verständigung," 209.
38. Helene Stöcker, "Volkerhaß und Presse," *Die neue Generation* 3 (1917): 83.
39. Ibid., 87.
40. Helene Stöcker, "Moderne Bevölkerungspolitik," *Die neue Generation* 3/4 (1916): 85.
41. Helene Stöcker, "Menschlichkeit," *Die neue Generation* 1/2 (1916): 13.
42. Stöcker, "Geschlechtspsychologie und Krieg," 293.

As a consequence of her pacifism, Stöcker abandoned her erst-while nationalism in favor of appeals to a seemingly universal humanity, and became a vocal critic of both the German state and even the very concept of the state itself. In her 1916 article, "Humanity"—a term that began to appear in sex reform jour-nals over the course of the First World War—Stöcker character-ized war as "the triumph of a state in its original form: [namely, as] an organization of power."[43] Stöcker repeatedly called upon all states to stop treating their citizens as "the fertilizer of civilization" (*Kulturdünger*), and instead treat them as "the carriers of culture" (*Kulturträger*). This shift in perspective, she insisted, would inhibit states from sacrificing their highest wealth: healthy, highly devel-oped humans.[44] However, Stöcker's pacifism and criticism of the state placed her in conflict with the majority of the League for the Protection of Mothers and Sexual Reform's membership.[45]

Similarly, at the beginning of the war, left-leaning sexologist and homosexual rights activist Magnus Hirschfeld displayed a surpris-ing degree of nationalist fervor. He counseled gay men and women who wished to serve in the military on how to pass as straight, and encouraged them to send him reports of their heroism so they could be published in the *Quarterly Reports of the Scientific Humanitar-ian Committee*.[46] Hirschfeld believed that such evidence would not only prove gay men and women's much-doubted courage and pa-triotism, but also secure a sense of belonging in the nation and per-haps even support for their political demands.[47] What biographer Elena Mancini refers to as the apogee of Hirschfeld's "naïve pa-triotism" came with the 1915 publication of his pamphlet, "Why Do Other Nations Hate Us?" in which he asserted that Germany's

43. Stöcker, "Menschlichkeit," 22.
44. Stöcker, "Moderne Bevölkerungspolitik," 86.
45. Nowacki, *Der Bund für Mutterschutz*, 83, 86.
46. Elena Mancini, *Magnus Hirschfeld and the Quest for Sexual Freedom: A History of the First International Sexual Freedom Movement* (New York: Palgrave Macmillan, 2010), 111.
47. Ibid. Note Mancini's citation of Charlotte Wolff's observation that Hirschfeld's nationalism could have been a strategic response to antisemitism (*Magnus Hirschfeld*, 112); however, it could have equally been a strategic response to the opportunity to advance LGBT rights.

enemies were envious of its desirable social, economic, and political conditions and fearful of its geopolitical potential.[48] It was not until Hirschfeld served as a Red Cross inspector at the war front in 1916 that he adopted an unwavering, unapologetic pacifist stance in response to the horrors he witnessed.[49] Thereafter Hirschfeld became a member of the League for a New Fatherland.[50]

As Stöcker and Hirschfeld's commitments to pacifism intimate, the war shook both male and female sexologists' faith in the beneficial outcomes of evolution, specifically in the idea that human evolution would inevitably lead to progressive improvements in sexual, social, and political life. Most sexologists believed that the war represented a kind of mass atavism, marking the triumph of primal urges and bloodlust over moderation, restraint, and reason. Although some naively believed early on that the war would have positive evolutionary effects, such hopes faded quickly as the war took its crushing toll, and such beliefs were instead replaced by the view that the war represented a major setback for human progress. Some sexologists saw the war as causing an active regression of humanity, including among supposedly civilized Europeans. The range of phenomena taken as symptomatic of degeneration highlights the fact that the diagnosis of war as atavism cut across political ideologies. Among the signs of degeneration male and female sexologists identified were women's abandonment of sexual ethics and "honor" on the home front; the sexual violence inflicted upon civilians by invading armies; the awakening of primitive bloodlust and erotic instincts on the battlefield; and reports of interracial relationships between white women and colonial soldiers on European soil. Regarding the latter point, physician Ike Spier characterized the attraction of "certain women to foreign, exotic men, colored soldiers, prisoners of war" as an "atavistic phenomenon" that represented a "relapse" into "the primeval times of spousal choice, where the most striking,

---

48. Mancini, *Magnus Hirschfeld*, 112.
49. Ibid.
50. Ralf Dose, *Magnus Hirschfeld: The Origins of the Gay Liberation Movement*, trans. Edward H. Willis (New York: Monthly Review Press, 2014), 47.

strongest, most bizarre, most full of sexual secrets and most prom-
ising [mates] were chosen."[51]

Intriguingly (and somewhat dishearteningly), instead of making European sexologists more circumspect about their place on
the evolutionary scale, the war made many *more* insistent on preserving their assumed place at the top, and more concerned with
supposedly race-based group differences. Sexologists' belief that
civilization itself was under threat (civilization of course being
a condition they thought had been realized only by Europeans)
made them fearful of a lapse into barbarity on the Continent,
which in turn would facilitate the triumph of other, supposedly
inferior races as hegemonic geopolitical forces. In fact, this perceived need to defend and safeguard civilization—or rather, European supremacy—fueled some sexologists' pacifist positions.

These tendencies are evident in August Forel's pacifist treatise,
The United States of Earth (1914). Here the reader confronts critical analyses of, among other topics, geopolitics, international political economy, and nationalism as an ideology and psychological
phenomenon. However, woven through these concerns are various
kinds of racial anxieties that betray their author's overt cosmo-
politan orientation. In *The United States of Earth*, Forel insisted
that peace could only be achieved through the cultural and social
disciplining of the "predator instinct" that lay dormant within all
humans. Although he maintained that "culture cannot change humanity's inherited nature," he nonetheless believed that "humans
can, through appropriate upbringing, be brought to experience
social sentiments, perform social work, be frugal and disciplined,
that is to say, can more or less be made to conform to social
duties."[52] Yet at the same time, Forel also maintained that a necessary precondition for taming primal, aggressive human instincts
was the achievement of a certain cultural status, one that he believed only Europeans had achieved. Forel clarified that the pacifist

---

51. Ike Spier, "Der Einfluss des Krieges auf das Geschlechtsleben," *Die neue
Generation* 5/6 (May/June 1916): 135.

52. August Forel, *Die Vereinigten Staaten der Erde: Ein Kulturprogramm* (Lausanne: Buchdruckerei Fr. Ruedi, 1914), 5.

program for a "United States of the Earth" was only to be applied to "civilized nations" (*Kulturnationen*); according to him, "Only an international agreement among all cultured nations on fair arrangements can thwart that danger [of war]; the end of the present war will offer a unique opportunity to achieve this end."[53] Aside from China, which Forel believed was "once again becoming a cultured nation," he maintained that "the rest of the barbaric or wild people barely come into consideration."[54] Moreover, Forel's insistence on the necessity of attaining a certain level of cultural evolution as a precondition for peace led him to justify the maintenance of colonies within his envisioned "United States of the Earth." Although he opined that it was difficult to know which groups could be taught the rudiments of culture, he nonetheless believed that certain races could only be "tamed" and taught to externally adapt "our culture" as long as they remained under the dominance of a higher race, lest they fall back into "sad barbarism."[55] In his view, "Our goal must be to make people everywhere happier by freeing them from barbarism and by ensuring at the same time their enjoyment of freedom to a degree that they can bear without jeopardizing the outstanding social value of all humanity."[56] According to Forel, those peoples that could not (or would not) adopt the standards of (European) culture would ultimately go extinct. He insisted that it was merely a fact of evolution that "the uncivilized people die out; culture rapidly conquers the rest of the world."[57] Similar attitudes toward race, peace, and civilization could be found in the writings of sexologists beyond German-speaking Europe, most notably in the work of Havelock Ellis.[58]

In addition to viewing the war as a major step backward for human progress, male and female sexologists also viewed the war as

---

53. Ibid., 9.
54. Ibid.
55. Ibid., 16, 20.
56. Ibid., 20.
57. Ibid., 7.
58. See Havelock Ellis, *Essays in War-Time* (London: Constable, 1916); Ellis, *The Philosophy of Conflict, and Other Essays in War Time. Second Series* (1919; Reprint, Freeport, NY: Books for Libraries Press, 1970).

highly dysgenic. Sexologists invested in racial hygiene warned that both the functional and the nervous sexual problems that afflicted some soldiers, such as impotence and the increasing spread of venereal diseases, were threatening men's fertility and potentially damaging the health and well-being of their wives and future children.[59] Moreover, they feared that instead of weeding out weaker men as previous wars had supposedly done, the indiscriminate and wide-ranging destruction of modern, technological warfare was exercising a disastrous eugenic counterselection by decimating even the fittest of soldiers. Many decried the massive loss of what was often referred to as blossoming life, and feared the demographic consequences of losing so many healthy men at the front. Sexologists foresaw a range of disastrous knock-on effects that would follow this loss of life. First, they noted the obvious: namely, that the war had dealt a disastrous blow to population numbers, which would take some time to recover. This effect was notably less worrying to eugenically inclined sexologists than to the pronatalist state: in fact, many sexologists maintained that a falling birthrate was a sign of higher evolution.[60] Second, sexologists argued that the war's high death toll would exacerbate the prewar demographic imbalance between men and women; specifically, it would increase the numbers of so-called surplus women of marriageable age who would not be able to find husbands. Third, sexologists prophesied that the war's impact on the population would give an unnatural and detrimental advantage to unfit men on the marriage market; that is, they worried that men afflicted with diseases or disabled by the war would, in the absence of fitter and more desirable male rivals, be able to reproduce, with supposedly disastrous results for future generations.[61]

---

59. See, for example, Ike Spier, "Der Einfluss des Krieges auf das Geschlechts-leben," 129–141; Wilhelm Stekel, "Kriegsliteratur: Prof. Friedl Pick, Über Sexu-alstörungen im Kriege," *Zeitschrift für Sexualwissenschaft* 5 (May 1918): 79–80.

60. For example, see Eduard David, "Der Krieg und das Bevölkerungsproblem," *Die neue Generation* 11 (November 1914): 469–480.

61. See, for example, Buschan, "Bücherbesprechungen: Geza von Hoffmann, 'Krieg und Rassenhygiene,'" *Zeitschrift für Sexualwissenschaft* 3, no. 5 (August 1916): 231.

In order to mitigate the war's dysgenic effects, sexologists advocated a range of reforms. Those who subscribed to a conservative interpretation of eugenics and racial hygiene continued their push for various invasive and prohibitive measures, including marriage restrictions on the "unfit," sterilization for those individuals deemed less valuable, and longer prison terms for convicted criminals. Additionally, they advocated ideological and cultural campaigns to shift public attitudes and thereby mold behavior. To this end, they encouraged both the social celebration of "child-rich" healthy families and the adoption of an attitude of sexual "revulsion toward less valuable races."[62]

Conversely, sexologist Hermann Rohleder and social democrat Eduard David stressed the importance of fostering better life chances among those children already alive. They therefore stressed the need to reduce the infant mortality rate and create better and healthier living conditions for the majority of people. As we will see, many of their proposals resembled those put forward before the war by writers like Grete Meisel-Hess. According to Eduard David, the population question would only be resolved if "better conditions of existence" were realized "for the masses: adequate food and nutrition, healthy homes, a reduction in working time, security against threats to health and accidents, and special protections for women, youth, and children—in short, the whole wide field of economic and social policy, focused to elevate the poorer social classes."[63] Both David and Rohleder called for the development of a comprehensive program of mother and child protection and the introduction of science-based sexual education in schools. Likewise, they insisted on the need to eliminate the social and material obstacles that prevented many men and women from marrying and starting a family, and advocated incentives such as an increase in civil servants' salaries and a reduction in compulsory military service for married men. Rohleder further insisted on the need to

---

62. Buschan, "Bücherbesprechung: Geza von Hoffmann," 231.

63. David, "Der Krieg und das Bevölkerungsproblem," 473. See also Eduard David, "Krieg und Bevölkerungspolitik," *Zeitschrift für Sexualwissenschaft* 4 (January/February 1917): 393–401.

"energetically fight venereal diseases . . . criminal abortions . . . [and] alcoholism," "remove the imposed celibacy rule on Catholic priests and female civil servants," and "restrict emigration."[64] These reforms were justified not only on humanitarian grounds, but on political-economic ones as well, specifically on appeals to national efficiency and productive potential. Rohleder and David both invoked Austrian sociologist Rudolf Goldscheid's influential concept of "human economy" (*Menschenökonomie*), which represented healthy human life as a form of foundational capital for the entire economy. Yet even these more environmentally oriented authors advocated sterilization among "people who are unfit for life, incurable, mentally ill, criminal, etc. just like in North America," where states such as Indiana (1907) and California (1909) had passed some of the world's first compulsory sterilization laws.[65]

Finally, male and female sexologists alike preoccupied themselves with the sexual-ethical consequences of the war. Many believed that the combination of long-term spousal separation and newfound sexual freedoms threatened not merely the institution of marriage, but the practice and value of monogamy itself. In particular, many male sexologists feared that as a result of their wartime freedoms, women would become less interested in marriage and lose their commitment to an ideal of monogamy. Sexologists also warned that the war was depressing the very will to have children on the part of both genders.[66] Although most sexologists agreed that sexual morals and values were declining, they disagreed—notably along gendered lines—on who was ultimately to blame for these developments. Many male sexologists maintained that women's promiscuity was responsible for wartime sexual degeneration. They attributed women's increased promiscuity to psychological

---

64. Hermann Rohleder, "Hebung der Geburtenziffer nach dem Kriege," *Zeitschrift für Sexualwissenschaft* 4 (April 1917): 16.

65. Ibid., 21.

66. See David, "Der Krieg und das Bevölkerungsproblem," 469–480; David, "Krieg und Bevölkerungspolitik, 393–401; Dr. M. Vaerting, "Über den Einfluß des Krieges auf Präventivverkehr und Fruchtabtreibung und seine eugenischen Folgen," *Zeitschrift für Sexualwissenschaft* 4 (July 1917): 137–138; Buschan, "Bücherbesprechung: Geza von Hoffmann," 231.

causes, such as newfound female sexual pathologies like "uniform fetishism" (*Uniformfetischismus*). Some even blamed the very nature of female sexual physiology itself. The latter is best exemplified by gynecologist E. Heinrich Kisch's notorious 1917 publication, *The Sexual Unfaithfulness of Women*, which asserted that women's promiscuity stemmed from their weak and suggestible sex drive.[67] Even if women's sexual behavior was attributable to biology or psychology, male sexologists nonetheless held "careless girls and women" responsible for seducing soldiers and spreading venereal diseases.[68] During the first months of the war, the journal *Sexual Problems* went so far as to publish reports of "undignified women" (*würdelose Weiber*) who intimately associated with prisoners of war.[69] As we will see, women sexologists offered notably different interpretations of the causes and perpetrators of the war's sexual ills.

The Difference Gender Made: Women, War, and Sexology

Although women's wartime sexual analyses largely constellated around the same set of issues that preoccupied their male colleagues, they diverged in significant ways that had everything to do with gender. Despite sharing common concerns about the war's impact on sexual morality, sexual relations, and population health and numbers, women sexologists offered unique analyses of the causes of these sexual problems and put forward different solutions. They rejected their male colleagues' efforts to blame women for wartime sexual degeneracy by offering sensitive portrayals

67. E. Heinrich Kisch, *Die sexuelle Untreue der Frau* (Bonn: A. Marcus and E. Webers Verlag, 1917).

68. See "Varia: Die 'Deutsche Gesellschaft zur Bekämpfung der Geschlechtskrankheiten' hat das folgende Merkblatt für Soldaten unter den ins Feld ziehenden Soldaten verbreiten lassen," *Zeitschrift für Sexualwissenschaft* 1 (November 1914): 336.

69. See, for example, "Würdelose Weiber" and "Noch mehr würdelose Weiber," *Sexual-Probleme* 10 (Sept. 1914): 619.

of women's intimate wartime experiences and holding men accountable for their own sexual excesses. They also offered alternative perspectives on the population question that pushed back against pronatalist demands. The extent and threat of the war arguably emboldened some women writers to insist on reforms to laws, morals, and institutions that had found only limited expression and acceptance before 1914, and even to put forward radical new solutions that aimed to empower women specifically by giving them greater control over their fertility. That is, they aimed to empower *certain* women: eugenics continued to infuse women sexologists' analyses and prescriptions. Although their eugenic investments arguably make strategic sense in light of the intensification of biopolitical anxieties during the war, the presence of eugenics in their analyses had the same familiar inhibiting implications for the scope and purchase of their ideas as it had before the war.

As mentioned earlier, women sexologists shared common anxieties with their male peers; however, they frequently understood these problems differently. They not only highlighted different underlying causes for, and aspects of, these sexual problems, but also drew attention to the different impacts they had on women. Moreover, they asserted authority over certain subjects that they claimed were of greater importance to women. Mathilde Vaerting for one declared that women had more reason to care, and more authority to comment upon, the population question because they were the ones who were primarily responsible for the "higher breeding of humanity," and would be most affected by the lack of men (*Männermangel*) following the war.[70] Certainly, subjects such as sexual ethics and heterosexual relations were not new to female sexual theorists, but the conditions of war exacerbated old problems, created new ones, and undoubtedly heightened the sense of urgency many women sexologists felt in their need to understand and remedy conditions they viewed as harmful to the community and especially to women.

---

70. Vaerting went so far as to call women the "eugenic rulers of humanity" (*Eugeniker des Menschengeschlechts*); Prof. Dr. M. T. Vaerting, "Die Frau, die erblich-organische Höherentwicklung und der Krieg," *Die neue Generation* 3/4 (March/April 1916): 68.

While they generally agreed that moral conditions were devolving and relations between men and women were deteriorating, women sexologists vehemently resisted male sexologists' assertions that women were primarily responsible for causing these conditions. Even when they were critical of some women's "irresponsible" and "immoral" sexual behavior during the war, women sexologists sought to understand the causes of such behavior. For her part, Grete Meisel-Hess argued that the war had increased women's sexual needs and intimate suffering by removing their husbands and partners.[71] It was their suffering, loneliness, and sexual needs, Meisel-Hess maintained, that chipped away at "the last bulwark of feminine dignity, strength, and reserve," and ultimately led women into promiscuity.[72] While sympathetic to women's plight, her judgment of such behavior was not neutral, as she believed it would have negative long-term consequences. She described her sexually active contemporaries as engaging in love like hetairas, the sophisticated and educated courtesans of ancient Greece. Her choice of metaphor, though esoteric to twenty-first-century readers, would have been familiar to an educated early twentieth-century audience, and was certainly apt for Meisel-Hess's rhetorical purposes: like the hetaira of ancient Greece, whose independence and intelligence placed her in a liminal space between the married woman and the common prostitute, Meisel-Hess asserted that promiscuous wartime women were blurring the distinctions between the respectable woman and the whore.[73] Consequently, she claimed that as a result of the war and its new opportunities, present-day society was "teeming with intermediate types" (*Grenztypen)* of women who were helping to degrade standards of sexual morality and relations between men and women.[74] Meisel-Hess's reactions and especially her investments in respectability may appear strange, even hypocritical, given her prewar support of women's sexual agency and premarital unions; however, they make sense in light of the fact

71. Grete Meisel-Hess, "Krieg und Ehe," *Die neue Generation* 6 (June 1915): 159–160.
72. Ibid., 160.
73. Ibid.
74. Ibid., 164.

that Meisel-Hess's enthusiasm for women's sexual freedom was always undergirded by a profound commitment to monogamy, and by her insistence upon an ethic of "racial responsibility" as a lodestar guiding sexual behavior. The perceived indiscriminate promiscuity of her female contemporaries was something she would not countenance.

Although writers like Meisel-Hess could prove judgmental regarding the changes happening in female sexuality, they were also quick to point out the fact that if sexual morality was declining, women alone were not responsible: men were just as much to blame. An important focus in women's wartime sexology was the war's negative impact on male sexuality. According to Meisel-Hess, the war unleashed and allowed men to succumb to the "hunger of an atavistic wild sexuality" that lay within all men, from "the leadings lights of society to its simple members."[75] Likewise, Helene Stöcker maintained that the war had strengthened men's deeply rooted, primitive instincts, desires, and drives.[76] For Stöcker, the destructiveness of the war had once and for all undermined the claim that reason and objectivity were exclusively masculine qualities: "The collapse of those powers, which one had hoped might de-escalate the war if not prevent it entirely:—the Christian world view, the socialist International, the 'Republic of Letters' of intellectuals from all nations—means for us women the collapse of our faith in the supposedly higher development of masculine objectivity, which we women had to strive towards if we were able to reach the heights of pure science (*Wissenschaft*). . . . Man should, after this experience, be a little more cautious and modest in his disparaging judgment about woman's lack of objectivity."[77] According to her, men's propensity for war proved that irrational instincts, drives, and desires are stronger in men than their logic, rationality, and wisdom.[78]

In Stöcker's view the war was not just deteriorating men and women's sexualities, but was regressing gender relations by sanctioning

---

75. Ibid., 162.
76. Stöcker, "Liebe oder Hassen?," 542.
77. Stöcker, "Geschlechtspsychologie und Krieg," 287, 290.
78. Ibid., 290.

misogyny. From the earliest days of the war, Stöcker exhibited a keen awareness of how the war made manifest pernicious attitudes toward women. These tendencies were abundantly clear, she maintained, in the public abuse of German women who exhibited kindness toward prisoners of war by bringing them chocolate and flowers. In Stöcker's view, such attacks were motivated not by patriotism but rather by a deep-seated hatred of women. The same men who spat in these women's faces were the very same prewar antifeminists who attacked the women's movement, she claimed—only now, they enjoyed even greater license and legitimacy.[79] Stöcker later connected the rise in misogyny leading up to and during the war to the rise of nationalism and patriotism, writing, "We therefore had to sadly note from the beginning of the war, how the old injustices, misrepresentations and prejudices have banded together with the current stirred-up nationalistic feelings against women."[80] Here she made connections between militarism, nationalism, and misogyny and framed them as products of innate masculine aggression, attributable to men's evolutionary development, specifically their "millennia of fighting for survival."[81] In her view, war represented "the strongest expression of the masculine principle of power (*Herrschaftsprinzip*) in the world."[82] In this time of war, which stirred up "primitive passions," it was not surprising to her that these old regressive instincts came to the fore.[83] In Stöcker's view, "It is naturally no accident that in this moment, when atavistic, animalistic instincts have been awoken . . . that a loss of sexual inhibitions has emerged among all people, and is accompanied by a deep degradation of woman. To speak of a reform of sexual ethics is laughable in this moment, when the primitive precondition of every moral—Thou shalt not kill!—is not yet obeyed."[84]

Beyond manifesting explicit misogyny, Stöcker maintained that the public's negative reaction to German women's compassion for prisoners of war exemplified the persistence of the sexual double

---

79. Stöcker, "Der Krieg und die Frauen," 423–424.
80. Stöcker, "Krieg und doppelte Moral," *Die neue Generation* 11 (1915): 229.
81. Stöcker, "Geschlechtspsychologie und Krieg," 294.
82. Ibid., 288.
83. Helene Stöcker, "Gewalt oder Verständigung," 200.
84. Stöcker, "Moderne Bevölkerungspolitik," 80.

standard, which found new expressions during the war. To make this case, she contrasted the penalization of any contact between German women and prisoners of war with the state's sanction and even facilitation of sexual relations between German soldiers and foreign sex workers at the front.[85] In an article entitled "The Sexual Double Standard in the War," Stöcker critically observed that "while brothels are being established for soldiers in enemy territories and relationships with female members of 'our enemies' are met with hardly any disapproval, to the extent that a discussion has started about providing financial state support to 'war children' who are the result of these relationships, women continuously receive jail sentences or are being threatened who only have friendly contact with war prisoners."[86] She pointed out that the temporary pleasures soldiers enjoyed during their brothel visits posed a greater public health and military risk than women's potential romantic relationships with prisoners of war. Indeed, she stressed that soldiers' state-sanctioned visits to prostitutes came at the expense of women at home, as such behavior rendered men vulnerable to venereal disease, which they could then pass along to their wives and future children.[87] To further stress the hypocrisy inherent in the public's negative reaction to German women's involvements with foreign prisoners of war, Stöcker pointed out that during times of peace, relations between German women and other European men were never a matter of concern or condemnation.[88]

To remedy wartime damages to sexual morality and sexual relations, women writers put forward an array of solutions. As we will see, many of the solutions proposed were actually demands they had made before the war, such as their call for an end to the prohibition on marriage for female civil servants, a comprehensive system of maternal welfare protections that did not discriminate against unwed mothers and so-called illegitimate children, and a sweeping overhaul of the ethics and practices of heterosexual

---

85. Stöcker, "Krieg und doppelte Moral," 232.

86. Stöcker, "Doppelte Moral im Kriege," *Die neue Generation* 3 (March 1917): 110.

87. Stöcker, "Krieg und doppelte Moral," 236–238.

88. Ibid., 232, 237.

monogamy.[89] They also supported some of the newly established
public health institutions that they believed would help improve
relations between men and women. As a longtime member of the
German Society for the Fight against Venereal Diseases, Henriette
Fürth voiced her support for the venereal disease advice and counseling clinics established during the war. In Fürth's view, the clinics would provide for the "timely detection, [and] early, thorough
and continued treatment" of diseases that would be necessary after
soldiers returned from the war.[90] She declared that these new clinics should combine medical, educational, social, and economic approaches in order to get at the root causes of the spread of venereal
diseases; however, she further insisted that, in order for the clinics
to work, people must be ready to speak about these diseases publicly, openly, and free from judgment and bias.[91] Above all, she
insisted that women must understand and forgive their partners for
any wartime sexual indiscretions to help mitigate the shame associated with venereal disease infection. To this end, Fürth encouraged
women to be empathetic, and consider men's suffering at the front.
Men could not be blamed for seeking temporary sexual pleasure
in a situation where they faced the constant threat of death and
experienced unrelenting nervous tension in the face of this reality,
she insisted: "In the rest between battles, inhibitions fall away, a
thirst for life grows, and he grasps at whatever he can get from
this life."[92] Instead of condemning their partners, Fürth enjoined
women to pursue facts about venereal diseases as a means of preventing their spread throughout the family and the broader population.[93] Curiously, she did not make similar demands upon men to
forgive their female partners' extramarital relations.

89. See Henriette Fürth, "Der Krieg und die Bevölkerungsfrage," *Zeitschrift für
Sexualwissenschaft* 3 (1916): 201, 198; Stöcker, "Moderne Bevölkerungspolitik,"
86; Grete Meisel-Hess, *Das Wesen der Geschlechtlichkeit: Die sexuelle Krise in
ihren Beziehungen zur sozialen Frage & zum Krieg, zu Moral, Rasse & Religion &
insbesondere zur Monogamie* (Jena: Eugen Diedrichs, 1916), 140, 174.
90. Henriette Fürth, "Die Bekämpfung der Geschlechtskrankheiten in und nach
dem Kriege und die Beratungstellen," *Zeitschrift für Sexualwissenschaft* 4 (1917): 71.
91. Ibid., 70.
92. Ibid., 76.
93. Ibid., 76–77.

In addition to institution building, many women advocated institutional reform, specifically marriage reform. Fürth reiterated feminists' prewar demand that female civil servants be allowed to marry and that the state legally recognize and support illegitimate children and their single mothers; however, like Hermann Rohleder, she now hinted at the possibility of allowing healthy military officers and even Catholic clergy to marry as a means of replenishing the postwar population, questioning what spiritual rule absolutely prevented priests from marrying.[94] To make marriage more attractive and materially possible, Fürth also advocated greater acceptance of women's work outside the home across all classes, and equal pay for women's work; to raise the birthrate, she supported an expansion of welfare provisions, including the introduction of state child support, child care, rental subsidies for civil servants with large families, free schooling, school meals, and financing for home building.[95] In addition to facilitating marriage, Fürth maintained that these measures would help strengthen men and women's "will to reproduce," and would thereby quantitatively and qualitatively enhance the population.[96]

Mathilde Vaerting went even further in her marriage reform proposals: across a number of different articles and publications she insisted that, in the name of population growth and improvement, older women ought to marry younger men, space births two and a half years apart, and have no more than five children.[97] She insisted that her prescribed pairings would produce highly valuable hereditary variations, and pointed to evidence that indicated most philosophical, scientific, and artistic geniuses were the offspring of younger fathers.[98] Notably absent from the rationale she provided

---

94. Fürth, "Der Krieg und die Bevölkerungsfrage," 195.

95. Ibid., 198–199.

96. Ibid., 201.

97. See Buschan, "Bücherbesprechungen: M. Vaerting, Wie ersetzt Deutschland am schnellsten die Kriegsverluste durch gesunden Nachwuchs?," *Zeitschrift für Sexualwissenschaft* 2 (1916): 435. Interestingly, because the author was stated as M. Vaerting, the reviewer assumed it was a man. His review of Vaerting's proposals was positive.

98. Vaerting, "Die Frau," 69.

was the feminist argument in favor of such an arrangement: after all, reversing the custom of older men marrying younger women could alter relations of power between husband and wife. To facilitate her envisioned marital reforms, Vaerting called on the state to improve wages and salaries for young men, provide state subsidies for marriage (*Heiratszuschuss*) funded by taxes levied on bachelors, and reduce the length of military service for married men. She recommended that young men marry ideally at age seventeen, women at age twenty.[99] Furthermore, she declared that women had a "eugenic duty" to give male youths priority in the "production" of their children, "just like the first mothers (*Urmütter*)," even though it may be "very difficult for women who have become degenerated by a desire for money and social status." Finally, Vaerting counseled women to delay marriage in order to allow their sexuality and bodies to come to full maturity for the benefit of their future children.[100]

As Fürth's and Vaerting's rationales for their proposed marriage reforms suggest, women sexologists were deeply invested in the population question. Like their male peers, they urgently sought to understand its causes and consequences, and to propose workable remedies to enhance population quality and quantity. However, their analyses of the population question stemmed not only from their eugenic commitments, but also from their gendered standpoint and feminist commitments. As a result of the latter, they highlighted concerns particularly germane to women. For example, both Mathilde Vaerting and Henriette Fürth drew attention to the war's negative effects on the sex ratio, particularly for young women at the age of peak fertility.[101] Both authors warned that a number of women would be forced to marry men rendered unfit for marriage as a result of disability or disease, while still other women would be precluded from marrying at all. They also

---

99. Buschan, "Bücherbesprechungen: M. Vaerting," 436.

100. Vaerting, "Die Frau," 75.

101. See Mathilde Vaerting, "Die rassenhygienischen Gefahren des Frauenüberschusses nach dem Kriege und Wege zur erhöhten Vermehrung des männlichen Geschlechts," *Zeitschrift für Sexualwissenschaft* 2 (February 1916): 397–404; 3 (March 1916): 445–452. Subsequent citations of this work appear parenthetically in the text.

worried that the postwar shortage of men would not only reduce the number of desirable marriage partners and the range of positive hereditary variations within the population, but also hamper the life choices and survival possibilities available to women.

Beyond marital prospects, writers like Fürth and Vaerting feared that a sexual imbalance would inhibit "the legitimate fulfillment of [women's] sexual desires"—a goal that women sexologists had long deemed a "biological right."[102] Lacking a "legitimate" outlet, Vaerting and Grete Meisel-Hess feared that women's sexual needs, when confronted with the lack of marriageable men, would ultimately lead them to abandon monogamy.[103] Vaerting went further and predicted that the surplus of women after the war would ultimately invert heterosexual courtship rituals and thereby endanger the population. How she made this connection, and why it provoked racial anxiety, require some unpacking here. As Vaerting pointed out, a surplus of sexually mature women would mean that there would not be enough men for every woman. This imbalance would undermine monogamy, she asserted, and would also contribute to the spread of venereal diseases. Even though many women would be unable to marry, they would not remain celibate: according to Vaerting, "The sex drive is the strongest human drive and propels women with an elemental force to seek its satisfaction. It is therefore natural that these sexually unprovided-for women (*geschlechtlich unversorgten Frauen*), especially when their sexual desires are at their peak and their prospects for marriage in light of the lack of men look bleak, take for themselves whatever they can get" ("Die rassenhygienischen Gefahren," 399). When women become less selective and less monogamous in the search for sexual satisfaction—that is, when they engage in what Vaerting called "secret prostitution"—they help accelerate the spread of venereal diseases. Vaerting insisted that her dire postwar prophecy was all the more likely in light of the war's impact on sexual ethics and

---

102. Henriette Fürth, "Sexuelle Kriegsfragen," *Zeitschrift für Sexualwissenschaft* 2 (1915/1916): 135.

103. Vaerting, "Die rassenhygienischen Gefahren," 399. See Meisel-Hess, "Krieg und Ehe," 159–160.

relationships: "The ground for such random sexual encounters is especially favorable as a result of the long-term separation of the sexes during the war, which loosened the requirement of monogamy for both sexes" (399). Beyond "secret prostitution," Vaerting also warned of an increase in "official prostitution" after the war, as economic conditions would force more women to sell sex to survive (399–400).

If women constituted the majority of the population, Vaerting claimed, they would become sexual aggressors, and thereby displace men from their role as the "competing element in sexual love" (400–401). Obliquely referencing sexual selection, she asserted that it was eugenically necessary for men to be the active force in sexual relations to ensure that women were brought to the "highest level of their lust, orgasm": according to Vaerting, a child conceived without a woman experiencing orgasm would be severely damaged (401). She further insisted that men should be numerically greater in the population and maintain their leading role in courtship in view of their sexual shortcomings when it came to women's satisfaction. "A man can barely satisfy at most one woman," Vaerting bluntly asserted. "However, a woman can easily satisfy many men. Prostitution is a powerful, if also disgusting piece of evidence for this fact" (401). If men were forced to satisfy too many women, it would heavily damage his vital "life powers," and ultimately degrade the race by producing ever-weaker offspring (401–402). In the name of sexual economy and eugenics, Vaerting maintained that the gender with the lowest sexual capacity must constitute the majority.

Another obvious difference between women sexologists and their male peers vis-à-vis the population question lay in women's thorough rejection of pronatalist demands, which they recognized fell squarely on women's shoulders.[104] Questions of reproductive

---

104. Mathilde Vaerting intimated that pronatalism was an inherently masculine ideology, one that derived from the nature of the male reproductive process: men's desire for large numbers of children supposedly sprang from their mass production of semen. (Conversely, women's supposedly innate inclination toward eugenic selection stemmed, Vaerting claimed, from the relative rarity of their ova.) See Vaerting, "Die Frau," 71–73, esp. 73.

rights and justice therefore constituted, as before, a major fault line between male and female sexologists. Although women sexologists believed in the need to regenerate Germany with "high-quality" individuals, they nonetheless vehemently resisted the pressure put on women to bear as many children as possible. Both Meisel-Hess and Stöcker took issue with their male colleagues like social hygienist Alfred Grotjahn, who insisted that it was women's duty to the fatherland to bear *at least* four children.[105] In Stöcker's view, Grotjahn did not "consider to give the appropriate rights to a woman who becomes aware of her considerable power to be able to either bear children for the state or not. But when one assesses the psychology of human beings correctly, one recognizes that relatively few children enter this world out of consideration for the duties which one owes to the state and even less out of considering that one will supply a lot of cannon fodder for the next war."[106] Stöcker argued that empowering women through legal access to safe contraception, material support in the form of maternal insurance, and legal and social recognition of illegitimate children and their mothers would have a more positive effect on the population than forcing them to have children through appeals to patriotic duty, or threats of criminal sanction: "To make women into healthy, strong, respected personalities, fully conscious of their special purpose . . . appears to me to be a much more effective way of encouraging a woman to bear multiple children (*mehrfacher Mutterschaft*), as opposed to legally forced reproduction (*polizeilich verfügte Gebärzwang*)."[107] Stöcker's argument points toward one of the major insights that distinguished women sexologists from their male colleagues: they stressed above all that women should *want* to have children. Somewhat surprisingly, it was Grete Meisel-Hess

---

105. Stöcker, "Moderne Bevölkerungspolitik," 80; Meisel-Hess also criticized Grotjahn's proposal, writing, "These demands, which bring the most private aspect of an individual's life under a tyrannical imperative, and which require not only a general passivity in the interest of the species, but also a general activity, require barely any commentary"; Meisel-Hess, *Das Wesen der Geschlechtlichkeit*, 122.
106. Stöcker, "Moderne Bevölkerungspolitik," 81.
107. Ibid., 82.

who cleverly and tersely observed that "no one will have . . . a child only because 'the race' wants one."[108]

To combat pronatalist thinking, women sexologists insisted that the population question should not focus exclusively on the birthrate itself because that number, out of context, was misleading. Instead, they argued that in order to get an overall sense of the population size and replacement needs, the falling birthrate must be understood in relation to the falling infant death rate.[109] Henriette Fürth insisted that a lower birthrate and smaller population were signs of evolutionary progress, and favorably compared the virtues of a smaller Germany to its enemy, the behemoth Russia, to prove this point. While some women acknowledged an immediate need for an increase in sheer numbers, they nonetheless asked, as Fürth put it, "What are numbers, if value does not stand behind them?"[110]

Fürth's pointed question not only illustrates once again the persistence of eugenics in informing women's wartime sexual theorizing, but also suggests some of the analytical and rhetorical work eugenics did for women sexologists. As her comments indicate, eugenic logics could helpfully combat pronatalist demands on women: by stressing quality over quantity, they could support arguments to limit fertility, specifically in ways that placed reproductive decision making in women's hands. The war also tested and demonstrated the malleability of eugenic arguments, and their ability to be reconciled with other discourses, including those of political economy and reproductive rights.

This observation certainly holds true for Grete Meisel-Hess, who more than anyone else in this book has illuminated eugenics' polyvalent potential for feminist sexual theorizing. This polyvalence is further illuminated by her wartime study, *The Nature of Sexuality* (1916), which sought to document and account for the changes happening to sexuality as a result of the war. In *The*

108. Meisel-Hess, *Das Wesen der Geschlechtlichkeit*, 139.

109. Fürth, "Der Krieg und die Bevölkerungsfrage," 202–205; Meisel-Hess, *Das Wesen der Geschlechtlichkeit*, 104.

110. Fürth, "Der Krieg und die Bevölkerungsfrage," 204.

Nature of Sexuality, Meisel-Hess dedicated particular attention to the population question and its solution. Like progressive eugenicists Eduard David and Hermann Rohleder, she insisted that the population would not experience any increase in either quantity or quality until living conditions for the majority had improved. Unlike David and Rohleder, she offered a detailed analysis of why this was the case. Building upon but departing somewhat from the analysis of sexual life she had elaborated before the war in texts like *The Sexual Crisis*, Meisel-Hess argued that the population question was inextricable from what she called the *Nahrungsproblem*, namely, the inability to secure the material necessaries of life. In this way, she was able to argue that the sexual crisis, the social crisis, and the war all shared a common root.[111] Meisel-Hess explicitly held capitalism responsible for creating social, political, and economic conditions that made an "unbounded increase in the population size" (*unbegrenzter Volksvermehrung*) undesirable. As a result of the "banditry" (*Banditismus*) of the capitalist state, she argued that most men and women confronted a restricted "social scope of securing the necessities of life" (*soziale Nahrungsspielraum*), which meant that

> in Germany, as in all other European states, there is now a high number of people who are not being fed because they cannot find sufficient, well-paid, permanent and regular work under the current economic principles. They have therefore no other choice but to either suppress their descendants or let them die an early death and are damned to what [Rudolf] Goldscheid accurately calls "sterile fertility." (90–91)

As Meisel-Hess pointed out, individuals restrict their fertility in response to their economic capacity: "A man in the civilized world remains indeed to a high degree unmarried, because he quite often cannot support a wife and her children . . . at least in those years which are most beneficial and appropriate for procreation" (84). Conditions within capitalist states thus contributed to unfavorable living conditions for their populations (98).

---

111. Meisel-Hess, *Das Wesen der Geschlechtlichkeit*, xxviii. Subsequent citations from this work appear parenthetically in the text.

The *Nahrungsfrage* Meisel-Hess identified had long preceded the war—in her view, it was responsible for *causing* the war. The struggle for the necessities of life was, in her view, an obvious consequence of capitalist exploitation that ultimately resulted in a race for empire, and consequently led to global conflict. "When people are being chased beyond their borders" as a result of a lack of work, she argued, "then an effort has to be made to acquire colonies ruthlessly, resulting in a struggle for the supremacy over the oceans and finally to war" (87).[112] Meisel-Hess maintained that this war would not have happened if economically just conditions had prevailed: "*Unjust wars arise from the legitimate dissatisfaction of people.* . . . Nations whose populations do not lack the most fundamental needs . . . will not start wars anymore" (94; emphasis in original). In light of her materialist diagnosis of the conjoined causes of war and sexual problems, Meisel-Hess vehemently opposed calls for an "unrestricted increase in population" to replace those lost in the war; she even prophesied that "a rush to an excessive increase in population would . . . most likely result in the next generation engaging in a world war" (87).

As a result of the war experience and her more explicitly materialist analysis of the population question, Meisel-Hess overcame some of her earlier ambivalence regarding contraceptives, and in *The Nature of Sexuality* she supported the use of contraception within the context of a monogamous relationship as a means of reducing infant mortality. For this reason, she now described contraception as a "life-promoting principle"; however, it is clear she believed that contraception ought to promote specific kinds of lives. As she put it, contraception would allow parents to "secure the well-being of two or three children they can raise properly instead of giving a great number of children who are biologically inferior and doomed to an early death" (104). If the state wanted to increase the fertility rate, Meisel-Hess argued, it must work to establish social and economic conditions that would enable

---

112. Curiously, on that same page Meisel-Hess wrote, "The colonization of foreign lands for the purpose of the expansion of race is only sensible if these lands are fertile and in good shape, so that the race can prosper."

husbands and wives to feed the children they bring into the world, as individuals were already restricting their fertility in response to their economic capacity. As she noted, the restriction of births was only a "provisional-practical solution" (*provisorisch-praktische Lösung*) that rested with the individual; the social solution lay in the realm of social politics and involved "the fight against pauperism and banditry in the state, through a just division of property and power, and . . . through a determination of how many people within a particular area (*Kulturzone*) could be provided for (*überhaupt ernährt werden können*), so that they can achieve an age of work (*Erwerbsalter*) and, at that point, find lasting work and nourishment" (84–85). Meisel-Hess's ideal vision of a postwar state was a socialistic one, premised upon a eugenic version of reproductive justice: that is, it would be a state wherein every *healthy* woman who wanted to become a mother could do so, and every child born was desired and had a fighting chance not only to reach maturity but to enjoy a baseline standard of welfare and social care (93).

Another unabashed, yet equally eugenic, defender of women's reproductive rights was Mathilde Vaerting, who insisted that it was the prohibition and lack of regulation of contraceptives and abortion that was truly damaging to the survival of the *Volk*. In her 1917 article, "On the Influence of the War on Sex with Contraceptives (*Präventivverkehr*) and Abortion and Their Eugenic Consequences," Vaerting argued that "the proper termination of a developing life that resulted from having sex with a defective contraceptive is urgently required for eugenic reasons" (176). While not necessarily an unequivocal champion of contraceptives, Vaerting pointed out that when good contraceptives are inaccessible, individuals resort to poor-quality substitutes, which she claimed not only failed to prevent births but also weakened and damaged the sperm that made it to the ovum and ultimately created "inferior quality" children (139). She further pointed out the damaging effects of nonmedical abortions on women's health and future fertility, and on the quality of children born following botched procedures (176). Instead of inhibiting the use of contraceptives and the provision of abortions, Vaerting argued that the state ought to exercise better regulation and quality control in the production of

contraceptives, and educate more people on the use of good technologies (177–178). As Vaerting pointed out, whether contraceptives or abortion was made legal or not, "an intelligent and talented
woman" who wants to terminate a pregnancy will find "means and
ways" to realize her goal (176). Vaerting insisted that her proposals would ultimately prove most successful in the long run, as they
would incite and support individuals' "free and inner wishes and
desires for children" (179). While Vaerting's proposals may have
been radical, she insisted that they were unquestionably necessary.
"Since the war has already damaged the quality of the population
to an unbelievable degree," she declared, "it is therefore our duty
to be doubly vigilant towards all further eugenic damages" (176).

Particularly when it comes to reproductive rights and freedoms,
the analyses, critiques, and reforms proposed by Vaerting, Fürth,
Meisel-Hess, and Stöcker between 1914 and 1918 appear empowering to women. They speak to the fact that the war provided a
unique opportunity to advance radical new analyses of sexual life
and demands for its reform—and that eugenics once again proved a
sturdy vehicle for their articulation. As was the case before the war,
these analyses reflected unequal evaluations of particular kinds of
lives, and were certainly not meant to serve as universal demands
on behalf of all women. For example, in her arguments on behalf of contraceptives and the legalization of abortion, Mathilde
Vaerting made the case that the criminalization of abortion was
effectively "a direct protective law for stupidity, because it exclusively favors the stronger reproduction of ungifted parents" ("Über
den Einfluß," 176). Moreover, the radicalization of women sexologists' demands for reproductive rights was not always a straightforwardly good thing. During the war, one begins to encounter
women openly championing sterilization as a means of preventing
the unfit from reproducing. Although Meisel-Hess did not generally support abortion, she did support involuntary abortions and
even sterilization among the "severely degenerated and serious
criminals" (*Das Wesen der Geschlechtlichkeit,* 179–182). For Henriette Fürth, forced sterilization was such an extreme intervention
into intimate life and so underresearched that she maintained that
laypeople must abstain from judging these measures; nevertheless,

she did maintain that there existed "a whole range of other cases," including "consumptives and other incurably burdened peoples," where "the use of contraception would be desirable for personal and racial political (*rassepolitischen*) reasons, yet the application of more violent methods [such as sterilization] would be absolutely impossible."[113] Fürth thus supported contraceptions on eugenic grounds, and cited "prominent scientists" and medical experts who opposed anticontraception laws to support her position.[114] It is not entirely clear that she viewed their use as voluntary.

Even the rehabilitation of monogamy was proposed as a means not just of ending widespread sexual excesses among men, but of eradicating what Grete Meisel-Hess had called "intermediate" types (*Grenztypen*) of women.[115] Meisel-Hess insisted that monogamy constituted the only means of cultivating and maintaining a "pure" and highly cultivated race, as monogamy itself was an evolutionary achievement representing the "highest cultural ideal" realized by "advanced races."[116] While eugenic thought once again proved productive and rhetorically powerful for female sexual theorists, its dangerous implications were exacerbated by the anxieties the war inspired, and by the perceived need for drastic remedies to rescue sexual morality and the population itself. The proposed solutions clearly would have unevenly impacted women based on their biopolitical desirability; yet even those women empowered by such reforms would only have benefited as a result of the subsumption of their rights claims within larger arguments regarding the health and well-being of the race. Despite women's sexologists' insistence that women be treated as ends in themselves, their reliance upon and investments in eugenics meant that women and

113. Fürth, "Der Krieg und die Bevölkerungsfrage," 205.
114. Ibid., 205–206.
115. Meisel-Hess, "Krieg und Ehe," 164.
116. Ibid., 165–166. On the discursive relationship between race, civilization, and claims of sexual evolution, see, for example, Julian Carter, *The Heart of Whiteness: Normal Sexuality and Race in America, 1880–1940* (Durham, NC: Duke University Press, 2007); Kirsten Leng, "Culture, Difference, and Sexual Progress in Fin-de-Siècle Europe: Cultural Othering and the German League for the Protection of Mothers and Sexual Reform, 1905–1914," *Journal of the History of Sexuality* 25, no. 1 (January 2016): 62–82.

their rights would once again be treated as means to an end, rendering the case that women deserved rights *as women* all the more difficult to make.

While the ideas, analyses, and even prescriptions offered by women sexologists over the course of the war bore many similarities to those of their male peers, their analyses of sexual problems and proposals for postwar reform differed significantly from those offered by men. Women's analyses gave greater credence to women's subjective experiences of the war and drew attention to the ways that agreed-upon problems impacted women differently. When it came to the perceived decline in sexual morality, women writers decried the double standard inherent in their male colleagues' frequent attempts to blame women for the war's sexual problems. While critical of women's sexual promiscuity, they also pointed to the degeneration of male sexuality and men's complicity in sexual decline. Moreover, while female sexual theorists proved equally anxious about the war's effect on the population, they rejected demands that women ought to have more children as a matter of patriotic duty. In defending women's rights to control their own fertility and determine the conditions of their maternity, women sexologists once again made good rhetorical use of eugenics, as they had before the war, with similar ambivalent implications. In response to these changing conditions, they proposed a mix of old and new, practical and arguably idiosyncratic, solutions that they maintained would benefit not only women, but also the race itself. Arguably, the sheer destructiveness of the war gave women sexologists hope that their ideas could play a role in postwar regeneration.

   The analyses and reform proposals they offered were developed with a sense of urgency, in a context of anxiety, despair, and perceived existential crisis. These texts represent attempts to comprehend the incomprehensible by using and reinterpreting analytic frameworks developed under much different political and social conditions. While I have been critical of women sexologists' tendency to stress the needs of the race above those of women, or to treat women's rights as a subset of larger racial goals, it perhaps reflects a very real and pressing conviction that the first order of business, when it came to dealing with the war's aftermath, was to prevent collective annihilation. It is worth recalling that the violence and loss of life during the First World War were unprecedented, and that no one knew how the war would end, or what the world would look like when it did. During the war years, women sexologists were analyzing the immanent, theorizing in uncertainty, and endeavoring to stave off anxieties about unknown collective fates.

When the war finally ended, this uncertainty remained, even though virtually everything had changed. The immediate conditions in Germany at the end of the war—marked by defeat, revolution, abdication, street violence, intraparty strife, stillborn soviets, mass death, and the return of injured and traumatized veterans—provided difficult foundations upon which to imagine better national futures. Despite all of this, some sexologists and reformers remained optimistic: in the October–November 1918 edition of *The New Generation*, Helene Stöcker echoed Maeterlinck as she looked upon the future, hopefully writing, "Up to this point was a bad dream. The beautiful starts now!'"[117]

Arguably, women felt the postwar mix of optimism and uncertainty most acutely. Despite their ascension to full citizenship following the Revolution, the memories of what they had endured throughout the war, and what they had lost and gained, loomed large. In the case of Grete Meisel-Hess, the war brought a series of personal tragedies: she lost both her husband and her economic security, and as a consequence sunk into a deep depression that led to her institutionalization in a psychiatric asylum. She died in 1922, at age forty-three. Beyond mourning such losses, women were also anxious and wary about what they might be forced to sacrifice in the new German Republic. Already toward the end of the war, male sexologists were calling for women to return to the home. In an article published in the June 1918 edition of the *Journal for Sexual Science*, Innsbruck-based physician Johannes Dück stressed women's primary roles and functions as mothers, and encouraged them to return to these exclusively domestic roles as part of their feminine duty and as a means of helping to solve the population

---

117. Helene Stöcker, "Wandlung," *Die neue Generation* 10/11 (October/November 1918): 343.

question. Sexual roles were predetermined by essential biological and psychological differences, he insisted, regardless of what women had accomplished during the war. Because the fate of the people (*Völkerschicksal*) was bound up with the fate of women (*Frauenschicksal*), Dück argued that Germany's fate rested with women's return to the home and their willingness to make reproduction their primary occupation without protest. As a salve, Dück insisted that women could influence public life through their husbands by wielding their "special power" within the home.[118] Dück's piece not only marked the resurrection of prewar anti-feminist discourse, but also foreshadowed the attempts to limit women's social, political, and economic roles in the years to come. Perhaps more importantly, it demonstrated the dangerous polyvalence of tying women's fate to that of the race.

Regardless of Dück's desires, a return to the old gender and sexual order was impossible; life had changed too profoundly. Through their participation in the unprecedented total war effort as laborers, administrators, and primary breadwinners, women had shown themselves capable of presumed masculine occupations and obligations in the economy and the family, thereby undermining beliefs regarding innate feminine weakness and dependence. The war marked a definitive break, but women's full emancipation and empowerment were by no means assured.

Sexology would also be profoundly transformed as a result of the war experience. The sexological field would be reinvigorated through its greater involvement in the new German state's biopolitical projects aimed at regenerating postwar populations, and through its embrace of new methods and approaches that interrogated the roles social, cultural, and psychological forces played in shaping sex. Women's contributions to sexology would be equally transformed by these new developments, and informed by the field's new preoccupations. Particularly in light of what women wrote during the First World War, it is important to note the degree to which they turned away from eugenic arguments and rationale, and

---

118. Johannes Dück, "Frauenschicksal-Völkerschicksal," *Zeitschrift für Sexualwissenschaft* 5, no. 3 (June 1918): 81–95.

toward psychology and other social sciences in order to understand sex. There are many reasons why eugenics may have lost some of its purchase with female sexual theorists following the war; perhaps in light of the retrenchment of women's social and economic rights after the war, women became wary of so closely entwining women's fate with that of the *Volk*. In any event, women would contribute to the paradigm shifts in sexology during the 1920s, and theorize sex in ways that appear strikingly contemporary to present-day readers: it is to these new ideas that we now turn.

7

Fluid Gender, Rigid Sexuality

Constrained Potential in the Postwar Period

Germany emerged from the war a fractured nation. Defeated, rev-
olutionized, and newly republican, it was immediately divided by
politics, ideology—and sex. The gender-differentiated experiences
of the First World War created palpable intimate and social conflicts between men and women. Many men resented the freedoms
and assumed safety women enjoyed on the home front; some even
blamed women for the war's disastrous end, and accused them of
delivering a fatal "stab in the back" by joining in the revolutionary
activities on the home front. Meanwhile, women resented being
forced by early republican law to relinquish their jobs (and thus
their independent incomes and public freedoms) in favor of men
returning from the war. This apparent crisis in gender relations
amplified existing anxieties regarding national regeneration and re-
population following the war.

Conditions were perhaps even more transformed in Austria,
which had been reduced from a multiethnic empire into a rump

republic. Austria was not only prevented from joining Germany, as it endeavored to do immediately following the war, but also lost the rich agricultural lands of Hungary and the Bohemian industrial sector that had been crucial to the empire's well-being. As was the case in Germany, state and civil society actors desired to rehabilitate the impoverished and traumatized body politic; however, here too changing gender roles and relations were viewed as significantly complicating the project of social rehabilitation. Especially vexing was the figure of the New Woman, who was accused of threatening the stability and productivity of marriage and the family through her pursuit of happiness and sexual freedom.

The challenges presented by revised gender roles, strained heterosexual relations, and ongoing biopolitical concerns would persist throughout the 1920s in both Germany and Austria. In the field of sexology, they inspired diverse new efforts to understand, theorize, and cope practically with these new realities. During this period, sexologists expanded their research into new areas, and increasingly focused their attention on topics such as the determination of sex and the origins and nature of sexual difference. They also began to take seriously the influence of social and cultural forces in shaping sex, possibly in response to the war and revolution's demonstration of the undeniable effects of human action and decision making in shaping sexual life.

Sexology's increasing focus on the role of society and culture in shaping sexual roles, relationships, and behaviors is evident in the writing of many women sexologists. In this chapter I examine texts written by two women, Mathilde Vaerting and Austrian individual psychologist Sofie Lazarsfeld, that engaged social sciences, above all sex psychology, to make strikingly new and original contributions to sexology, specifically to discussions of sexual difference. These texts also mark a notable move away from eugenics and explicit engagement with biopolitical concerns. Both Mathilde Vaerting's two-volume *New Foundation for the Psychology of Man and Woman* (1921, 1923) and Sofie Lazarsfeld's *Woman's Experience of the Male* (1931) were highly influential texts in their own time: they were translated into multiple languages and, in Lazarsfeld's case, reprinted over a thirty-year period.[1] Lazarsfeld's text actually references Vaerting's work; this fact, in addition to their shared themes and similar analytical frameworks, bolsters the case for analyzing these texts together, despite the fact that one originated in Germany and the other in Austria.

Social scientific approaches to the study of sex proved productive for both Vaerting and Lazarsfeld. In their celebrated texts, Vaerting and Lazarsfeld deployed psychology and other social scientific fields to destabilize existing understandings of femininity and masculinity. Although many female sexual theorists held gender and sexuality to be variable, nonbinary, and subject to dramatic transformation even before the war, their theories were based upon a biologically based understanding of sex as the bedrock of gender and sexuality. In this chapter, we find women sexologists insisting on a fundamental disconnect between gender and sexed bodies, and playing up the role of environmental influences on gender roles, relations, and performances. Vaerting's texts went so far as to attack the very idea that femininity and masculinity were essential traits emanating from particularly sexed bodies, and to suggest that gender categories were above all functional categories. In these ways, Vaerting and Lazarsfeld seem to depart dramatically from preceding sexological work. And yet, both texts retreat to essentialism when it comes to sexuality: in both texts the radical contingency of gender they espouse seems tethered to a foundation of naturalized heterosexuality.

---

1. See Mathilde Vaerting and Mathias Vaerting, *The Dominant Sex: A Study in the Sociology of Sex Differentiation*, trans. Eden Paul and Cedar Paul (New York: George H. Doran, 1923); Mathilde Vaerting, *Il sesso dominante* (Milan: Bompiani, 1935). Sofie Lazarsfeld, *Wie die Frau den Mann erlebt: Fremde Bekenntnisse und eigene Betrachtungen* (Leipzig: Schneider, 1931). Lazarsfeld's text was translated into Croatian, Dutch, Danish, Italian, and English. The English translation bore two different titles: *Rhythm of Life: A Guide to Sexual Harmony for Women* (New York: Greenberg, 1934), and *Woman's Experience of the Male*, published by London Torch Press in 1934 and the Encyclopaedic Press in 1955 and 1967. The publishing house Francis Aldor also released numerous English reprints of *Woman's Experience of the Male*, though their dates of publication are unclear. I have worked with an undated Francis Aldor version of Lazarsfeld's text.

Why would it not seem incongruous to Vaerting and Lazarsfeld to posit gender as a cultural construct that was fluid and determined by the ebb and flow of history and hegemony, while uncritically maintaining sexuality as natural and resistant to change, even subject to the evaluative criteria of deviancy and pathology? How can we make sense of this apparent tension in their work? I address these questions by analyzing Vaerting's and Lazarsfeld's texts contextually, and read them as manifestations of the changes and anxieties surrounding gender and (hetero)sexuality in 1920s Germany and Austria. I argue that these texts can be read as attempting to assuage concerns regarding changing postwar gender roles by linking them to a bedrock of sexual constancy that would ensure an enduring bond between men and women. I further maintain that the complexities of these texts manifest the ways in which postwar changes to the sexual order were putting pressure on understandings of sex itself. The meaning of sex had already been subject to decades of sexological (and feminist) scrutiny and deconstruction; Vaerting's and Lazarsfeld's work marks the halting, uneven ways in which sex was breaking apart into distinctive categories of gender and sexuality, and becoming subject to sociological investigations that held sex to be an effect of power. Vaerting's and Lazarsfeld's texts raise questions about the historical and social conditions in which gender and sexuality can become open to new forms of scrutiny and analysis. Furthermore, the tensions between gender and sexuality in their work once again instantiate the confounding blend of possibility and constraint that runs through much of women's sexological writing.

Sex and Sexology in 1920s Germany and Austria

The dramatic changes in gender and sexuality effected by the war made them the subjects of widespread interest and anxiety from the very beginning of the postwar era. In the eyes of some commentators, the changes wrought by the war signaled an incipient "sexual crisis"—one that, as Kathleen Canning has argued, symbolized the crisis of the Republic itself, and was distinct from the sexual crisis identified by figures like Grete Meisel-Hess before the war.[2] Particularly vexing were the changes in women's roles, symbolized in the ubiquitous figure of the much-maligned New Woman. Women's new republican civil rights and freedoms, their greater public visibility, and their increased economic independence were interpreted by some as threats to the family and social order, and engendered calls for a return to prewar gender and family roles in the name of social stability. In the early years of the German Republic, the state seemed responsive to such fears and passed various laws and policies that aimed to reinstate patriarchal authority and reaffirm male privileges. The demobilization decrees, which removed married women from their jobs in favor of men returned from the war, are a fitting example.[3] By the end of the 1920s, it seemed that reactionary critics had won the day, as women returned to more traditionally feminine fashions and seemed to prepare themselves for a return to what Marxist feminist and individual psychologist Alice Rühle Gerstel sarcastically referred to as the "good old days."[4]

Myriad other political, social, economic, and cultural changes ensured that no such "return" was possible, however—including key founding acts of the Republic itself, namely, the extension of the rights to vote and stand for public office to women.[5] Among the major changes that reshaped women's lives in the 1920s were increased university enrollment, expanded employment within the white-collar labor force, growing participation in the burgeoning consumer culture and emergent "Girl Kultur," and greater (but still highly restricted) access to birth control through the new marriage

---

2. Kathleen Canning, "Women and the Politics of Gender," in *Weimar Germany*, ed. Anthony McElligott, (Oxford: Oxford University Press, 2009), 167, 146.

3. Renate Bridenthal, Atina Grossmann, and Marion Kaplan, "Introduction," in *When Biology Became Destiny: Women in Weimar and Nazi Germany*, ed. Renate Bridenthal, Atina Grossmann, and Marion Kaplan (New York: Monthly Review Press, 1984), 7. See also Susanne Rouette, "Mothers and Citizens: Gender and Social Policy in Germany after the First World War," *Central European History* 30 (1997): 48–66.

4. Alice Rühle Gerstel, "Zurück zur guten alten Zeit?," *Die literarische Welt* 9 (27 January 1933): 5–6.

5. Canning, "Women and the Politics of Gender," 154.

and sex counseling centers.[6] Sexuality was a major site of (highly contested) change for heterosexual women and lesbians alike. Women, and especially gay women, benefited from the emergence of new sexual publics undergirded by a proliferation of bars, clubs, cafés, newspapers, journals, and political and social organizations, as well as new fashion trends that enabled the subversion of masculine and feminine aesthetic norms.[7]

Sexuality was also a major factor inhibiting any return to the prewar order. In addition to the aforementioned developments, the war had placed a significant strain on intimate heterosexual relationships. One telltale sign can be found in the divorce rate, which reached historic levels as many husbands and wives encountered each other as strangers following the war.[8] Such developments, alongside the intense backlash against women's social and political gains, have led some historians to characterize relations between men and women during the early years of the Weimar Republic as antagonistic.[9] Intriguingly, both contemporary and retrospective analyses of the state of heterosexuality postwar seem to neglect the fraught state of sexual relations between men and women before the war, as the work of Edward Ross Dickinson and others has illustrated.

6. See Katharina von Ankum, ed., *Women in the Metropolis: Gender and Modernity in Weimar Culture* (Berkeley: University of California Press, 1997); Kristine von Soden, *Die Sexualberatungsstellen der Weimarer Republik, 1919–1933* (Berlin: Hentrich, 1988); Atina Grossmann, "Girlkultur or Thoroughly Rationalized Female: A New Woman in Weimar Germany?," in *Women in Culture and Politics: A Century of Change*, ed. Judith Friedlander (Bloomington: Indiana University Press, 1986), 62–80; Joachim S. Hohmann, *Sexualforschung und -aufklärung in der Weimarer Republik: Eine Übersicht in Materialien und Dokumenten* (Frankfurt am Main: Foerster Verlag, 1985).

7. On queer life in Weimar Germany, see Marti Lybeck, "Gender, Sexuality, and Belonging: Female Homosexuality in Germany, 1890–1933" (PhD diss., University of Michigan, 2007); Marti M. Lybeck, *Desiring Emancipation: New Women and Homosexuality in Germany, 1890–1933* (Albany: State University of New York Press, 2014); Laurie Marhoefer, *German Homosexual Emancipation and the Rise of the Nazis* (Toronto: University of Toronto Press, 2015); Katie Sutton, *The Masculine New Woman in Weimar Germany* (Oxford: Berghahn Books, 2011).

8. Bridenthal et al., "Introduction," 7.

9. Ibid.

These negative postwar trends in heterosexuality not only amplified the discourse of sexual crisis sparked by changes in women's roles, but also exacerbated biopolitical fears regarding the fate of the national population. State and civil society actors became increasingly convinced of the need to shore up monogamous (and hopefully reproductive) heterosexuality as a matter of national interest. In their view, if the changes in gender relations could not be reversed, they could at least be mitigated and rehabilitated through various forms of intervention in the intimate lives of men and especially women. Consequently, the German state enacted a range of population policies, from maternal welfare to school-based sexual education to continued restrictions on abortion that aimed to regulate women's bodies and ensure that women continued to serve as "mothers of the nation."[10] The state, along with various civil society actors, also introduced and administered a network of sex and marriage advice counseling centers.[11] The 1920s also witnessed the birth of a new popular medical genre: the marital sex guide, which aimed to scientifically advise couples on how to achieve mutually pleasurable erotic (and reproductive) lives.[12]

Conditions in Austria paralleled those prevailing in Germany. As was the case in Weimar Germany, gender was a fraught topic within the new Austrian Republic, and sexuality was also invested with desires for collective regeneration and social transformation. The dramatic changes to the very constitution of the Austrian state made the prospect of a return to prewar conditions as remote as it was in Germany, also newly republican. As Maria Mesner has noted, the defeat and breakdown of the Hapsburg Empire undermined the influence of former authorities, including the Catholic Church (although the Christian Social Party dominated the national

10. See Cornelie Usborne, *The Politics of the Body in Weimar Germany: Women's Reproductive Rights and Duties* (Ann Arbor: University of Michigan Press, 1992).

11. Atina Grossman, *Reforming Sex: The German Movement for Birth Control and Abortion Reform, 1920–1950* (Oxford: Oxford University Press, 1995).

12. On the emergence of this genre and its contributions to the larger project of shoring up heterosexuality, see Annamarie Jagose, *Orgasmology* (Durham, NC: Duke University Press, 2012), 40–77.

government). In the city of Vienna, under the leadership of the Social Democratic Workers' Party elected in 1919, conditions were
particularly ripe for new forms of social and political experimentation.[13] Over the course of the 1920s, Viennese city officials and sex
reform activists established a network of sex and marriage advice
counseling centers that aimed to support heterosexual and potentially reproductive couples. A "Health Advice Center for Engaged
Couples" was even established in Vienna's city hall in June 1922.[14]
Beyond the sex and marriage advice centers, municipal administrators established a range of other institutions aimed at supporting
families and shaping a productive new generation from the cradle
to young adulthood, including kindergartens, advice centers for
mothers, child transfer centers and foster homes for children with
behavioral problems, school medical services, and clinics for testing and treating sexually transmitted diseases.[15] They also introduced long-term rent control and public housing with communal
facilities like laundries, baths, kindergartens, libraries, groceries,
playgrounds, swimming pools, and medical and dental clinics.[16]

Viennese sex and marriage advice centers endeavored to stabilize
heterosexual relationships under the conditions of a new gender
order. State-run counseling services were fundamentally informed

13. According to historian Helmut Gruber, "In Vienna between 1920 and 1934
the Socialist party (SDAP) attempted to create a comprehensive workers' culture
that was antithetical to bourgeois forms and that heralded the socialist future before the revolution. It was the largest and most ambitious attempt in interwar Europe to create a socialist culture that went to the roots of everyday life. In their
aim at a total transformation of workers' culture, the socialists erased the boundaries between the public and the private spheres, between the social and the sexual"; Helmut Gruber, "Sexuality in 'Red Vienna': Socialist Party Conceptions and
Programs and Working-Class Life, 1920–34," *International Labor and Working-
Class History* 31 (Spring 1987): 37.

14. Maria Mesner, "Educating Reasonable Lovers: Sex Counseling in Austria
in the First Half of the Twentieth Century," in *Sexuality in Austria*, ed. Gunter
Bischof, Anton Pelinka, and Dagmar Herzog (New Brunswick, NJ: Transaction
Publishers, 2007), 48.

15. Ibid., 51.

16. Gruber, "Sexuality in 'Red Vienna,'" 38; Britta McEwen, *Sexual Knowledge:
Feeling, Fact, and Social Reform in Vienna, 1900–1934* (New York: Berghahn,
2012), 35–36.

by the logic of Rudolf Goldscheid's "human economy": they aimed to restore "organic capital" following the devastating loss of life during the war. To this end, they offered monogamous heterosexual couples information about chronic diseases and the hereditary effects of alcohol and drug addiction, in addition to expert medical advice, in the hopes that individuals would make "good" decisions regarding marriage and reproduction on these bases.[17] While it is important to acknowledge the biopolitical logic that underwrote the opening of state sex and marriage advice centers, it is also worth noting that the founders' intentions did not exclusively determine their use: Mesner points out that many clients using the consultation centers did not intend to marry, but rather sought reliable, detailed information about contraceptives and how to use them.[18] Such subversive use of municipal centers is perhaps not surprising given that abortion remained illegal.[19]

Moreover, many sex and marriage centers approached the task of healing gender rifts and heterosexual dysfunctions with different objectives that subordinated biopolitical imperatives and targeted particular populations. Centers run by the Association for Birth Control, for example, were more concerned with preventing "coerced motherhood" and providing contraceptives to poor and working-class girls and women than they were with realizing strictly eugenic objectives.[20] Meanwhile, counseling centers run by Wilhelm Reich and Marie Frischauf's Socialist Society for Sexual Advice and Sexual Research aimed to help blue-collar and lower-level white-collar workers by providing counseling and hygienic information, including information about masturbation and birth control.[21] As Mesner observes, the Socialist Society's centers were informed by Reich's views on "correct" sexuality, which dictated that "sexual activity should be liberated from bourgeois sexual repression and be, therefore, regular, joyful, satisfying, and—as unspoken as obvious—heterosexual as well as oriented towards

17. Mesner, "Educating Reasonable Lovers," 52.
18. Ibid., 53.
19. Gruber, "Sexuality in 'Red Vienna,'" 42.
20. Mesner, "Educating Reasonable Lovers," 55–56.
21. Ibid., 57–58.

orgasm. Sexual activities deviating from this scheme were deroga-
torily call[ed] 'neurotic.'" Indeed, Reich believed homosexuality
was a sickness that resulted from a developmental disorder. Thus,
even advice centers that were not oriented toward biopolitical objectives could prove remarkably normative: as Mesner notes, the
Socialist Society combined "the rhetoric of emancipation on the
one hand and authoritative instructions on the other."[22]

As suggested by the role of psychoanalysis in the Socialist Society's sex and marriage advice centers, sexology played an important role within the variegated postwar efforts to rehabilitate sex
and gender relations in both countries. Indeed, in Vienna, individual psychologists (such as Sofie Lazarsfeld), who followed the
teachings of Freudian dissident Alfred Adler, assumed increasingly
authoritative social and political roles. Adlerian individual psychology, which stressed cooperation as the most important human
trait and highlighted the role of social hierarchy in creating psychic problems, was very popular among Austrian social democrats.
Adler himself was invited by the city of Vienna to direct an experimental teaching college.[23]

The 1920s arguably marked a renaissance for the sexological
field. Thanks to a relaxation of censorship restrictions that allowed
for more open public discussions and representations of sex and
sexuality, professional sexological organizations and their journals were revived and even expanded their activities. For the first
time, sexologists created their own center for research and education, namely, Magnus Hirschfeld's famous Institute for Sexual
Science. Moreover, new professional organizations and journals
proliferated, particularly within psychoanalysis, which enjoyed
heighted legitimacy and public interest during the 1920s thanks
in part to its work with so-called war hysterics.[24] These dynamic

---

22. Ibid., 58–59.

23. McEwen, *Sexual Knowledge*, 12.

24. See Paul Lerner, *Hysterical Men: War, Psychiatry, and the Politics of Trauma
in Germany, 1890–1930* (Ithaca, NY: Cornell University Press, 2003). Despite the
increasingly independent and variegated institutionalization of psychoanalysis,
psychoanalysts continued to play significant roles in the sexological field. Psychoanalysts not only belonged to professional sexological organizations and presented

efforts at institution building led sexual researchers, theorists, and reformers from abroad to once again view German-speaking Europe (and especially Berlin and Vienna) as the international headquarters of sexological research; tellingly, it was in Berlin that the first meeting of what became the World League for Sexual Reform occurred.[25]

In addition to renewed efforts at institutionalization and professionalization, the sexological field also expanded its objects of inquiry during the 1920s. Aside from its perennial preoccupation with reproduction, sexology was increasingly animated by investigations into the determination of sex and the origins and causes of sex difference.[26] Perhaps more significantly, in a marked divergence from prewar sexology, postwar analysts began to consider the effects of social and cultural conditions in shaping sex, both in addition to and independent of biology. This development marks epistemological and paradigmatic changes within the field itself, possibly catalyzed by postwar sociopolitical conditions and concerns. Postwar studies of sex difference and sex determination were informed by a number of new scientific developments, including new research into hormones and "flexible heredity" conducted by Eugen Steinach and Paul Kammerer;[27] psychoanalysis and individual psychology, which viewed gender roles as the products of a developmental process that was shaped not only by drives but also by

---

at their meetings, but also published regularly in sexological journals. For example, Alfred Adler and other individual psychologists published in the *Journal for Sexual Science* and took part in meetings of the International Society for Sexual Research. On psychoanalysis in Weimar Germany, see Veronika Feuchtner, *Berlin Psychoanalytic: Psychoanalysis and Culture in Weimar Republic Germany and Beyond* (Berkeley: University of California Press, 2011).

25. For details of the conference proceedings, see Dr. A. Weil, ed., *Sexualreform und Sexualwissenschaft* (Stuttgart: Julius Püttmann, 1922).

26. See M. Vaerting, "Literarische Berichte: Paul Kammerer, *Geschlechtsbestimmung und Geschlechtsverwandlung*," *Die neue Generation* 2 (February 1919): 86–90; "Die Bestimmung des embryonalen Geschlechtscharakters," *Die neue Generation* 8 (August 1919): 402–403.

27. On Steinach and Kammerer's innovations, see Cheryl A. Logan, *Hormones, Heredity, and Race: Spectacular Failure in Interwar Vienna* (New Brunswick, NJ: Rutgers University Press, 2013).

environment and social relations;[28] and social scientific research, especially work in anthropology, such as Margaret Mead's famous *Coming of Age in Samoa* (1928), that drew attention to cultural variability in sexual norms and practices.[29] The work of Mathilde Vaerting and Sofie Lazarsfeld demonstrates the impact of the field's preoccupation with the flexibility of sex roles and sex differences, as well as the impacts of the increasing turn to social and cultural factors on understandings of sex, gender, and sexuality.

Mathilde Vaerting and the *New Foundation for the Psychology of Man and Woman*

Mathilde Vaerting is a complex yet little-known figure in the history of sexology. She began publishing in sexological journals in 1914, much later than many of the other writers examined in this book. Vaerting proved remarkably prolific during the war, when her texts were overwhelmingly preoccupied with biopolitical questions such as the best reproductive age of parents to ensure superior intellectual capacity in their offspring, and the racial dangers stemming from a surplus of women after the war.[30] These articles were saturated with eugenic ideas, assumptions, and desires.

---

28. Psychoanalysis was a major vehicle for investigation into the formation of sex roles: it was during this time that Freudian psychoanalysts were embroiled in their own "woman question," marked by the groundbreaking work of Karen Horney and Melanie Klein, among others.

29. See Andrew P. Lyons and Harriet D. Lyons, *Irregular Connections: A History of Anthropology and Sexuality* (Lincoln: University of Nebraska Press, 2004), esp. chap. 7 ("Margaret Mead, the Future of Language, and Lost Opportunities") and chap. 6 ("Malinowski as 'Reluctant Sexologist'").

30. See Mathilde Vaerting, "Die rassenhygienischen Gefahren des Frauenüberschusses nach dem Kriege und Wege zur erhöhten Vermehrung des männlichen Geschlechts," *Zeitschrift für Sexualwissenschaft* 2 (February 1916): 397–405; and *Zeitschrift für Sexualwissenschaft* 3 (March 1916): 445–452; Prof. Dr. M. T. Vaerting, "Die Frau, die erblich-organische Höherentwicklung und der Krieg," *Die neue Generation* 3/4 (March/April 1916): 67–75; Dr. M. Vaerting, "Über den Einfluß des Krieges auf Präventivverkehr und Fruchtabtreibung und seine eugenischen Folgen," *Zeitschrift für Sexualwissenschaft* 4 (July 1917): 137–144; (August 1917): 176–179; Mathilde Vaerting, "Der Nachwuchs der begabten Frauen," *Die neue Generation* 9 (September 1919): 426–433.

While eugenic concerns and theories consistently and thoroughly imbued her sexological contributions between 1914 and 1919, they are notably absent—at least on the surface—from *New Foundation for the Psychology of Man and Woman*. *New Foundation* was comprised of two volumes: *Female Character in the Male State and Male Character in the Female State* (1921) and *Truth and Misconception in Sex Psychology* (1923) (henceforth, I will refer to these volumes as *Female Character* and *Truth and Misconception*). Beginning with *Female Character*, Vaerting's analytic focus seems to have shifted decisively to questions of power and oppression, which she argued stemmed from socially rather than biologically based inequalities.[31] It is unclear exactly what precipitated this change. Further research will hopefully yield more than speculative answers; however, the aforementioned tendencies in sexology and the lessons the war taught regarding the impact of human actions on sexuality likely played roles in causing this shift. The first volume of *New Foundation*, *Female Character*, was originally published as the coauthored works of "Mathilde and Mathias Vaerting," whom many reviewers assumed to be a married couple. However, Vaerting's status as a female civil servant would have prohibited her from marrying, and to date there exists no record of a brother named Mathias.[32]

The *New Foundation* series attracted international scientific and political attention. The volumes comprising *New Foundation* were reviewed in a wide range of journals between 1921 and 1933 that

31. See also Mathilde Vaerting, *Soziologie und Psychologie der Macht: Die Macht der Massen* (Berlin: Dr. M. Pfeiffer, 1928); Prof. Dr. M. T. Vaerting, *Die Frau in unserer Zeit* (Darmstadt-Eberstadt: Themis-Verlag, 1952).

32. Some later editions of the volumes comprising *New Foundation* were published exclusively under the name of "Dr. M. Vaerting." It is interesting to speculate about the reasons why Vaerting initially chose to represent the texts as the work of a male-female couple. Was it out of concern for the reception of the text as a work of science? Was it meant to instantiate the texts' claims regarding sexual equality, or its affirmation of heterosexuality? At this point it is impossible to know. Katharina Leppänen confirms that she has not been able to find traces of a "Mathias" Vaerting, and suspects he does not exist. See Katharina Leppänen, *Elin Wägner's Alarm Clock: Ecofeminist Theory in the Interwar Era* (Lanham, MD: Lexington Books, 2008), 41.

addressed audiences interested in sexology, psychology, medicine, sociology, eugenics, pedagogy, criminology, and women's rights.[33] Both volumes elicited a range of critical responses that very much reflected the position of the reviewer and her or his envisioned readership. Very few reviews were as straightforwardly dismissive and condescending as the three-line notice that appeared in the *Archive for Racial and Social Biology*, which characterized *Truth and Misconception* as revealing more about the psychology of its author than anything else.[34] Some notices, such as Max Marcuse's review of the same text in the *Journal for Sexual Science*, veered toward the patronizing. While noting that many of the ideas presented were "very correct" and their formulation "rather striking," Marcuse nonetheless criticized Vaerting's approach as "dilettantish" and "tendentious." He offered the book the backhanded compliment that it could provide "material for scientific work."[35] Nevertheless, most reviewers conceded that Vaerting's work could not and should not be ignored. Regarding *Female Character*, a review for the *Journal for Sexual Science* declared the volume a "diligent compilation and processing of facts" that is "enjoyable to read."[36] While criticizing the vagueness of *Truth and Misconception*, sexual researcher and theorist Else Voigtländer concluded her review by stating, "The book contains, without doubt, very important findings and points of view" that could help "eliminat[e] mistakes in the field of psychological research and . . . provid[e] access to truth. " "All in all," she insisted, "no one who is involved with

33. In addition to the reviews cited herein, Vaerting's work was also reviewed in other notable publications, including *Deutsche medizinische Wochenschrift, Neue Zuricher Zeitung, Archiv für Sozialwissenschaft und Sozialpolitik, Monatsschrift für Kriminalpsychologie, Die neue Generation, Zeitschrift für Psychologische Forschung, Das neue Deutschland, Der Tag, Die Frau in der Gegenwart, Die Frau, Volksbildung, Fortschritte der Medizin, Zeitschrift für Völkerrecht, Vossische Zeitung, Natur und Gesellschaft, Berliner Tageblatt,* and the *Neue freie Presse*.

34. Fetscher, *Archiv für Rassen und Gesellschaftsbiologie* 17 (1925): 345.

35. Max Marcuse, "Wahrheit und Irrtum der Geschlechterpsychologie," *Zeitschrift für Sexualwissenschaft* 18 (1932): 490.

36. Karl Urbach, "Vaerting, M.: *Neubegründung der Psychologie von Mann und Weib*, Bd. I, *Die weibliche Eigenart im Männerstaat und die männliche Eigenart im Frauenstaat*," *Zeitschrift für Sexualwissenschaft* 8 (February 1922): 363.

these relevant questions could possibly ignore this book."[37] Similar assessments that mixed critique with praise were made in more strictly "scientific" journals, such as the *Archive of Comprehensive Psychology*, the *Journal for Psychology and Physiology of the Sensory Organs,* and the *Journal for Applied Psychology.*[38] These latter reviews addressed the 1932 reissue of the *New Foundation* volumes, which affirms the study's popularity and renown.

Among certain audiences *New Foundation* was rapturously received. Writing for the socialist journal *The Struggle,* feminist theorist Therese Schlesinger heralded Vaerting's work as no less important for sexual psychology than the work of Adler.[39] Helene Stöcker asserted that the study constituted "a prerequisite for the true equal valuation (*Gleichbewertung*) of the sexes" and was "therefore for our movement of particular importance."[40] Likewise, the American *Birth Control Review* declared that, in *Female Character,* "Mathilde and Mathias Vaerting" had "blazed a new trail."[41] Writing in the progressive feminist journal *The Woman in the State,* Helene Rosenau hailed both volumes as providing "not only explanation and support, but also incentive to aim for unrestricted equality"—and, hinting at some of the tensions of Vaerting's

37. Else Voigtländer, "Bücherbesprechung: Vaerting, M., *Wahrheit und Irrtum in der Geschlechterpsychologie,* II. Band der *Neubegründung der Psychologie von Mann und Weib,*" *Zeitschrift für Sexualwissenschaft* 11 (1924): 107.

38. See H. Triepel, "Literaturbericht: Mathilde Vaerting, *Wahrheit und Irrtum in der Geschlechterpsychologie,*" *Archiv für gesamte Psychology* 47 (1924): 227–229; Georg Schwarz, "Literaturbericht: Mathilde Vaerting, *Wahrheit und Irrtum in der Geschlechterpsychologie,*" *Zeitschrift für Psychologie und Physiologie der Sinnesorgane* 127 (1932): 372; Paul Plaut, "Beiträge zur Soziologie," *Zeitschrift für angewandte Psychologie* 42 (1932): 515.

39. Therese Schlesinger, "Zur Psychologie der Geschlechter," *Der Kampf* 6 (1925): 226.

40. See Helene Stöcker's editorial footnote to Mathilde Vaerting's article, "Der Kampf gegen die historischen Spuren der Frauenherrschaft," in *Die neue Generation* 11/12 (November/December 1921): 353. For similar expressions of feminist enthusiasm, see Helene Rosenau, "Die Krisis der Frauenbewegung: Zur Kritik M. Vaertings 'Neubegründung der Psychologie von Mann und Weib,'" *Die Frau im Staat* 8 (1926): 8–11; Schlesinger, "Zur Psychologie der Geschlechter," 225–229; Miriam Van Waters, "Book Reviews: *The Dominant Sex,* by Mathilde and Mathias Vaerting," *Birth Control Review* 6 (October 1923): 273.

41. Van Waters, "Book Reviews," 273.

work, argued that the book proved that, "sexually, woman and man are indeed equal, insofar as both are heterosexual."[42] The *Archive for Gynaecology and Constitutional Research* lavishly praised *Truth and Misconception*, proclaiming that "everybody who reads this will be extremely stimulated, and for many it will shine like a light in the dark of his subconscious."[43]

As the aforementioned reviews suggest, *New Foundation* was clearly a far from insignificant contribution to 1920s-era sexology. Vaerting's texts were not only well received but also treated as authoritative by contemporaries who engaged and appropriated her ideas. They were especially popular among feminists and sex reformers, including Paul Krische and Elin Wägner of Sweden.[44] They also attracted the attention of the famous British sexologist Havelock Ellis, who helped facilitate their English translation.[45]

In *Female Character*, Vaerting mobilized historical and anthropological evidence to articulate a pioneering social constructionist and radically antiessentialist analysis of gender.[46] Here she builds the argument that supposedly sex-differentiated roles, norms, and behaviors are not universal, unchanging, or fundamentally rooted in

42. Rosenau, "Die Krisis der Frauenbewegung," 10, 11, 7.

43. [Max] Westenhöfer, "M. Vaerting: *Wahrheit und Irrtum in der Geschlechterpsychologie*," *Archiv für Frauenkunde und Konstitutionsforschung* 10 (June 1924): 193.

44. See Lepännen, *Elin Wägner's Alarm Clock*. As Peter Davies notes, Krische actually dedicated his study to Vaerting. See Peter Davies, *Myth, Matriarchy, and Modernity: Johann Jakob Bachofen in German Culture, 1860–1945* (New York: De Gruyter, 2010), 140.

45. Mathilde Vaerting and Mathias Vaerting, *The Dominant Sex: A Study in the Sociology of Sex Differentiation*, trans. Eden Paul and Cedar Paul (New York: George H. Doran, 1923), viii. I have taken quotes here from the English translation of the first volume of Vaerting's study.

46. The role of history, anthropology, ethnology, and related disciplines has been largely overlooked within histories of sexology; however, it is worth noting that these disciplines played important roles in studies such as Havelock Ellis's *Man and Woman* (1894) and Iwan Bloch's landmark *The Sexual Life of Our Time* (1908), and inspired Sigmund Freud's *Totem and Taboo* (1913). Moreover, anthropologists such as Friedrich Krauss and Freiherr Ferdinand von Reitzenstein published often within sexological journals such as *Sexual Problems, The New Generation*, and the *Journal for Sexual Science*; Krauss even belonged to the editorial board of *Sexual Problems*.

biology. Instead, she insists they are profoundly malleable imposi-
tions and historically contingent manifestations of power relations
in society. Masculinity and femininity therefore do not constitute
essences, but rather empty categories that have historically recapitulated binary, unequal relationships between dominant and subordinate classes. The historical evidence Vaerting used in *Female
Character* was largely dependent upon the explosion of German
Orientalist studies into "ancient civilizations" such as Egypt and
India from the nineteenth and early twentieth centuries.[47] This
knowledge base of course raises its own provocative questions regarding the role of Germany's erstwhile imperialist project in un-
derwriting her gender analysis, which deserve fuller attention.

Vaerting opened *Female Character* with a blunt critique of past
and current studies of sex psychology by pointing out their fundamental methodological and epistemological failings. These studies
have been wrong, she insisted, because they are based on shaky
foundations and false equivalents. As Vaerting noted, previous research was conducted within a sociopolitical context wherein one
sex enjoyed social, political, and economic power and privileges
over the other. These studies did not proceed from neutral, equal
grounds, nor did they compare like objects. As a result, Vaerting
observed, "the differences shown to exist between such groups are
just as likely to depend upon sociological causes, and to be the
outcome of the reciprocal position of the sexes, as to be due to
congenital divergencies."[48] She further argued that this basic methodological oversight was the result of masculine bias; in so doing,
she prefigured the metacritique of contemporary sexology that she
developed more fully in the second volume of *New Foundation*.

To be in a position to identify "truly congenital differentiae of
sex," Vaerting maintained that "we must compare the sexes when
their position is precisely similar": namely, across comparable relations of power. She insisted that researchers "are only entitled to

---

47. On the history of German Orientalism, see Suzanne Marchard, *German
Orientalism in the Age of Empire: Religion, Race, and Scholarship* (Cambridge:
Cambridge University Press, 2010).

48. Vaerting and Vaerting, *Dominant Sex*, xiii. Subsequent citations of this
work appear parenthetically in the text.

compare dominant men with dominant women, subordinate men with subordinate women, or the two sexes under absolutely equal rights" (*Dominant Sex*, xiv). *Female Character* endeavored to serve as a model of how such research ought to be undertaken, and what its results would be. Here, Vaerting based her comparative analysis upon evidence from past civilizations and cultures she alternately referred to as female dominant (*weibliche Vorherrschaft*) or as "women's states" (*Frauenstaaten*). Importantly, Vaerting does not use the language of "matriarchy" or "patriarchy," though many scholars identify her as a matriarchal theorist; in fact, in some of the cultures and civilizations she identifies as female dominant, like ancient Egypt, men held positions of formal political power.[49] Rather, what Vaerting seems to be describing is a situation of hegemony.

According to Vaerting, comparing qualities ascribed to masculinity and femininity under "women's states" and "men's states," respectively, reveals an "extremely important fundamental law": that "the contemporary peculiarities of women are mainly determined by the existence of the Men's State, and that they are accurately and fully paralleled by the peculiarities of men in the Women's State" (*Dominant Sex*, xiv-xv). "Sex differentiation is merely the outcome of the position of dominance or subjection," she declared, "and is not a product of inborn biological characteristics" (51). Vaerting's objective in *Female Character* was to "show that there is not a single 'masculine quality' which cannot be paralleled as a 'feminine quality' in the history of one race or another" (24). To this end, Vaerting endeavored to demonstrate how sex roles developed under conditions of male dominance constitute reversals of those that prevailed in female-dominant polities. She teased out sex norms and expectations by analyzing a range of social institutions and practices wherein sex differences are most prominent, including marriage, family forms and laws, courtship rituals, and divisions of labor. In addition, she examined moral codes, attitudes toward war, property laws, and religious systems.

---

49. See Vaerting and Vaerting, *The Dominant Sex*, 188–201, for an explanation.

Under conditions of female dominance, Vaerting claimed, one repeatedly confronts women in roles occupied by men in male-dominant societies: woman is the "wooer," and enjoys unbounded sexual freedom; she determines her children's status, inheritance, and name; she controls property and monopolizes the right of ownership; she is the one to "carry on occupations outside the home" (*Dominant Sex*, 22, 25, 27, 64–66, 71, 75). Conversely, within such societies man is the one who is wooed, who is considered sexually modest and expected to obey standards of chastity, and who is eroticized and praised for his beauty rather than his brains. He is also singularly responsible for the household and care for the family, and is denied rights of property and ownership (121, 123–127, 139). Beyond these findings, Vaerting's comparative method led her to undermine other essentialist assumptions, including those held dear by many of her feminist contemporaries. She asserted that women are not pacifists by nature by highlighting the warlike character of many female-dominant states (chap. 15, esp. p. 210). Even more radically, she challenged the notion of inherent *physiological* differences between the sexes, and argued that anatomical particularities themselves arise from the division of labor (90–91, 100–113). Vaerting maintained that under a system of equal rights, the "natural resemblances" between the sexes in their stature, form, and clothing would be reasserted (114).

Based upon the evidence presented, Vaerting concluded that "the mere fact that the members of the respective sexes exhibit almost identical peculiarities as dominants or as subordinates, shows that there must be a very close similarity in the inborn psychical aptitudes of men and women. . . . The psychical trends that appear both in men and in women when one sex dominates the other are universally human and not specifically masculine or feminine." Sexual inequality itself must constitute "the decisive factor in the formation of masculine and feminine peculiarities that are apparent in any epoch" (220). Masculinity and femininity constitute nothing more than variable manifestations of social relations of dominance and subordination when one sex is dominant.

It is for these reasons that Vaerting championed sexual equality as the only condition that would lead to "the abrogation of the division of labour on sexual lines," and thus enable truly individual development (94). Instead of "repress[ing] individual peculiarities in order to form two artificially divergent sexual types" and enforcing conformity *within* the sexes, sexual equality would liberate "men from manliness" and women from womanliness (222). Although Vaerting believed that sexual equality was inevitable, at least for a time, as a result of the "Pendulum Theory" of sexual dominance she articulated toward the end of *Female Character*, she believed that the challenge would lie in "discover[ing] ways and means for the permanent realisation of the ideal of sex equality, and for the prevention of either type of monosexual dominance" (268).[50]

As an added benefit, Vaerting further insisted that sexual equality would improve sexual morality, given the role that relations of power play in determining sexual customs (49). In her view, power determines not only sexual roles but also sexual norms, values, and relations. According to Vaerting, a sexual double standard is inevitable in states when one sex dominates (41, 48).[51] She maintained that, just as in male-dominant societies, female-dominant societies ascribe complete sexual freedom to the dominant sex (in this case women) while intensely regulating the sexual behavior of the subordinate sex (men) through laws, norms, and assumptions. Within "women's states," men are idealized when sexually "pure" and modest, and their sexual purity (which Vaerting deems a "slave's virtue") is treated as a desirable quality by women (228–229). In

---

50. According to Vaerting's pendulum theory, the history of sexual relations is "undulatory," swinging from one form of sexual domination to the other. This constant shift from one form of dominance to another, she claimed, was due to what she called "the psychological law of action and reaction—the psychological law of power." One form of sexual domination was ultimately overthrown, she claimed, because of the excesses and abuses of power by one sex over the other. Yet in the "swing" from one form of domination to the other, Vaerting maintained that a society necessarily "traverses the stage in which there is a balance of power between the sexes," which constitutes the "phase of equal rights." She believed that her own society was in a state of transition between forms of dominance. Although she declared that "power alone can make women free," she cautioned against taking this power to an "extreme" and recapitulating the errors of the past. See *Dominant Sex*, chap. 18, "The Pendulum Movement of Monosexual Dominance."

51. This claim is elaborated in chapter 3 in this book.

Vaerting's view, sexual inequality tends toward degeneracy, although she does not explicitly clarify what she means by this term. Sexual equality would, she insisted, allow men and women both to become sexually free, and to be judged by the same moral standard. Furthermore, Vaerting claimed that sexual equality would increase the happiness of married men and women, eliminate prostitution, elevate the status and treatment of illegitimate children, and, in a nod to her earlier eugenic work, contribute to an "improvement in the quality of offspring" (233–234). She even suggested that sexual equality could lead to the acceptance of abortion (which she maintained is commonplace within female-dominant societies) (57–59). Finally, by enabling men and women to authentically relate to one another as individuals, sexual equality would enhance harmony and intimacy between men and women, and would prevent men and especially women from "enter[ing] the pathways of the unnatural sexual life," whose hallmarks according to Vaerting are "self-gratification" and "Lesbian love" (228). In such instances the reader can begin to see how Vaerting's analysis of sex roles is bound up with assumptions regarding sexuality.

Female Character would seem to offer a strong, coherent, and internally consistent theory of sexual difference that required no further elaboration. Yet Vaerting's provocative analysis and arguments raise a number of important questions. First, if her claims are true, why had no one previously realized and publicized these facts? And second, why had the perception of binary sexual differences, regardless of their particular configuration, persisted as a seemingly transcultural, transhistorical phenomenon? Vaerting began formulating an answer to the first question in *Female Character* by identifying the ways in which the subjectivity and ideologies of the dominant sex influence the reading of evidence, and thus the production of knowledge (193, 196–197, 237–238). She further asserted that historical records documenting a particular form of sex dominance are routinely altered by the usurping rulers to reflect new relations of power (193, 196–199). It was not until she released *Truth and Misconception*, the second volume of *New Foundation*, that she fully addressed both questions.

In *Truth and Misconception*, Vaerting focused on two factors she claimed have caused sex psychology to become "a psychology of errors": namely, sexual inequality and the lack of recognition of a psychological mechanism she called the "sexual component."[52] According to Vaerting, these two factors are interrelated, and understanding their interaction and effects would have profound implications for sexual psychology, as well as practical consequences for women's employment and education, and broader demands for equality. Whereas her argument regarding sexual inequality clearly proceeds from the analysis she initiated in *Female Character*, her concept of the sexual component represents a marked deviation from her social constructionist approach. As we will soon discover, it is premised upon essentialist assumptions regarding sexuality.

The first part of *Truth and Misconception* offers a thorough and persuasive analysis of the ways in which sexual inequality influences the production of knowledge and, according to Vaerting, has led to glaring errors. Her case rests on her critique of early twentieth-century psychological studies of men and women. Vaerting argued that inequalities of power eliminate the possibility of objective knowledge, as the standpoint from which a researcher interprets the world is not neutral. To support this argument, she advanced three supporting claims. First, she noted that researchers proceeding from a position of dominance tend to establish their group as the measure of all things. Though in Weimar Germany this insight implicates male researchers, Vaerting took pains to note that women are subject to the same vulnerabilities when they occupy positions of power. She declared this subjective bias a *human* mistake that she named "the master's subjectivity" (*Herrschersubjektivität*) (*Wahrheit und Irrtum*, 2).

Second, she noted that research conducted by members of sexually dominant groups tends to exaggerate the differences between the ruling and ruled groups while diminishing similarities. This tendency, Vaerting argued, aims to create distance between the ruling

---

52. Mathilde Vaerting, *Wahrheit und Irrtum in der Geschlechterpsychologie* (Karlsruhe: G. Braun, 1923), vii. Subsequent citations of this work appear parenthetically in the text.

and the ruled and illuminate supposedly innate superior and inferior traits, thereby preserving prevailing relations of power. She
pointed out, for example, that in a study which found 41.4 percent
of men to be objective compared to 34.1 percent of women, most
(male) analysts focus on the 7 percent difference, rather than their
overwhelming similarity (7).

Third, Vaerting observed that researchers from the dominant
sex focus on flaws identified in the subordinated group and apply
them to all members of that group, whereas they only focus on the
strengths of their own group and apply them to all members of
their group. As a result of the exclusive focus on flaws on one side
and strengths on the other, analysts from the dominant group tend
to assume that activities or occupations that their members find
challenging, for example, math, must be impossible for the subordinated group. Vaerting referred to this tendency as the "ruler's
argument by analogy" (*Herrscheranalogieschluss*) (34-40).

Taken together, Vaerting claimed, the effects of power on knowledge make it impossible to accept existing scientific assessments of
sexual difference as truthful and objective. The dynamics of dominance and subordination ensure that the powerful will find what
they want to find, and these findings in turn will support the status
quo by denigrating the subordinated group. It is for these reasons,
Vaerting maintained, that women in male-dominated states are described as docile, less intelligent, emotional, gossipy, and unjust,
among other unflattering inferior traits that supposedly make them
incapable of relating to men as equals. Consequently, in Vaerting's
view, "there is only one factor which can remove this distance, that
is power" (4).

So far, over the course of the two volumes comprising *New
Foundation*, Vaerting has articulated a compelling, provocative argument regarding the fundamental contingency of sexual norms,
attributes, roles, and behaviors, treating them as nothing more
than expressions of particular, malleable configurations of power.
She has also developed an incisive critique of knowledge, and has
shown the ways in which inequalities of power thoroughly bias
scientific studies of sex psychology. Up to this point, however, her
analysis has been unable to explain why differences between the

sexes continue to be identified, and why sex has provided such a consistent staging ground for contests over power. To answer such questions, in *Truth and Misconception* Vaerting developed the concept of the sexual component, which she asserted "necessitates not only a fundamental change in current sex psychology, but is also at the same time of far-reaching importance for the whole field of applied psychology" (vii).

According to Vaerting, the sexual component can explain differences between the sexes that power alone cannot. She described the sexual component as a consequence of the "dual sexed nature of humanity" (*Zweigeschlechtlichkeit der Menschheit*), which imparts to the soul of every man and woman a "double-face" (*doppeltes Gesicht*) that causes the psyche to react very differently toward the opposite sex than toward its own. Specifically, the sexual component causes a person to act in a "sexually inflected" (*geschlechtsbetonten*) way toward a member of the opposite sex. Because of the sexual component, Vaerting argued, the possibility of a "sexual influence" on behavior always exists whenever men and women come into intellectual contact with one another, though she conceded that the sexual component can remain latent and inactive in some individuals (vii, 46). She further described the expression of the sexual component as either positive or negative, "namely leaning toward emphasizing lust or apathy (*Lust- oder Unlustbetonung*)." As such, the sexual component could have two opposite effects: inhibiting and arousing (*hemmend und erregend*) (46). However, Vaerting insisted that people behave "neutrally," or rather in a nonemotional, nonsexually inflected way, toward members of their same sex (47). For her, sexual influence never comes into question between "normal" individuals of the same sex.

Vaerting maintained that the sexual component has particularly strong effects on the emotions and "ability to think" (*Denkleistungsfähgikeit*)—that it encourages the expression of emotion between the sexes while inhibiting reason (90). In her view, the sexual component exercises a particularly strong influence over girls (94–95). According to Vaerting, the sexual component explains why, for example, women may appear to men to be more emotional, and why they would be less capable of intellectual achievement when educated solely by men and forced to engage with male-dominated cultural and educational institutions (50–53, 59, 62–71, 73–84, 226–237).[53] It is for this reason, she asserted, that girls tend to excel academically under the guidance of female teachers (46, 90–91).

The sexual component served to further explain why a female researcher studying women would arrive at different findings than a male researcher studying women, and vice versa (54–57, 72, 97–98). By way of proof, she cites the work of American psychologist Helen Thompson, whose studies in comparative sex psychology contradicted the findings advanced by her male colleagues (53–57). Vaerting pointed out that not only positive but also strongly negative emotional reactions could be attributed to the workings of the sexual component; however, she insisted that these negative reactions are often signs of sexual abnormality. In her words, "A negative direction of the sexual component" can arise as "the result of a sick or confused sexuality" (71).

Vaerting never clarifies in the text exactly what kind of entity the sexual component *is*; it figures as a nebulous essence of human existence. Yet many of Vaerting's assertions regarding the nature and working of the sexual component indicate that it has something to do with sex and sexuality. Specifically, as something that binds men and women to an inexorable, dynamic, emotional, and implicitly eroticized interaction with one another, it would seem that the sexual component is a synonym for naturalized heterosexuality. It is perhaps telling that she uses the adjective "sexual" rather than "geschlecht" to describe the component, as "geschlecht" gestures to an understanding of sex more in line with what would today be called gender. Equally revealing is the fact that Vaerting characterized the component as working to either "arouse" or "inhibit" one's "lust or apathy" toward a person of the opposite sex. Furthermore, Vaerting specified that the sexual component can only

---

53. Importantly, Vaerting believed that this dynamic held true for men as well— that is, that they behaved more emotionally and less rationally toward women. However, she claimed that, thanks to their current dominance, men can neglect this "weakness" in themselves, as it would potentially undermine their power.

take effect between men and women—that is, between "healthy and normal" men and women whose sexuality is not "sick" or "confused."

Tellingly, Vaerting maintained that "sexuality is overall the driving force behind emotional life," and that therefore "the sexual component undoubtedly has a very strong emotional effect on psychic phenomena" (50). Speaking of women, Vaerting wrote that "the woman feels as a sexual being—when her sexual component is aroused. . . . She has then consciously or unconsciously a tendency to show a man her feelings first and then her intellect, because she perceives a male in this situation as a sexual being and builds a bridge to this being by way of her feelings" (108). Conversely, Vaerting explicitly, albeit briefly, addressed the role of the sexual component in same-sex desiring individuals. She bluntly described the working of the sexual component among homosexual women as "pathological abnormalities of the sexual influence." While she did not view homosexual men and women to be immune to the workings of the sexual component, she believed that in these individuals, "the positive orientation of the component . . . is completely directed towards its own sex," while negative emotional responses are directed toward the opposite sex (111). Neutrality strangely does not seem to be an option here. Although she maintained that the sexual component in homosexual men and women requires further investigation, even suggesting that functional observations of the sexual component could be used to identify latent homosexuality, she stopped herself, saying that she didn't "want to go into it any further" (111–112). Instead, she focused her attention on the effects of the sexual component upon the feelings that "healthy individuals" bear toward homosexuality (111).

Bearing in mind the arguments made in both volumes of the *New Foundation*, by the conclusion of *Truth and Misconception* the reader finds herself in a complicated position: on the one hand, gender differences are attributed to the workings of power, as determined by larger social structures and the functional demands they imply; on the other hand, the phenomenon of difference itself is naturalized as an essential, unavoidable consequence of heterosexuality. Men and women seem destined to react to one another in certain emotionally and sexually overdetermined ways, regardless of the particular constellations of gender and power relations. Vaerting claimed that it is impossible to eradicate the effects of the sexual component, given how fundamental the component is to the souls of sexed human beings. She concluded the second volume by declaring, "It would be fairer not to make any sex responsible for the sins of dominance by one sex, because both sexes are, as a whole, victims of evolution" (253).

The best that can be done, in Vaerting's view, is to try and mitigate the effects of the sexual component where and when they matter in the lives of individual men and women, and in the study of sexual differences. To achieve these ends, she proposed new methodologies for the study of sex psychology that would require participation and input from male *and* female researchers, along with reforms in the education and upbringing (*Erziehung*) of boys and girls (166–172, 176–181, 217–225). Perhaps even more radically, like feminist sex reformers such as Grete Meisel-Hess she advocated greater sexual freedom for women as a means of furthering their intellectual achievement (241–244). Yet because of the sexual component, Vaerting discounted the possibility of same-sex desire, attraction, and identification as viable options within a state of sexual equality. Individuals must behave neutrally or rationally toward members of their same sex; positive erotic feelings, desires, and interactions can only serve as signs of pathology and degeneration within this framework.

Sofie Lazarsfeld and the *Woman's Experience of the Male*

First published in the early 1930s, Sofie Lazarsfeld's *Woman's Experience of the Male* was among the sexological studies of sex and sexual difference that drew upon Vaerting's groundbreaking work.[54] Lazarsfeld directly cited Vaerting to support her own arguments based in Adlerian individual psychology.[55] Lazarsfeld's

54. Here and below I cite from the English translation of Lazarsfeld's work.

55. Sofie Lazarsfeld explicitly discusses Mathilde Vaerting's work in chap. 7 ("Woman's Erotic Personality") of *Woman's Experience of the Male* (London:

work strikingly resembles Vaerting's in the tensions it manifests between the denaturalization of gender on the one hand and the essentialization of heterosexuality on the other. The interconnections between these texts and their similar treatment of gender and sexuality in spite of their different approaches, generic forms, and places of publication indicate the influence of broader social and cultural dynamics on sexological knowledge.

Like Mathilde Vaerting, Sofie Lazarsfeld has received little attention from scholars until recently. The first book-length biography of Lazarsfeld was only published in 2015, and bears the subtitle *The Rediscovery of a Pioneer of Individual Psychology.* Sofie Lazarsfeld (née Munk) was born in 1881 in Troppau, part of the Austrian section of Schlesien (now Czech Republic). Even though she lacked university education, following her move to Vienna, she and her husband became part of the city's socialist-intellectual milieu, and she proved an avid autodidact. Through her friendships with Margarete Hilferding and Alfred Adler, Lazarsfeld became interested in individual psychology and pursued its study. At this time, women made up 50 percent of the Viennese Association for Individual Psychology's membership.[56] Upon qualification, she dedicated her career to issues concerning women's and children's sexuality. In 1925, Lazarsfeld opened up a sex and marriage counseling center in her apartment and began writing a sex advice column. She later assumed leading roles in professional organizations dedicated to individual psychology in the United States, following her forced emigration because of her ethnicity and socialist politics.

Like Vaerting's *New Foundation, Woman's Experience of the Male* was widely reviewed in journals addressing diverse audiences, including *Biological Healing Arts, The Woman in the State, The New Generation, New Home Economics, The Struggle, Journal for Applied Psychology, Journal for School Health and Social Hygiene*, and, perhaps not surprisingly, the *Journal for Individual*

Francis Aldor, n.d). Echoes of Vaerting's ideas can also be found on pp. 56–57, 62, 102–104, 174.

56. Martina Siems, *Sofie Lazarsfeld: Die Wiederentdeckung einer individual-psychologischen Pionerin* (Göttigen: V & R Unipress, 2015), 11.

Psychology. The early English translation of her book, entitled
Rhythm of Life, was also reviewed in the *Journal of Personality*.[57]
As was the case with *New Foundation, Woman's Experience of the
Male* was no stranger to condescending commentary. The British
Journal of Personality's review of Lazarsfeld's book disparagingly
referred to it as "a rather strange though interesting conglomera-
tion of quotations from medical authorities, philosophers, psychologists, and poets on the one hand, and some practical experiences
in, and statistics on, an Austrian 'marital advice bureau,' written
in a typically journalistic style." Although it noted that Lazarsfeld
"took a leading part in one of those Central European bureaus
which . . . give advice before the final decision to marry is taken,"
and that she "kept careful statistics on the cases treated," it also
stated that she "quote[d] extensively" authors "whose views she
found in agreement with her own observations."[58] Aside from
this dismissive review, on the whole the book was positively received. Writing for the feminist journal *The Woman in the State*, E.
Paulsen exclaimed in the very first lines of her review, "An important book! Every woman read it!"[59] Paulsen noted that the book
was firmly grounded in experience and clinical evidence, and written in a lively, accessible way. She especially celebrated Lazarsfeld's
theory that men's feeling of sexual inferiority was the origin of
many social phenomena, including women's oppression, which I
outline below.[60] Although this aspect of *Woman's Experience of
the Male* was downplayed in the review that appeared in the *Journal for Applied Psychology*, its author, H. Keller, nonetheless declared that the book should be comprehensively studied by men as
well as women.[61] Writing for *Biological Healing Arts*, Dr. Werner

57. R. S., "Books on Sex and Marriage," *Journal of Personality* 3, no. 2 (December 1934): 172.

58. Ibid.

59. E. Paulsen, "Bücherbesprechung: Sofie Lazarsfeld: *Wie die Frau den Mann
erlebt*," *Frau im Staat* 13 (1931): 12.

60. Ibid.

61. H. Keller, "Sofie Lazarsfeld: *Wie die Frau den Mann erlebt*," *Zeitschrift
für angewandte Psychologie* 40 (1931): 537. According to Keller, "The work does
not want to turn against the man—although it speaks here and there about the

Becker pointed out that although the author sympathetically identified with the sexual condition of women, and that as a "highly
modern" woman she stressed the equality of the sexes, Lazarsfeld
never lost the impartiality needed for this work, and did not assign
blame for sexual dysfunction exclusively to one sex. Becker ultimately recommended reading *Woman's Experience of the Male*,
noting that everyone could learn from Lazarsfeld and her wealth
of experience.[62]

Unlike *New Foundation*, Lazarsfeld's *Woman's Experience of the
Male* was not meant to be an academic contribution to the study of
sex and sexual difference. Rather, Lazarsfeld aimed to write a sexological guidebook by a woman for women, based on her knowledge and experience as an Adlerian psychologist. Although less
familiar than Freudian or even Jungian psychoanalytic traditions,
Adlerian or individual psychology was an important and influential movement, particularly in 1920s Vienna. Unlike Freudian or
Jungian traditions, Adlerian psychology stresses the importance of
the total environment on the development of an individual's personality. The individual is treated holistically, not as a collection of
drives or instincts, although Adlerians attribute much importance
to the motivating forces of aggression and feelings of inferiority.
Adlerians are responsible for developing the concepts of the "inferiority complex" and "overcompensation." They were much more
attuned to relations of power and social relations in shaping subjectivity, including an individual's sense of masculinity or femininity,
than many other psychologists at the time.[63] Adlerians also heavily

---

physiological inferiority of the man—rather, it stresses women's independence, and
wants to make the woman uninhibited in regards to sexual things as well" (536).

62. Dr. Werner H. Becker, "*Wie die Frau den Mann erlebt* von Sofie Lazarsfeld," *Biologische Heilkunst* 12 (1931): 531.

63. On Adlerian theories of sexual subjectivity, including the pivotal role of the
so-called Masculine Protest, see Bernard Handlbauer, "Psychoanalytikerinnen und
Individualpsychologinnen im Roten Wien," in *Die Revolutionierung des Alltags:
Zur intellektuellen Kultur von Frauen im Wien der Zwischenkriegszeit*, ed. Doris
Ingrisch, Ilse Korotin, and Charlotte Zwiauer (Frankfurt am Main: Peter Lang,
2004), 75–100; Andrea Capovilla, *Entwürfe weiblicher Identität in der Moderne:
Milena Jesenská, Vicki Baum, Gina Kraus, Alice Rühle-Gerstel: Studien zu Leben
und Werk* (Oldenburg: Igel Verlag, 2004); Siems, *Sofie Lazarsfeld*, 125–134.

stressed the importance of self-awareness and individual willpower as means of developing a productive, fulfilling lifestyle that would enable a person to realize her or his fullest sense of self. For this reason, Adlerians heavily stressed the importance of taking responsibility for one's choices and one's life path.

In the introduction to *Woman's Experience of the Male*, Lazarsfeld bemoaned the lack of sexological texts written by women, writing that "in so far as [sexological texts] are founded upon real knowledge and practical experience of life, they are written by men and for men, from the male point of view. They show clearly the traces of the man, favoring as they do the civilization in which woman plays a subordinate role, and they betray a certain condescension" (18). "Even where the investigations have been carried out conscientiously, and have led to the conclusion that the sexes are equal," she noted that "the male author's unconscious acceptance of the subordination of the female sex becomes apparent again and again" (105). What was needed, she claimed, was a book like hers: a sexological text written by a woman for women, one that combined "feminine attitude" with specialist knowledge gained from practical, professional experience. Lazarsfeld positioned herself as the ideal author of such a work by appealing not only to her gender, but also to her experience running a sex and marriage advice center in Vienna. Books like hers, she insisted, would correct studies written by men: bringing women's experience to bear on existing facts and theories would remedy sexual half-truths and ultimately enable women to determine their future as autonomous sexual agents.

One of Lazarsfeld's major interventions in *Woman's Experience of the Male* was her challenge to two general attitudes toward sex and sexuality that she claimed shaped the existing "erotic atmosphere": first, that "sex and sexuality represent . . . rigid, immutable principle[s]," and second, that "woman's sexual role is . . . inferior" (95). Lazarsfeld was particularly critical of the essentialization of femininity, and the ways in which "natural laws" were mobilized in order to "justify the subordination of women" (102). In her view, it was essential to attack these attitudes not only because they "have caused and continue to cause a great deal of harm," but also

because they were unfounded and had been disproven by "both scientific investigation and practical experience" (95). From the outset
of her text, she expressed criticism of the notion of absolute sex differences, writing that "we are very careful not to describe anything
as 'typically masculine,' because we are convinced that there is no
such thing in the psychological sense, and because we are of the
opinion that it is hardly correct to speak of 'men' or 'women' on the
basis of such distinctions at all. Actually, the difference between one
woman and another may be far greater than that between a man
and a woman" (21).

In support of her argument that gender distinctions are not
natural phenomena, Lazarsfeld appealed to a range of social and
natural scientific resources. She drew upon new findings in biology, which she claimed were proving that distinctions between the
sexes did not exist, or were at least found to be of degree rather
than kind (104–105). According to Lazarsfeld, cutting-edge biology proved "that none of these distinctions apply naturally as between the sexes, and that in so far as they existed they were due
to an imposed and enforced status and mode of life" (102). As a
supplement, she invoked "ethnological investigations into the matriarchate," including Vaerting's studies of hegemonically female
societies, which demonstrated that gender roles, norms, and performances varied according to the given relations of power in a
social order (103). To further prove her point, Lazarsfeld referenced new research on hormones, which she claimed affirmed the
malleability of gender, as it proved that "it is possible to change a
woman almost completely into a male or a man into a female, at
least theoretically" (49). The very physiology associated with masculinity and femininity, such as degrees of fat accumulation and
skeletal build, was variable, she insisted, and was proven by "experience" through the example of "masculinized" American women
(200–201). Even in instances when physiological differences may
have distinctively shaped male and female sexuality, Lazarsfeld
asserted that they had been incorrectly interpreted against wom-
en's interests and pleasure. Using the examples of women's sexual
desires during menstruation, she drew upon her experience as a
sexual consultant and the expertise of the British sexologist Marie

Stopes to prove that women "particularly sought sexual contact" during menstruation, and that they "enjoy[ed] it with far greater intensity than usual" (135). "All this had to be said in some detail," she maintained, "because it is essential to disprove the hypocritical argument concerning the biological inferiority of women which is so glibly used to support the tendency of suppressing the development of the feminine personality. Modern science has definitely destroyed that argument, and has proved that there is no 'feminine biological tragedy' and women can be independent. Nor is there any doubt that women could make themselves independent if they wanted to do so" (222–223). Because the idea of biological inequality between men and women was a myth, Lazarsfeld believed that contemporary women ought to find "assurance and confidence in the knowledge of the *natural* equality of the sexes" (205; emphasis in original).

Undermining arguments regarding essential sex differences and drawing upon individual psychology enabled Lazarsfeld not only to argue on behalf of sexual equality, but also to theorize alternate accounts of men's sexual oppression of women that, while not ignoring the body, stressed the importance of psychological and social motivations. Lazarsfeld's analysis proceeded from a fundamental premise of individual psychology: namely, that fear is the motivating factor behind human action and behavior, and that this "life fear" produces a sense of inferiority (98–99). In terms of sexuality, fears of sexual inferiority lead a person to overinflate the importance of sex, and to treat sex as a realm in which to pursue personal power over others. Both tendencies, she insisted, were especially evident in men (101–102). Consequently, Lazarsfeld argued, "Sexual life in our man-ruled world is built on the subordination of the woman, and this situation is maintained and convulsively adhered to despite the harm resulting from it to the man as well as the woman" (101).

But why should men feel inferior, given that, as Lazarsfeld noted, they enjoy "every privilege, [play] the leading role in every sphere, ha[ve] every opportunity for the full development of [their] personality and [do] not occupy a position of inferiority anywhere"? (108). The answer, she declared, lies in man's sense of inferiority

regarding his sexual capacity. She identified certain physical limitations on male sexuality that do not exist for women:

> His capacity for sexual pleasure depends on certain physiological condi-
> tions; hers does not; his ability to engage in sexual contact is conditional
> upon his achieving an erection; hers is not thus limited. Therefore, the
> man's activity depends on and is limited by certain physiological condi-
> tions, while the woman is always capable of sexual contact; repetition is
> not always possible to the man, but always possible to the woman. (111)

It is out of a sense of physiological lack, Lazarsfeld declared, that
men are led to "overcompensate" by insisting on their dominance
over women. According to Lazarsfeld, "Out of man's consciousness of the woman's physiological superiority there has developed
a whole fear complex which makes itself felt not only in every aspect of our sexual life, but in the very structure of society. It is
the man's fear of sexual failure, sexual defeat"—and ultimately,
she insisted, men's fear of the "entire female sex"—that "really
governs our lives" (111–113). This fear is further responsible for
denigrating women's sexual role through theories such as that of
penis envy, which, Lazarsfeld maintained, "springs from the over-
compensation of masculine sexual inadequacy due to physiological
causes" (116). "Actually," Lazarsfeld noted, "what women desire
is not the possession of a penis in their own organism, but rather
the power and privileges which the possessors of a penis have secured for themselves by way of over-compensation for the physiological inadequacy of that organ" (117).

According to Lazarsfeld, then, if there were no intrinsic, essential differences between men and women, it followed that women
had as much capacity for sexual pleasure and sexual agency as
men. In addition to using biology to debunk prevailing stereo-
types, Lazarsfeld also mobilized psychology as a way to highlight
the sexual potential that lay dormant in all people. In line with her
training in Adlerian psychology, Lazarsfeld stressed that sexual
personality was individualized, not overdetermined by gender; it
was influenced by a person's erotic atmosphere, and thus changeable. In Lazarsfeld's words, individual sexuality "is not fixed, but
variable, and it is therefore up to him to develop it; everyone has

the kind of sexuality which he or she deserves" (118). In order to establish more authentic sexual subjectivities, untethered from essentialist ideas regarding gender, Lazarsfeld stressed the need particularly for women to develop what individual psychologists call a "life plan," and advocated that women work outside the home to build their self-confidence and free themselves from a gendered sense of inferiority (191–192). In her view, "The full development of the human personality, both masculine and feminine, demands both love and work" (233). Lazarsfeld therefore called for a transformation of the broader erotic environment that shaped sexuality.

Lazarsfeld did not believe that pursuing professional work was enough in itself, however: she further insisted that women must be paid equally with men for their labor. According to her, "A really satisfactory sexual relationship between men and women in the future can only be achieved if female labor is rated just as highly as male labor, and women attain economic independence of their sexual partner" (256). Equally paid employment would provide women not only with greater confidence, but also greater material independence; both, Lazarsfeld believed, would reduce the burden on demands for fulfillment through sex, and would reduce inhibitions between sexual partners, critical to any pleasurable sexual experience (231–232). Here it is worth noting that the demand for women's economic independence—whether through (equally) paid labor outside the home, or through maternal welfare schemes—has been a constant demand of female sexual theorists, and has been consistently identified as a fundamental precondition for healthy sexual relations between men and women. Lazarsfeld further called for a new education for girls and boys that would train girls to embrace work outside the home and its psychological benefits, and teach boys to appreciate women and desire equality between the sexes. "It is to be hoped," she declared, "that the rational education of boys will cause at some future time all men to realize that perfect sexual happiness for both sexes lies not in antagonistic opposition but in cooperation on equal terms. . . . That time will relieve the men of their exaggerated and totally unfounded sexual fear of women, and will free both sexes from the many troubles from which we are at present suffering as a result of this fear" (264).

Lazarsfeld's engagement with individual psychology and its stress on social forces, power relations, and the motivating force of feelings like fear, aggression, and inferiority all enabled her to destabilize the naturalization of gender and especially the essentialization of female sexuality. Individual psychology also supported Lazarsfeld's calls for sexual equality and the need to individualize sexuality. As the preceding paragraph suggests, however, Lazarsfeld's goals in writing *Woman's Experience of the Male* were not limited to deconstructing sex roles and providing women readers with gender-specific sexological guidance. Perhaps even more importantly, Lazarsfeld endeavored to rehabilitate heterosexual relations between men and women to ensure that both parties could enjoy a mutually satisfactory sex life (144–148). After all, this book was informed not just by Lazarsfeld's training in individual psychology, but also by her experiences running a sex and marriage advice center and penning a sex advice column (19–22). For Lazarsfeld, it was necessary to abandon essentialist understandings of sex roles precisely in order to create healthier heterosexual unions. For Adlerians, as Lazarsfeld pointed out, "it is decisive for the happiness of any conjugal or sexual relationship that each partner should recognise the separate personality of the other and his or her absolute right to decide the conditions of his or her love" (26; see also 27, 36).

On its surface, the goal of improving sexual relations between men and women may seem benign, especially when paired with demands for sexual equality and women's empowerment in the workforce. Yet the fact that Lazarsfeld's destabilization of gender is linked so closely to the affirmation of heterosexuality should give the reader pause. In Lazarsfeld's view, heterosexual relations constituted the bedrock of social, cultural, and psychological life. According to her, "The destiny of the individual, as well as that of the nations, to a considerable extent depends on that relationship [between a man and a woman]" (53). She even maintained that the "relationship between man and woman comprises every form of relationship that may exist between one human and another," including "the erotic and sexual relationship," reproduction, and labor (54–55).[64] Heterosexual relations informed not only social structure but also spiritual life, and even shaped the most fundamental trait of the human psyche (from an Adlerian point of view), the urge for personal power (55). According to Lazarsfeld, only with the emergence of sexual science were researchers and laypeople alike coming to realize not only the centrality but also the *necessity* of heterosexuality for human survival and social order—and that the security of this institution was not something to be taken for granted, given the myriad sexual problems of the present day.[65]

Accompanying Lazarsfeld's insistence on and celebration of heterosexuality was her rather damning (though sometimes ambivalent) presentation of female homosexuality as a pathological consequence of unsatisfactory heterosexual relations (307). Though she refrained from "enter[ing] into the medical dispute as to whether homosexuality is congenital," she nonetheless maintained that "homosexuality in many cases arises from defects in education" (304). More specifically, she asserted that in her clinical work, she was "frequently able to trace a childhood situation which, via passive discouragement or active defiance led to a deflection of the sexual bent" (304). In the case of female homosexuality, she declared that in many cases it was caused by a "dis-satisfaction with the feminine sexual role in early girlhood," or the particulars of family dynamics: "a brilliant or too insignificant mother,

64. Intriguingly, in her discussion of reproduction, Lazarsfeld insisted on distinguishing the reproductive from the sexual drives in ways that resembled the arguments of the women sexologists whose ideas were examined in chapter 2: "It is frequently said that there is such a thing as the instinct of reproduction and a hypocritical science that places this on a footing of equality with the sexual urge. That, of course, is sheer nonsense. We all know that sexual relationships are generally entered into without the least thought of reproduction, and sometimes with the express intention of avoiding reproduction. . . . In any case, it is quite certain that the sexual urge has become separated and entirely independent of the urge for reproduction"; Lazarsfeld, *Woman's Experience of the Male*, 54–55.

65. "Curiously enough, science took a long time to establish the vital significance of this problem. It seems as though science, too, was prevented by a certain reluctance, a certain inner resistance, from settling down to its proper investigation"; Lazarsfeld, *Woman's Experience of the Male*, 53.

neglect in favour of a pretty sister, manifested disappointment of parents, who wanted a boy instead of a girl" (304–305). Here, she referenced Radclyffe Hall's novel *The Well of Loneliness* (1928) to support her claims.

In Lazarsfeld's view, "acquired homosexuality" could be cured through psychotherapy; yet without overt surprise or frustration, she noted that "many women so afflicted do not wish to be cured," as "they feel just as happy in their abnormal associations as do the heterosexuals in theirs" (305). Lazarsfeld observed that "homosexual women do not feel inferior to their normal sisters," but rather "feel superior, as though they possessed something that the others lack"—an observation that is all the more fascinating in light of the theories of homosexuality advanced by early twentieth-century women sexologists (305). Lazarsfeld claimed that this sense of superiority and contentedness with one's homosexuality was what distinguished homosexual women from men, as the latter were driven to "despair, even suicide" as a result of the legal prohibitions on sex acts between men (305). Another distinguishing feature she identified was the fact that homosexuality was, in her view, "completely unconquerable" in a man, whereas a woman's sexuality could be reformed; after all, she declared that over the course of her practice she had met "many women who were capable both of heterosexual and homosexual love" (307).

Despite this belief in some women's innate bisexuality, Lazarsfeld reiterated her observation that the women she counseled—even women who were "good wives and mothers, and . . . by no means insensible to normal love"—"always preferred homosexual love" (307). Whether this was a result of congenital factors or of unsatisfactory heterosexual experiences, Lazarsfeld could not say, as "the women mentioned above were quite normal, [and did not] complain of lack of potency on the part of their male partners" (307). In a startling admission, she even conceded that in the course of her clinical practice, she had "never come across a single case of heterosexual love that could compare in devotion and tenderness with the usual homosexual association between two women" (307).

Lest one think this last statement constituted approval and acceptance of homosexuality, in the very next sentence Lazarsfeld was quick to add, "I need hardly say that I am not praising this form of love. As I have shown throughout this book, the only completely satisfactory sexual life for a woman is a permanent association with a normally potent and sexually skilled man" (307). The only reason to even address homosexuality in women, she maintained, was "that there is no sense in shutting our eyes to realities. It undoubtedly exists, and the fact must be faced. My experience has taught me that much evil is caused by clinging to pleasant fictions and that only good can come from . . . facing up to realities" (308). Although this statement may be read as ambivalent—here she claims to simply be pointing out a "fact," without judgment—elsewhere in her text she proved less neutral. In response to a letter from an inquirer named "Carl H.," for example, she advised,

> It is quite possible that the woman in question has, perhaps without being conscious of it, carried within her a deep love for the deceased, and has now transferred it to his mistress. That frequently happens, and arises out of the vague feeling that love for another man is forbidden, but love for a woman is natural and permissible. The science of psychology knows that this is not the case, for it is precisely such associations that frequently prove to be more destructive than any others, thereby constituting a real danger. Perhaps it may be possible to persuade the woman in question to undergo psychological treatment. (33)

Despite conceding the fact that most female homosexuals are quite happy with their lives, do not wish treatment, and view themselves as possessing something "normal" women lack, so strong was Lazarsfeld's conviction regarding the necessity of heterosexuality as a foundational social and psychological institution that she recommended psychological counseling to straighten out women like the object of Carl H.'s concern.

In addition to denying what she herself acknowledged was the psychological good health of her lesbian clients, at certain points in *Woman's Experience of the Male*, Lazarsfeld even sacrificed her deconstructionist view of gender in order to ensure the smooth functioning of heterosexual relations, specifically to protect men's egos. Curiously, despite her stress on the importance of individualizing one's sex role and sexuality, Lazarsfeld insisted that women ought to continue performing feminine subordination and observing hegemonic beauty standards in order to satisfy their male partners. While stressing the importance of women's professional work for personal fulfillment, self-confidence, and the formation of a personality independent of sex, Lazarsfeld warned that the professional woman must not lose her (hetero)sexual attractiveness, and must "do everything in her power to enhance her feminine charm and make herself desirable" (247; see also 231, 233, 256). Because she claimed that "there are few men to-day with sufficient courage and self-confidence to forgive feminine progress" (255), she advised women to "pretend to be a little more dependent, a little weaker" than they actually were, as "nothing can be gained by 'rubbing it in'" (259). After all, she pointed out, "the masculine world inflicts a punishment on the woman who dares to develop and assert herself, and grows into a better individual than the men consider desirable"; consequently "women must therefore endeavor to reconcile the men to the change" (254–255). In the strictly sexual realm, Lazarsfeld insisted that women had to recognize that the success of heterosexual encounters rested on the "correct behavior on the part of the woman" (127): by this she meant that women must not "commit the blunder of giving expression to their subjective desire" (148). Precisely because women's sexual needs were greater than men's ability to satisfy them, Lazarsfeld maintained that "women must adjust themselves to the man and refrain from doing or saying anything that might interfere with his rest or might be an attempt to excite him again" (150).

Ultimately, Lazarsfeld's approach to gender and sexuality demonstrates tensions and conflicts similar to those identified in Vaerting's work. On the one hand, Lazarsfeld was well aware that gender is not biologically rooted, and drew upon a diverse body of scientific evidence to support this insight. As an Adlerian and a socialist, she was, like Vaerting, a supporter of the view that gender or "sex roles" are socially constructed or conditioned. For this reason, she supported the idea that an individual's personality ought to be free to develop independently of socially determined sex roles, and even advanced feminist demands for sexual and social reform. On the other hand, it quickly becomes clear that Lazarsfeld's approach to gender was closely linked to her broader goal of "healing" hetero-sexual relations. "Authentic" personalities free from gender roles are needed for both partners in a heterosexual union to enjoy mutual satisfaction. As was true of Vaerting's work, Lazarsfeld's naturalization of heterosexuality was also tied to her pathologization of homosexuality, which she treated as a consequence of inauthentic gender and heterosexuality gone wrong. Lazarsfeld went so far as to prescribe the continued performance of conventional, unequal gender roles to ensure heterosexual harmony, both through obedience to hegemonic feminine beauty standards and subordination to men's sexual needs in the bedroom (precisely the thing she seemed to argue was at the root of women's oppression in the first place!). *Woman's Experience of the Male*, like *New Foundation for the Psychology of Men and Women*, demonstrates how nascent antiessentialist, social constructionist approaches to gender were undermined by recapitulations of binary sexual difference as the inevitable consequence of heterosexual imperatives.

Both *New Foundation for the Psychology of Men and Women* and *Woman's Experience of the Male* contributed to dynamic sexological discussions regarding the determination of sex and the nature of sexual difference, discussions that took place amid the highly vexed, volatile sexual politics of 1920s Germany and Austria. In both texts, one can identify echoes of the long-standing feminist insight, dating back at least to the time of Mary Wollstonecraft, that social conditions determined the existential possibilities of womanhood; however, Vaerting and Lazarsfeld are arguably more groundbreaking and subversive because of their insistence on the role of social power in determining and *creating* masculinity and femininity themselves. Vaerting in particular put forward a thoroughgoing refutation of the idea that sexual character or psychology was overdetermined by physiology almost thirty years before the publication of Simone de Beauvoir's *The Second Sex* (1949). By arguing that "masculinity" and "femininity" were merely instantiations of shifting power relations between dominant and subordinate groups, Vaerting effectively questioned whether they exist as anything other than merely functional categories. Meanwhile,

Lazarsfeld's denaturalization of gender, along with her stress on the dynamics of socialization and Adlerian analysis of sexual psychological mechanisms, opened up the possibility of greater sexual self-determination and individualized personal development.

Both *New Foundation* and *Woman's Experience of the Male* offer interpretations of gender as fundamentally contingent on power relations—views that were controversial in the 1920s and that seem strikingly modern and progressive. Nevertheless, I have demonstrated that the arguments regarding gender advanced in both texts are ultimately tethered to constraining claims regarding sexuality in at least two ways. For both Vaerting and Lazarsfeld, the project of critically examining gender roles was legitimized by claiming that so doing would help rehabilitate heterosexuality. Moreover, both authors ultimately reified the existence of binary sexual difference as a necessary effect of heterosexuality. Vaerting and Lazarsfeld treated heterosexuality as a stable, essential feature of human existence that ensures the persistence of difference and the continued relationship between men and women. They treated homosexuality as pathological and even, in Vaerting's case, as a potential obstacle to sexual equality. Ultimately, both *New Foundation* and *Woman's Experience of the Male* present a confounding mix of constructionist and essentialist (to say nothing of homophobic) arguments.

To make sense of the tensions between constructed gender and essentialized sexuality, I have suggested that these texts must be firmly situated in their historical context. By the 1920s, understandings of sex as a unified concept signifying physiology, social roles, and sexual desires were breaking down within sexology, albeit haltingly, as a result of broader social changes, greater consideration of social and cultural factors in shaping sex, and new scientific developments and trends. As writers concerned with the advancement of women's social rights and roles, both Vaerting and Lazarsfeld arguably endeavored to prove that changing gender roles, such as those demonstrated by the rise of the New Woman, need not exacerbate the "crisis" in heterosexual relations that was the cause of widespread anxiety following the First World War. The tensions between Vaerting's and Lazarsfeld's treatments of gender and sexuality provide further evidence of the historical contingency of understandings and theorizations of sex, gender, and sexuality. Specifically, they raise questions about the kinds of social, cultural, political, and economic conditions that had to be present for intellectuals to begin simultaneously deconstructing gender and sexuality as effects of power relations. Appreciating the contingency of intellectual possibility when it comes to thinking about sex ultimately contributes to a richer understanding of the ambivalent course of sexual theorizing, as well as a recognition of both the potential and the limits of the sexological field as a site for such thought experiments.

CONCLUSION

This book has endeavored to be a number of things simultaneously: a critical intellectual history of women's contributions to sexology; an intervention into the existing historiography and secondary literature concerning sexology itself; an interrogation of the historically and culturally specific feminist possibilities latent in the scientization of sex; and an investigation into the epistemological difference that gender and a commitment to feminist politics made in the creation of sexual scientific knowledge.

Borrowing a concept from the sociology of knowledge, in this work I have characterized sexology as a field in order to draw attention to the diverse participants involved in the creation of sexual scientific knowledge, and to the proliferation of competing ideas, theories, and evidence often flattened or elided by the representation of sexology as discourse. Treating sexology as a field opens it up and allows for new observations and insights: critically for this project, it enables us to identify women's contributions. In the preceding chapters, I demonstrated through a detailed examination of women's ideas and texts how they contributed to the scientization of sex throughout the first decades of the twentieth century, and how their work reconceptualized gender, heterosexuality, same-sex desire, and motherhood. For some women, sexology offered a site for the elaboration of novel, utopian visions of subjectivity and desire that augured personal and social transformation. Science and its readings of nature provided these women with resources to envision and articulate new, unconventional possibilities for women's existence; they were also able to leverage science's authority to legitimize alternative organizations of social and intimate relations that would empower women as independent, self-determining sexual agents.

By recovering and analyzing women's engagements with sexology, *Sexual Politics and Feminist Science* has not only drawn attention to women's overlooked and fascinating contributions to early twentieth-century sexual science. It has also revealed that early twentieth-century understandings of gender and sexuality were remarkably unsettled, and that the course of their development was contingent upon scientific, social, and political developments. Attending to women's sexological work thus opens up new ways of understanding gendered and sexual pasts, and allows us to tell new kinds of stories about the meanings and legacies of sex's scientization. Furthermore, it challenges historical interpretations of sexology that frame it as an exclusively male governmental project aimed at enhancing the productive potential of bodies for the benefit of the state and capital.

And yet, as I have insisted throughout this book, women's visions were deeply problematic. The ideas they put forward were fundamentally informed by sexology's project of identifying healthy sexual subjects; consequently, only those subjects deemed healthy were treated as the legitimate bearers of rights and freedoms and deserving of political advocacy. Women sexologists were complicit in establishing hierarchies of valuable life and creating new registers of power-laden differences that mapped onto existing stratifications of class and race. Moreover, insisting on health and nature as the fundamental criteria defining legitimate (if subversive) sexualities helped establish what today would be called an "ableist" rationale for sexual empowerment that, as many theorists in disability studies have stressed, would render certain subjects improperly sexual and unsuited for sexual agency. This legacy of women's sexological writing (and sexology generally) has been largely unexamined, and arguably persists into the present.

In raising these issues, my intent is not to censure misguided past actors. I have insisted throughout on grappling with the complexities of women sexologists' ideas, specifically the possibilities they envisioned *and* the limitations they imposed. I maintain that these ideas deserve attention, in spite of all the ambivalence they provoke, because they represent important attempts at challenging the masculine overdetermination of female sexualities and gender possibilities.

While I've spoken of sexology in general terms here, the history of sexology explored in this book is specific to early twentieth-century Germany and, laterally, Austria. I have insisted that the German sexological field was forged beyond the academy by a range of actors with varying degrees of education and access to clinical experience. Specifically, I have argued that sex reform organizations played a pivotal role in forging sexology as a unique field of knowledge production. The sex reform organizations that sprang up in the late 1890s and early years of the first decade of the twentieth century embraced science as providing a path to the truth of sex, as well as a solid basis upon which to demand their desired reforms. These organizations helped create epistemic communities of men and women committed to knowing and reforming sex along scientific lines, as well as media that would publish and disseminate the knowledge they produced. The links sexual reform groups established between knowledge and politics influenced subsequent reform movements that mobilized science as a means of effecting change, such as the World League for Sexual Reform. It took time for specifically sexological journals and professional organizations to establish themselves and their expertise independently of sex reform organizations and their media. Even following the establishment of professional sexological associations, many leading professional sexologists like Magnus Hirschfeld continued to be deeply involved in sex reform activism. The ties between the worlds of sexual science and politics persisted despite the efforts of some to submerge them.

All of this came to a dramatic end with the Nazis' assumption of power in 1933. Sexological texts, portrayed by the Nazis as manifestations of a "degenerate" and "Jewish" science, were used as kindling in mass book burnings, and the destruction of Hirschfeld's Institute for Sexual Science was one of the first acts of the regime. Both sex reform and feminist organizations, including the moderate League of German Women's Associations, were forced to cease operation. Many of the most radical voices in German sexology and sex reform were driven into exile as a result of their ethnicity and their politics, as Atina Grossmann has chronicled in heartbreaking detail.[1] This was the fate, sadly, of many of the women at the heart of this book. Some, like Helene Stöcker, sought refuge abroad, shuttling from country to country, and settling and dying in unfamiliar and alien environments. Others, like Mathilde Vaerting, were forced into internal exile. Vaerting was stripped of her university post and barred not only from publishing, but also from leaving the country. Consequently, she was unable to take up the various academic positions abroad that colleagues had arranged for her. Although she would live into her late nineties and attempt to establish an independent institute for sociological research, she never again held an academic post. Rare was the woman like Anna Rüling, who continued to work during the Third Reich by accommodating to its new rules—in Rüling's case, as a journalist chronicling the performing arts, not as a writer on sexuality. Rüling's fate makes sense in light of her swing to the political right during the First World War, a move that was rare among female sexual theorists.[2] Most women who did not die earlier (like Ruth

---

1. Atina Grossmann, *Reforming Sex: The German Movement for Birth Control and Abortion Reform, 1920–1950* (New York: Oxford University Press, 1995), 136–188.

2. Christiane Leidinger, "'Anna Rüling': A Problematic Foremother of Lesbian Herstory," *Journal of the History of Sexuality* 13, no. 4 (October 2004): 488–493. Käthe Schirmacher is another, high-profile example of a German feminist whose politics shifted to the right during and after the First World War. On right-wing women in Germany, see Raffael Scheck, *Mothers of the Nation: Right-Wing Women in Weimar Germany* (New York: Berg, 2004); and Elizabeth Harvey, "Visions of the Volk: German Women and the Far Right from Kaiserreich to Third Reich," *Journal of Women's History* 16 (2004): 152–167.

Bré and Grete Meisel-Hess, in 1912 and 1922, respectively) did so under Nazi rule and under forced retreat from public life, including Henriette Fürth (d. 1938), Rosa Mayreder (d. 1938), and Johanna Elberskirchen (d. 1943). After 1933, Fürth was banned from holding public office, and two of her children were murdered at Auschwitz. Sofie Lazarsfeld's successful postwar individual psychology practice in New York City was exceptional, though she too had to flee her home and lost her husband over the course of emigration.[3] The unhappy endings most of these women met following the rise of the Nazis—exiled, disillusioned, censored, repressed, and alienated—certainly militate against any easy or straightforward interpretation of their work as laying an intellectual foundation for fascist racism. Their fates speak to the consequences faced by women who demanded sexual powers and freedoms when placed under extreme right-wing domination.

Given the Nazis' efforts to destroy all records of sexological and sex reform agitation, along with the scattering of personal papers and possessions following forced exile and war, it is perhaps not surprising that women's sexological texts were forgotten. At the same time, however, it is important to note that women published in many of the same journals as the men whose work has been rediscovered in recent decades. Women's exclusion from existing histories of sexology speaks volumes about a priori assumptions regarding who was a sexologist, and about women's role in scientific knowledge production during a period when women's access to postsecondary education and professional positions was uneven. However, including women within our histories of sexual science reveals sexology to be much more complex than previously thought, and shows that the full range of sexology's potential (and danger) cannot be captured by the analytics of governmentality and disciplinary discourses alone. It entreats scholars to consider the effects of subjectivity and struggles over power and authority

---

3. On Sofie Lazarsfeld's later career in New York, I am grateful to information provided by her granddaughter, Dr. Lotte Bailyn; Dr. Lotte Bailyn, in discussion with the author, 12 June 2014. See also Martina Siems, *Sofie Lazarsfeld: Die Wiederentdeckung einer individualpsychologischen Pionierin* (Göttingen: V&R Unipress, 2015), 77–80.

upon the creation of sexual scientific knowledge. Women's contributions demonstrate that sexology was heteroglossic and contested, and that a great deal of this contestation was provoked by the gendered question of who could claim expertise over sex. Highlighting women's contributions to sexology not only acknowledges these women as sexologists in their own right, but also reframes sexology itself as unstable, dynamic, and politicized.

Beyond challenging and expanding existing frameworks and narratives, the history of ideas constructed in this book provides the foundation for a larger study of women's engagement with sexual science and sexual politics throughout the twentieth century. The work of scholars like Lucy Bland and Michiko Suzuki suggests that women's involvement in creating, contesting, and challenging knowledge about gender and sexuality was an international phenomenon in the early twentieth century; as histories of gender and sexuality become more international and transnational, it is likely that we will learn more about women's involvement in sexual knowledge production, especially as scholars expand their definitions of what sexology was and who produced it.[4] Evidence of women's involvement in sexual knowledge production can in fact already be found throughout the twentieth century. Without too much effort, names like Charlotte Wolff, Shere Hite, Anne Koedt, Virginia Johnson, "Dr. Ruth" Westheimer, and Leonore Tiefer quickly come to mind.[5] Scholars are now beginning to flesh out the story of Second Wave feminist engagements with sexual

---

4. See Lucy Bland, *Banishing the Beast: Feminism, Sex, and Morality* (London: I. B. Tauris, 2001); Lesley A. Hall, *Outspoken Women: An Anthology of Women's Writing on Sex, 1870–1969* (London: Routledge, 2005); Michiko Suzuki, *Becoming Modern Women: Love and Female Identity in Prewar Japanese Literature and Culture* (Stanford, CA: Stanford University Press, 2009).

5. See, for example, Charlotte Wolff, *Love between Women* (New York: St. Martin's Press, 1971); Wolff, *Bisexuality: A Study* (London: Quartet Books, 1979); William Masters and Virginia Johnson, *Human Sexual Response* (New York: Little, Brown, 1966); Anne Koedt, *The Myth of the Vaginal Orgasm* (Somerville, MA: Free Press, 1970); Boston Women's Health Book Collective, *Our Bodies, Ourselves* (New York: Simon and Schuster, 1973); Shere Hite, *The Hite Report: A Nationwide Study of Female Sexuality* (1976; New York: Seven Stories Press, 2004); Ruth K. Westheimer, *Dr. Ruth's Guide to Good Sex* (New York: Warner Books, 1984); Leonore Tiefer, *Sex Is Not a Natural Act, and Other Essays* (Boulder, CO:

science and technology; the larger, longer, fractured, trans- and international twentieth-century history of the complex interactions between women, gender, sexual knowledge, and sexual politics has yet to be fully explored.[6]

Historical investigations into the intersections of sex, gender, feminism, and science are especially important at this particular moment in time as feminist theorists are once again turning to science as an intellectual resource. Curiously, following decades of sustained feminist critique of the epistemology, ideology, and practices of the sciences, eminent feminist theorists are now embracing evolutionary theory, biology, and neuroscience, and are demanding that feminists engage more openly and positively with science, nature, and materiality.[7] Briefly taking stock of twenty-first-century feminists' turn to the sciences and their embrace of nature and matter illuminates some of the reasons why science exercises such an enduring appeal for resistant politics. Moreover, reviewing the claims made by contemporary feminists demonstrates the need to consider some of the lessons the past can teach the present.

The recent turn to science, nature, and matter in feminist theorizing, which has cohered under the rubric of "new materialist feminism," includes an array of thinkers whose approaches to science and matter and the relationship between nature and culture vary in significant ways.[8] Despite their differences, proponents of new ma-

---

Westview Press, 1995). Then there is, of course, Dr. Ruth's career-making radio and television show, *Sexually Speaking*.

6. However, see Michelle Murphy, *Seizing the Means of Reproduction: Feminism, Health, and Technoscience* (Durham, NC: Duke University Press, 2012); Wendy Kline, *Bodies of Knowledge: Sexuality, Reproduction, and Women's Health in the Second Wave* (Chicago: University of Chicago Press, 2010).

7. Notably, this new movement in feminist theory does not engage with feminist science studies scholars, such as Emily Martin, Anne Fausto-Sterling, Donna Haraway, Evelyn Fox Keller, or Rebecca Jordan Young, to name a few. On this point, see Sara Ahmed, "Open Forum: Imaginary Prohibitions; Some Preliminary Remarks on the Founding Gestures of the 'New Materialism,'" *European Journal of Women's Studies* 15 (2008): 27.

8. To clarify, here I am focusing specifically on work that is still concerned primarily with *human* biology and *human* culture. There is, for example, a strong "posthumanist" strand that focuses on the hybridities of humans and technology, as well as a literature that challenges the human/animal dichotomy.

terialist feminism agree that feminists should embrace science and
questions of nature and materiality in order to overcome the "im-
passe" feminist theory has reached as a result of "the contemporary linguistic turn in feminist thought."[9] According to proponents
of new materialist feminism like Stacy Alaimo and Susan Hekman,
postmodernist perspectives and their greater attention to language
and discourse have "not fulfilled [their] promise as a theoretical
grounding for feminism" because they have supposedly maintained
a dichotomy between language and reality.[10] Conversely, Alaimo
and Hekman argue, new materialist approaches reclaim ontology
by engaging with matter and nature, which they position as the
true loci of reality.[11]

New materialist feminists believe that the postmodern linguistic turn has had particularly damaging consequences for feminist
study of bodies and embodiment. They maintain that feminists'
"retreat from materiality" has led to the elision of "lived, material
bodies and evolving corporeal practices."[12] Unlike postmodern approaches, which they claim treat material human bodies as inert
and passive surfaces upon which meaning is imposed, new materialists seek to engage the materiality of human bodies as a "positive
event rather than a negated origin,"[13] and aim to develop a "way to
talk about the materiality of the body as itself an active, sometimes
recalcitrant force . . . [as a] lived experience, corporeal practice,
and biological substance."[14] Thus, new materialist feminism would
restore to matter agency, dynamism, and the capacity for change.

Much like early twentieth-century female sexual theorists,
twenty-first-century feminists seem to view the body as possessing

9. Stacy Alaimo and Susan Hekman, "Introduction: Emerging Models of Materiality in Feminist Theory," in *Material Feminisms*, ed. Alaimo and Hekman
(Bloomington: Indiana University Press, 2008), 1.
10. Ibid., 2.
11. Ibid., 5, 7.
12. Ibid., 3.
13. A. Bray and C. Colebrook, "The Haunted Flesh: Corporeal Feminism and
the Politics of (Dis)Embodiment," *Signs: Journal of Women in Culture and Society*
24 (1998): 57; quoted in Myra J. Hird, "Feminist Matters: New Materialist Considerations of Sexual Difference," *Feminist Theory* 5 (2004): 228.
14. Alaimo and Hekman, "Introduction," 4.

innate political potential and meaning; and yet, in spite of their critiques of postmodern approaches, among new materialist feminists the body is treated like a text requiring exegesis—and like women sexologists of the early twentieth century, they treat science as providing essential interpretive resources for this work. Indeed, one of new materialist feminism's most intriguing claims, in light of the history this book has explored, is that feminists ought not be inhibited when it comes to "engag[ing] with medicine [and] science in innovative, productive, or affirmative ways."[15] According to Alaimo and Hekman, new materialist feminists are invested in understanding "how we can define the 'real' in science and how we can describe nonhuman agency in a scientific context."[16] In contrast to the (supposed) antibiologism of much feminist theory, new materialist feminists view natural science as "crucial" for "understanding issues of critical concern to feminist theory and practice."[17] Intriguingly, this same argument is being advanced within popular feminist media as well.[18] According to Elizabeth Wilson, feminist critiques "premised on a primary oppositional relation to the sciences or premised on antibiologism, antiessentialism, or antiutilitarianism are losing their critical and political purchase—not necessarily because they are wholly mistaken, but because they have relied on, and reauthorized, a separation between the inside and the outside, the static and the changeable, the natural and the political, the chromosomal and the cultural."[19]

In fact, new materialist feminists claim that their approaches "go beyond" even the work of feminist science studies scholars, who have developed an impressive critical literature on the intersections of sex, gender, and scientific knowledge and practices over

15. Ibid.
16. Ibid., 7.
17. Hird, "Feminist Matters," 225.
18. See, for example, Catherine O'Grady, "Born This Way? Why an Evidence-Based Stance on Sex and Gender Is Good for Science and for Feminism," *Bitch Magazine* 65 (Winter 2015): 28–33.
19. Elizabeth Wilson, *Neural Geographies: Feminism and the Microstructure of Cognition* (London: Routledge, 1998), 200; quoted in Hird, "Feminist Matters," 225.

the past forty years. In Myra J. Hird's view, feminist science studies display "a hesitation to delve into the actual physical processes through which differentiation and change take place," whereas new materialists embrace new developments within the natural sciences that "suggest that there is openness and play within the living *and* nonliving world, contesting previous paradigms which posited a changeable culture against a stable and inert nature."[20] Embracing science would thus enable feminists to liberate the political and ethical possibilities they believe to inhere in evolution via natural selection, specifically nonlinearity, indeterminism, and dynamism.[21] Renowned feminist theorist Elizabeth Grosz, whose work over the past decade has been marked by an intense and enthusiastic engagement with Darwin, has enjoined feminists to seriously engage with evolutionary theories and consider whether "these discourses provide theoretical models, methods, questions, frameworks, or insights that . . ., in spite of their recognizable limitations, could be of some use in understanding and transforming the prevailing structures of (patriarchal) power and in refining and complexifying feminist analyses of and responses to these structures."[22]

While the question itself may be a valid and worthy one, it is unsettled by Grosz's recognition of the theories' "recognizable limitations." In fact, Grosz explicitly eschews critique of the sexist and racist elements of Darwin's theories. Surveying a few selected studies by feminist science studies scholars Janet Sayers, Patricia Gowaty, and Sue V. Rosser, she maintains that focusing on sexism and bias evades the true value of Darwin's work, and offers reduced, flattened, and partial views of his theories. In defense of her position, Grosz asserts that "critique of texts never actually transforms texts or even necessarily produces better, more elaborated and developed texts," but rather "tends to function as a form of dismissal of

20. Myra Hird, "From the Culture of Matter to the Matter of Culture: Feminist Explorations of Nature and Science," *Sociological Research Online* 8 (2003), emphasis in original, http://www.socresonline.org.uk/8/1/hird.html.

21. Hird, "Feminist Matters," 227.

22. Elizabeth Grosz, *Time Travels: Feminism, Nature, Power* (Durham, NC: Duke University Press, 2005), 17.

texts."[23] She further claims that "any discourse written before the development of feminism as a theoretical and political movement" tends to "[privilege] the masculine and [position] the feminine as its subordinated and complementary counterpart."[24] Contrary to existing critical feminist practice, Grosz insists on the value of theoretical work that "seize[s] and develop[s] what is of use in a text or position, even in acknowledging its potentially problematic claims or assumptions," noting that "no text or position is without problems, contradictions, weaknesses, points of uneasiness."[25]

Notably, Grosz's affirmative position is not unique to her: commentators have noted that new materialist feminists' turn to nature and science has facilitated a deliberate "rejection of critique."[26] Such a posture, some claim, renders feminist theory "freer" and "more positive" than its supposedly negative antecedents.[27] Unlike language- and discourse-centric feminist theories, which supposedly "have not yielded social and political change," new materialist approaches claim to offer a generative approach to politics and ethics—as well as a more "affirmative orientation towards the theories of selected key Western male philosophers and scientists."[28]

New materialist feminist texts are marked by the enthusiasm of a field designated "new," yet their embrace of science as revealer of "the real" feels rather familiar. Indeed, in light of the history examined in this book, Elizabeth Grosz's enthusiasm for Darwinian sexual selection as a vital resource for contemporary feminist theorizing is at once intriguing and arresting.[29] Feminism's historically complex entanglements with science raise numerous questions about the implications of new materialist feminism for sexual politics. Will new materialist feminists be able to successfully

---

23. Ibid., 2–3.
24. Ibid., 17.
25. Ibid., 3.
26. Maureen McNeil, "Post-Millenial Feminist Theory: Encounters with Humanism, Materialism, Critique, Nature, Biology, and Darwin," *Journal for Cultural Research* 14 (October 2010): 427, 432–433.
27. Ibid., 427–428.
28. Ibid., 432–433.
29. Elizabeth Grosz, *Becoming Undone: Darwinian Reflections on Life, Politics, and Art* (Durham, NC: Duke University Press, 2011), 7.

318

Sexual Politics and Feminist Science

mobilize scientific knowledge for political ends while simultaneously maintaining a critical stance toward the processes of its creation? Will they find a way to be "both complicit with data and skeptical of its mainstream uses," as Kylie Valentine asks?[30] These questions are particularly urgent because, as Angie Willey observes, "data [alone] neither reveals nor engenders possibilities for materialities with which we can live."[31] In their embrace of nature and matter, will new materialist feminists avoid transforming them into "fetish objects" and sources of "moral authority," as was evident among the women sexologists explored in this book?[32] Will they avoid lapsing into an uncritical celebration and prioritization of "healthy," stable, and able bodies? Already, Valentine has pointed out that many of these new biologically and scientifically "affirmative" texts tend to focus on "a relatively narrow range of age and embodiment."[33] As part of their effort to embrace science "positively" (that is, uncritically), will feminist scholars avoid recapitulating and reiterating the racialism, homophobia, and ableism of their forebearers, who also sought to productively engage science for feminist ends?

In the rush to reclaim ontology, new materialist feminists seem to have dismissed the value of critical analysis that can reveal latent assumptions and normativities that may be counterproductive for feminist goals. As generations of feminist science studies scholars have demonstrated, scientific knowledge is not neutral. Undoubtedly, the natural sciences have important knowledge and insights to offer; nonetheless, it is critical that we continue to interrogate

---

30. Kylie Valentine, "After Antagonism: Feminist Theory and Science," *Feminist Theory* 9 (2008): 363. For a similar but more thoroughgoing critique of the turn to science, nature, and biology within feminist theory that attends to race and racism, see Claire Peta Blencowe, "Biology, Contingency, and the Problem of Racism in Feminist Discourse," *Theory, Culture, and Society* 28 (2011): 3–27.

31. Angela Willey, "Biopossibility: A Queer Feminist Materialist Science Studies Manifesto, with Special Reference to the Question of Monogamous Behavior," *Signs: A Journal of Women and Culture* 41, no. 3 (Spring 2016): 573.

32. Ahmed, "Open Forum," 35. There is a worrisome tendency to treat "nature" as a singular agent, subject, and even category of analysis. For an example of the latter usage, see Alaimo and Hekman, "Introduction," 12.

33. Valentine, "After Antagonism," 363.

the production of scientific knowledge. Researchers' worldviews, norms, and values influence the construction of studies, the methodologies used, the outcomes inferred, and the findings reported. Subjective factors play a role not just in what we know, but in what we believe to be "objectively" real and true.[34] This is particularly the case for scientific studies of sexuality and sexual difference, which scholars such as Ann Fausto-Sterling and Rebecca Jordan Young have demonstrated to be profoundly informed by gender bias, even at the level of research design and methodology.[35] It is therefore worth asking whether Darwin's attitudes toward sex, gender, and sexuality (not to mention race) were incidental to, and not bound up with, his theorization of evolution, and whether his subjectivity can be easily parsed from his intellectual output. Did it matter that, in Erika Milam's words, Darwin's theory of sexual selection in particular "built on his assumptions about normative relations between men and women and the place of Victorian England in the pantheon of great civilizations"?[36] That his understandings of sexual difference, fundamental to his theorization of sexual selection, recapitulated what Cynthia Eagle Russett calls "a familiar Victorian litany," with males excelling in courage, pugnacity, energy, and intelligence, and females characterized as intuitive, self-less, emotional, and imitative?[37] Although Darwin summoned the observation of Mungo Park and other travelers as to the presence of these traits among "even the savages," Russett notes that Darwin had no other evidence of a sexual disparity in

---

34. For lucid discussions of this point, see Helen Longino, "Introduction: Good Science, Bad Science," in *Science as Social Knowledge: Values and Objectivity in Scientific Inquiry* (Princeton, NJ: Princeton University Press, 1990), 3–15.

35. See Anne Fausto-Sterling, *Myths of Gender: Biological Theories about Women and Men* (New York: Basic Books, 1986); Anne Fausto-Sterling, *Sexing the Body: Gender Politics and the Construction of Sexuality* (New York: Basic Books, 2000); Rebecca Jordan Young, *Brain Storm: The Flaws in the Science of Sex Differences* (Cambridge, MA: Harvard University Press, 2010).

36. Erika Milam, *Looking for a Few Good Males: Female Choice in Evolutionary Biology* (Baltimore: Johns Hopkins University Press, 2010), 10.

37. Charles Darwin, *The Descent of Man, and Selection in Relation to Sex*, 2nd ed. (New York: P. F. Collier and Son, 1900), 586–587; cited in Cynthia Eagle Russett, *Sexual Science: The Victorian Construction of Womanhood* (Cambridge, MA: Harvard University Press, 1989), 40–41.

temperament.[38] Did Darwin's views on gender shape the way he interpreted what he observed in nature and how he understood mating rituals and the reproduction of species? Did these, in turn, have implications for his theories? Excavating the sexual ideology underlying Darwin's work, of course, does not mean that people ought to condemn and discard evolutionary theory; however, knowing this history should caution feminists against uncritically embracing science, and should also attune us to the limits of any "tactically polyvalent" engagement with science. At the very least, the examination of early twentieth-century sexology presented in this book should encourage present-day feminists to acknowledge that scientific knowledge is not "innocent," to once again draw upon Donna Haraway's phrasing. Engaging science for feminist ends is a tricky business; it ought to be difficult to resolutely and definitively embrace any theory or research for political ends—and to try and parse theories from their contexts. In any event, in refusing to critically engage with the production of scientific knowledge and choosing instead to selectively embrace claims and hypotheses that may be theoretically productive or interesting, feminists may be taking on and perpetuating undesirable ontological baggage.

It remains to be asked why science, nature, and matter are so politically urgent and intellectually appealing to feminists now. After all, as Sara Ahmed astutely notes, "there is a politics to how we distribute our attention."[39] What kinds of change or transformation do present-day feminists hope to realize by using scientific knowledge to understand and illuminate the inextricability of nature and culture? The political possibilities and implications of new materialist feminism and its insistence on the interconnections of nature and culture and biology and sociality are currently in the process of being worked out. Will its theorists escape the problems of the past? I hope that the history explored in this book will contribute some sense of both the promise and the perils, as well as the benefits and the costs, of using science for feminist ends, and of investing too much political faith in the "truth" of nature.

---

38. Russett, *Sexual Science*, 41.
39. Ahmed, "Open Forum," 30.

Appendix

Brief Biographies of Key Figures

Elisabeth Bouness, a.k.a Ruth Bré (?–1912) Little is known about Elisabeth Bouness, who wrote under the pseudonym Ruth Bré and was based in the Silesian town of Hermsdorf am Kynast. Bré's primary causes included a fight against the proscription of marriage among female civil servants in Prussia, and the plight of unwed mothers and their children. These issues were personal for Bré as a teacher and the daughter of an unwed mother. She was involved in the creation of the League for the Protection of Mothers and Sexual Reform, although her actual role remains unclear and controversial. Bré's vision for the league was eugenic and imperial: she envisioned settling "healthy" young single mothers and their children in colonies established in eastern Europe. These colonies aimed not only to provide a good life for these women and their children, but also to strengthen the German population by fostering "valuable" life. Bré ultimately broke with the league when the rest of its members rejected her racialist utopian objectives.

Aside from the league, Bré is not known to have been involved in any other organizations within the German women's movement. In spite of her historical liminality, Bré produced a number of contemporarily influential and provocative texts, including *The Right to Motherhood* (*Das Recht auf die Mutterschaft*, 1903), *Wards of the State or the Right of the Mother?* (*Staatskinder oder Mutterrecht?* 1904), and *Ecce Mater!* (1905).

For further information, see Bernd Nowacki, *Der Bund für Mutterschutz (1905–1933)* (Husum: Matthiesen Verlag, 1983); Catherine Dollard, *The Surplus Woman: Unmarried Women in Imperial Germany, 1871–1918* (New York: Berghahn Books, 2009).

Johanna Elberskirchen (1864–1943) Elberskirchen was born into a lower-middle-class merchant family in Bonn. In her early twenties she worked as a bookkeeper until she entered academia. Elberskirchen belonged to the generation of women who, barred from studying at German universities, pursued higher education in Switzerland. She studied medicine, natural sciences, anatomy, physiology, and philosophy at the University of Bern before switching to law and jurisprudence at the University of Zurich. Upon returning to Bonn, she became involved in left-leaning organizations such as the Progressive Association (Fortschrittlicher Verein), as well as women's suffrage organizations like the Prussian Regional Association for Women's Right to Vote (Preussischer Landesverein für Frauenstimmenrecht) and the German Association for Women's Right to Vote (Reichsverein für Frauenstimmenrecht), which she founded in 1912. Elberskirchen was one of the only "out" lesbians among German feminists, and in 1914 she became one of only four female chairs of the Scientific Humanitarian Committee (Wissenschaftlich-humanitäres Komitee), the first organization in the world to publicly campaign for the decriminalization of homosexual acts. She later became involved in the Social Democratic Party and the World League for Sexual Reform. In 1915 she moved to Berlin, where she worked in infant care; five years later, Elberskirchen and her long-term partner, teacher and Communist Party member Hildegard Moniac (1891–1967), moved to Rüdersdorf outside of Berlin, where Elberskirchen ran a homeopathic practice until her death on 17 May 1943. Elberskirchen produced a remarkable body of work written under her own name and under her male pseudonym, Hans Carolan. Her texts addressed marital reform, prostitution, women's emancipation, homosexuality and heterosexuality, maternal welfare, eugenics and even subjective male bias within scientific knowledge production.

For further information, see Christiane Leidinger, *Keine Tochter aus gutem Hause: Johanna Elberskirchen (1864–1943)* (Konstanz: UVK Verlagsgesellschaft, 2008).

Henriette Fürth (1861–1938) Henriette Katzenstein was born to a comfortably middle-class Jewish family in Giessen. In 1880 she relocated to Frankfurt with her husband, Wilhelm Fürth. It was in Frankfurt that she became involved in feminist and sexual reform movements such as the German Society for the Fight against Venereal Diseases and the League for the Protection of Mothers and Sexual Reform—all while caring for six daughters and two sons. During her years of public engagement, Fürth produced an impressive corpus covering diverse themes, sometimes under her own name and sometimes under her pseudonym, G. Stein. Her prolific output included books, articles, and pamphlets on topics including social and racial hygiene, women's suffrage, home economy, women's work, maternal insurance and welfare, infant welfare, sexual morality, and abortion. Aside from her feminist and sex reform activism, Fürth was a member of numerous Jewish organizations including the Central Association of German Citizens of Jewish Faith (Centralverein deutscher Staatsbürger jüdischen Glaubens) and the Jewish Women's Association (Jüdische Frauenbund). She held strong social democratic sympathies and ultimately joined the German Social Democratic Party. Between 1919 and 1924 she served as a city councilor (*Stadtverordnete*) in Frankfurt, where she focused on municipal finances, schools, and health. Despite her lack of academic credentials, Fürth became the first female member of the German Society for Sociology (Deutsche Gesellschaft für

Soziologie). Although she was honored by the city of Frankfurt on her seventieth birthday in 1932, her death in Bad Ems in 1938 was not noted.

For further information, see Angelika Epple, *Henriette Fürth und die Frauenbewegung im deutschen Kaiserreich: Eine Sozialbiographie* (Pfaffenweiler: Centaurus Verlagsgesellschaft, 1996); Henriette Fürth, *Streifzüge durch das Land eines Lebens: Autobiographie einer deutsch-jüdischen Soziologin, Sozialpolitikerin, und Frauenrechtlerin (1861–1938)*, ed. Monika Graulich et al. (Wiesbaden: Kommission für die Geschichte der Juden in Hessen, 2010).

Sofie Lazarsfeld (1881–1976) Sofie Munk was born in Troppau, part of the Austrian section of Schlesien (now the Czech Republic). Following her father's death, she and her mother moved to Vienna. She later married lawyer Robert Lazarsfeld and had two children: the renowned sociologist Paul Lazarsfeld, and psychologist and translator Elisabeth Lazarsfeld (later Zerner). Lazarsfeld and her husband were deeply committed socialists, and their apartment was a well-known meeting place among comrades. Leading social democrats Otto and Helene Bauer and Rudolf and Margarethe Hilferding were among their close friends. It was through Margarethe Hilferding that Lazarsfeld became acquainted with individual psychology and met its *leitfigur*, Alfred Adler, who became a close colleague and family friend. In 1924 Lazarsfeld began her career as a writer and psychologist. Her texts analyzed problems related to women's sexuality, marriage, sexual education, and child rearing through the lens of individual or Adlerian psychology. In addition to her writing, Lazarsfeld engaged in practical sexological work: she opened up a sex and marriage counseling center in her apartment in 1925. As her most famous text, *Woman's Experience of the Male* (*Wie die Frau den Mann erlebt*, 1931), relays, she also wrote a sex advice column. In 1932 she organized the first individual psychology summer school. As a consequence of their socialist activities, the Lazarsfelds were temporarily arrested during the Austrian civil war in 1934. Thereafter, they withdrew from overt political activity. Lazarsfeld wrote some of her most famous articles during this period, including "Dare to Be Less Than Perfect" (1936) and "Did Oedipus Have an Oedipal Complex?" (1944). Following the Nazis' annexation of Austria in 1938, the Lazarsfelds fled to France, where Robert Lazarsfeld died in 1941. Sofie Lazarsfeld moved once more, this time to New York City, where her son, Paul, had already taken up a position at Columbia University. She eventually became an American citizen, and remained active in individual psychology circles in New York. Lazarsfeld ultimately became the vice president of the US-based Individual Psychology Association. She died in New York in 1976.

For further information, see Martina Siems, *Sofie Lazarsfeld: Die Wiederentdeckung einer individualpsychologischen Pionieren* (Göttingen: V&R Unipress, 2015).

Rosa Mayreder (1858–1938) Rosa Obermayer was born to a large Catholic family in Vienna, and was one of twelve brothers and sisters. Her father, a wealthy restaurant owner, did not believe in education for girls; consequently, her education was limited to the arts and modern languages. She nevertheless proved a disciplined autodidact, and also learned what she could from her brothers' lessons. In 1881 she married the architect Karl Mayreder, with whom she had a complex relationship: Karl suffered depression for over twenty years—and, some speculate, the psychological effects of syphilis. In 1902, Mayreder helped found the General Austrian Women's Organization (Allgemeine Österreichischer Frauenverein), the central organization of the Austrian women's movement, and *Documents of Woman* (*Dokumente der Frau*), a key Austrian feminist journal. She was especially active in feminist campaigns against the state regulation of prostitution and in the Austrian branch of the League for the Protection of Mothers and Sexual Reform. Following the outbreak of the First World War, Mayreder became heavily involved in the peace movement, particularly the International Women's League for Peace and Freedom. During her own lifetime, Mayreder was renowned as a feminist philosopher, thanks in particular to her influential studies

Towards a Critique of Femininity (*Zur Kritik der Weiblichkeit*, 1905) and *Sex and Culture* (*Geschlecht und Kultur,* 1923). She also wrote librettos, including the libretto for Hugo Wolf's opera *The Corregidor* (*Der Corregidor*, 1896), and novels such as *From My Youth* (*Aus meiner Jugend,* 1908). Like Henriette Fürth, despite her lack of formal academic training she was one of the few female members of Vienna's Sociological Society. Mayreder's image was at one time featured on the 500 Austrian schilling note, and schools and parks in Vienna bear her name.

For further information, see Harriet Anderson, *Utopian Feminism: Women's Movements in Fin-de-Siècle Vienna* (New Haven, CT: Yale University Press, 1992); Agatha Schwartz, *Shifting Voices: Feminist Thought and Women's Writing in Fin-de-Siècle Austria and Hungary* (Montreal: McGill-Queen's University Press, 2007).

Grete Meisel-Hess (1879–1922) Grete Meisel was born in Prague to a middle-class Jewish family. She grew up in Vienna, where she later attended university and studied philosophy, sociology, and biology. After a brief marriage to journalist Peter Hess in 1900, she moved to Berlin in 1908; a year later she married the architect Oskar Gellert. While in Berlin, she became involved in various sex reform organizations, including the League for the Protection of Mothers and Sexual Reform. Following her husband's death in the First World War, Meisel-Hess suffered from psychological illness and loss of economic status. She died quite young, and severely depressed, in Berlin in 1922. In her brief life she published numerous important texts across a variety of genres, all of which addressed feminist issues and sex reform. Her 1909 study, *The Sexual Crisis* (*Die sexuelle Krise*), was especially influential, eventually gaining an international readership. Other key texts include novels such as *Fanny Roth* (1902) and *The Intellectuals* (*Die Intellektuellen,* 1911), and nonfiction treatises such as *In the Modern World View* (*In der modernen Weltanschauung*, 1901), "Sexual Rights" ("Sexuelle Rechte," 1912), *Observations regarding the Woman Question* (*Betrachtungen zur Frauenfrage*, 1914), "War and Marriage" ("Krieg und Ehe," 1915), *The Essence* *of Sexuality* (*Das Wesen der Geschlechtlichkeit*, 1916), and *The Meaning of Monogamy* (*Die Bedeutung der Monogamie*, 1917).

For further information, see Harriet Anderson, *Utopian Feminism*; Elinor Melander, "Toward the Sexual and Economic Emancipation of Women: The Philosophy of Grete Meisel-Hess," *History of European Ideas* 14 (1992): 695–713; Agatha Schwartz, *Shifting Voices: Feminist Thought and Women's Writing in Fin-de-Siècle Austria and Hungary* (Montreal: McGill-Queen's University Press, 2007).

Anna Rüling (1880–1953) Based on Christiane Leidinger's painstaking research, historians now know that Anna Rüling was a pseudonym for the writer and journalist Theo Anna Sprüngli. Sprüngli was born in Hamburg to a Swiss businessman and his wife. Like Johanna Elberskirchen, Rüling was one of the few feminists who agitated on behalf of homosexual acceptance. With Elberskirchen, Rüling was one of the few woman members of the Scientific Humanitarian Committee, and actually served as a "chairman" on the committee (other female "chairmen" included Helene Stöcker and the poet Toni Schwabe). In addition to her speech, "What Interest Does the Women's Movement Have in the Homosexual Problem?" she wrote a short story collection in 1906, *Which of You Is without Sin?* (*Welcher unter Euch ohne Sünde ist*) that featured love stories between women with happy endings. For most of her life, Rüling lived in Düsseldorf. Over the course of the First World War, she became quite conservative and nationalist in her convictions. Rüling supported the war and joined the Düsseldorf branch of the Naval Association of German Women (Flottenbunde deutscher Frauen). She also became active in the right-leaning German Housewives Association (Reichsverband Deutscher Hausfrauenvereine). In spite of her earlier political work and writing, Rüling somehow managed to remain active as a journalist throughout the Third Reich and Second World War, although it does not appear that she was a member of the Nazi Party. She died in Delmenhorst in 1953 as one of Germany's oldest female journalists.

For further information, see Christiane Leidinger, "'Anna Rüling':
A Problematic Foremother of Lesbian Herstory," *Journal of the
History of Sexuality* 13, no. 4 (October 2004): 477–499.

Helene Stöcker (1869–1943) Stöcker was perhaps one of the most
famous radical feminists in early twentieth-century Germany. She
was born in Wuppertal to a strict Calvinist household. She moved to
Berlin to continue her studies, and ultimately moved to Switzerland
to pursue graduate education at the University of Bern. Stöcker later
became one of the first German women to receive her doctorate in
philosophy. Upon returning to Berlin, she became a member of the
Union of Progressive Women's Associations and in 1905 helped
to establish the League for the Protection of Mothers and Sexual
Reform. Until the organization's dissolution in 1933, she was
editor of the league's journal, *The New Generation* (1908–33).
Additionally, she was one of only four female chairpersons of
the Scientific Humanitarian Committee, and became publicly
involved in the fight against the criminalization of same-sex behavior
between women. Stöcker never married, but maintained a long-
term relationship with lawyer and league member Bruno Springer.
Before the First World War, Stöcker's main philosophical project was
the elaboration of what she called the New Ethic, a new approach
to sexuality and sexual relations that supported her demands for
women's sexual empowerment, the recognition and equality of so-
called illegitimate children and their mothers, the legalization of
abortion, and sexual education. The New Ethic was heavily influenced
by Stöcker's embrace of Nietzschean philosophy. Stöcker viewed
the establishment of the New Ethic as an essential precondition for
establishing authentic, deeper, mutually satisfying relations between
men and women, and for the realization of women's political and
social equality. Beyond sexual reform and feminist activities, Stöcker
was also heavily involved in the pacifist movement. Although her
pacifist activities preceded the First World War, they intensified
between 1914 and 1918 and complemented her feminist and sex
reform activities during the Weimar era. In 1921 she helped establish
War Resisters' International. Following the Nazis' ascension to

power in 1933, Stöcker fled to Switzerland, England, and ultimately to the United States. She died of cancer in New York City in 1943. In addition to her myriad articles and editorial work, she published the monographs *Love and Women* (*Die Liebe und die Frauen*, 1906), *The Love of the Future* (*Die Liebe der Zukunft*, 1920), *Love: A Novel* (*Liebe: Roman*, 1922), and *Erotic and Altruism* (*Erotik und Altruismus*, 1924).

For further information, see Christl Wickert, *Helene Stöcker, 1869–1943: Frauenrechtlerin, Sexualreformerin und Pazifistin; Eine Biographie* (Bonn: J. H. W. Dietz, 1991); Kristin McGuire, "Activism, Intimacy, and the Politics of Selfhood: The Gendered Terms of Citizenship in Poland and Germany, 1890–1918" (PhD diss., University of Michigan, 2004); Tracie Matysik, *Reforming the Moral Subject: Ethics and Sexuality in Central Europe, 1890–1930* (Ithaca, NY: Cornell University Press, 2008).

Mathilde Vaerting (1884–1977) The life and work of Mathilde Vaerting have been largely overlooked by English-language scholars. This elision is somewhat surprising, given her historical importance as one of Germany's first female professors. It is this achievement that has attracted the attention of German researchers. Even within German-language scholarship, research into Vaerting's work as a sexual researcher and theorist and its influence is lacking, even though at the time she was hailed as "among the most profound and original investigators of eugenic and sociological problems at present working on the continent of Europe" in the United States–based journal *Critic and Guide* 25, no. 6 (June 1922): 235.

Vaerting was born in Messingen in 1884, and was the fifth of ten children born to a well-off Catholic family. Her parents, both farmers (*Landwirte*), placed considerable value on their children's education, and provided them with a private tutor. Vaerting ultimately pursued one of the few professions open to intelligent and ambitious German women at the turn of the century: teaching. She successfully passed her teaching exam in Münster in 1903, and took up her first position in Düsseldorf that same year. Four years later, Vaerting, a woman of seemingly great energy and initiative, began studying math, philosophy, physics, and chemistry at universities in Bonn, Munich, Marburg, and Giessen. In 1910, she passed the exam to become a senior teacher (*Oberlehrerin*) in math, physics, and chemistry, and only a year later obtained her doctorate from the University of Bonn. Vaerting moved to Berlin in 1913, where she took up a position as *Oberlehrerin* in the working-class district of Neukölln. There she became involved in radical education reform movements, sex reform movements such as the League for the Protection of Mothers and Sexual Reform, and sexological associations like the International Society for Sexual Research.

In 1923 Vaerting was named professor in the new chair of *Erziehungswissenschaft,* which roughly translates to pedagogy, at the University of Jena. At the time, she was thirty-nine years old. Her appointment by the Social Democratic state government of Thuringia was strongly resisted by most of her male colleagues, who referred to her as a "coerced professor" (*Zwangsprofessorin*) and dismissed her scholarship as "feminism in the guise of science." Vaerting lost her professorship when the Nazis came to power, as a result of Paragraph 4 of the Nazis' Law for the Reestablishment of the Civil Service Profession (Gesetz zur Wiederherstellung des Berufsbeamtentums). During the Third Reich she was placed under a travel ban, and was consequently unable to travel to the United States or the Netherlands, where colleagues had endeavored to arrange new faculty positions for her.

Following her forced retirement she retreated from public life, and did not publish during the Third Reich. In 1944 a bomb attack destroyed her unpublished manuscripts and works in progress. Following the Second World War, she attempted to reestablish an academic career, with no success. Between 1953 and 1971, she published regularly in the *Journal for State Sociology (Zeitschrift für Staatssoziologie*), and helped to found the International Institute for Politics and State Sociology (Internationale Institut für Politik und Staatssoziologie). Mathilde Vaerting died in 1977, at the age of ninety-three, in Schönau im Schwarzwald.

For further information, see Christina Herkommen, "Mathilde Vaerting (1884–1977)," in *Personenlexikon der Sexualforschung,* ed. Volkmar Sigusch and Günter Grau (Frankfurt am Main: Campus Verlag, 2009), 715–717; Markus Seltzer, *Mathilde Vaerting: Biographische Forschungs-Arbeit zum Kampf einer Professorin am Anfang des 20. Jahrhunderts* (Tübingen: Eberhard-Karls-Universität, 2002); Elisabeth Dickmann and Eva Schöck-Quinteros, eds., *Barrieren und Karrieren: Die Anfänge des Frauenstudiums in Deutschland; Dokumentationsband der Konferenz, 100 Jahre Frauen in der Wissenschaft im Februar 1997 an der Universität Bremen* (Berlin: trafo verlag, 2000).

BIBLIOGRAPHY

Archival Sources

British Library Manuscripts and Archives, London
  Havelock Ellis Papers
Bundesarchiv, Koblenz
  Nachlass Adele Schreiber
Geheimes Staatsarchiv preussischer Kulturbesitz, Berlin
  I. HA Rep. 76 Kultusministerium VIII A. Nr. 4151
  I. HA Rep. 76 Kultusministerium VIII B Nr. 2006
  I. HA Rep. 76 Kultusministerium VIII B Nr. 2017
  I. HA Rep. 76 Kultusministerium VIII B Nr. 2762
  I. HA Rep. 76 Kultusministerium VIII B Nr. 2763
  I. HA Rep 77 Ministerium des Innern Tit. 662 Nr. 123 (Bund für Mutterschutz)
  Beiakte 4 (Deutsche Gesellschaft zur Bekämpfung der Geschlechtskrankheiten)
  Ministerium des Innern II. Abtheilung Rep. 77 Tit. 662 Nr. 44
Internationaal Instituut voor Sociale Geschiedenis, Amsterdam
  Kollektion August Bebel
  Kollektion Minna Cauer
  Kollektion Henriette Fürth
  Sozialistische Monatshefte Kollektion

Landesarchiv Berlin, Helene-Lange Archiv
  Allgemeiner Deutscher Frauenvereine
  Bund Deutscher Frauenvereine
  Nachlass Helene Lange
  Nachlass Anna Pappritz
  Verband Fortschrittlicher Frauenvereine
  Verein 'Frauenwohl'
Österreichische Nationalbibliothek, Vienna
  Teilnachlass Rosa Mayreder
Sächsisches Staatsarchiv Hauptstaatsarchiv, Dresden
  Internationale Hygieneausstellung in Dresden 1911
Sheffield Archives
  Edward Carpenter Collection
Staatsbibliothek zu Berlin—Preussischer Kulturbesitz Handschriftenabteilung
  Autogr. I/4009–1
  Autogr. I/4009–7
  Autogr. I/4009–8
  Autogr. I/4009–9
  Hirsch Nachlaß
  Nachl. Hans von Müller, Briefslg. III, Mp. 64, Bl. 13–26
University College, University of London, Special Collections
  Pearson Papers
Wienbibliothek im Rathaus
  Auguste Fickert
  Rosa Mayreder

Primary Sources

Adler, Otto. *Die mangelhafte Geschlechtsempfindung des Weibes*. Berlin: Fischers med. Buchandlung, 1911.

Alafberg, Friedrich. "Büchertisch: Grete Meisel-Heß, Die sexuelle Krise." *Das freie Worte* 9 (1909): 527–528.

Alexander, Carl. "Sexual-Hygiene, Frauen-Proteste, und Libido Sexualis." *Monatschrift für Harnkrankheiten, Psychopathia sexualis, und sexuelle Hygiene* 1, no. 4 (1904): 163–175.

Arduin, Dr. phil. "Die Frauenfrage und die sexuellen Zwischenstufen." *Jahrbuch für sexuelle Zwischenstufen* 2 (1900): 211–223.

Baars. "Grete Meisel-Hess, *Die sexuelle Krise*." *Sexual-Probleme* 6 (1910): 73–76.

Beauvoir, Simone de. *The Second Sex*. Translated by Constance Borde and Sheila Malovany-Chevallier. New York: Vintage Books, 2010. Ebook ed.

Bebel, August. *Die Frau und der Sozialismus.* 50th ed. Stuttgart: J. W. Dietz, 1910.

Becker, Dr. Werner H. "*Wie die Frau den Mann erlebt* von Sofie Lazarsfeld." *Biologische Heilkunst* 12 (1931): 531.

Bibliotheks-Kommission des Vereins "Frauenwohl Berlin," eds. *Katalog der Bibliothek zur Frauenfrage des Vereins Frauenwohl.* Berlin: G. Bernstein, 1897.

Bloch, Iwan. "Aufgaben und Ziele der Sexualwissenschaft." *Zeitschrift für Sexualwissenschaft* 1 (April 1914): 2–11.

———. *Das Sexualleben unserer Zeit, in seiner Beziehungen zur modernen Kultur.* Berlin: Louis Marcus, 1908.

———. *The Sexual Life of Our Time.* Translated by Eden Paul. New York: Allied Book, 1908.

Bluhm, Agnes. "Ethik und Eugenik." In *Frauenbewegung und Sexualethik: Beiträge zur modernen Ehekritik,* edited by Getrud Bäumer et al., 118–131. Heilbronn: Verlag von Eugen Salzer, 1909.

———. "Geschlechtliche Enthaltsamkeit und Frauenleiden: Aerztliche Randbemerkungen zu Ruth Bré's 'Das Recht auf Mutterschaft.'" *Die Frauenbewegung* 10, no. 3 (February 1904): 18–20.

———. "Zur Erwiderung auf den Artikel von Ruth Bré: 'Ist erzwungene unfreiwillige Enthaltsamkeit und Kinderlosigkeit für das gesunde, normale Weib schädlich?'" *Deutsche medizinische Presse* 5 (1904): 34–35.

Bré, Ruth. "Ist erzwungene, unfreiwillige Enthaltsamkeit und Kinderlosigkeit für das gesunde, normale Weib schädlich?" *Deutsche medizinische Presse* 4 (1904): 27–29.

———. *Das Recht auf die Mutterschaft: Eine Forderung zur Bekämpfung der Prostitution der Frauen- und Geschlechtskrankheiten.* Leipzig: Verlag der Frauen-Rundschau, 1903.

———. "Schlusswort zu der Erwiderung von Dr. Agnes Bluhm." *Deutsche medizinische Presse* 6 (1904): 41–42.

Brewster, E. T. "Studying the Animal Mind in Laboratories." *McClure's Magazine* 33 (1909): 383–387.

Burchard, E. "Sexuelle Fragen zur Kriegszeit." *Zeitschrift für Sexualwissenschaft* 1 (Jan. 1915): 373–380.

Buschan. "Bücherbesprechungen: Geza von Hoffmann, "Krieg und Rassenhygiene." *Zeitschrift für Sexualwissenschaft* 3, no. 5 (August 1916): 231.

———. "Bücherbesprechungen: M. Vaerting, Wie ersetzt erst Deutschland am schnellsten die Kriegsverluste durch gesunden Nachwuchs?" *Zeitschrift für Sexualwissenschaft* 2, no. 11 (February 1916): 434–436.

Carpenter, Edward. *The Intermediate Sex: A Study of Some Transitional Types of Men and Women.* London: Swan Sonnenschein, 1908.

———. *Love's Coming of Age: A Series of Papers on the Relations of the Sexes.* Manchester: The Labour Press, 1896.

Clouston, Thomas Smith. *Clinical Lectures on Mental Diseases.* Philadelphia: Lea Brothers, 1897.

Darwin, Charles. *The Descent of Man, and Selection in Relation to Sex.* Vol. 2. London: John Murray, 1871.

Dauthendey, Elisabeth. *Vom neuen Weibe und seiner Liebe: Ein Buch für reife Geister.* Berlin: Schuster u. Loeffler, 1900.

David, Eduard. "Krieg und Bevölkerungspolitik." *Zeitschrift für Sexualwissenschaft* 4 (January/February 1917): 393–401.

———. "Der Krieg und das Bevölkerungsproblem. " *Die neue Generation* 11 (November 1914): 469–480.

Dohm, Hedwig. "Von der biologischen Liebe." *Sozialistische Monatshefte* 13, no. 23 (1909): 1493–1495.

Duc, Aimee. *Sind es Frauen?* 1901. Reprint, Berlin: Amazonen Frauenverlag, 1976.

Dück, Johannes. "Frauenschicksal-Völkerschicksal." *Zeitschrift für Sexualwissenschaft* 5, no. 3 (June 1918): 81–95.

Eken, Anne van den. *Mannweiber-Weibmänner und der §175: Eine Schrift für denkende Frauen.* Leipzig: Verlag von Max Spohr, 1906.

Elberskirchen, Johanna. *Feminismus und Wissenschaft.* 2nd ed. Leipzig: Magazine Verlag Jacques Hegner, 1903.

———. *Geschlechtsleben und Geschlechtsenthaltsamkeit des Weibes.* Munich: Seitz & Schauer, 1905.

———. "Das Geschlechtsleben des Weibes." In *Mann und Weib: Ihre Beziehungen zueinander und zum Kulturleben der Gegenwart,* edited by Dr. R. Kossmann and Dr. Julius Weiss, 187–230. Stuttgart: Union Deutsche Verlagsgesellschaft, 1908.

———. *Die Liebe des dritten Geschlechts: Homosexualität, eine bisexuelle Varietät keine Entartung—keine Schuld.* Leipzig: Max Sport Verlag, 1904.

———. *Mutter! II. Geschlechtliche Aufklärung des Weibes.* Munich: Seitz und Schauer, 1905.

———. "Offener Brief an Fräulein Dr. phil. Ella Mensch." *Frauen Rundschau* 5, no. 12 (1904): 376–382.

———. *Die Sexualempfindung bei Weib und Mann: Betrachtet vom physiologisch-soziologisch Standpunkte.* Berlin: R. Jacobsthal Verlag, 1903.

———. *Was hat der Mann aus Weib, Kind und sich gemacht? Revolution und Erlösung des Weibes: Eine Abrechnung mit dem Mann—ein Wegweiser in die Zukunft!* 3rd ed. N.p: Magazin-Verlag, 1904.

———. "Was ist Homosexualität?" *Die Freundin: Wochenschrift für ideale Frauenfreundschaft,* 10, 17, 24 July 1929.

Ellis, Havelock. *Essays in War-Time.* London: Constable, 1916.

———. *Man and Woman: A Study of Human Secondary Sexual Characteristics.* London: Walter Scott, 1894.

———. *The Philosophy of Conflict, and Other Essays in War Time.* Second Series. 1919. Reprint, Freeport, NY: Books for Libraries Press, 1970.

———. *The Problem of Race-Regeneration.* London: Cassells, 1911.

———. "The Sexual Impulse in Women." *American Journal of Dermatology* 6, no. 3 (March 1902): 47–57.

——. *Studies in the Psychology of Sex.* Vol. 3, *Analysis of the Sexual Impulse.* Philadelphia: F. A. Davis, 1903.

——. *Studies in the Psychology of Sex.* Vol. 3, *Analysis of the Sexual Impulse, Love and Pain, the Sexual Impulse in Women.* 2nd ed., rev. and enl. ed. Philadelphia: F. A. Davis, 1913.

——. *Studies in the Psychology of Sex: Erotic Symbolism, the Mechanism of Detumescence, the Psychic State in Pregnancy.* 1906. Reprint, Philadelphia: F. A. Davis, 1920.

——. *The Task of Social Hygiene.* London: Constable, 1912.

Ellis, Havelock, and John Addington Symonds. *Sexual Inversion: A Critical Edition.* Edited by Ivan Crozier. London: Palgrave Macmillan, 2009.

Eulenberg, Albert. "Leitsätze zu dem Referate: 'Die sexuelle Abstinenz und die modern Kultur.'" In *Mutterschutz und Sexualreform: Referate und Leitsätze des I. Internationalen Kongresses für Mutterschutz und Sexualreform in Dresden 28./30. September 1911,* edited Dr. Max Rosenthal, 112–114. Breslau: Verlag von Preuss und Jünger, 1912.

Fantl, Grete. "Männlicher und Weibliche Eros." *Die neue Generation* 8 (August 1919): 384–387.

Fetscher. *Archiv für Rassen und Gesellschaftsbiologie* 17 (1925): 345.

Fischer, H. C., and Dr. E. X. DuBois. *Sexual Life during the War.* London: Francis Aldor, 1937.

Forel, August. *The Sexual Question: A Scientific, Psychological, Hygienic, and Sociological Study for the Cultured Classes.* Translated by C. F. Marshall, M.D. London: Rebman, 1908.

——. *Die sexuelle Frage: Eine naturwissenschaftliche, psychologische, hygienische und soziologische Studie für Gebildete.* Munich: Ernst Reinhardt, 1905.

——. *Die Vereinigten Staaten der Erde: Ein Kulturprogramm.* Lausanne: Buchdruckerei Fr. Ruedi, 1914.

Freud, Sigmund. "Die kulturelle Sexualmoral und die moderne Nervosität." *Sexual-Probleme* 4 (1908): 107–129.

——. "Modern Sexual Morality and Modern Nervousness." *American Journal of Urology and Sexology* 11 (October 1915): 391–405.

——. *Three Contributions to the Theory of Sexuality.* Translated by A. A. Brill. 2nd ed. New York: Nervous and Mental Disease Publishing, 1920.

——. *Three Essays on the Theory of Sexuality.* In *The Freud Reader,* edited by Peter Gay, 239–297. New York: W. W. Norton, 1989.

Fürth, Henriette. "Der Aufklärungsunterricht: Ein Beitrag zur Sexualpädagogik." *Sozialistische Monatshefte* 12 (1908): 243–246.

——. "Die Bekämpfung der Geschlechtskrankheiten in und nach dem Kriege und die Beratungstellen." *Zeitschrift für Sexualwissenschaft* 4 (1917): 65–77.

——. "Die Frauenbewegung und was ihr not tun." *Neues Frauenleben* 17 (1905): 2–10.

——. *Das Geschlechtsproblem und die moderne Moral.* Gautsch b. Leipzig: Felix Dietrich, 1908.

——. "Der Krieg und die Bevölkerungsfrage." *Zeitschrift für Sexualwissenschaft* 3 (1916): 193–214.

——. *Die Prostitution: Ursachen und Wege zur Abshilfe.* N.d.

——. "Sexualpädagogik und Sexualethik." *Sozialistische Monatshefte* 12 (1908): 564–568.

——. "Sexuelle Kriegsfragen." *Zeitschrift für Sexualwissenschaft* 2 (1915/1916): 133–137.

——. *Staat und Sittlichkeit.* Leipzig: Hans Wehner, 1912.

Gerhard, Adele, and Helene Simon. *Mutterschaft und geistige Arbeit: Eine psychologische u. soziologische Studie auf Grundlage einer internationalen Erhebung mit Berücksichtigung der geschichtliche Entwicklung.* Berlin: G. Reimer, 1901.

Gnauck-Kühne, Elisabeth. *Die deutsche Frau um die Jahrhundertwende: Statistische Studie zur Frauenfrage.* 2nd ed. Berlin: Verlag von Otto Liebmann, 1907.

Goldscheid, Rudolf. *Frauenfrage und Menschenökonomie.* Vienna: Anzengruber, 1914.

——. *Höherentwicklung und Menschenökonomie: Grundlegung der Sozialbiologie.* Leipzig: Klinkhardt, 1911.

Grassl, Dr. "Die Mutterschaft und die finanztechnische Hilfe für die Mutter." *Zeitschrift für Medizinalbeamte: Zentralblatt für das gesamte Gesundheitswesen für gerichtliche Medizin, Psychiatrie und Irrenwesen* 22, no. 8 (20 April 1909): 292–299.

Hallermeyer, Aya. "Über die rassenbiologisches Bedeutung der Krieg." *Sexual-Probleme* 10 (Jan. 1914): 11–30.

Hammer, Wilhelm. "Über gleichgeschlechtliche Frauenliebe mit besonderer Berücksicthigung der Frauenbewegung." *Monatsschrift für Harnkrankheiten und sexuelle Hygiene* 4 (1907): 394–404.

Hartung, Dr. [Christopher]. *Homosexualität und Frauenemanzipation: Ein Beitrag zur Lösung der Frage.* Leipzig: Max Spohr Verlag, 1910.

Hegar, Alfred. *Der Geschlechtstrieb: Eine social-medicinische Studie.* Stuttgart: Verlag von Ferdinand Enke, 1894.

Heymann, Lida Gustava. "III. Kongreß der deutschen Gesellschaft zur Bekämpfung der Geschlechtskrankheiten." *Der Abolitionist* 3 (1904): 65–66.

Hirschfeld, Magnus. *Die Homosexualität des Mannes und Weibes.* Berlin: L. Marcus, 1914.

——. "Die objective Diagnose der Homosexualität." *Jahrbuch für sexuelle Zwischenstufen* 1 (1899): 4–35.

——. *The Sexual History of the World War.* New York: Falstaff Press, 1937.

——. "Sexualwissenschaft als Grundlage der Sexualreform." In *Mutterschutz und Sexualreform: Referate und Leitsätze des I. Internationalen Kongresses für Mutterschutz und Sexualreform in Dresden 28./30. September 1911,* edited by Dr. Max Rosenthal, 75–84. Breslau: Verlag von Preuss und Jünger, 1912.

——. "Sexualwissenschaft als Grundlage der Sexualreform." *Die neue Generation* 8 (1912): 115–126.

——. "Sind sexuelle Zwischenstufen zur Ehe geeignet?" *Jahrbuch für sexuelle Zwischenstufen* 3 (1901): 37–71.

——. *Sittengeschichte des Weltkrieges.* Leipzig: Schneider, 1930.

——. *Der urnische Mensch.* Leipzig: Max Spohr, 1903.

——. "Die Vergeistigung des Geschlehctstriebes." *Die neue Generation* 7, no. 10 (October 1911): 411–421.

——. "Vorwort." *Jahrbuch für sexuelle Zwischenstufen* 1 (1899): 1–3.

——. "Zur Methodik der Sexualwissenschaft." *Zeitschrift für Sexualwissenschaft* 1 (1908): 681–705.

Keller, H. "Sofie Lazarsfeld: *Wie die Frau den Mann erlebt.*" *Zeitschrift für angewandte Psychologie* 40 (1931): 535–537.

Kisch, E. Heinrich. *Die sexuelle Untreue der Frau.* Bonn: A. Marcus and E. Webers Verlag, 1917.

Krafft-Ebing, Richard von. *Lehrbuch der Psychiatrie auf klinischer Grundlage für praktische Ärzte und Studirende.* Bd. I, *Die allgemeine Pathologie und Therapie des Irreseins.* 2nd ed. Stuttgart: Ferdinand Enke, 1883.

——. "Neuen Studien auf dem Gebiete der Homosexualität." *Jahrbuch für sexuelle Zwischenstufen* 3 (1901): 1–36.

——. *Psychopathia Sexualis, with Especial Reference to Contrary Sexual Instinct: A Medico-Legal Study.* Translated by Charles Gilbert Chaddock. 7th ed. Philadelphia: F. A. Davis, 1894.

——. *Psychopathia Sexualis: Mit besonderer Berücksichtigung der Conträren Sexualempfindung; Eine klinisch-forensische Studie.* Stuttgart: Verlag von Ferdinand Enke, 1888.

Krause, E. "Die Wahrheit über mich." *Jahrbuch für sexuelle Zwischenstufen* 3 (1901): 292–307.

Landesverein Preußischer Volksschullehrerinnen. *Die verheiratete Lehrerin: Verhandlungen der ersten Internationalen Lehrerinnen-Versammlung in Deutschland, berufen im Anschluss an den Internationalen Frauenkongreß im Juni 1904.* Berlin: Walther, 1905.

Lange, Helene. "Die Frauenbewegung und die moderne Ehekritik." In *Frauenbewegung und Sexualethik: Beiträge zur modernen Ehekritik,* edited by Gertrud Bäumer et al., 78–102. Heilbronn: Verlag von Eugen Salzer, 1909.

——. *Intellektuelle Grenzlinien zwischen Mann und Frau.* 2nd ed. Berlin: W. Moeser Hofbuchdruckerei, n.d.

Lazarsfeld, Sofie. *Rhythm of Life: A Guide to Sexual Harmony for Women.* New York: Greenberg, 1934.

——. *Wie die Frau den Mann erlebt: Fremde Bekenntnisse und eigene Betrachtungen.* Leipzig: Schneider, 1931.

——. *Woman's Experience of the Male.* London: Francis Aldor, n.d.

Lischnewska, Maria. "Die geschlechtliche Belehrung der Kinder: Zur Geschichte und Methodik des Gedankens." *Mutterschutz* 1 (1905): 137–170.

Marcuse, Max. "Rundschau: Johanna Elberskirchen, Geschlechtsempfindung und Liebe." *Sexual-Probleme* 4 (1908): 153.

——. "Wahrheit und Irrtum der Geschlechterpsychologie." *Zeitschrift für Sexualwissenschaft* 18 (1932): 490.

——. "Ein Wort zur Einführung." *Sexual-Probleme* 4 (Jan. 1908): 1–5.

Mayreder, Rosa. *A Survey of the Woman Problem*. Translated by Herman Scheffauer. London: Heinemann, 1913.

——. *Zur Kritik der Weiblichkeit: Essays*. Jena: Eugen Diedrichs, 1905.

Meisel-Hess, Grete. *In der modernen Weltanschauung*. Leipzig: Hermann Seemann Nachfolger, 1901.

——. "Krieg und Ehe." *Die neue Generation* 6 (June 1915): 159–174.

——. *The Sexual Crisis: A Critique of Our Sexual Life*. Translated by Eden Paul and Cedar Paul. New York: Critic and Guide, 1917.

——. "Die Sexualmoral der Frau—von heute und später." In *Ehe? Zur Reform der sexuellen Moral*, edited by Hedwig Dohm, 97–110. Berlin: Internationale Verlag, 1911.

——. *Die sexuelle Krise: Eine sozialpsychologische Untersuchung*. Jena: Diedrichs, 1909.

——. "Sexuelle Rechte." *Die neue Generation* 8 (1912): 181–198.

——. *Das Wesen der Geschlechtlichkeit: Die sexuelle Krise in ihren Beziehungen zur sozialen Frage & zum Krieg, zu Moral, Rasse & Religion & insbesondere zur Monogamie*. Jena: Eugen Diedrichs, 1916.

——. *Weiberhaß und Weiberverachtung: Eine Erwiderung auf die in Dr. Otto Weiningers Buche "Geschlecht und Charakter" geäußerten Anschauungen über "Die Frau und ihre Frage."* 2nd ed. Vienna: Verlag Die Wage, 1904.

Mensch, Ella. *Bilderstürmer in der Berliner Frauenbewegung*. Berlin: Hermann Seemann, 1906.

——. "Perspektiven von Dr. Ella Mensch." *Frauen Rundschau* 5, no. 9 (1904): 257–259.

M. F. "Wie ich es sehe." *Jahrbuch für sexuelle Zwischenstufen* 3 (1901): 308–312.

Moll, Albert. *Handbuch der Sexualwissenschaft, mit besonderer Berücksichtigung der kulturgeschichtlichen Beziehungen*. Leipzig: F. C. W. Vogel, 1912.

Müller, Robert. *Das Problem der sekundaren Geschlechtsmerkmale und die Tierzucht: Eine wissenschaftliche Untersuchung*. Stuttgart: Verlag von Ferdinand Enke, 1908.

Müller-Lyer, Franz. *Phasen der Liebe: Eine Soziologie des Verhältnisses der Geschlechter*. Munich: Albert Langen, 1913.

Näcke, Paul. "Kleinere Mitteilungen: 12. Geschlechstrieb und Mutterinstinkt bei der Frau." In *Archiv für Kriminal-Anthropologie und Kriminalistik*, 20:186–187. Leipzig: Verlag von F. C. W. Vogel, 1905.

"Neugründung zur Sexualwissenschaft." *Die neue Generation* 5 (May 1914): 287–289.

Nordau, Max. *Degeneration*. 9th ed. London: William Heinemann, 1896.

Pappritz, Anna. "Gibt es geborene Prostituierte?" *Der Abolitionist* 2 (1903): 63–67.

———. *Herrenmoral*. Leipzig: Verlag der Frauen Rundschau, n.d.

———. "Die Zwecke und Ziele der Internationalen Abolitionistischen Föderation." *Der Abolitionist* 1 (1902): 2–5.

Pataky, Sophie, ed. *Lexikon deutscher Frauen der Feder: Eine Zusammenstellung der seit dem Jahre 1840 erschienenen Werke weiblicher Autoren, nebst Biographien der lebenden und einem Verzeichnis der Pseudonyme.* Berlin: Verlagsbuchhandung von Carl Pataky, 1898.

Paulsen, E. "Bücherbesprechung: Sofie Lazarsfeld: *Wie die Frau den Mann erlebt.*" *Frau im Staat* 13 (1931): 12–13.

Plaut, Paul. "Beiträge zur Soziologie." *Zeitschrift für angewandte Psychologie* 42 (1932): 514–515.

"Referate: Prof. Neisser, *Krieg, Prostitution und Geschlechtskrankheiten.*" *Zeitschrift für Sexualwissenschaft* 2 (May 1915): 68.

Rohleder, Hermann. "Hebung der Geburtenziffer nach dem Kriege." *Zeitschrift für Sexualwissenschaft* 4 (April 1917): 13–22.

———. "Die sexuelle Veranlagung der Frauen." *Die neue Generation* 7 (July 1911): 259–272.

Rosenau, Helene. "Die Krisis der Frauenbewegung: Zur Kritik M. Vaertings 'Neubegründung der Psychologie von Mann und Weib.'" *Die Frau im Staat* 8 (1926): 8–11.

R. S. "Books on Sex and Marriage." *Journal of Personality* 3, no. 2 (December 1934): 170–172.

Rühle Gerstel, Alice. "Zurück zur guten alten Zeit?" *Die literarische Welt* 9 (27 January 1933): 5–6.

Rüling, Anna. *Welcher unter Euch ohne Sünde ist . . . Bücher von der Schattenseite.* Leipzig: Max Spohr, 1906.

———. "Welches Interesse hat die Frauenbewegung an der Lösung des homosexuellen Problems?" *Jahrbuch für sexuelle Zwischenstufen* 7 (1905): 131–151.

———. "What Interest Does the Women's Movement Have in the Homosexual Question?" In *We Are Everywhere: A Historical Sourcebook of Gay and Lesbian Politics*, edited by Mark Blasius and Shane Phelan, 143–150. London: Routledge, 1997.

Runge, Max. *Das Weib in seiner geschlechtlichen Eigenart.* 4th ed. Berlin: Verlag von Julius Springer, 1900.

Schlesinger, Therese. "Zur Psychologie der Geschlechter." *Der Kampf* 6 (1925): 225–229.

Schreiber, Adele. *Der Bund für Mutterschutz und seine Gegner.* Leipzig: Felix Dietrich, 1909.

———. "Ehereform." *Die Umschau* 12 (7 March 1908): 181–185.

———. *Mutterschaft: Ein Sammelwerk für die Probleme des Weibes als Mutter.* Munich: Langen, 1912.

Schwarz, Georg. "Literaturbericht: Mathilde Vaerting, *Wahrheit und Irrtum in der Geschlechterpsychologie.*" *Zeitschrift für Psychologie und Physiologie der Sinnesorgane* 127 (1932): 372.

Snyder, J. Ross. "The Status of the Child: Chairman's Address before the Section on Diseases of Children at the Fifty-Eighth Annual Session, American

Medical Association, 1907." *Journal of the American Medical Association* 49, no. 5 (3 August 1907): 363–365.

Spier, Ike. "Der Einfluss des Krieges auf das Geschlechtsleben." *Die neue Generation* 5/6 (May/June 1916): 129–141.

St., L. [likely Lydia Stöcker]. "Literarische Bericht: M. Vaerting. Der Männermangel nach dem Krieg," *Die neue Generation* no. 4 (April 1917): 152–155.

Stekel, Wilhelm. "Kriegsliteratur: Prof. Friedl Pick, Über Sexualstörungen im Kriege." *Zeitschrift für Sexualwissenschaft* 5 (May 1918): 79–80.

Stöcker, Helene. "An unsere Leser!" *Die neue Generation* 1 (1915): 1.

——. "An unsere Leser!" *Die neue Generation* 8/9 (14 August 1914): 409–410.

——. "Geschlechtspsychologie und Krieg." *Die neue Generation* 1 (1915): 286–300.

——. "Gewalt oder Verständigung." *Die neue Generation* 5 (1917): 199–210.

——. "Der Krieg und die Frauen." *Die neue Generation* 8/9 (14 August 1914): 422–427.

——. "Krieg und doppelte Moral." *Die neue Generation* 11 (1915): 229–238.

——. "Kriegstagung des Deutschen BfM." *Die neue Generation* 1 (1915): 345–356.

——. *Die Liebe und die Frauen.* Minden: J. C. C. Bruns' Verlag, 1906.

——. "Liebe oder Hassen? " *Die neue Generation* 12 (1914): 530–546.

——. "Menschlichkeit." *Die neue Generation* 1/2 (1916): 11–31.

——. "Moderne Bevölkerungspolitik." *Die neue Generation* 3/4 (1916): 76–87.

——. "Volkerhaß und Presse." *Die neue Generation* 3 (1917): 78–88.

——. "Von Kongressen und Gründungen." *Die neue Generation* 9 (October 1912): 547–548.

——. "Wandlung." *Die neue Generation* 10/11 (October/November 1918): 337–343.

——. "Zur Reform der sexuellen Ethik." *Mutterschutz* 1, no. 1 (1905): 3–12.

Stöcker, Helene, Lily Braun, Ellen Key, et al. *Bund für Mutterschutz.* Berlin: Pan-Verlag, 1905.

Stritt, Marie. "Nachschrift." *Centralblatt des Bundes deutscher Frauenvereine* 9 (15 November 1907): 123.

Thal, Max. *Mutterrecht: Frauenfrage und Weltanschauung.* Breslau: Schlesische Verlags-Anstalt v. S. Schottlaender, 1903.

Triepel, H. "Literaturbericht: Mathilde Vaerting, *Wahrheit und Irrtum in der Geschlechterpsychologie.*" *Archiv für gesamte Psychology* 47 (1924): 227–229.

Troll-Borostyani, Irma von. *Die Gleichstellung der Geschlechter und die Reform der Jugend Erziehung: Die Mission unseres Jahrhunderts.* Zurich: Schabelitz, 1888.

[Trosse, Emma.] *Der Konträrsexualismus inbezug auf Ehe und Frauenfrage.* Leipzig: Verlag von Max Spohr, 1895.

Ulrichs, Karl Heinrich. *The Riddle of "Man-Manly" Love: The Pioneering Work on Male Homosexuality I.* Translated by Michael A. Lombardi-Nash. Buffalo: Prometheus Books, 1994.

Urbach, Karl. "Vaerting, M.: *Neubegründung der Psychologie von Mann und Weib*, Bd. I, *Die weibliche Eigenart im Männerstaat und die männliche Eigenart im Frauenstaat.*" *Zeitschrift für Sexualwissenschaft* 8 (February 1922): 362–363.

Vaerting, Dr. *Das günstigste elterliche Zeugungsalter für die geistigen Fähigkeiten der Nachkommen.* Würzburg: Curt Kabitzsch, Kgl. Universitäts-Verlagsbuchhändler, 1913.

Vaerting, Dr. M. "Die Frau, die erblich-organische Höherentwicklung und der Krieg." *Die neue Generation* 3/4 (March/April 1916): 67–75.

———. "Über den Einfluß des Krieges auf Präventivverkehr und Fruchtabtreibung und seine eugenischen Folgen." *Zeitschrift für Sexualwissenschaft* 4 (July 1917): 137–144; (August 1917): 176–179.

Vaerting, Mathilde. "Die eugenische Bedeutung des Orgasmus." *Zeitschrift für Sexualwissenschaft* 2 (Sept. 1915): 185–194.

———. "Der Kampf gegen die historischen Spuren der Frauenherrschaft." *Die neue Generation* 11/12 (November/December 1921): 353–371.

———. "Der Nachwuchs der begabten Frauen." *Die neue Generation* 9 (September 1919): 426–433.

———. "Physiologische Ursachen geistiger Höchstleistungen bei Mann und Weib." In *Abhandlungen aus dem Gebiete der Sexualforschung*, edited by Max Marcuse. Bonn: Marcus & E. Webers Verlag, 1922.

———. "Die rassenhygienischen Gefahren des Frauenüberschusses nach dem Kriege und Wege zur erhöhten Vermehrung des männlichen Geschlechts." *Zeitschrift für Sexualwissenschaft* 2 (February 1916): 397–405; 3 (March 1916): 445–452.

———. *Soziologie und Psychologie der Macht: Die Macht der Massen.* Berlin: Dr. M. Pfeiffer, 1928.

———. *Wahrheit und Irrtum in der Geschlechterpsychologie.* Karlsruhe: G. Braun, 1923.

———. *Die weibliche Eigenart im Männerstaat und die männliche Eigenart im Frauenstaat.* Karlsruhe: G. Braun, 1921.

Vaerting, Mathilde, and Mathias Vaerting. *The Dominant Sex: A Study in the Sociology of Sex Differentiation.* Translated by Eden Paul and Cedar Paul. New York: George H. Doran, 1923.

Vaerting, Prof. Dr. M. T. *Die Frau in unserer Zeit.* Darmstadt-Eberstadt: Themis-Verlag, 1952.

Van Waters, Miriam. "Book Reviews: *The Dominant Sex*, by Mathilde and Mathias Vaerting." *Birth Control Review* 6 (October 1923): 273.

"Varia: Die 'Deutsche Gesellschaft zur Bekämpfung der Geschlechtskrankheiten' hat das folgende Merkblatt für Soldaten unter den ins Feld ziehenden Soldaten verbreiten lassen." *Zeitschrift für Sexualwissenschaft* 1 (November 1914): 336.

Verhandlungen des [ersten bis achten] Jahresversammlung der Deutschen Gesellschaft zur Bekämpfung der Geschlechtskrankheiten. Edited by the Vorstande der Gesellschaft. Leipzig: Verlag von Johann Ambrosius Barth, 1911.

Voigtländer, Else. "Bücherbesprechungen: Vaerting, M., *Wahrheit und Irrtum in der Geschlechterpsychologie*, II. Band der *Neubegründung der Psychologie von Mann und Weib.*" *Zeitschrift für Sexualwissenschaft* 11 (1924): 105–107.

——. "Zur Problematik der Geschlechtsunterschiede." *Zeitschrift für Sexualwissenschaft* 10 (July 1923): 89–99.

Weber, Marianne. "Sexualethische Prinzipienfragen." In *Frauenbewegung und Sexualethik: Beiträge zur modernen Ehekritik*, edited by Gertrud Bäumer et al., 27–44. Heilbronn: Eugen Salzer, 1909.

Weil, Dr. A., ed. *Sexualreform und Sexualwissenschaft.* Stuttgart: Julius Püttmann, 1922.

Weininger, Otto. *Sex and Character: An Investigation of Fundamental Principles.* Translated by Ladislaus Löb. Indianapolis: Indiana University Press, 2005.

Westenhöfer, [Max]. "M. Vaerting: *Wahrheit und Irrtum in der Geschlechterpsychologie.*" *Archiv für Frauenkunde und Konstitutionsforschung* 10 (June 1924): 192–193.

Westphal, Carl. "Die conträre Sexualempfindung: Symptom eines neuropathischen (psychopathsichen) Zustandes." *Archiv für Psychiatrie und Nervenkrankheiten* 2 (1870): 73–108.

Willard, Elizabeth Osgood Goodrich. *Sexology as the Philosophy of Life: Implying Social Organization and Government.* Chicago: J. R. Walsh, 1867.

"Würdelose Weiber." *Sexual-Probleme* 10 (Sept. 1914): 619.

Secondary Sources

Abrams, Lynn. "Prostitutes in Imperial Germany, 1870–1918: Working Girls or Social Outcasts?" In *The German Underworld: Deviants and Outcasts in Germany History*, edited by Richard J. Evans, 189–209. London: Routledge, 1988.

Ahmed, Sara. "Open Forum: Imaginary Prohibitions; Some Preliminary Remarks on the Founding Gestures of the 'New Materialism.'" *European Journal of Women's Studies* 15 (2008): 23–39.

Alaimo, Stacy, and Susan Hekman, eds. *Material Feminisms.* Bloomington: Indiana University Press, 2008.

Allen, Ann Taylor. "Feminism and Eugenics in Germany and Britain, 1900–1940: A Comparative Perspective." *German Studies Review* 23, no. 3 (October 2000): 477–505.

——. *Feminism and Motherhood in Germany, 1800–1914.* New Brunswick, NJ: Rutgers University Press, 1991.

——. *Feminism and Motherhood in Western Europe, 1890–1970: The Maternal Dilemma.* London: Palgrave Macmillan, 2005.

——. "Feminism, Social Science, and the Meanings of Modernity: The Debate on the Origins of the Family in Europe and the United States, 1860–1914." *American Historical Review* 104, no. 4 (October 1999): 1085–1113.

———. "Feminism, Venereal Disease, and the State in Germany, 1890–1918." *Journal of the History of Sexuality* 4 (July 1993): 27–50.

———. "German Radical Feminism and Eugenics, 1900–1908." *German Studies Review* 11, no. 1 (February 1988): 31–56.

———. "Mothers of the New Generation: Adele Schreiber, Helene Stöcker, and the Evolution of a New German Idea of Motherhood, 1900–1914." *Signs* 10, no. 3 (Spring 1985): 418–438.

———. "Patriarchy and Its Discontents: The Debate on the Origins of the Family in the German-Speaking World, 1860–1930." In *Germany at the Fin-de Siècle: Culture, Politics, and Ideas*, edited by Suzanne Marchand and David Lindenfeld, 81–101. Baton Rouge: Louisiana State University Press, 2004.

Allen, Judith. "Men Interminably in Crisis? Historians on Masculinity, Sexual Boundaries, and Manhood." *Radical History Review* 82, no. 1 (Winter 2002): 191–207.

Anderson, Harriet, ed. *Rosa Mayreder Tagebücher 1873–1937*. Frankfurt: Insel Verlag, 1988.

———. *Utopian Feminism: Women's Movements in Fin-de-Siècle Vienna*. New Haven, CT: Yale University Press, 1992.

Ankum, Katharina von, ed. *Women in the Metropolis: Gender and Modernity in Weimar Culture*. Berkeley: University of California Press, 1997.

Badinter, Elisabeth. *The Myth of Motherhood: An Historical View of the Maternal Instinct*. Translated by Roger DeGaris. London: Souvenir Press, 1981.

Bashford, Alison, and Philippa Levine, eds. *The Oxford Handbook of the History of Eugenics*. Oxford: Oxford University Press, 2010.

Bauer, Heike. *English Literary Sexology: Translations of Inversion, 1860–1930*. London: Palgrave Macmillan, 2009.

———. "Theorizing Female Inversion: Sexology, Discipline, and Gender at the Fin de Siècle." *Journal of the History of Sexuality* 18 (January 2009): 84–102.

Beachy, Robert. *Gay Berlin: Birthplace of a Modern Identity*. New York: Knopf, 2014.

———. "The German Invention of Homosexuality." *Journal of Modern History* 82 (2010): 801–838.

Beccalossi, Chiara. *Female Sexual Inversion: Same-Sex Desires in Italian and British Sexology, c. 1870–1920*. London: Palgrave Macmillan, 2012.

Berghahn, Volker R. *Imperial Germany, 1871–1914: Economy, Society, and Politics*. Rev. and exp. ed. New York: Berghahn Books, 2005.

Berlin, Isaiah. "Two Concepts of Liberty." In *Liberty: Incorporating Four Essays on Liberty*, edited by Henry Hardy, 166–217. Oxford: Oxford University Press, 2002.

Blackbourn, David. "Europeanizing German History: Comment on the Eighteenth Annual Lecture of the GHI, November 18, 2004." *GHI Bulletin* 36 (Spring 2005): 25–31.

———. *History of Germany, 1789–1914: The Long Nineteenth Century*. Malden, MA : Blackwell, 2003.

Bland, Lucy. *Banishing the Beast: Feminism, Sex, and Morality.* London: I. B. Tauris, 2001.

——. "Introduction [Gender and Sexual Difference]." In *Sexology Uncensored: The Documents of Sexual Science*, edited by Lucy Bland and Laura Doan, 11–14. Chicago: University of Chicago Press, 1998.

Blencowe, Claire Peta. "Biology, Contingency, and the Problem of Racism in Feminist Discourse." *Theory, Culture, and Society* 28 (2011): 3–27.

Borelli, Siegfried, Hermann-Joseph Vogt, and Michael Kreis, eds. *Geschichte der Deutschen Gesellschaft zur Bekämpfung der Geschlechtskrankheiten.* Berlin: Blackwell, 1992.

Bourdieu, Pierre. "The Specificity of the Scientific Field and the Social Conditions of the Progress of Reason." *Social Science Information* 14 (December 1975): 19–47.

Braker, Regina. "Helene Stöcker's Pacifism: International Intersections." *Peace and Change* 23 (October 1998): 455–465.

——. "Helene Stöcker's Pacifism in the Weimar Republic: Between Ideal and Reality." *Journal of Women's History* 13 (Autumn 2001): 70–97.

Bridenthal, Renate, Atina Grossmann, and Marion Kaplan, eds. *Women in Weimar and Nazi Germany.* New York: Monthly Review Press, 1984.

Briggs, Laura. *Reproducing Empire: Race, Sex, Science, and US Imperialism in Puerto Rico.* Berkeley: University of California Press, 2002.

Bullough, Vern. *Science in the Bedroom: A History of Sex Research.* New York: Basic Books, 1995.

Canning, Kathleen. *Gender History in Practice: Historical Perspectives on Bodies, Class, and Citizenship.* Ithaca, NY: Cornell University Press, 2006.

——. *Languages of Labor and Gender: Female Factory Work in Germany, 1850–1914.* Ann Arbor: University of Michigan Press, 2002.

——. "Women and the Politics of Gender." In *Weimar Germany*, edited by Anthony McElligott, 146–174. Oxford: Oxford University Press, 2009.

Canning, Kathleen, Kerstin Barndt, and Kristin McGuire, eds. *Weimar Publics/Weimar Subjects: Rethinking the Political Culture of Germany in the 1920s.* New York: Berghahn, 2010.

Capovilla, Andrea. *Entwürfe weiblicher Identität in der Moderne: Milena Jesenská, Vicki Baum, Gina Kraus, Alice Rühle-Gerstel; Studien zu Leben und Werk.* Oldenburg: Igel Verlag, 2004.

Carter, Julian. *The Heart of Whiteness: Normal Sexuality and Race in America, 1880–1940.* Durham, NC: Duke University Press, 2007.

Chiang, Howard. "Double Alterity and the Global Historiography of Sexuality: China, Europe, and the Emergence of Sexuality as a Global Possibility." *e-pisteme* 2 (2009): 33–52.

——. "Epistemic Modernity and the Emergence of Homosexuality in China." *Gender and History* 22 (2010): 629–657.

——. "Liberating Sex, Knowing Desire: *Scientia Sexualis* and Epistemic Turning Points in the History of Sexuality." *History of the Human Sciences* 23, no. 5 (2010): 42–69.

———, ed. "Revisiting *The History of Sexuality*: Thinking with Foucault at Forty." Special issue, *Cultural History* 5, no. 2 (October 2016): 115–121.

Cocks, H. G. "Historiographical Review: Modernity and the Self in the History of Sexuality." *Historical Journal* 49 (2006): 1211–1227.

Cohen, Deborah. *Family Secrets: Shame and Privacy in Modern Britain*. New York: Oxford University Press, 2013.

Cooter, Roger, and Stephen Pumfey. "Separate Spheres and Public Spaces: Reflections on the History of Science Popularization and Science in Popular Culture." *History of Science* 32 (September 1994): 237–267.

Crew, David F. *Germans on Welfare: From Weimar to Hitler*. Oxford: Oxford University Press, 1998.

Cunningham, Gail. "He-Notes: Reconstructing Masculinity." In *The New Woman in Fiction and in Fact: Fin-de-Siècle Feminisms*, edited by Angelique Richardson and Chris Willis, 94–106. London: Palgrave, 2001.

Daston, Lorraine, and Fernando Vidal, eds. *The Moral Authority of Nature*. Chicago: University of Chicago Press, 2004.

Daum, Andreas. "Varieties of Popular Science and the Transformations of Public Knowledge: Some Historical Reflections." *Isis* 100, no. 2 (June 2009): 319–332.

Davidson, Arnold I. *The Emergence of Sexuality: Historical Epistemology and the Formation of Concepts*. Cambridge, MA: Harvard University Press, 2001.

Davidson, Roger, and Lesley A. Hall. "Introduction." In *Sex, Sin, and Suffering: Venereal Disease and European Society since 1870*, edited by Roger Davidson and Lesley A. Hall, 1–14. London: Routledge, 2001.

Davies, Peter. "Introduction: 'Crisis' or 'Hegemony'? Approaches to Masculinity." In *Edinburgh German Yearbook*, vol. 2, *Masculinities in German Culture*, edited by Sarah Colvin and Peter Davies, 1–19. Rochester: Camden House, 2008.

———. *Myth, Matriarchy, and Modernity: Johann Jakob Bachofen in German Culture, 1860–1945*. New York: De Gruyter, 2010.

de Blécourt, Willem, ed. *Sisters of Subversion: Histories of Women, Tales of Gender*. Amsterdam: AMB Press, 2008.

Deutscher, Penelope. "Foucault's *History of Sexuality, Volume I*: Re-reading Its Reproduction." *Theory, Culture, and Society* 29 (January 2012): 119–137.

Dickinson, Edward Ross. "Biopolitics, Fascism, Democracy: Reflections on Our Discourse About 'Modernity.'" *Central European History* 37 (2004): 1–48.

———. "'A Dark, Impenetrable Wall of Complete Incomprehension': The Impossibility of Heterosexual Love in Imperial Germany." *Central European History* 40 (2007): 467–497.

———. "The Men's Christian Morality Movement in Germany, 1880–1914: Some Reflections on Politics, Sex, and Sexual Politics." *Journal of Modern History* 75, no. 1 (March 2003): 59–110.

———. "Not So Scary after All? Reform in Imperial and Weimar Germany." *Central European History* 43 (2010): 149–172.

——. "Reflections on Feminism and Monism in the Kaiserreich, 1900–1913." *Central European History* 34, no. 2 (2001): 191–230.

Dickinson, Edward Ross, and Richard F. Wetzell. "The Historiography of Sexuality in Modern Germany." *German History* 23, no. 3 (2005): 292–305.

Dickmann, Elisabeth, and Eva Schöck-Quinteros. *Barrieren und Karrieren: Die Anfänge des Frauenstudiums in Deutschland; Dokumentationsband der Konferenz, 100 Jahre Frauen in der Wissenschaft im Februar 1997 an der Universität Bremen.* Berlin: trafo verlag, 2000.

Dobler, Jens. *Prolegomena zu Magnus Hirschfelds Jahrbuch für sexuelle Zwischenstufen (1899 bis 1923).* Neumünster: von Bockel Verlag, 2004.

Domansky, Elizabeth. "Militarization and Reproduction in World War One Germany." In *Society, Culture, and the State in Germany, 1870–1930*, edited by Geoff Eley, 427–464. Ann Arbor: University of Michigan Press, 1997.

Dose, Ralf. *Magnus Hirschfeld: The Origins of the Gay Liberation Movement.* Translated by Edward H. Willis. New York: Monthly Review Press, 2014.

——. "The World League for Sexual Reform: Some Possible Approaches." *Journal of the History of Sexuality* 12 (2003): 1–15.

Duberman, Martin B., Martha Vicinus, and George Chauncey, eds. *Hidden from History: Reclaiming the Gay and Lesbian Past.* New York: New American Library, 1989.

Dworschak, Herta. "Rosa Obermayer-Mayreder: Leben und Werk." PhD diss., University of Vienna, 1949.

Eder, Franz X., Lesley A. Hall, and Gert Hekma, eds. *Sexual Cultures in Europe: National Histories.* Manchester: Manchester University Press, 1999.

——. *Sexual Cultures in Europe: Themes in Sexuality.* Manchester: Manchester University Press, 1999.

Eley, Geoff. "'An Embarrassment to the Family, to the Public, and to the State': Liberalism and the Rights of Women, 1860–1914." In *Wilhelmine Germany and Edwardian Britain: Essays on Cultural Affinity*, edited by Dominik Geppert and Robert Gerwarth, 143–172. Oxford: Oxford University Press, 2008.

——. "Introduction 1: Is There a History of the *Kaiserreich*?" In *Society, Culture, and the State in Germany, 1870–1930*, edited by Geoff Eley, 1–42. Ann Arbor: University of Michigan Press, 1996.

Eley, Geoff, and James Retallack, eds. *Wilhelmism and Its Legacies: German Modernities, Imperialism, and the Meanings of Reform, 1890–1930.* Oxford: Berghahn, 2003.

Epple, Angelika. *Henriette Fürth und die Frauenbewegung im deutschen Kaiserreich: Eine Sozialbiographie.* Pfaffenweiler: Centaurus Verlaggesellschaft, 1996.

Epstein, Steven. *Impure Science: AIDS, Activism, and the Politics of Knowledge.* Berkeley: University of California Press, 1996.

Evans, Richard J. *Comrades and Sisters: Feminism, Socialism, and Pacifism in Europe, 1870–1945.* New York: St. Martin's Press, 1987.

———. *The Feminist Movement in Germany, 1894–1933*. London: Sage Publications, 1976.

Ewald, Francois. "Norms, Discipline, and the Law." *Representations* 30 (Spring 1990): 138–161.

Exner, Gudrun. "Rudolf Goldscheid (1870–1931) and the Economy of Human Beings." *Vienna Yearbook of Population Research*, 2004, 283–301.

Faderman, Lillian. "The Morbidifcation of Love between Women by 19th-Century Sexologists." *Journal of Homosexuality* 4 (1978): 73–90.

Fausto-Sterling, Anne. *Myths of Gender: Biological Theories about Women and Men*. New York: Basic Books, 1986.

———. *Sexing the Body: Gender Politics and the Construction of Sexuality*. New York: Basic Books, 2000.

Fell, Alison, and Ingrid Sharp, eds. *The Women's Movement in Wartime: International Perspectives, 1914–1919*. New York: Palgrave Macmillan, 2007.

Felski, Rita. "Introduction." *Sexology in Culture: Labelling Bodies and Desires*, edited by Lucy Bland and Laura Doan, 1–8. Chicago: University of Chicago Press, 1998.

Ferdinand, Ursula. *Das Malthusische Erbe: Entwicklungsstränge der Bevölkerungstheorie im 19. Jahrhundert und deren Einfluss auf die radikale Frauenbewegung in Deutschland*. Münster: LIT Verlag, 1999.

Ferdinand, Ursula, Andreas Pretzel, and Andreas Seeck, eds. *Verqueere Wissenschaft? Zum Verhältnis von Sexualwissenschaft und Sexualreformbewegung in Geschichte und Gegenwart*. Münster: LIT Verlag, 1998.

Ferree, Myra Marx. *Varieties of Feminism: German Gender Politics in Global Perspective*. Stanford, CA: Stanford University Press, 2012.

Fischer, Lila, and Emil Brix, eds. *Die Frauen der Wiener Moderne*. Vienna: Verlag für Geschichte und Politik, 1997.

"Forum: The 'German Question' in the History of Science and the 'Science Question' in German History." *German History* 29 (2011): 628–639.

Foucault, Michel. *The Birth of Biopolitics: Lectures at the Collège de France, 1978–1979*. Edited by Michel Senellart, translated by Graham Burchell. New York: Picador, 2008.

———. "Governmentality." In *The Foucault Effect: Studies in Governmentality*, edited by Graham Burchell, Colin Gordon, and Peter Miller, 87–104. Chicago: University of Chicago Press, 1991.

———. *The History of Sexuality*. Vol. 1. Translated by Robert Hurley. New York, Vintage, 1990.

———. "The Subject and Power." In *Michel Foucault: Beyond Structure and Hermeneutics*, edited by Hubert Dreyfus and Paul Rabinow, 208–228. Chicago: University of Chicago Press, 1982.

Fout, John C. "Sexual Politics in Wilhelmine Germany: The Male Gender Crisis, Moral Purity, and Homophobia." *Journal of the History of Sexuality* 2 (January 1992): 388–421.

Fox Keller, Evelyn. *Reflections on Gender and Science*. New Haven, CT: Yale University Press, 1985.

Fox Keller, Evelyn, and Helen E. Longino, eds. *Feminism and Science*. Oxford: Oxford University Press, 1996.

Frevert, Ute. "Europeanizing Germany's Twentieth Century." *History and Memory* 17 (Spring/Summer 2005): 87–116.

Friebus, Dorothee. "Sofie Lazarsfeld oder 'Wie die Frau den Mann erlebt.'" In *Gestalten um Alfred Adler: Pioniere der Individualpsychologie*, 157–174. Würzburg: Königshausen & Neumann, 2002.

Fritzen, Florentine. *Gesünder Leben: Die Lebensreformbewegung im 20. Jahrhundert*. Stuttgart: Steiner, 2006.

Frühstück, Sabine. *Colonizing Sex: Sexology and Social Control in Modern Japan*. Berkeley: University of California Press, 2003.

Fuechtner, Veronika. *Berlin Psychoanalytic: Psychoanalysis and Culture in Weimar Republic Germany and Beyond*. Berkeley: University of California Press, 2011.

Gerhard, Ute. *Unerhört: Die Geschichte der deutschen Frauenbewegung*. Hamburg: Rowohlt Taschenbuch Verlag, 1990.

Gibson, Margaret. "The Masculine Degenerate: American Doctors' Portrayals of the Lesbian Intellect, 1880–1949." *Journal of Women's History* 9 (Winter 1998): 78–103.

Gillerman, Sharon. *Germans into Jews: Remaking the Jewish Social Body in the Weimar Republic*. Palo Alto, CA: Stanford University Press, 2009.

Good, David F., Margarete Grandner, and Mary Jo Maynes, eds. *Frauen in Österreich: Beiträge zu ihrer Situation in 20. Jahrhundert*. Vienna: Böhlau Verlag, 1994.

Göttert, Margit. "Zwischen Betroffenheit, Abscheu und Sympathie: Die alte Frauenbewegung und das 'heikles' Thema Homosexualität." *Ariadne: Almanach des Archivs der deutschen Frauenbewegung* 29 (May 1996): 14–21.

Grayzel, Susan. *Women's Identities at War: Gender, Motherhood, and Politics in Britain and France during the First World War*. Chapel Hill: University of North Carolina Press, 1999.

Greenway, Judy. "It's What You Do with It That Counts: Interpretations of Otto Weininger." In *Sexology in Culture: Labeling Bodies and Desires*, edited by Lucy Bland and Laura Doan, 27–43. London: Polity Press, 2008.

Greer, Germaine. *The Female Eunuch*. St. Albans: Paladin, 1971.

Grigg, Russell, Dominique Hecq, and Craig Smith, eds. *Female Sexuality: The Early Psychoanalytic Controversies*. New York: Other Press, 1999.

Grosskurth, Phyllis. *Havelock Ellis: A Biography*. New York: Knopf, 1980.

Grossman, Atina. "Continuities and Ruptures: Sexuality in Twentieth-Century Germany; Historiography and Its Discontents." In *Gendering Modern German History: Rewriting Historiography*, edited by Karen Hagemann and Jean H. Quatert, 208–227. Oxford: Berghahn Books, 2007.

——. "Girlkultur or Thoroughly Rationalized Female: A New Woman in Weimar Germany?" *Women in Culture and Politics: A Century of Change*, edited by Judith Friedlander, 62–80. Bloomington: Indiana University Press, 1986.

——. *Reforming Sex: The German Movement for Birth Control and Abortion Reform, 1920–1950.* New York: Oxford University Press, 1995.

Grosz, Elizabeth. *Becoming Undone: Darwinian Reflections on Life, Politics, and Art.* Durham, NC: Duke University Press, 2011.

——. *Time Travels: Feminism, Nature, Power.* Durham, NC: Duke University Press, 2005.

Gruber, Helmut. "Sexuality in 'Red Vienna': Socialist Party Conceptions and Programs and Working-Class Life, 1920–34." *International Labor and Working-Class History* 31 (Spring 1987): 37–68.

Gullace, Nicoletta. *The Blood of Our Sons: Men, Women, and the Renegotiation of British Citizenship during the Great War.* New York: Palgrave Macmillan, 2002.

Haas, Peter. "Introduction: Epistemic Communities and International Policy Coordination." *International Organization* 46, no. 1 (Winter 1992): 1–35.

Hahn, Barbara, ed. *Frauen in den Kulturwissenschaften von Lou Andreas-Salome bis Hannah Arendt.* Munich: C. H. Beck, 1994.

Hall, Lesley A. *Outspoken Women: An Anthology of Women's Writing on Sex, 1870–1969.* London: Routledge, 2005.

——. "Stella Browne and the German Radical Sex Reform Tradition." In *Sisters of Subversion: Histories of Women, Tales of Gender*, edited by Willem de Blécourt, 152–161. Amsterdam: AMB, 2008.

Halperin, David. *How to Do the History of Homosexuality.* Chicago: University of Chicago Press, 2004.

Handlbauer, Bernhard. *Die Entstehungsgeschichte der Individualpsychologie Alfred Adlers.* Vienna: Geyer-Edition, 1984.

——. "Psychoanalytikerinnen und Individualpsychologinnen im Roten Wien." In *Die Revolutionierung des Alltags: Zur intellektuellen Kultur von Frauen im Wien der Zwischenkriegszeit*, edited by Doris Ingrisch, Ilse Korotin, and Charlotte Zwiauer, 75–100. Frankfurt am Main: Peter Lang, 2004.

Haraway, Donna. "Situated Knowledges: The Science Question in Feminism and the Privilege of Partial Perspective." In *The Feminist Standpoint Theory Reader: Intellectual and Political Controversies*, edited by Sandra Harding, 81–102. New York: Routledge, 2004.

Harding, Sandra. *The Science Question in Feminism.* Ithaca, NY: Cornell University Press, 1986.

Hark, Sabine. *Dissident Partizipation.* Frankfurt am Main: Suhrkamp, 2005.

——. "'Welches Interesse hat die Frauenbewegung an der Lösung des homosexuellen Problems?'—zur Sexualpolitik der bürgerlichen Frauenbewegung im Deutschland des Kaiserreichs." *Beiträge: Zur feministischen Theorie und Praxis* 12, no. 25/25 (1989): 19–28.

Harvey, Elizabeth. "Pilgrimages to the 'Bleeding Border': Gender and Rituals of Nationalist Protest in Germany, 1919–39." *Women's History Review* 9 (2000): 201–229.

Hau, Michael. *The Cult of Health and Beauty in Germany: A Social History, 1890–1930.* Chicago: University of Chicago Press, 2003.

Heberer, Eva-Maria. *Prostitution: An Economic Perspective on Its Past, Present, and Future.* Wiesbaden: Springer Science and Business Media, 2014.

Hekma, Gert. "'A Female Soul in a Male Body': Sexual Inversion as Gender Inversion in Nineteenth-Century Sexology." In *Third Sex, Third Gender: Beyond Sexual Dimorphism in Culture and History,* edited by Gilbert Herdt, 213–239. New York: Zone Books, 1994.

Herzer, Manfred. *Magnus Hirschfeld: Leben und Werk eines jüdischen, schwulen und sozialistischen Sexologen.* Frankfurt am Main: Campus Verlag, 1992.

Herzog, Dagmar. "Syncopated Sex: Transforming Sexual Cultures." *American Historical Review* 114, no. 5 (December 2009): 1287–1308.

Hird, Myra J. "Feminist Matters: New Materialist Considerations of Sexual Difference." *Feminist Theory* 5 (2004): 223–232.

——. "From The Culture of Matter to the Matter of Culture: Feminist Explorations of Nature and Science." *Sociological Research Online* 8 (2003). http://www.socresonline.org.uk/8/1/hird.html.

Hodge, Jonathan, and Gregory Radick, eds. *The Cambridge Companion to Darwin.* Cambridge: Cambridge University Press, 2003.

Hohmann, Joachim S. *Sexualforschung und -aufklärung in der Weimarer Republik: Eine Übersicht in Materialien und Dokumenten.* Frankfurt am Main: Foerster Verlag, 1985.

Holland-Cunz, Barbara. *Die alte neue Frauenfrage.* Frankfurt am Main: Suhrkamp Verlag, 2003.

Hong, Young Sun. "Gender, Citizenship, and the Welfare State: Social Work and the Politics of Femininity in the Weimar Republic." *Central European History* 30, no. 1 (1997): 1–24.

Hrdy, Sarah Blaffer. *Mother Nature: Maternal Instincts and How They Shape the Human Species.* New York: Ballantine Books, 1999.

Hull, Isabel V. *Sexuality, State, and Civil Society in Germany, 1700–1815.* Ithaca, NY: Cornell University Press, 1996.

Izenberg, Gerald N. *Modernism and Masculinity: Mann, Wedekind, Kandinsky through World War I.* Chicago: University of Chicago Press, 2000.

Jackson, Margaret. *The Real Facts of Life: Feminism and the Politics of Sexuality c. 1850–1940.* London: Taylor and Francis, 1994.

Jacobus, Mary, Evelyn Fox Keller, and Sally Shuttleworth. "Introduction." In *Body/Politics: Women, Literature, and the Discourse of Science,* edited by Mary Jacobus, Evelyn Fox Keller, and Sally Shuttleworth, 1–10. London: Routledge, 1990.

Jagose, Annamarie. *Orgasmology.* Durham, NC: Duke University Press, 2012.

Janssen-Jurreit, Marielouise, ed. *Frauen und Sexualmoral.* Frankfurt am Main: Fischer Taschenbuch Verlag, 1986.

——. "Sexualreform und Geburtenrückgang—über die Zusammenhänge von Bevölkerungspolitik und Frauenbewegung um die Jahrhundertwende." In *Frauen in der Geschichte,* edited by Annette Kuhn and Gerhard Schneider, 56–81. Düsseldorf: Schwann, 1979.

Jazbinsek, Dietmar. "Lebensgeschichte und Eigensinn: Über die Biographie und die Biographieforschung des Dirnenarztes Wilhelm Hammer." *Mitteilungen der Magnus Hirschfeld Gesellschaft* 37/38 (2007): 32–57.

Jeffreys, Sheila. *The Spinster and Her Enemies: Feminism and Sexuality, 1880–1930.* London: Pandora Press, 1985.

Johns, Alessa. "Feminism and Utopianism." In *The Cambridge Companion to Utopian Literature*, edited by Gregory Claeys, 174–199. Cambridge: Cambridge University Press, 2010.

Jusek, Karin. "Entmystifizierung des Körpers? Feministinnen im sexuellen Diskurs der Moderne." In *Frauen der Wiener Moderne*, edited by Lisa Fischer, 110–123. Munich: Verlag für Geschichte und Politik, 1997.

Katz, Jonathan Ned. *The Invention of Heterosexuality.* Chicago: University of Chicago Press, 1995.

Kelly, Alfred. *The Descent of Darwin: The Popularization of Darwinism, 1860–1914.* Chapel Hill: University of North Carolina Press, 1981.

Kenner, Clara. *Der zerrissene Himmel: Emigration und Exil der Wiener Individualpsychologie.* Göttingen: Vandenhoeck & Ruprecht, 2007.

Kline, Wendy. *Bodies of Knowledge: Sexuality, Reproduction, and Women's Health in the Second Wave.* Chicago: University of Chicago Press, 2010.

Kokula, Ilse. "Helene Stöcker, der Bund für Mutterschutz und die Sexualreformbewegung." *Mitteilungen der Magnus Hirschfeld Gesellschaft* 6 (August 1985): 5–25.

———. *Weibliche Homosexualität um 1900 in zeitgenössichen Dokumenten.* Munich: Frauenoffensive, 1984.

Koven, Seth, and Sonya Michel. "Womanly Duties: Maternalist Politics and the Origins of the Welfare States in France, Germany, Great Britain, and the United States, 1880–1920." *American Historical Review* 95, no. 4 (Oct. 1990): 1076–1108.

Kozma, Liat. "Sexology in the Yishuv: The Rise and Decline of Sexual Consultation in Tel Aviv, 1930–1939." *International Journal of Middle East Studies* 42 (2010): 231–249.

———. "We, the Sexologists . . . Arabic Medical Writing on Sexuality, 1897–1943." *Journal of the History of Sexuality* 22, no. 3 (September 2013): 426–445.

Kubes-Hofmann, Ursula. "'Etwas an der Männlichkeit ist nicht in Ordnung': Intellektuelle Frauen am Beispiel Rosa Mayreder und Helene von Druskowitz." In *Die Frauen der Wiener Moderne*, edited by Lisa Fischer, 124–136. Vienna: Verlag für Geschichte und Politik, 1997.

Kundrus, Birthe. "Gender Wars: The First World War and the Construction of Gender Relations in the Weimar Republic." In *Home/Front: The Military, War, and Gender in Twentieth-Century Germany*, edited by Karen Hagemann and Stefanie Schüller-Springorum, 159–179. Oxford: Berg, 2002.

Laslett, Barbara, Sally Gregory Kohlstedt, Helen Longino, and Evelynn Hammonds, eds. *Gender and Scientific Authority.* Chicago: University of Chicago Press, 1996.

Lees, Andrew. *Cities, Sin, and Social Reform in Imperial Germany.* Ann Arbor: University of Michigan Press, 2002.

Lehmstedt, Mark. *Bücher für das dritte Geschlecht: Der Max Spohr Verlag in Leipzig; Verlagsgeschichte und Bibliographie, 1881–1941.* Wiesbaden: Harrassowitz, 2002.

——. "Selektive Wahrnehmung: Die Publikations- und Rezeptionsgeschichte der Schriften von Edward Carpenter in Deutschland zwischen 1895 und 1930." *Mitteilungen der Magnus Hirschfeld Gesellschaft* 26, no. 2 (July 1998): 31–127.

Leidinger, Christiane. "'Anna Rüling': A Problematic Foremother of Lesbian Herstory." *Journal of the History of Sexuality* 13, no. 4 (October 2004): 477–499.

——. *Keine Tochter aus gutem Hause: Johanna Elberskirchen (1864–1943).* Konstanz: UVK Verlagsgesellschaft, 2008.

——. "Theo A[nna] Sprüngli (1880–1953) alias Anna Rüling/Th. Rüling/Th. A. Rüling—erste biographische Mosaiksteine zu einer zwiespältigen Ahnin lesbischer Herstory." *Mitteilungen der Magnus Hirschfeld Gesellschaft* 35/36 (2003): 28–39.

Lemke, Thomas. *Biopolitics: An Advanced Introduction.* New York: New York University Press, 2011.

Leng, Kirsten. "Culture, Difference, and Sexual Progress in Turn-of-the-Century Europe: Cultural Othering and the German League for the Protection of Mothers and Sexual Reform, 1905–1914." *Journal of the History of Sexuality* 25, no. 1 (January 2016): 62–82.

——. "The Personal Is Scientific: Women, Gender, and the Production of Sexological Knowledge in Germany and Austria, 1900–1931." *History of Psychology* 18, no. 3 (August 2015): 238–251.

Leppänen, Katharina. *Elin Wägner's Alarm Clock: Ecofeminist Theory in the Interwar Era.* Lanham, MD: Lexington Books, 2008.

Lerner, Paul. *Hysterical Men: War, Psychiatry, and the Politics of Trauma in Germany, 1890–1930.* Ithaca, NY: Cornell University Press, 2003.

Levine, Philippa. *Prostitution, Race, and Politics: Policing Venereal Disease in the British Empire.* New York: Routledge, 2003.

Levitas, Ruth. *Utopia as Method: The Imaginary Reconstitution of Society.* London: Palgrave Macmillan, 2013.

Lightman, Bernard. *Victorian Popularizers of Science: Designing Nature for New Audiences.* Chicago: University of Chicago Press, 2007.

Lightman, Bernard, and Aileen Fyfe, eds. *Science in the Marketplace: Nineteenth-Century Sites and Experiences.* Chicago: University of Chicago Press, 2007.

Logan, Cheryl A. *Hormones, Heredity, and Race: Spectacular Failure in Interwar Vienna.* New Brunswick, NJ: Rutgers University Press, 2013.

Longino, Helen. *Science as Social Knowledge: Values and Objectivity in Scientific Inquiry.* Princeton, NJ: Princeton University Press, 1990.

Lorde, Audre. "The Uses of the Erotic: The Erotic as Power." In *Sister Outsider: Essays and Speeches,* 53–59. 1984. New York: Ten Speed Press, 2007.

Lybeck, Marti M. "Gender, Sexuality, and Belonging: Female Homosexuality in Germany, 1890–1933," PhD diss., University of Michigan, 2007.

Lyons, Andrew P., and Harriet D. Lyons. *Irregular Connections: A History of Anthropology and Sexuality*. Lincoln: University of Nebraska Press, 2004.

Maclaren, Angus. *Trials of Masculinity: Policing Sexual Boundaries, 1870–1930*. Chicago: University of Chicago Press, 1997.

Mancini, Elena. *Magnus Hirschfeld and the Quest for Sexual Freedom: A History of the First International Sexual Freedom Movement*. New York: Palgrave Macmillan, 2010.

Marchand, Suzanne. *German Orientalism in the Age of Empire: Religion, Race, and Scholarship*. Cambridge: Cambridge University Press, 2010.

Marchand, Suzanne, and David Lindenfeld, eds. *Germany at the Fin de Siècle: Culture, Politics, and Ideas*. Baton Rouge: Louisiana State University, 2004.

Marhoefer, Laurie. *Sex and the Weimar Republic: German Homosexual Emancipation and the Rise of the Nazis*. Toronto: University of Toronto Press, 2015.

Martin, Biddy. "Extraordinary Homosexuals and the Fear of Being Ordinary." *differences* 6 (1994): 101–125.

Martin, Emily. "The Egg and the Sperm: How Science Has Constructed a Romance Based on Stereotypical Male-Female Roles." *Signs* 16, no. 3 (Spring 1991): 485–501.

Matte, Nicholas. "International Sexual Reform and Sexology in Europe, 1897–1933." *Canadian Bulletin of Medical History* 22 (2005): 253–270.

Matysik, Tracie. "Beyond Freedom: A Return to Subjectivity in the History of Sexuality." In *After the History of Sexuality: German Genealogies with and beyond Foucault*, edited by Scott Spector, Helmut Puff, and Dagmar Herzog, 185–201. New York: Berghahn Books, 2012.

——. *Reforming the Moral Subject: Ethics and Sexuality in Central Europe, 1890–1930*. Ithaca, NY: Cornell University Press, 2008.

McEwen, Britta. *Sexual Knowledge: Feeling, Fact, and Social Reform in Vienna, 1900–1934*. New York: Berghahn Books, 2012.

McGuire, Kristin. "Activism, Intimacy, and the Politics of Selfhood: The Gendered Terms of Citizenship in Poland and Germany, 1890–1918." PhD diss., University of Michigan, 2004.

McNeil, Maureen. "Post-Millennial Feminist Theory: Encounters with Humanism, Materialism, Critique, Nature, Biology, and Darwin." *Journal for Cultural Research* 14 (October 2010): 427–437.

McRuer, Robert. "Compulsory Able-Bodiedness and Queer/Disabled Existence." In *The Disability Studies Reader*, edited by Lennard J. Davis, 369–380. 4th ed. London: Taylor and Francis, 2013.

——. *Crip Theory: Cultural Signs of Queerness and Disability*. New York: New York University Press, 2006.

McRuer, Robert, and Anna Mollow, eds. *Sex and Disability*. Durham, NC: Duke University Press, 2012.

Melander, Ellinor. "Towards the Sexual and Economic Emancipation of Women: The Philosophy of Grete Meisel-Hess." *History of European Ideas* 14, no. 5 (1992): 695–711.

Mesner, Maria. "Educating Reasonable Lovers: Sex Counselling in Austria in the First Half of the Twentieth Century." In *Sexuality in Austria*, edited by Gunter Bischof, Anton Pelinka, and Dagmar Herzog, 48–64. New Brunswick, NJ: Transaction Publishers, 2007.

Milam, Erika. *Looking for a Few Good Males: Female Choice in Evolutionary Biology*. Baltimore: Johns Hopkins University Press, 2010.

Minton, Henry L. *Departing from Deviance: A History of Homosexual Rights and Emancipatory Science in America*. Chicago: University of Chicago Press, 2002.

Mitchell, Michele. *Righteous Propagation: African Americans and the Politics of Racial Destiny after Reconstruction*. Chapel Hill: University of North Carolina Press, 2004.

Mosse, George. *The Image of Man: The Creation of Modern Masculinity*. Oxford: Oxford University Press, 1996.

———. *Nationalism and Sexuality: Respectability and Abnormal Sexuality in Modern Europe*. New York: H. Fertig, 1985.

Murphy, Kevin, and Jennifer M. Spear. "Historicising Sexuality and Gender." *Gender and History* 22, no. 3 (November 2010): 527–537.

Murphy, Michelle. *Seizing the Means of Reproduction: Feminism, Health, and Technoscience*. Durham, NC: Duke University Press, 2012.

Nelson, Claudia, and Ann Sumner Holmes, eds. *Maternal Instincts: Visions of Motherhood and Sexuality in Britain, 1875–1925*. London: Macmillan, 1997.

Nelson, Lynn Hankinson. "Epistemic Communities." In *Feminist Epistemologies*, edited by Linda Alcoff and Elizabeth Potter, 121–160. New York: Routledge, 2013.

Newton, Esther. "The Mythic Mannish Lesbian: Radclyffe Hall and the New Woman." In *Hidden from History: Reclaiming the Gay and Lesbian Past*, edited by Martin Bauml Duberman, Martha Vicinus, and George Chauncey, 281–293. New York: Penguin, 1990.

Nitzschke, Bernd, Annelise Heigel-Evers, and Franz Heigl. "'Wo es in einer Sache nur Gegner oder Anhänger gibt': Ein bisher unbekannter Brief Sigmund Freuds an Max Marcuse." *Zeitschrift für Sexualforschung* 8 (1995): 241–248.

Nowacki, Bernd. *Der Bund für Mutterschutz (1905–1933)*. Husum: Matthiesen Verlag, 1983.

Nye, Robert. "The History of Sexuality in Context: National Sexological Traditions." *Science in Context* 4 (1991): 387–406.

Oertzen, Christine von, Maria Rentetzi, and Elizabeth S. Watkins. "Finding Science in Surprising Places: Gender and the Geography of Scientific Knowledge; Introduction to 'Beyond the Academy: Histories of Gender and Knowledge.'" Special issue, *Centaurus: An International Journal of the History of Science and Its Cultural Aspects* 55 (May 2013): 73–80.

Offen, Karen. "Defining Feminism: A Comparative Historical Approach." *Signs* 14, no. 1 (Autumn 1988): 119–157.

——. *European Feminisms, 1700–1950: A Political History*. Palo Alto, CA: Stanford University Press, 2000.

O'Grady, Catherine. "Born This Way? Why an Evidence-Based Stance on Sex and Gender Is Good for Science and for Feminism." *Bitch Magazine* 65 (Winter 2015): 28–33.

Olson, Richard. *Science and Scientism in Nineteenth-Century Europe*. Urbana: University of Illinois Press, 2008.

Oosterhuis, Harry. *Stepchildren of Nature: Krafft-Ebing, Psychiatry, and the Making of Sexual Identity*. Chicago: University of Chicago Press, 2000.

Opitz-Belakhal, Claudia. "'Krise der Männlichkeit'—ein nützliches Konzept der Geschlechtergeschichte?" *L'Homme* 19 (2008): 31–50.

Paletschek, Sylvia, and Bianka Pietrow-Ennker, eds. *Women's Emancipation Movements in the Nineteenth Century: A European Perspective*. Stanford, CA: Stanford University Press, 2004.

Pateman, Carole. *The Sexual Contract*. Stanford, CA: Stanford University Press, 1988.

Penny, H. Glenn. "The Civic Uses of Science: Ethnology and Civil Society in Imperial Germany." *Osiris* 17, no. 2 (2002): 228–252.

Peukert, Detlev. "The Genesis of the 'Final Solution' from the Spirit of Science." In *Reevaluating the Third Reich*, edited by Thomas Childers and Jane Caplan, 234–252. New York: Holmes and Meier, 1993.

Pick, Daniel. *Faces of Degeneration: A European Disorder, c. 1848–c. 1918*. Cambridge: Cambridge University Press, 1989.

Poovey, Mary. "Speaking of the Body: Mid-Victorian Constructions of Female Desire." In *Body/Politics: Women, Literature, and the Discourse of Science*, edited by Mary Jacobus, Evelyn Fox Keller, and Sally Shuttleworth, 29–46. London: Routledge, 1990.

Porter, Roy, and Lesley A. Hall. *The Facts of Life: The Creation of Sexual Knowledge in Britain, 1650–1950*. New Haven, CT: Yale University Press, 1995.

Porter, Roy, and Mikulás Teich, eds. *Sexual Knowledge, Sexual Science: The History of Attitudes to Sexuality*. Cambridge: Cambridge University Press, 1994.

Porter, Theodore M. "How Science Became Technical." *Isis* 100, no. 2 (June 2009): 292–309.

Pretzel, Andreas. "Zur Geschichte der 'Ärztliche Gesellschaft für Sexualwissenschaft' (1913–1933): Dokumentation und Forschungsbericht." *Mitteilungen der Magnus Hirschfeld Gesellschaft* 24/25 (October 1997): 35–120.

Quataert, Jean. *Reluctant Feminists in German Social Democracy, 1885–1917*. Princeton, NJ: Princeton University Press, 1979.

Radicalesbians. "The Woman-Identified Woman." Pittsburgh: Know, 1970.

Reinert, Kirsten. *Frauen und Sexualmoral*. Herzbolzheim: Centaurus Verlag, 2000.

Repp, Kevin. *Reformers, Critics, and the Paths of German Modernity: Anti-Politics and the Search for Alternatives, 1890–1914*. Cambridge, MA: Harvard University Press, 2000.

——. "Sexualkrise und Rasse: Feminist Eugenics at the Fin-de-Siècle." In *Germany at the Fin de Siècle: Culture, Politics, Ideas*, edited by Suzanne Marchand and David Lindenfeld, 102–126. Baton Rouge: Louisiana State University Press, 2004.

Rich, Adrienne. "Compulsory Heterosexuality and Lesbian Existence." *Signs* 5 (1980): 631–660.

Riley, Denise. *"Am I That Name?" Feminism and the Category of "Women" in History*. Minneapolis: University of Minnesota Press, 2003.

Robb, George. "Race Motherhood: Moral Eugenics vs. Progressive Eugenics, 1880–1920." In *Maternal Instincts: Visions of Motherhood and Sexuality in Britain, 1875–1925*, edited by Claudia Nelson and Ann Sumner Holmes, 57–71. London: Macmillan, 1997.

Roebling, Irmgard. "Grete Meisel-Hess: Sexualreform zwischen Nietzschekult, Freudrezeption und Rassenhygiene." In *Freiburger literaturpsychologische Gespräche*, Bd. 12, *Literarische Entwürfe weiblicher Sexualität*, edited by Johannes Gemeius, Wolfram Maiser, Carl Pietzcker, and Frederick Wyatt, 205–230. Würzburg: Königshausen and Neumann, 1993.

——, ed. *Lulu, Lilith, Mona Lisa . . . Frauenbilder der Jahrhundertwende*. Pfaffenweiler: Centaurus-Verlagsgesellschaft, 1989.

Rose, Nikolas. "The Politics of Life Itself." *Theory, Culture, and Society* 18, no. 6 (2001): 1–30.

Rossiter, Margaret. "Which Science? Which Women?" *Osiris* 12 (1997): 169–185.

Rouette, Susanne. "Mothers and Citizens: Gender and Social Policy in Germany after the First World War." *Central European History* 30 (1997): 48–66.

Rowbotham, Sheila. *Edward Carpenter: A Life of Liberty and Love*. New York: Verso, 2008.

Rowbotham, Sheila, and Jeffrey Weeks. *Socialism and the New Life: The Personal and Sexual Politics of Edward Carpenter and Havelock Ellis*. London: Pluto Press, 1977.

Roy, Deboleena. "Feminist Theory in Science: Working toward a Practical Transformation." *Hypatia* 19 (2004): 255–279.

Rubin, Gayle. "Thinking Sex: Notes for a Radical Theory of the Politics of Sexuality." In *Pleasure and Danger: Exploring Female Sexuality*, edited by Carole Vance, 267–319. London: Routledge, Kegan and Paul, 1984.

Rupp, Leila J. "Sexuality and Politics in the Early Twentieth Century: The Case of the International Women's Movement." *Feminist Studies* 23 (1997): 577–605.

Russett, Cynthia Eagle. *Sexual Science: The Victorian Construction of Womanhood*. Cambridge, MA: Harvard University Press, 1989.

Sauerteig, Lutz. "'The Fatherland Is in Danger, Save the Fatherland!': Venereal Disease, Sexuality, and Gender in Imperial and Weimar Germany." In

Sex, Sin, and Suffering: Venereal Disease and European Society since 1870, edited by Roger Davidson and Lesley A. Hall, 76–92. London: Routledge, 2001.

Sayers, Janet. *Biological Politics: Feminist and Anti-Feminist Perspectives*. London: Tavistock, 1982.

Scheck, Raffael. *Mothers of the Nation: Right-Wing Women in Weimar Germany*. New York: Berg, 2004

Schick, I. C. *The Erotic Margin: Sexuality and Spatiality in Alterist Discourse*. New York: Verso, 1999.

Schiebiner, Londa. *Nature's Body: Gender and the Making of Modern Science*. 2nd ed. New Brunswick, NJ: Rutgers University Press, 2003.

Schwartz, Agatha. "Austrian Fin-de-Siècle Gender Heteroglossia: The Dialogism of Misogyny, Feminism, and Viriphobia." *German Studies Review* 28, no. 2 (May 2005): 347–366.

———. "Sexual Cripples and Moral Degenerates: Fin-de-Siècle Austrian Women Writers on Male Sexuality and Masculinity." *Seminar: A Journal of Germanic Studies* 44, no. 1 (February 2008): 53–67.

Sedgwick, Eve Kosofsky. *Epistemology of the Closet*. Berkeley: University of California Press, 1990.

Seeck, Andreas. "Aufklärung oder Rückfall? Das Projekt der Etablierung einer 'Sexualwissenschaft' und deren Konzeption als Teil der Biologie." In *Durch Wissenschaft zur Gerechtigkeit? Textsammung zur kritischen Rezeption des Schaffens von Magnus Hirschfeld*, edited by Andreas Seeck, 173–206. Münster: LIT Verlag, 2003.

Seltzer, Markus. *Mathilde Vaerting: Biographische Forschungs-Arbeit zum Kampf einer Professorin am Anfang des 20. Jahrhunderts*. Tübingen: Eberhard-Karls-Universität, 2002.

Showalter, Elaine. *Sexual Anarchy: Gender and Culture at the Fin de Siècle*. New York: Viking, 1990.

Siems, Martina. *Sofie Lazarsfeld: Die Wiederentdeckung einer individualpsychologischen Pionierin*. Göttingen: V&R Unipress, 2015.

Sigusch, Volkmar. "Eugenisches Denken in der Sexologie: Einige Exempel." In *Durch Wissenschaft zur Gerechtigkeit? Textsammlung zur kritischen Rezeption des Schaffens von Magnus Hirschfeld*, edited by Andreas Seeck, 57–62. Münster: LIT Verlag, 2003.

———. *Geschichte der Sexualwissenschaft*. Frankfurt am Main: Campus Verlag, 2008.

———. "Der Sexualforscher Max Marcuse in bisher unveröffentlichen Selbstzeugnissen." *Zeitschrift für Sexualforschung* 21 (2008): 124–164.

Sigusch, Volkmar, and Günter Grau, eds. *Personenlexikon der Sexualforschung*. Frankfurt am Main: Campus Verlag, 2009.

Smith, Andrew. *Victorian Demons: Medicine, Masculinity, and the Gothic at the Fin de Siècle*. Manchester: Manchester University Press, 2004.

Smith-Rosenberg, Carroll. "Discourses of Sexuality and Subjectivity: The New Woman, 1870–1936." In *Hidden from History: Reclaiming the Gay and Lesbian Past*, edited by Martin Bauml Duberman, Martha Vicinus, and George Chauncey, 264–280. New York: Penguin, 1990.

Soden, Kristine von. *Die Sexualberatungsstellen der Weimarer Republik, 1919–1933*. Berlin: Hentrich, 1988.

Soloway, Richard. *Demography and Degeneration: Eugenics and the Declining Birthrate in Twentieth-Century Britain*. Chapel Hill: University of North Carolina Press, 1990.

Somerville, Siobhan. *Queering the Color Line: Race and the Invention of Homosexuality in American Culture*. Durham, NC: Duke University Press, 2000.

Spector, Scott, Helmut Puff, and Dagmar Herzog, eds. *After the History of Sexuality: German Genealogies with and beyond Foucault*. New York: Berghahn Books, 2012.

Steakley, James D. "Iconography of a Scandal: Political Cartoons and the Eulenburg Affair in Wilhelmine Germany." In *Hidden from History: Reclaiming the Gay and Lesbian Past*, edited by Martin Duberman, Martha Vicinus, and George Chauncey J., 233–263. New York: Meridian, 1990.

Stepan, Nancy. *The Idea of Race in Science: Great Britain, 1800–1960*. Hamden, CT: Archon Books, 1982.

Stoler, Ann Laura. *Carnal Knowledge and Imperial Power: Race and the Intimate in Colonial Rule*. Berkeley: University of California Press, 2002.

——. *Race and the Education of Desire: Foucault's "History of Sexuality" and the Colonial Order of Things*. Durham, NC: Duke University Press, 1995.

Summers, Anne. "Which Women? What Europe? Josephine Butler and the International Abolitionist Federation." *History Workshop Journal* 62 (Autumn 2006): 214–231.

Suzuki, Michiko. *Becoming Modern Women: Love and Female Identity in Prewar Japanese Literature and Culture*. Stanford, CA: Stanford University Press, 2009.

Thomas, Keith. "The Double Standard." *Journal of the History of Ideas* 20 (1959): 195–216.

Todd, Lisa. "Sexual Treason: State Surveillance of Immortality and Infidelity in World War I Germany." PhD diss., University of Toronto, 2005.

Usborne, Cornelie. *The Politics of the Body in Weimar Germany: Women's Reproductive Rights and Duties*. Ann Arbor: University of Michigan Press, 1992.

Valentine, Kylie. "After Antagonism: Feminist Theory and Science." *Feminist Theory* 9 (2008): 355–365.

Vance, Carole, ed. *Pleasure and Danger: Exploring Female Sexuality*. New York: Routledge and Kegan Paul, 1984.

Wake, Naoko. *Private Practices: Harry Stack Sullivan, the Science of Homosexuality, and American Liberalism*. New Brunswick, NJ: Rutgers University Press, 2011.

Walkowitz, Judith. *City of Dreadful Delight: Narratives of Sexual Danger in Late Victorian London*. Chicago: University of Chicago Press, 1992.

——. *Prostitution and Victorian Society*. Cambridge: Cambridge University Press, 1980.

Warner, Michael. *The Trouble with Normal: Sex, Politics, and the Ethics of Queer Life*. Cambridge, MA: Harvard University Press, 1999.

Weeks, Jeffrey. "Foucault for Historians." *History Workshop Journal* 14 (1982): 106–119.

Weinbaum, Alys Eve, et al., eds. *The Modern Girl around the World*. Durham, NC: Duke University Press, 2008.

Weinberger, Joel, and Jeffrey Stein. "The Drive Theory." In *The Freud Encyclopedia: Theory, Therapy, and Culture*, edited by Edward Erwin, 161–165. New York: Routledge, 2002.

Weindling, Paul. *Health, Race, and German Politics between National Unification and Nazism, 1870–1945*. Cambridge: Cambridge University Press, 1993.

——. "Theories of the Cell State in Imperial Germany." In *Biology, Medicine, and Society, 1840–1940*, edited by Charles Webster, 99–155. Cambridge: Cambridge University Press, 1981.

Wickert, Christl. *Helene Stöcker, 1869–1943: Frauenrechtlerin, Sexualreformerin und Pazifistin; Eine Biographie*. Bonn: J. H. W. Dietz, 1991.

Willey, Angela. "Biopossibility: A Queer Feminist Materialist Science Studies Manifesto, with Special Reference to the Question of Monogamous Behavior." *Signs: A Journal of Women and Culture* 41, no. 3 (Spring 2016): 553–577.

Williams, John Alexander. *Turning to Nature in Germany: Hiking, Nudism, and Conservation, 1900–1940*. Stanford, CA: Stanford University Press, 2007.

Wilson, Elizabeth. *Psychosomatic: Feminism and the Neurological Body*. Durham, NC: Duke University Press, 2004.

Wobbe, Theresa. *Gleichheit und Differenz: Politische Strategien von Frauenrechtlerinnen um die Jahrhundertwende*. Frankfurt am Main: Campus Verlag, 1989.

Wolff, Charlotte. *Magnus Hirschfeld: A Portrait of a Pioneer in Sexology*. London: Quartet Books, 1986.

Wolff, Kerstin. "Herrenmoral: Anna Pappritz and Abolitionism in Germany." *Women's History Review* 17, no. 2 (2008): 225–237.

Young, Rebecca Jordan. *Brain Storm: The Flaws in the Science of Sex Differences*. Cambridge, MA: Harvard University Press, 2010.

INDEX

Meisel-Hess, Grete *(continued)*
hygiene, eugenics, and the body
politic, 188–89, 195, 202–17,
218–19; sex reform proposals
of, 97–100, 103, 173, 177–78,
208–14; sexology in early twentieth-
century Germany and, 44; Stöcker
compared, 219; Vaerting compared,
290; on women cohabiting, 212n57;
in women's history, 6; works,
reception, and influences, 202–5;
writings and research of, 6
Meisel-Hess, Grete, works: *The
Intellectuals* (1911), 202; *In the
Modern Worldview* (1901), 202,
205; *The Nature of Sexuality*
(1916), 254–56; *The Sexual Crisis*
(1909), 12, 44, 87, 90, 95, 202–4,
205, 213–14, 255; "The Sexual
Morality of Woman—of Today
and Later" (1911), 204–5; "Sexual
Rights" (1912), 205
Men's Alliance for Combating Public
Immorality, 50
Mensch, Ella, *Iconoclasts in the Berlin
Women's Movement* (1906), 133
Mesner, Maria, 270, 272, 273
Michel, Sonya, 130
misogyny, 13, 57, 126, 166, 178, 246
Moll, Albert: on female sex drive, 92;
on homosexuality, 119, 125, 126,
128, 138, 150; *Research on the
Libido Sexualis* (1897), 76; sexology
in early twentieth century and, 15,
32, 58, 60, 62
Monism and Monists, 23n46, 102
monogamous female/polygamous male
discourse, 70, 163
monogamy, 97, 98, 100, 110, 207,
241, 251, 259, 270
*Monthly Journal for Urinary Illness
and Sexual Hygiene,* 85–86
moral purity and sex reform
movements, 45, 48–56
Morel, Bénédict Augustin, *Physical,
Intellectual, and Moral Traits of
Degeneration in the Human Species*
(1857), 156, 192

Mosse, George, 155, 156
motherhood. *See* marriage and
reproduction
Müller, Paula, 27n58
Müller, Robert, 210
Müller-Lyer, Franz, 67n6
Munk, Sofie. *See* Lazarsfeld, Sofie

Näcke, Paul, 163
Napoleonic law, 71
National Women's Service, 227–28
natural selection, 192, 206, 208, 316
nature and the natural: female sex
drive as natural physiological
necessity, 87–90, 93–95, 102–3,
107–8; feminist debate over the
good versus the natural, 107–8;
heterosexuality as purportedly
natural norm, 110; new materialist
feminism and, 313–20. *See also*
racial hygiene, eugenics, and the
body politic
Naval Association of German Women
(Flottenbund deutscher Frauen), 134
Nazis and Nazism, 38, 217, 310–11
Neisser, Albert, 52, 90n81, 158n22,
161
neo-Malthusianism, 192, 200, 216
New Ethic, 200–201
The New Generation (journal), 1–2,
53, 56, 197, 202, 203, 221, 261,
279n46, 291
New Home Economics, 291
new materialist feminism, 313–20
New Woman, 123n14, 265, 268, 305
Nietzsche, Friedrich, 23, 200, 201, 203
nonnormative female subjectivities.
See homosexuality
Nordau, Max, *Degeneration* (1892),
156
Nowacki, Bernd, 60
nymphomania, 110

Ober, Eduard, 52
Obermayer, Rosa. *See* Mayreder, Rosa
Offen, Karen, 130, 132
Office for Mother Protection (Büro für
Mutterschutz), 75

venereal diseases: criminalization of sexual transmission of, 161–62, 231–32; in First World War, 226, 230, 248; German Society for the Fight against Venereal Diseases, 7, 52, 55–56, 63, 74, 87, 157, 160–61; male (hetero)sexuality critiqued and, 154, 157–62; males as vector of, 154, 158–60; as moral issue, 157–58; treatment clinics, 230, 248

VFF (Union of Progressive Women's Associations or Verband Fortschrittlicher Frauenvereine), 26, 72

Vidal, Fernando, 10

Viennese Association for Individual Psychology, 291

Virchow, Rudolf, 8, 23n46

Voigtländer, Else, 277–78

Wägner, Elin, 279

Wagner, Richard, 178

Weber, Marianne, 109; "Sexual-Ethical Principal Questions" (1909), 107

Weber, Max, 198

Weindling, Paul, 22, 30, 45–46, 47, 196, 229n21

Weininger, Otto, 126, 127, 136, 138, 149

welfare state in Germany: creation of, 46, 191; First World War and, 229–30, 240–41, 250; postwar period, 270

Westheimer, Ruth, 312

White Cross League, 50

Wilde, Oscar, 156

Wilhelm II (Kaiser), 39, 49, 118, 229

Willard, Elizabeth Osgood Goodrich, 17n26

Wilson, Elizabeth, 315

Wolff, Charlotte, 151, 235n47, 312

Wolff, Julius, 58, 60

Wollstonecraft, Mary, 304

The Woman in the State (journal), 278, 291, 292

women sexologists in Germany and Austria (1900–1933), 1–42, 307–20; appeal of scientific knowledge about

sex for women, 8–12, 29–32, 307–8; Austria and Germany, cultural and intellectual interconnectedness of, 4–6; biopolitics and, 21–25, 34–38; cognitive biases and social prejudices of, 13–14, 35–38; definition, origins, and historical development of sexology, 15–20, 39; field, sexology treated as, 33–34, 307; Foucault's historiography of sexuality and, 14–15, 20–25, 30, 31, 34; gender politics as lens for reconceptualizing sexology, 14–15, 32–34; German cultural and intellectual ties with Austria and Europe generally, 4–6; historiographical attention, importance of, 32, 311–13; legal position of women in early twentieth-century Germany, 9–10, 27, 261, 268; Nazis and Nazism, 38, 217, 310–11; new materialist feminism and, 313–20; power and authority, sexology as focal point for, 8–9, 24–25; role of, 6, 12–13, 31–32, 57–62; significance of time period, 1–2; similarities and differences of women studied, 6–8; treatment of women in sexual research, critiques of, 2–4, 11, 104–5, 285–86; "the woman question" and German women's movement, 25–29. *See also* female sex drive; feminism and women's movements; First World War; homosexuality; male (hetero) sexuality critiqued; postwar era; racial hygiene, eugenics, and the body politic; sexology in early twentieth century

women's movements. *See* feminism and women's movements

World League for Sexual Reform, 44, 139, 274, 309

World War I. *See* First World War

Yearbook for Sexual Intermediaries, 55, 129

Young, Rebecca Jordan, 319

www.ingramcontent.com/pod-product-compliance
Lightning Source LLC
Chambersburg PA
CBHW022258280326
41932CB00010B/910